IN TERNAL AUDIT

r Uni

INTERNAL AUDIT

Third edition

Julian Venables BA, MEd, IPFA, MBIM
Vice Principal (Finance and Industrial Relations),
Bourneville College of Further Education

Ken Impey FCA
Formerly Head of Internal Audit, Reed International PLC

Butterworths
London, Dublin and Edinburgh
1991

United Kingdom	Butterworth & Co (Publishers) Ltd, 88 Kingsway, LONDON WC2B 6AB and 4 Hill Street, EDINBURGH EH2 3JZ
Australia	Butterworths Pty Ltd, SYDNEY, MELBOURNE, BRISBANE, ADELAIDE, PERTH, CANBERRA and HOBART
Canada	Butterworths Canada Ltd, TORONTO and VANCOUVER
Ireland	Butterworths (Ireland) Ltd, DUBLIN
Malaysia	Malayan Law Journal Sdn Bhd, KUALA LUMPUR
New Zealand	Butterworths of New Zealand Ltd, WELLINGTON and AUCKLAND
Puerto Rico	Equity de Puerto Rico, Inc, HATO REY
Singapore	Malayan Law Journal Pte Ltd, SINGAPORE
USA	Butterworth Legal Publishers, AUSTIN, Texas; BOSTON, Massachusetts; CLEARWATER, Florida (D & S Publishers); ORFORD, New Hampshire (Equity Publishing); ST PAUL, Minnesota; and SEATTLE, Washington

A CIP Catalogue record for this book is available from the British Library.

First edition 1985
Second edition 1988

ISBN 0 406 00205 3

Typeset by Phoenix Photosetting, Chatham, Kent
Printed and bound by Mackays of Chatham PLC, Chatham, Kent

To Anne and Betty in appreciation

Acknowledgments

The authors gratefully acknowledge the assistance, advice and co-operation given by the following in the preparation of the first and second editions of this book:

Individuals

Eric Corns BA, IPFA—*Principal Lecturer,*
Southampton Institute of Higher Education
Jim Francis FMCA, J DIP MA, INST AM—*Audit Manager,*
Reed International PLC
David Hewett MSC, IPFA *Principal Lecturer*
Southampton Institute of Higher Education
Tim Hickson BA, ACA—*Lead Auditor,*
Reed International PLC
Alan Speed BSC, ACMA—*Computer Auditor,*
Southern Gas
Gerald Thomas LLB—*Senior Lecturer,*
Southampton Institute of Higher Education
Brenda Watts BA, MA, Barrister—*Senior Lecturer,*
Southampton Institute of Higher Education

Professional bodies

Chartered Association of Certified Accountants (*CACA*)
Chartered Institute of Management Accountants (*CIMA*)
Chartered Institute of Public Finance and Accountancy (*CIPFA*)
Institute of Chartered Accountants in England and Wales (*ICAEW*)
Institute of Internal Auditors—United Kingdom (*IIA–UK*)

Organisations

Audit Commission
Reed International PLC
Stoy Hayward & Co, *Chartered Accountants*
Grant Thornton & Co, *Chartered Accountants*

1988

Preface

The need for a professional internal audit function emerged with the growth in size and complexity of organisations in both the private and public sectors. There was a need to reassure accountable managers that complex fabrics of management obligations were being properly discharged and also to make a positive contribution to the achievement of organisational objectives. By identifying and evaluating opportunities and risks, the internal auditor is in a unique position to stimulate change leading to enhanced operational performance.

This book, which is the result of much research gleaned from many sources, concentrates the thoughts of many into one readable text. It covers all general internal auditing topics and examines a selection of specialist audits.

For the student it provides an authentic textbook encompassing the examination syllabuses of CIMA, CIPFA, IIA and AAT, but without sacrificing readability and with added enlightenment from diagrams and practical examples. For the practitioner it offers guidance on developing the practical application of internal audit techniques. External auditors will also find it helpful in appraising internal audit work.

It will be particularly useful to senior executives when defining corporate internal audit policy. Special attention is paid to the pursuit of improved operational performance and reassurance to management about the conduct of its operations. General managers will appreciate the concept of internal audit as an effective management tool, capable of contributing positively to improved performance by promoting sound control in critical risk areas and by uncovering new opportunities for gain.

Since publication of the second edition, important developments in public attitudes have been gathering momentum and these changes can be expected to have considerable impact on the role of internal auditing. The text of this third edition has been updated and rearranged to reflect these changes in attitudes and to give due emphasis to current legislation and developments which affect internal audit practice. In particular, it addresses the impact of three significant developments. Firstly, growing world-wide concern to protect the environment is progressively influencing the strategies and management policies pursued by all organisations. Secondly, there has been a relatively high level of corporate failures in 1990, in some cases associated with unlawful or unacceptable practices. This has focused public attention on the quality of corporate governance and the effectiveness of the regulatory framework introduced by the Companies Act 1989. Thirdly, concern about effective control of public spending has resulted in legislation which aims to strengthen accountability and to establish the pursuit of value for money as a primary objective in public sector activity, such as the changes introduced by the National Health and Community Care Act 1990. Each of these developments imposes new and onerous obligations on managements who will look to their internal audit functions for reassurance that the control system is adequate and effective in ensuring that these obligations are being properly discharged. This edition analyses these developing management obligations and offers ideas to assist internal auditors to meet the new challenges which they generate.

Julian Venables
Ken Impey
May 1991

Contents

CHAPTER 1   Introduction

Objectives	To introduce the positive contribution that internal audit can make to the management of the organisation
Contents	The nature of internal audit; an agent for change; an evolving role
Summary	Internal audit provides a supporting service to management which is independent of operational responsibilities and is used to provide objective analyses, counsel and recommendations concerning activities appraised, leading to enhanced efficiency and effectiveness

1.0   THE NATURE OF INTERNAL AUDIT

The auditor is 'a watchdog not a bloodhound'. This celebrated quotation from auditing case law is as pertinent to internal auditors as to statutory auditors. Nevertheless an image of the internal auditor as a bloodhound persists. It portrays the auditor unnecessarily raking over the past and pouncing on every minor mistake to uncover it as a serious misdemeanour. As with all stereotyping there may be a grain of truth and it is unfortunate that such an image persists largely through the auditor's backwardness at public relations.

It has to be a false image: it implies a presumption of wrong-doing, even of fraud; a suggestion that those whose work is to be subjected to audit examination are assumed to be guilty until proven otherwise.

Internal audit is a service to management. It is a function which management will have chosen to establish as part of the process of monitoring performance to help achieve the operational targets and plans adopted. The bloodhound image is not compatible with the management service concept: it conflicts with the basic philosophy of team management where motivation is based upon trust and responsibility. As a management service the function has to be recognised as an integral part of the management structure and part of the fabric of trust.

The role of the internal auditor has moved on from just checking that duties are being performed in compliance with instructions, although this remains a cornerstone for the work. It is now concerned with analysing the ability of the organisation to react to changing circumstances and with providing impartial advice to senior management on all aspects of policy implementation. It is at once a protective role, providing positive reassurance to all levels of management, and an activating role, contributing to

1

improvements in operational performance: the watchdog has become a guide dog. The breadth and depth of this role means that it requires definition by senior management to fulfil given objectives in the context of each particular organisation.

Nor is this role restricted to the examination of financial systems. Finance may be regarded as a common factor binding the range of different functions which are essential to each particular activity into a single cohesive organisation, providing channels of communication and a means of measuring performance. The disciplines essential for effective financial control can also often be applied to non-financial operations in the pursuit of improved efficiency and effectiveness.

Throughout this book emphasis has been placed on the positive role that internal auditors have to play in identifying opportunities and risks and in giving reassurance to management that a complex fabric of management objectives is being fulfilled.

The internal audit function must be separate from all other management functions to preserve the element of independence necessary for making impartial and objective judgements. Internal auditors must identify totally with the objectives of the managements they serve but they should have no authority to change anything: their role is to observe and recommend. It is nevertheless a responsible role and the responsibility can be onerous. Some internal audit recommendations may have far-reaching implications. The internal auditor needs to appraise potential opportunities and risks and acknowledge a share of responsibility in contributing to the decision-making process.

When accountable managers accept internal audit assurances and recommendations they are placing considerable confidence in the auditor's judgement. There has to be a sound basis for such confidence. The internal auditor must not only have competence in the audit skills of penetrating observation, meaningful analysis and rational judgement, he must also demonstrate perceptive understanding of the operations and the management philosophy by offering sound recommendations which are also feasible.

2.0   AGENT FOR CHANGE

Internal audit is a management function.

Management is about motivating, organising and leading a team of people so that their collective activities achieve a defined corporate objective.

The survival of every such organisation in a competitive world depends upon its ability to fulfil its objective efficiently.

This is valid whether success is measured in terms of profit, service to customers or service to the public.

Economies of scale result in organisations of ever increasing size and this increases the complexity of the management task.

This increase in complexity is compounded by an ever growing body of legislation designed to protect the rights of individuals against unfair use of the power inherent in large organisations. Consequently, the freedom of such organisations to act is restricted by laws for protecting the environment, the consumer, the employee, the investor and so on.

In a large organisation management has to be developed through a formal structure which identifies separate functions with responsibility for specific areas of the overall objectives. The complexity is further compounded as each area is sub-divided.

Day-to-day management is a continuous decision-making activity which must occur when and where the operations to be managed are taking place. In a large organisation this activity is inevitably fragmented but the means must be retained for ensuring that every management decision made is consistent with the corporate objective and contributes to its achievement.

Formal systems for operational procedures and effective communication are clearly essential and it is important that these systems are so designed for all functions to be contributing fully to corporate objectives.

It is equally important to ensure that the formal procedures are being properly observed.

Organisations have to be dynamic to respond to changing environments. Objectives change, organisational structures change, people change, systems and procedures may have to be flexible to cope with these changes or to take advantage of opportunities as they occur. In the process of change important links may be lost or signalling markers may get eliminated. Drift may occur in the observance of procedures.

Internal audit is the management function which monitors the continuing validity of management control systems and effective compliance. In fulfilling this role the internal auditor has an excellent viewpoint from which to recognise opportunities for strengthening systems and procedures, for improving methods and for achieving greater efficiency all with the object of increasing the contribution each management sector can make towards achieving corporate objectives.

Throughout this book we have referred to the internal auditor's special position as an agent for change. All organisations must change to survive in a changing environment. Achieving change is one of the most demanding of management tasks. In a large organisation it will usually involve a reorientation of the attitudes of many individuals. It will demand the application of a considerable degree of management skill to influence them effectively in order to overcome inertia and maintain motivation in a new direction.

This is not a new challenge and was probably never better described than by Nicolo Machiavelli in the sixteenth century:

> 'There is nothing more difficult to carry out, or more doubtful of success, nor more dangerous to handle, than to initiate a new order of things. For the reformer has enemies in all those who profit by the old order, and only lukewarm defenders in all those who would profit by the new order. This arises partly from the incredulity of mankind, who do not believe in anything new until they have had actual experience of it.'

The internal auditor who acknowledges this is most likely to contribute positively to the process of change.

3.0 AN EVOLVING ROLE

The Companies Acts and other legislation impose ever increasing obligations on the directors of public companies. There is a primary duty of accountability to shareholders to maintain capital intact and make it work to earn a good return. But there are many additional responsibilities imposed by law which may relate to employment, health and safety, fair trading, the environment and so on. These burdens are additional to the contractual obligations and commercial risks of the enterprise. Likewise, senior executives of public sector organisations have increasing burdens of similar obligations, in both those imposed upon them by law and those arising from the specific public functions involved. The primary emphasis here may be on accountability for public funds and achieving value for money in their application.

The management task of ensuring that the organisation lawfully discharges all its obligations while actively pursuing its objectives will be dependent upon the system of internal control being adequate and effective. It is a key internal audit role to give positive assurance on this question or to identify weakness or gaps and to recommend a suitable remedy.

A report of The hundred group of Finance Directors 'Audit: The Client's View' (1981) contained the following comment recognising this aspect of the internal audit role.

> 'It is generally recognised that the proper organisation, staffing and methodology of internal audit presents the Board with the best means of focusing on its obligation to ensure proper controls in the business . . .'

All modern organisations are having to adapt to rapid fundamental change in various forms such as environmental changes, technological breakthrough and global market opportunities and risks. It all adds to the ever increasing complexity of the management task and has led to a much broader role for internal audit. Initially, it was mainly concerned with financial security; subsequently, the scope of internal auditing has been progressively widened to encompass audit appraisal of every aspect of corporate activity. It encompasses continuous assessment of how effectively the system of internal control contributes towards the achievement of corporate objectives and also evaluation of operational efficiency. This development has created a need for mature internal auditors with the personal stature, professional competence and experience necessary to command management respect for their audit judgements.

A survey of internal auditing in the UK and Eire conducted in 1985 by the Institute of Internal Auditors (IIA)–UK found that around half of the organisations participating were planning increased scope for computer audits and increased general audit scope. One-third of the organisations were planning expanded scope for operational audits.

However, the survey found that a lack of suitably qualified and experienced staff to meet this expanding role, was a major problem area which all organisations had to address. One of the principal objectives of this book has been to contribute towards resolving this problem. Since publication of the first edition, the complexities and diversification of modern organisations have continued to evolve and the role of internal audit has had to develop correspondingly.

Consequently this third edition also aims to address the progressive requirement for appropriate training and development of internal auditors. The supporting role is presented positively by focusing on the appraisal of both operational and administrative activity from the management viewpoint. Due emphasis continues to be placed on operational audit and also on information management and particularly computerised control systems.

The role of internal audit is defined in the Auditing Guideline 'Guidance for internal auditors' developed by the Auditing Practices Committee of CCAB Limited (June 1990) as follows:

> 'Internal audit is an independent appraisal function established by the management of an organisation for the review of the internal control system as a service to the organisation. It objectively examines, evaluates and reports on the adequacy of internal control as a contribution to the proper economic, efficient and effective use of resources.'

It is similarly defined in the 'Statement of Responsibilities' published by the Institute of Internal Auditors–UK in *Standards and guidelines for the professional practice of internal auditing* August 1988 as amended May 1991 as follows:

> 'Internal auditing is an independent appraisal function established within an organisation to evaluate its activities as a service to the organisation.'

This definition leads on to a 'statement of objective and scope' as follows:

> 'The objective of internal auditing is to assist members of the organisation including those in management and on the board in the effective discharge of their responsibilities. To this end, internal auditing furnishes them with analyses, appraisals, recommendations, counsel and information concerning the activities reviewed.'

This book is devoted to the pursuit of these objectives. Internal audit is presented throughout as an invaluable tool of management for improving performance with the supportive role of providing reassurance, where appropriate, that control systems are adequate and effective.

The subject matter can be divided into three parts.

3.1 Professional considerations

Chapters 1 to 5 deal with the professional aspects of internal auditing. The five separate chapters in turn: introduce the function; define its role; consider first directing the function; and next the resources needed to fulfil the role; and then examine the principal techniques in the context of evaluating control systems.

3.2 Management perspective

Chapters 6 to 11 focus on management objectives and analyse the internal audit task in the context of the control principles which apply in six key management areas. A separate chapter is devoted to each: information management; computer security; financial security; contract management; operational management; and corporate management.

Special involvement

Chapters 12 to 14 deal comprehensively with three areas where internal audit concern or involvement has special significance. These are respectively: the role in relation to external audit, audit committees and corporate governance; public sector organisations; and finally, prevention and detection of fraud.

Further reading

Brink, V Z and Witt, H *Modern internal auditing* (1982) (Wiley).

Chambers, A, Selim, G and Vinten, G *Internal auditing* (2nd edn, 1979) (Pitman).

Stearn, H J and Impey, K W, in association with IIA–UK and ICSA, *Manual of internal audit practice* (1990) (ICSA Publishing).

CHAPTER 2　　The role of internal audit

Objectives	To analyse the role of internal auditing in terms of its underlying concepts and established standards of professional practice
Contents	The need for internal auditing. The concept of control. Essential requirements. Internal auditing practice
Summary	Internal auditing has become a critical support function for management control and accountability. Authority, independence, and resources are all essential for its effectiveness. The concept of control is fundamental to internal audit. A professional discipline with standards of best practice helps to ensure consistent quality in the service provided

1.0　THE NEED FOR INTERNAL AUDIT

Professor W J M Mackenzie, in the foreword to *The Accountability and Audit of Governments* (E L Normanton) concisely states:

> 'Without audit, no accountability' without accountability, no control; and if there is no control, where is the seat of power?'

As long ago as 1941, J B Thurston as first president of the Institute of Internal Auditors–USA, said:

> 'with the ever increasing complexity of organisations, senior management are more removed from the places where prime entry is made. It is as an arm of management that internal audit has its most brilliant future.'

In both the USA and Canada the need for internal audit has long been recognised. In the USA, following a number of notorious corporate scandals and failures, The Foreign Corrupt Practices Act 1977 imposed upon corporate managements a statutory responsibility to maintain adequate internal control systems with severe penalties for failing to do so. This development emphasised the need for effective internal auditing to provide assurance that internal control systems remained adequate and effective.

Development of internal auditing in the UK, however, tended to lag behind North America, but it is now acknowledged generally as an important management tool which contributes most effectively in the implementation of corporate policies and the achievement of management objectives.

7

To be effective, the internal audit function must be independent of the operations subject to audit, but it is expected to advise the management on ways of improving organisational performance.

This means internal auditors should have unrestricted right to observe and make enquiries, in order to express informed opinions and to offer recommendations to those responsible, but they should have no authority to make changes of any kind. It is a key element of their role to reassure management about the adequacy and effectiveness of internal control when appropriate. And if not, then to recommend improvements which are feasible and which would aid achievement of the organisation's goals. Thus, internal auditing is an invaluable tool to support management endeavours by improving the quality of control. There follow some specific examples:

1.1   Error prevention and detection

Managers need reliable information to monitor performance continuously within their areas of responsibility. Errors in the collection, processing or reporting of monitoring information will undermine its reliability and usefulness and lead to ineffective control. There is then a need to detect errors and to prevent their recurrence.

Errors may be caused by deviation from the rules of the organisation due to failure of established checks. Such errors may occur because of carelessness or inadequate checking due to lack of discipline; they may be the result of weak procedures or failure to observe them; or there may be an absence of effective control procedures.

Internal auditors are expected to have expert knowledge of control procedures and to be able to offer sound advice. Internal checks, and prevention and detection of errors are management responsibilities. Managers are entitled to rely on the internal audit function for guidance and reassurance when ensuring that adequate internal checks are provided and that when errors are detected they are rectified promptly.

1.2   Waste elimination

Management success is judged by performance in the achievement of clearly defined objectives. The ultimate objective may be related to maximum profitability as in private sector organisations or optimum use of resources as in the public sector. In all cases waste will diminish the achievement.

Waste occurs wherever control is lacking. Waste can result from:

1 Organisational weakness wherever accountability is not matched with authority or skills with tasks.
2 Poor decision quality wherever monitoring is unreliable.
3 Inefficient use of resources wherever operations are inadequately planned and co-ordinated.
4 Excessive employment costs wherever motivation is overlooked, direction unclear or supervision inadequate.
5 Procurement risks wherever specification is imprecise or negotiation weak.
6 Extravagant consumption wherever standards are imprecise or monitoring unreliable.

7 Stock shrinkage wherever security is lax.
8 Erosion of asset values and other resources wherever the need for protection is overlooked.
9 Fraud, theft and other irregularities wherever the management fails actively to promote honesty and fraud prevention.

The scope of modern internal auditing encompasses operational review including critical examination of value for money. This work involves examining how effectively management policy is being implemented; assessing the economy and efficiency of operations; and evaluating the results in terms of achieving management objectives.

By identifying where waste is occurring and quantifying it, those areas of the control system which need strengthening can be ranked for priority of remedial action. In this way an experienced operational auditor provides an invaluable service in assisting management to achieve improved operational performance.

1.3 Reliable monitoring

Management reporting may be undermined as a result of system weaknesses which give rise to inaccurate or incomplete information or even excessive information which overloads management so that the wood cannot be seen for the trees. System weaknesses could be due to faulty design, a need for modification to accommodate changed circumstances or to lapses in application. The resulting information may be meaningless or misleading.

Such reporting failures lead to poor management decisions. Consequently, there is a prudent need to challenge continuously and to verify the reliability of all monitoring information used as a basis for management decisions. This is a key role for internal audit. Prevention of monitoring failures as well as identification and correction of reporting weaknesses, all help management to direct the organisation's affairs more effectively and to make more efficient use of resources.

1.4 Compliance with the law

The law imposes an increasing burden of statutory obligations on all organisations. These range from requirements to collect and account for taxes, to measures intended for protection of the environment, the general public, consumers, employees and shareholders. Corporate management carries the burden of responsibility for fulfilling all such obligations and must be able to place reliance on systems of internal control designed to ensure compliance.

This is another key role for internal audit to examine the adequacy and effectiveness of such systems. This examination will expose for rectification, weaknesses or gaps where they do occur, but perhaps more importantly it will give management appropriate assurance where the fabric of control for statutory compliance is satisfactory.

In those areas where the external auditor may need to conduct a similar examination, every endeavour should be made to avoid wasting resources by the duplication of effort which could otherwise occur.

1.5   Fraud prevention and detection

Imperfections in the moral character of any of those entrusted with authority to commit the organisation or with custody of its resources may result in dishonesty and fraudulent activity to the disadvantage of the organisation.

Internal audit presence is a deterrent to lapses in integrity or breaches of trust, provided internal auditors are perceived as part of the fabric of trust. Audit enquiries have to be seen to be based on a presumption that no breach of trust has occurred by way of collusion or otherwise. Internal auditors must avoid presumption of fraud. Such an attitude would destroy their credibility and alienate them from everyone in positions of trust. Nevertheless, every internal auditor has to be alert at all times to the possibilities of irregularity.

Theft, misappropriation, embezzlement, fraud and other unlawful acts committed against the organisation are manifestations of waste and inefficiency. As with all other threats to management achievement, the probability of occurrence and the potential damage have to be evaluated and ranked for priority of corrective action by strengthening the control system. However, an important factor in assessing the potential for damage is the contagious nature of crime; it is most likely to proliferate in an environment where it is not discouraged.

Fraud prevention is a management responsibility. Within the organisation it is necessary to promote a climate of honesty and trust which discourages wrong-doing. This is achieved primarily by demonstrating management integrity and trustworthiness through exemplary behaviour and probity. It is also necessary to deal firmly but fairly with every lapse uncovered and to make this known. The internal audit function has an important role in reinforcing these management objectives. It should also be competent to provide expert advice on procedures to prevent fraud and to lead any investigation to detect fraud when there is reason to believe it has occurred.

1.6   Benefits and responsibilities

Top management needs to know that its policies are understood and being pursued throughout the organisation and that all statutory obligations are being fulfilled. The more complex the organisation the greater is the need for this assurance.

The quality of management decisions to determine future prosperity will reflect the reliability of the financial reports on which they may be based. Unreliable financial reporting is unlikely to be meaningful and could mislead.

The internal auditor has to make judgements as to the adequacy and effectiveness of systems of internal control. These are expert judgements and the internal auditor will expect the accountable management to place reliance on any assurance given. Similarly, recommendations for change may have significant and far-reaching implications but they must be feasible and the internal auditor is entitled to expect that they will be taken seriously by the accountable managements to whom they are addressed. Although not expected to be infallible, the internal auditor will not build and sustain credibility except on the basis of a track record of proven sound judgements.

Supporting management throughout the organisation from an impartial viewpoint places the internal auditor in a unique position to perceive opportunities for improvement. When problems are encountered, by applying the benefit of experience of how similar problems have been resolved elsewhere, the internal auditor is able to perform a pro-active role as an agent for change.

These are onerous responsibilities for the internal audit function, requiring particular skills and personal qualities in all those who undertake internal audit work. Such skills and qualities need to be embodied in a professional discipline with defined standards of practice as a basis for assurance on the quality of service provided.

2.0 THE CONCEPT OF CONTROL

2.1 The nature of control

In the context of management, to control means to regulate. It describes a key element of management activity.

Management is a cyclical activity with a recurring pattern of:

1 Defining the objectives.
2 Planning the activity necessary to achieve the objectives.
3 Organising resources and directing performance.
4 Monitoring results.
5 Regulating by reviewing and adjusting plans or directives.

The concept that control is the regulating process, implies procedures for adjusting plans or directives as may appear necessary as a result of reviewing them in the light of the monitoring information.

Thus, a control is a regulatory device, but this term can refer to management activity encompassing rather more than a regulatory element. And it may also describe the status resulting from such activity. For example:

> 'A control is any action taken by management to enhance the likelihood that established objectives and goals will be achieved. Management plans, organises and directs the performance of sufficient actions to provide reasonable assurance that objectives and goals will be achieved. Thus, control is the result of proper planning, organising and directing by management.' (IIA–UK, 'Standards and guidelines' 300.06)

2.1.1 *Control specification*

Peter F Drucker (1988) lists seven criteria for specifying control which are explained here.

Control must be:

1 *Economical*—The fewer controls required, the more effective they will be. Regulation should be minimal to achieve the desired result and cost should be commensurate with benefit.

2 *Meaningful*—Activities being regulated must be significant in relation to the purpose of the operation.

3 *Appropriate*—The effect of the control must be appropriate to the nature of the operation.

4 *Congruent*—Monitoring must be directly related to the activity being controlled and sufficiently accurate to allow sound decision making.

5 *Timely*—The availability of feedback must permit timely corrective action. Continuous monitoring is advisable for critical activities.

6 *Simple*—Complicated controls do not work, they confuse. They divert attention from the activity to be controlled to the mechanism for controlling it.

7 *Operational*—Controls must focus on activity rather than information. The information must reach the person capable of acting on it and must be comprehensible to that person.

2.1.2 *Categories of control*

Controls may be classified according to purpose. The three categories are here defined and illustrated with typical examples:

1 **Directive controls** are designed to cause or encourage a desired result.
Examples:
Routine training programmes
Sales billing generated from dispatch documentation

2 **Preventive controls** are designed to deter the occurrence of unwanted events.
Examples:
Segregation of duties
Computer access passwords

3 **Corrective controls** are designed to detect and rectify undesirable events which have occurred.
Examples:
Validation checks
Exception reporting

2.2 Organisational control

Relationships between people working together must be based upon trust, loyalty and respect for formally established authority. The necessary conditions are defined by the organisational structure in terms of authority and responsibility. Co-ordinating the endeavours of all involved so as to achieve corporate objectives is the role of management, and control is an element of the management process.

Control, in the context of corporate management depends upon certain basic principles of organisation being observed. These are:

1 *Delegation*—Responsibilities must be matched with delegated authority and should carry accountability. Failure to observe this principle will undermine the basis of trust.

2 *Motivation*—Responsibility is a powerful motivator. It should be defined in terms of contribution to achieving corporate objectives and management goals and then allocated the necessary authority. Personal initiative is a force which is capable of supporting or opposing corporate objectives; excessive regulation alienates it.

3 *Clarity*—The scope and limits of delegated authority must be clearly defined. Uncertainty will lead to misuse of authority by individuals, either in failing to act when they should or in committing the organisation beyond their competence. Such occurrences put the achievement of corporate objectives at risk.

4 *Communication*—The lines for delegation of authority define the channels of communication for corporate policy and management directives from the top down and for management reporting from the bottom up. These channels must be identical with no ambiguity. Clear communication of policy and directives and reporting back are crucial to effective management. When these are lacking in any respect, control is impaired and could become impossible.

5 *Functional influence*—Where specialist functions have been established to advise and guideline managers their role must be restricted to influencing. Line management authority must not be usurped. Any dilution of line management authority destroys the basis of accountability.

Corporate management for an organisation structured on these principles is then likely to be exercised as follows:

1 *Defining objectives*—This phase takes the form of strategic planning by top management. The result is a package of corporate policy objectives which is communicated to operational management as the parameters for corporate planning. Individual management centres then expand the corporate policy objectives by adding their own operational objectives.

2 *Planning the activities*—In this phase, operational managements prepare operational plans built up from detailed departmental budgets. The operational plans have then to be approved by top management and consolidated into a corporate plan. Some adjustments may be required and will have to be negotiated if necessary; for example, to match planned growth with available resources.

3 *Organising resources and directing performance*—These activities are the essential concern of operational management.

4 *Monitoring results*—The key to this phase is in collection and processing of data. Performance data on critical activities needs to be captured continuously where and when these activities occur. Processing involves selectively storing, accumulating, analysing and reporting from the data collected. A well designed management information system, or network of systems, is a critical requirement for ensuring that appropriate, reliable, and timely monitoring information is available to every critical decision point. This requirement applies throughout the organisation up to the highest level. The level determines what is appropriate with a trend to more consolidation, less detail and less frequent reporting at each higher level.

5 *Reviewing and regulating*—This is the control phase and can be exercised at every decision point throughout the organisation.

In some cases the control adjustments are made automatically. These are closed control systems; they may be adopted where there is no judgemental element in the control decision. In these cases drift from standard or programmed performance is automatically corrected immediately it reaches predetermined parameters or tolerances.

In other cases operatives receive monitoring information to enable them to correct deviations from planned or budgeted performance. These are open control systems and they allow judgemental discretion to be exercised.

Operational managers control by exception using variance reports to identify trends needing correction. Top management needs monitoring information to review corporate performance measured against corporate objectives: corporate plans may need reconsideration to respond to unforeseen environmental changes.

2.3   Internal control

Control is defined by IIA–UK, *Standards and guidelines for the professional practice of internal auditing* (August 1988 as amended May 1991) as:

'. . . any action taken by management to enhance the likelihood that established objectives and goals will be achieved . . .'

adding that:

'For the purpose of this statement, internal control is considered synonymous with control within the organisation.'

Internal control is defined by APC *Auditing Guideline 308 – Guidance for internal auditors* (1990) as:

'The regulation of activities in an organisation through systems designed and implemented to facilitate the achievement of management objectives.'

Internal control system is defined by CIMA *Official terminology* (1st edn, 1982) as:

'The whole system of controls, financial and otherwise, established by the management in order to carry on the business of the organisation in an orderly and efficient manner, ensure adherence to management policies, safeguard assets and secure as far as possible the completeness and accuracy of records. The individual components of an internal control system are known as "controls" or "internal controls".'

The APC guidance adopts this definition as appropriate for all CCAB member bodies adding the further comment:

'These [controls] ensure that processes work to meet the system's objectives.'

2.3.1   *Elements of internal control*

It is a management responsibility to establish control procedures designed to assist in achieving defined goals and objectives and to ensure compliance with policies, plans and applicable laws and regulations. The following elements are fundamental design requirements for effective internal control:

1 *Sound organisational structure*—The soundness of the structure depends upon observing all the organisational control principles outlined above. Control is unlikely to be adequate unless critical operations are afforded appropriate status in terms of authority, and accountability. Those who take control decisions must be seen to have appropriate authority. All activity must be clearly identifiable with specific areas of responsibility within the organisation.

2 *Management support*—Control systems are designed, developed and implemented to assist the achievement of management objectives. The design and development of such systems requires specialist skills. It is then essential that full commitment is secured from accountable managers for the ideas and procedures proposed during the development process and before implementation. Without this commitment it is doubtful whether the accountable management will apply the due weight of their authority in enforcing the disciplines of the system; drift is then likely to occur and control will be eroded.

3 *Adequate staffing*—Adequacy in staffing depends not only upon quality and quantity but also on motivation. There must be sufficient numbers to match the workload and they need to be competent for the work and trustworthy. These requirements establish criteria for selection in recruitment and for suitable training arrangements. Performance is unlikely to achieve high standards unless staff are well motivated. Motivation reflects job satisfaction, remuneration and prospects, working conditions and the quality of management and supervision.

4 *Segregation of duties*—This is achieved by dividing each operation into a series of sub-operations, each to be undertaken by a different person. This allows internal checks to be introduced. This control element should not be assumed to eliminate the risk of error or irregularity passing undetected, but it can reduce that risk significantly.

   The scope for segregation of duties may be limited in a small organisation. This element of control may then by partly achieved by sensible rotation of duties.

5 *Internal check*—This is a form of quality control. Checking routines of one kind or another are present in all control procedures. Continuous checking as processing proceeds enables errors or faulty work to be identified and rectified or rejected before further work is done on it.

   Checking disciplines often result from segregation of duties requiring the work of each individual to be checked by the next individual before accepting that work for performing the next process on it. Where this is not feasible, specific quality control checks may have to be introduced. Normally the checking procedure is designed to validate the end result of the previous process rather than the processing. Automated production processes usually have automatic quality control tests with correction devices designed into the control system.

   Internal checks in information processing are often designed adopting techniques such as batch pre-listing, cross casting or reconciliation. Internal checks are especially important in computerised information systems.

The checks for batch controlled processing may be similar to those for clerical procedures where there is good segregation of duties. However, for real time systems, control is achieved through restricted access devices, data integrity checks and check digit verification on transmission of data, critical validation of all input against predetermined parameters, strict protection of master files against unauthorised amendment and strictly controlled distribution of output.

3.0   ESSENTIAL REQUIREMENTS

For internal auditing to be effective it must have clearly defined objectives, authority, independence, and appropriate resources. The role of the internal auditing function of an organisation needs to be described in a formally adopted internal audit charter defining the objectives and scope of the function. It should also define the arrangements for ensuring independence and specify rights of access, responsibilities and duties of internal auditors. Adoption of the charter confirms the source of authority. The chief internal auditor should then ensure, in agreement with top management, that the resources needed to satisfy the defined objectives are available.

3.1   Objectives

Unless the internal auditing requirement is prescribed by law, objectives will have been determined by management when establishing the function, having regard to perceived risks. These objectives will determine the scope for internal auditing and should be defined in the internal audit charter.

Internal auditing must identify with corporate objectives and its aims are best expressed in terms of supporting specific management endeavours. These may include endeavouring to ensure any or all of the following:

1 Accuracy of records.

2 Security of assets.

3 Prevention of waste, errors or fraud.

4 Compliance with established control procedures.

5 Adherence to policy directives.

6 Reliability of management reporting.

7 Adequacy and effectiveness of control systems.

8 Economy, efficiency and effectiveness of operations.

3.2   Authority

Authority is needed in two forms. First, delegated authority within the organisational structure is necessary to undertake the work. Then, professional authority based upon skill, knowledge and experience and professional standards of practice, is necessary to fulfil the responsibilities.

Internal auditors need delegated authority to enter premises, to interview staff, to examine documents and to observe processes in order to collect audit evidence. In certain cases there is statutory authority but in most cases the function will have been established by the directorate to assist in the achievement of corporate objectives. The authority is then confirmed by board resolution.

In all cases it is necessary for top management to ensure that the role and purpose of the internal audit function is understood throughout the organisation. The internal auditors' rights of access to information, to personnel and to premises must be made known and any limitations must be clearly specified.

To fulfil the responsibilities of the internal audit function it is necessary for internal auditors to form judgements from their interpretation of the evidence collected. The effectiveness of the internal audit service will depend upon its credibility. This depends on how managers of the areas subject to audit, assess the internal auditor's competence to make such judgements about the operations for which they are responsible. For these judgements to command respect for their professional authority, the internal audit function must be staffed with individuals who have appropriate stature, skills, knowledge and experience.

Internal auditors should have no authority to change anything in the areas subject to audit. Change is a matter for the exclusive discretion of the responsible management; the internal auditor's role is to observe and make recommendations.

Here are some examples of the source of authority for internal audit in different types of organisation.

3.2.1 *Private sector organisations*

Authority and responsibility for internal audit in private sector corporations are determined by directives from top management.

An internal audit function will only be established in a private sector organisation where the directors have perceived a need for it. Its role is then determined by the authority of the board and preferably defined in an internal audit charter. The charter authorises the internal audit right of access to information, people, processes and premises with clearly defined limits if any are considered appropriate. It also specifies the scope of internal audit examinations and the reporting responsibilities.

3.2.2 *National Health Service*

Authority and scope for internal audit in the National Health Service are determined by directives from the Secretary of State for Health.

The need for internal audit was formally recognised in 1956 by the Minister of Health in Circular HN (56) 85 which defines the role of the health service treasurer as including the task of maintaining an internal audit function. This directive designated specific responsibilities for maintaining an adequate system of internal check and providing for constant supervision of the system. It then identified the areas of risk to which internal audit attention should be directed as follows:

1 Failure to account for income.
2 Failure to control the issue of cheques.
3 Insufficient separation of duties.

4 Weakness in the supervision of cash floats and balances.
5 Poor recording and care of hospital property.
6 Inadequate stores records and security.
7 Unsupervised handling of patients' money.

The Salmon Report (1983) covered both internal and external audit in the National Health Service and recommended that greater emphasis be placed on computer audit, contract audit and value for money examinations.

The National Health Service Internal Audit Manual has since been developed to cover all of these requirements. It is very extensive and one of the most comprehensive manuals for the practice of internal auditing in a specific organisation.

The National Health Service and Community Care Act 1990 introduced fundamental changes in the management structure to provide a more effective basis for accountability. This Act also changed the arrangements for audit, specifically requiring value for money examination of all key areas of activity by the Audit Commission. While this legislation does not explicitly extend the scope for internal auditing in the National Health Service, extending the concept of accountability inevitably adds an additional dimension to the work.

3.2.3   *Higher education*

The Education Reform Act 1988 created a new framework for funding higher education. Universities, polytechnics and colleges of higher education now have to comply with financial regulations established by the Universities Funding Committee (UFC). These regulations require provision to be made for both internal and external audit.

The Universities Funding Committee has issued a code of practice for internal and external audit (Ref UFC 19/91) which identifies the following criteria:

1 Sound systems of financial and management control need to have been established.
2 Terms of reference have to allow for provision of adequate internal audit.
3 The internal audit resource has to provide a continuous independent appraisal of all operations as a service to management.
4 There must be appropriate channels of communication to senior management.
5 A system based approach has to be adopted.

Failure to comply with these conditions may result in grant being withheld.

3.2.4   *Central government*

Authority for internal audit in central government flows from recommendations by the Committee for Public Accounts (CPA).

The 9th Report of CPA (1980–81) recommended improvement in the standard of central government audit. Again in 1983, CPA strongly criticised the lack of professionalism in internal audit in central government and requested the Treasury to increase the number of qualified staff. The Treasury and the Government Accounting Service (GAS) were jointly urged to define the establishment of fully-qualified staff necessary for providing a modern efficient internal audit.

The introduction to the *Government Internal Audit Manual* (GIAM) (HMSO 1983) states that it is issued by the Treasury to provide direction, advice and information on internal audit to government departments and non-departmental public bodies. It covers objectives, standards, and practice and incorporates a glossary of terms and a bibliography.

The Treasury has adopted the *Computer Audit Guidelines* of the Chartered Institute of Public Finance and Accountancy (CIPFA) as a companion volume to the *Government Internal Audit Manual*.

3.2.5 *Local government*

The authority for internal audit in local government is statutory with responsibilities defined by regulations issued by the Secretary of State for the Environment.

The Local Government Act 1972, s 151 requires a local authority to maintain proper arrangements for the administration of its affairs and to nominate an officer responsible for its financial affairs. The Secretary of State may issue regulations under s 166 to facilitate these arrangements.

The Accounts and Audit Regulations (1983) reinforced the 1974 regulations which first specified a requirement for internal audit. They require the responsible financial officer to maintain an adequate and effective internal audit of the accounts of the body and provide the necessary right of access to documents and a right to require information and explanations from any officer.

The Local Government Finance Act 1982 and the National Audit Act 1983 require external auditors to consider the provision of value for money when conducting public authority audits. For local authorities this is the responsibility of the Audit Commission whose *Code of Local Government Audit Practice* (1983) refers to the internal audit role concerning value for money.

3.2.6 *Building societies*

Authority and responsibility for internal audit in building societies are defined by statute.

The Building Societies Act 1986 reinforces the provisions of the 1962 Act requiring every building society to operate effective control systems for inspecting its books of account; supervising its cash handling; and safeguarding all title documents.

The internal audit responsibility is defined as ensuring that there are branch procedures in operation which are adequate and also effectively applied, for:

1 monitoring and reviewing control systems;
2 providing management information; and
3 preventing fraud, error and waste.

These statutory requirements are supported by the *Building Societies Commission Prudential Note* (1987) which gives detailed guidance to directors and auditors.

3.3 Professional standards

Internal auditing has become an established professional service for supporting management. The concept of internal auditing as a profession implies more than a general understanding of its purpose and how to achieve it. There is an expectation of consistency and dependability in providing the service which has to be based upon an agreed set of principles and a disciplined approach to the techniques and practices adopted in applying them.

As recipient of the internal audit service, management expects to be able to place considerable reliance in the assurances it offers. Such confidence can only be justified on the basis of effective quality control against standards for the practice of internal auditing which are both sound and consistently adopted.

The Institute of Internal Auditors, having provided the principal forum for debate about internal auditing principles, published a code of practice which is universally applicable. A UK edition is embodied in *Standards and guidelines for the professional practice of internal auditing* (IIA–UK August 1988 as amended May 1991). Familiarity with this publication is recommended for all involved in internal audit practice. Extracts quoted in this text are identified by the reference '(IIA–UK)'.

The professional bodies which comprise the Consultative Committee of Accountancy Bodies (CCAB) have issued guidance for members undertaking internal auditing responsibilities. This guidance is embodied in *Auditing Guideline 308 – Guidance for internal auditors* (APC 1990). Extracts quoted in this text are identified by the reference '(APC)'.

H M Treasury has issued the *Government Internal Audit Manual* (HMSO 1983) to provide direction, advice and information on internal audit to government departments and non-departmental public bodies. It incorporates statements of standards which are intended to represent good practice and to indicate the criteria by which the operation of internal audit should be measured and evaluated. Extracts quoted in this text are identified by the reference '(GIAM)'.

There are differences of emphasis in the standards and guidance which these three sources provide but there is much common ground and no conflicting issues. The comments here on aspects of internal audit practice take account of all three sources of guidance.

3.4   Independence

'The internal auditor should have the independence in terms of organisational status and personal objectivity which permits the proper performance of his duties.' (APC)

In order to serve a constructive purpose, internal audit judgements have to be unbiased and therefore can only be made by taking an objective view from an impartial viewpoint.

Independence for the internal audit function means:

1 Freedom to plan and carry out the work.
2 Access to the highest level of management.
3 Freedom from all operating responsibility.
4 Freedom to determine the appointment or removal, promotion and remuneration of all internal audit staff.

Internal auditors must be totally independent of the operations being audited and must be seen to be independent. Any suggestion of conflicting interests undermines the credibility of the advice or recommendations offered. Internal auditors must have personal integrity and an honest belief in the product of the work they do.

The internal audit function has to protect and preserve its independence to ensure it remains capable of making impartial audit judgements which can be perceived as objective. It must never usurp the operational manager's role.

Independence is achieved through organisational status and the personal objectivity of each individual internal auditor.

3.4.1 *Conditions for independence*

To ensure the independence of the internal audit function:

1 It must be so positioned in the organisational structure, that it is subject to authority from top management and free from any supervisory control or influence from the management of any operational area to be audited.
2 It must have the full support of management in all sectors.
3 Appointment or removal of the chief internal auditor should be a matter for decision by the chief executive.
4 Appointment or removal of internal audit staff should be a matter for decision by the chief internal auditor.
5 The chief internal auditor should be free to determine the priorities for the function in consultation with the chief executive.
6 The chief internal auditor should have unrestricted access to all senior management including members of the board and the audit committee.
7 Each internal auditor should have an objective attitude of mind and be free from conflicts of interest so as to be able to make judgements and express opinions with impartiality.
8 Internal auditors must be free from conflicts of interest arising from professional or personal relationships or from any pecuniary or other interest in any area subject to audit.
9 Internal auditors must be free from undue influences which could significantly affect the scope of their work, or their judgement as to the content of the internal audit report.

3.4.2 *Conflict of interests*

Careful consideration has to be given to all areas where a possible conflict of interest could occur.

Significant modifications often have to be made to the internal control system or to specific procedures to accommodate changed requirements. It is then usual and indeed advisable to consult the internal audit function for assurance that the systems proposed will provide an adequate basis for control and an effective means of fulfilling management objectives. Then, if further modification is found to be necessary it can still be incorporated at the design stage. Such involvement need not prejudice the objectivity of the internal auditor concerned in reviewing these systems subsequently.

Management resources in a small organisation are often severely stretched and the internal auditor may be one of a small team of non-operational staff who has critical knowledge or experience or who happens to be professionally qualified. In such circumstances the internal auditor may be required to participate in the management of operations at times of peak activity or when specific problems occur. An internal auditor in this sort of situation must make clear to the management that undertaking management tasks will not be internal audit work and the involvement in operational activity risks compromising the independence and credibility of the internal audit function.

3.5   Resources

It is necessary to ensure that appropriate resources are available to fulfil the objectives specified in the internal audit charter. Effective internal auditing depends upon suitable staff with appropriate skills and experience. This is the essential resource. In allocating corporate resources, the budget for internal auditing needs to take account of the cost of recruitment, training and motivation of the internal audit staff.

3.5.1   *Staffing*

'The internal audit unit should be appropriately staffed in terms of numbers, grades, qualifications and experience, having regard to its responsibilities and objectives.' (APC)

The internal audit function should be headed by a chief internal auditor who should be responsible for the management of the function. The ideal chief internal auditor will be suitably qualified with proven management experience and a sound grasp of internal audit principles. This role includes planning, directing and controlling the work of the department and building, sustaining and motivating the internal audit team.

Depending on the size of the organisation, there should be a team of internal auditors with suitable personal qualities and expertise to match the scope of the audit work to be undertaken and to fulfil its purpose. Internal audit work requires personal integrity and particular aptitudes, professional skills and experience.)

3.5.2   *Personal qualities and skills*

Key personal qualities are:

1 Leadership and the ability to work on own initiative.
2 Courage, integrity and honesty.
3 Intelligence, an enquiring mind, ability to learn quickly and to comprehend and appraise complex systems.
4 Decisiveness and the ability to make rational judgements.

Necessary skills, knowledge and experience include:

1 Well developed communication and interpersonal skills, ability to gain co-operation from others and to present ideas clearly and cogently in both verbal and written reports.
2 A sound grasp of the principles of control based upon specialist training in at least one control discipline such as finance, information technology, management science, industrial engineering, etc.
3 Training in the theory and practice of internal auditing.
4 A degree of knowledge and experience of the auditee organisation's management culture, structure and control systems, personnel, operations, products and markets.

This is an extensive range of qualities, skills and other attributes. The internal audit team is likely to be drawn from a variety of disciplines and will normally be comprised of individuals who have reached differing levels of competence in terms of skill, knowledge and experience. Hence provision for continuous staff training is a fundamental requirement.

3.5.3 *Training and development*

'the internal auditor should be properly trained to fulfil all his responsibilities.' (APC)

It is necessary to ensure internal auditors receive the training required for the performance of their full range of duties. Such training should include both the theoretical knowledge and its practical application under supervision of a suitably competent and experienced member of the team.

Training should be designed to match the needs of each individual internal auditor and it should be planned as a continuous process. There are three distinct stages to be planned in succession as appropriate:

1 Basic training providing knowledge of basic internal auditing principles and practice.
2 Development training in general internal audit skills, techniques and behavioural aspects.
3 Training for specialisation.

All internal auditors have individual responsibility to keep abreast of current developments and new techniques and practices in internal auditing.

3.5.4 *Due care*

'The internal auditor should exercise due care in fulfilling his responsibilities.' (APC)

Internal auditors have a duty to exercise due care in carrying out their work. In order to demonstrate that due care has been exercised it is necessary to show that the work has been performed in a way consistent with generally accepted standards of best practice.

Internal auditors are not infalliable and cannot be expected to give absolute assurance that there is no control weakness or that no irregularities have occurred. They do have a duty to exercise reasonable care and skill appropriate to the characteristics and complexities of the activity subject to audit. And they are expected to apply sound professional judgement in performing appropriate tests and in interpreting the evidence from them. The standard of care must involve having an adequate understanding of the organisation and up-to-date knowledge of the relevant legal requirements and professional standards of practice.

Professional proficiency is a personal responsibility of each internal auditor and the collective responsibility of the internal auditing function.

The chief internal auditor is normally custodian of the collective responsibility by reason of his job specification. The internal auditing department should possess or obtain the knowledge, skills and disciplines necessary to fulfil its audit responsibilities. It should also allocate to each internal audit assignment persons who collectively are proficient in the skills and disciplines required to conduct the audit properly.

For the individual, the expectation includes compliance with the published ethical guidelines of the appropriate professional body.

3.5.5   *Ethical conduct*

Many individuals engaged in the professional practice of internal auditing in the UK are qualified as members of the Institute of Internal Auditors–UK or are one of the CCAB professional bodies. The published ethical guidelines of all these professional organisations are appropriate for the practice of internal auditing.
Compliance with this ethical guidance entails:

1   A duty of loyalty to the organisation and to the management so far as this does not involve participation in any unlawful or improper activity.
2   A duty to be impartial and not allow any bias, prejudice or undue influence to limit or override objectivity.
3   A duty of care not to disclose improperly, information received in the course of the internal audit work.
4   An obligation not to conceal, nor to support any unlawful activity and a duty to advise management of concern regarding dubious activity.
5   An obligation to apply honesty, objectivity and diligence in the performance of internal audit duties and in meeting the associated responsibilities.
6   A responsibility to behave with integrity and to practise conduct which is beyond reproach at all times.
7   An obligation to refrain from activity which may conflict with the interests of the organisation.
8   An obligation not to accept gifts.
9   A responsibility to apply generally accepted standards of best professional practice in performing internal audit work.
10 A responsibility to undertake only work which can reasonably be expected to be completed within the scope of the internal auditor's professional competence.
11 A responsibility to strive continuously for improvement in the quality of the internal audit service provided.
12 An obligation to abide by the rules of membership of the relevant professional body and to give full support to its endeavours in promoting the highest standards of personal integrity and professional competence.

3.5.6   *Relationships*

'The internal auditor should seek to foster constructive working relationships and mutual understanding with management, with external auditors, with any other review agencies, and where one exists, the audit committee.' (APC)

The effectiveness of the internal audit service will depend upon the confidence operational managers and their staff feel able to place in the internal auditor who has examined their operations. Such confidence will be based upon the mutual understanding which should develop from constructive working relationships. The onus is on the internal auditor to foster such relationships not only with the auditee management and staff but also with external auditors and any other review agencies.
When preparing the internal audit plan it is necessary to consult with accountable managers for each of the operational areas subject to audit. The purpose of this consultation is to establish scope and timing for each internal audit assignment and to allow it to focus on critical management concerns at the most appropriate time.
Arrangements for internal audit visits should be agreed in advance with

the local manager except in special cases where a surprise visit is intended as an essential feature of the audit approach.

Arrangements for issuing each internal audit report should provide for the accountable manager to have sight of a draft report before completion for formal distribution. All matters raised in the report should have been discussed at the exit meeting and the report should contain no surprises.

This is a practice which helps to avoid circumstances which could put working relationships at risk. Sight of the draft report allows any errors of fact or misplaced emphasis to be corrected. It may allow management responses to be incorporated in the final version. It provides an opportunity for the accountable manager to alert senior management, if appropriate, about what to expect; internal audit reports must not assume a communication role in the line of command.

Internal auditors must be particularly careful to observe rules of responsible behaviour. They must respect the confidential nature of the information to which they have privileged access. When visiting auditees' premises they must respect the house rules established for the convenience and safety of those who work there. They must show common courtesy and due consideration for the workloads of auditee staff when planning and conducting interviews.

Liaison between internal and external auditors can be advantageous for both and for the auditee organisation. The aim should be for each to gain understanding and respect for the role and responsibilities of the other. Each can then plan their work to take acount of any relevant work undertaken by the other; audit visits can be arranged to avoid clashing and potential duplication in gathering audit evidence can be avoided.

External auditors may wish to establish a basis of confidence in those internal control systems which are critical to the financial statements on which they are required to give an opinion. Recent internal audit evaluation of the systems may be relevant but the external auditor must consider critically the reliance he can place on internal audit assurance. The review process needs to be seen by both parties as a necessary part of the working relationship.

4.0 INTERNAL AUDIT PRACTICE

Mautz and Sharaf *The philosophy of auditing* (American Accounting Association 1961) describe auditing as a critique involving three fundamental procedures:

1 Obtaining evidence.
2 Forming judgements and opinions based on the evidence.
3 Reporting those opinions.

Audit evidence has to be obtained in a disciplined way for it to be suitable as a basis for sound judgements. In practice the fact finding examination work needs to be carefully planned and performed in a controlled way and the process has to be scrupulously recorded. Internal audit judgements are primarily concerned with evaluating the adequacy and effectiveness of internal control.

4.1   Evidence

'The internal auditor should obtain sufficient, relative and reliable evidence on which to base reasonable conclusions and recommendations.' (APC)

4.1.1   *Definition*

Evidence—ground for belief; data on which to base proof or establish truth or falesehood, *Collins English Dictionary* (2nd edn).

Internal audit evidence is factual information collected by internal auditors which when analysed and interpreted enables them to reach conclusions on which to base recommendations. The collection process must be properly controlled for the evidence collected to be acceptable as valid for the purpose of making internal audit judgements.

Internal audit evidence is obtained by inspection, observation, enquiry, analysis, computation and confirmation. Sources include accounting and other systems and underlying documentation, tangible assets, management and staff and third parties who have dealings with the organisation.

The internal auditor has first to exercise judgement to determine what evidence will be necessary to form conclusions which are relevant to the objectives of the internal audit assignment. Factors which may influence this judgement are the scope of the assignment, the nature of available information and the cost or the time needed to get the evidence. Available information may be obtainable from various sources including observation, oral explanations and documentation which can be internal or third party.

The processes of collection, analysis and interpretation of internal audit evidence must be properly recorded, supervised and reviewed. This is necessary to provide reasonable assurance that the internal auditor's objectivity is maintained and the objective and scope of the internal audit assignment satisfied.

4.1.2   *Sufficiency*

'Sufficient information is factual, adequate and convincing so that a prudent informed person would reach the same conclusions as the internal auditor.' (IIA–UK)

Whether or not evidence is sufficient is a matter of judgement for the internal auditor taking account of the reliability of the evidence, the degree of risk involved and the level of assurance needed. Each of these factors has to be considered in the context of the objectives and scope of the internal audit assignment.

Care is necessary to maintain a reasonable balance between quality and quantity since the value of evidence may be reduced if it is excessive.

4.1.3   *Relevance*

'Information should be collected on all matters related to the objectives and scope of the internal audit assignment.' (GIAM)

'Relevant information supports the internal audit findings and recommendations and is consistent with the objectives of the audit assignment.' (IIA–UK)

The relevance of internal audit evidence is a matter for judgement by the internal auditor in relation to the objectives of the internal audit assignment. To be of use the evidence must be relevant to the matter on which opinion is to be formed. Information which can contribute to arriving at a conclusion will be relevant evidence.

4.1.4 *Reliability*

'In order to place reliance on evidence an internal auditor should be satisfied with its nature, extent, adequacy, consistency and relevance to the internal audit assignment and with the methods governing its collection.' (APC)

This concept of reliability forms the basis upon which the internal auditor must judge whether or not evidence is reliable. There are, however, some practical indicators:

1 Documentary or written evidence is usually more reliable than oral evidence.
2 Evidence obtained from third parties or sources outside the area subject to audit is usually more reliable than that from those with a direct interest or involvement.
3 Evidence originated by the internal auditor by analysis inspection or observation is usually more reliable than evidence obtained from others.
4 When evidence obtained from different sources appears inconsistent the reliability of each remains in doubt until the inconsistency has been resolved.
5 When individual pieces of evidence relating to a specific issue are all consistent the degree of confidence from all is greater than the sum of that from the parts.

'Reliable evidence can be achieved through the use of appropriate internal auditing techniques which should be selected in advance where practical and modified, if necessary during the course of the internal audit assignment.' (APC)

'Information which is reliable and the best attainable through the use of appropriate techniques is competent information. That which helps the organisation achieve its objectives is useful information.' (IIA–UK)

4.2 Planning, controlling and recording

'The internal auditor should adequately plan, control and record his work.' (APC)

4.2.1 *Planning*

Planning is a key element of internal audit management which is the primary responsibility of the chief internal auditor. It involves judgements about risks and opportunities and the degree of internal audit assurance expected by management. The internal auditor needs to have a thorough knowledge and sound understanding of all aspects of the organisation, in order to plan an effective service to the management. Internal audit plans must be prepared in consultation with the management they are intended to serve and should be agreed with those managements before implementation.

The planning process should include the following stages:

1 Identify the objectives of the organisation.
2 Define the objectives of the internal audit function.
3 Assess the current state of knowledge of the organisation.
4 Consider the impact of external influences.
5 Consider the impact of all major changes in control systems.
6 Ascertain management expectations and concerns.
7 Consider known strengths and weaknesses in control.
8 Identify, evaluate and rank risks.
9 Define priority areas for internal audit attention.
10 Take note of external audit plans.
11 Specify the resources needed and the basis of allocation.
12 Schedule the internal audit work to be done.
13 Secure appropriate management agreement to the plan.
14 Communicate the plan contents to all concerned.

Three levels of planning are required; strategic, periodic and operational.

The **strategic plan** should cover a period of three to five years ahead. It is developed from reviewing the corporate plans of the organisation in the context of internal audit objectives as specified in the internal audit charter. The purpose is to identify principal risks, and assess the internal audit support management will need in addressing them. This establishes the priorities and the resource requirement. It should be agreed with top management.

The **period plan** normally covers one year ahead. It translates the strategic plan into a programme of the internal audit assignments and specifies the scope and timing of each and the staff allocation. It should be prepared in consultation with operational management and approved by top management.

Operational plans are the detailed work programmes for each internal audit assignment. They are prepared by the internal auditor allocated to lead the assignment before starting the work. They should confirm the objective, define the scope and specify the areas to be examined indicating the techniques to be used. Operational plans should also allocate staff to specific tasks, provide for supervision and review, and incorporate a time budget.

4.2.2   *Controlling*

Having established what audit work has to be done it is then necessary to identify the audit staff who are to do it and to direct and supervise them.

Managing the internal audit team and directing the function in pursuit of its objectives are essential tasks within the responsibility of the chief internal auditor. This responsibility includes defining standards and disciplines for completing the operational plans and ensuring they are properly applied.

The chief internal auditor's role in directing the function comprises the following tasks:

1 Allocate assignments to suitable staff.
2 Ensure staff understand objectives and responsibilities.

3 Inform and agree audit scope and work programmes with staff.
4 Ensure guidance, supervision and review are documented.
5 Ensure adequate working papers are maintained.
6 Ensure compliance with internal audit plan.

It is also part of the role of the chief internal auditor to evaluate the performance of the function in terms of how effectively it is meeting its objectives.

Controlling internal audit work involves ensuring that the work is carried out efficiently and in accordance with defined standards and that the audit objectives are achieved. This means effective supervision of the internal audit staff and proper review of their work.

The review procedures provide the key to maintaining quality standards and are thus crucial to the quality of assurance given by the internal audit function. A structured discipline for reviews at different levels is advisable, including appropriate arrangements for periodic external reviews.

Completing the operational audit plan for each internal audit assignment is the task of the internal auditor in charge of that assignment. The most important audit conclusions from any internal audit assignment will be those based upon judgement by the individual auditors who have done the examination work.

4.2.3 *Recording*

Complete and reliable records of the work done and of the evidence collected are an essential feature of an effective internal audit service for the following reasons:

1 Audit judgements should be based upon consideration of a comprehensive and reliable record of the relevant facts. Unrecorded evidence is at risk of being overlooked.
2 Effective review of the work done is not feasible in the absence of a complete and reliable record of that work.
3 Any challenge of the reported findings or internal audit judgements will require the supporting evidence to be produced.
4 Audit planning is assisted by comprehensive working papers that provide information on each assignment which may be critical for subsequent assignments in the same area.
5 A methodical approach to the work is encouraged from each internal auditor by the discipline of having to maintain an orderly and complete record of work done.
6 A reliable record of the work done is necessary to determine whether or not the tests undertaken and the evidence obtained are adequate for the purposes of the audit assignment.

It is for the chief internal auditor to prescribe standards and procedures for maintaining proper working papers and to establish disciplines to ensure they are observed. Adopting standard formats of working papers for all assignments simplifies the task of subsequent reference. Standard formats also lead to efficiency in conducting the audit by saving time designing records, facilitating delegation and assisting review.

Working papers should be compiled as the work proceeds. They need to be sufficiently detailed to enable an experienced internal auditor to ascertain from them exactly what work has been done and the results of that work.

4.3　Evaluating internal control

'The internal auditor should identify and evaluate the organisation's internal control system as a basis for reporting upon its adequacy and effectiveness.' (APC)

'Internal control is the regulation of activities in an organisation through systems designed and implemented to facilitate the achievement of management objectives.

'A system is a series of inter-related procedures composed of processes and controls designed to operate together to achieve a planned objective. Controls ensure that processes act to achieve the system's objectives.' (APC)

Specific objectives for internal control are:

1 Ensuring management policies and directives are properly observed.
2 Preventing waste, error and irregularity.
3 Ensuring reliability and integrity of management information based upon complete and accurate records.
4 Safeguarding assets.
5 Ensuring compliance with the law.

Internal audit evaluation of internal control must be based upon examination of the systems in operation with a view to judging and reporting on how effectively they contribute to the achievement of management objectives. There are three critical questions:

1 *Goal congruence*—Is the system's purpose identified with implementing management policy?
2 *Basis for control*—Does the system's design provide a sound basis for effective control in achieving its purpose?
3 *Compliance*—Are the system's procedures being properly observed?

The internal auditor addresses these questions by working through a sequence of clearly defined stages which together comprise the process of systems evaluation. When this has been done the internal auditor will be in a position to give an opinion on the adequacy and reliability of each system and how well it is contributing to achievement of the objectives management expect of it.

4.3.1　*Stages in systems evaluation*

1 Identifying and understanding management objectives.
2 Identifying the systems in operation and their purposes.
3 Assessing alignment of purpose with management policy.
4 Identifying the operational parameters of each system.
5 Recording the system for subsequent reference and analysis.
6 Reviewing system procedures to identify control features.
7 Testing the system for adequacy of control.
8 Testing compliance with procedures.
9 Judging adequacy and effectiveness.
10 Reporting the result of evaluation.

4.4 Reporting and follow-up

'Internal auditors should report the results of their work. A signed, written report should be issued after the audit examination is completed. Interim reports may be written or oral and may be transmitted formally or informally.' (IIA–UK)

Internal audit reports should be objective, clear, concise, constructive and timely.

'1 *Objective* reports are factual, unbiased, and free from distortion. Findings, conclusions and recommendations should be included without prejudice.

2 *Clear* reports are easily understood and logical. Clarity can be improved by avoiding unnecessary technical language and providing sufficient supportive information.

3 *Concise* reports are to the point and avoid unnecessary detail. They express thoughts completely in the fewest possible words.

4 *Constructive* reports are those which as a result of their content and tone help the auditee and the organisation and lead to improvements where needed.

5 *Timely* reports are those which are issued without undue delay and enable prompt effective action.' (IIA–UK)

'The internal auditor should ensure that findings, conclusions and recommendations arising from each internal audit assignment are communicated promptly to the appropriate level of management and he should actively seek a response. He should ensure that arrangements are made to follow up audit recommendations to monitor what action has been taken on them.' (APC)

Reporting is a fundamental element of auditing. There is a basic requirement to report the results of every internal audit assignment to the accountable manager who has the authority to accept or reject the recommendations and to take the appropriate action.

4.4.1 *Interim reporting*

Interim written reports may be appropriate when the audit assignment extends over a long period. Informally reporting progress verbally is a feature of cultivating a good working relationship between internal auditor and accountable manager. When the audit examination uncovers significant weakness there is a need to alert the responsible management as early as possible. In every case there should be a meeting between internal auditor and management at the end of the field work to consider the audit findings and to present conclusions and recommendations before preparing the formal report.

4.4.2 *Final reporting*

In all cases there must be a final report which is formal, written and signed, and addressed to the manager who has responsibility for the subject area.

This report should deal comprehensively with the audit findings of the whole assignment.

It should state the objective and scope of the assignment and then the findings, conclusions and recommendations. Conclusions should be expressed boldly and unambiguously and recommendations must be feasible courses of action. When corrective action has been initiated by the management it should be acknowledged in the report. It is helpful to incorporate considered management comments, when available, in the formal audit report.

The formal report should be issued promptly after completion of the field work. It is normal and helpful practice to submit the report in draft to the management for factual confirmation. If opinions differ about the relevance of any facts, and the difference cannot be resolved, the report will need to refer to this.

All internal audit reports should request a response. The internal auditor should not regard the assignment as complete until all recommendations have been either accepted and implemented or carefully considered and consciously set aside.

4.4.3   *Role of audit reports*

The formal audit report fulfils a number of important purposes:

1 A competent, impartial and objective view on the adequacy and effectiveness of control in the areas examined should be both constructively critical and reassuring for the accountable management.
2 It is intended to prompt management action which will result in more effective control and improved performance.
3 It is the authentic permanent record of what the internal auditor has examined, his findings, conclusions and recommendations.
4 It confirms matters discussed between internal auditor and accountable manager at the end of the audit examination.
5 It records recommendations, which when accepted, become a programme of action to be taken.
6 It establishes the base from which subsequent audit work may be planned.
7 It is the means of informing other interested parties of the results of the audit assignment.

4.4.4   *Distribution of audit reports*

Internal audit reports are likely to contain confidential and sensitive information. The internal auditor has a duty to respect this confidentiality and must take care not to communicate the contents of the report to anyone who is not entitled to have access to it.

Reports should be addressed initially to the accountable manager for the management centre, subject to audit, who may nominate subordinates to receive additional copies. In many organisations there are senior executives with responsibilities over a number of management centres. Those who by virtue of their position have a right to know and some power to influence action will be entitled to receive copies. It is also a sound practice to make copies available to external auditors and to the audit committee.

The chief internal auditor should agree the arrangements for distribution of internal audit reports with the appropriate levels of management. Every internal audit report should disclose its distribution list in full. Every copy should be dispatched in a sealed envelope prominently marked 'Private and confidential' both outside and inside.

4.4.5   *Follow-up*

It is a management responsibility to ensure that proper consideration is given to all internal audit reports. The internal auditor should ensure that appropriate arrangements are made to determine whether action has been taken on internal audit recommendations or that management has understood and assumed the risk of not taking action.

Further reading

Auditing and reporting 1990/91, UK auditing standards, guidelines and exposure drafts (1990) (ICAEW).

Drucker, P J *Management: tasks, responsibilities and practices* (1988) (Heinemann).

H M Treasury *Government internal audit manual* (1983) (HMSO).

Standards and guidelines for the professional practice of internal auditing (1988 as amended May 1991) (IIA–UK).

CHAPTER 3 Internal audit management

Objectives	To examine the procedures used to apply the theory and principles in the practice of internal audit
Contents	Planning; appraisal of risk; status in the organisation Departmental structure; job descriptions; cost; staffing requirements; management training Directing; briefing; objectives; audit approaches Controlling; quality assurance; task analysis; use of computers
Summary	Senior management must define the policy for internal audit and give the function full support to enable it to make a positive contribution to the organisation. The direction and guidance provided by the chief internal auditor in administering the department efficiently with defined resources will then allow internal audit to be effective

1.0 INTRODUCTION

The following statement is one of five general standards issued by the IIA for the professional practice of internal auditing.

'The chief internal auditor should properly manage the internal auditing department.' (IIA Standard 500)

Audit management is concerned with planning, organising, directing and controlling the department and through these activities creating an environment that allows for an effective audit provision.

2.0 PLANNING

'The planning process involves establishing goals, audit work schedules, staffing plans, activity reports. (IIA Guideline 520.02).

These activities involve the establishment of the audit function within the organisation, its purpose, authority and responsibilities. IIA–UK have published a *Statement of Responsibilities* which gives professional guidance upon the function of internal audit within the organisation. With such guidance the head of internal audit can prepare a suitable charter for the department to specify appropriate terms of reference. It is important that the internal audit charter takes a written format and is approved by senior management. Such approval provides internal audit with the appropriate recognition of its importance to the organisation. Furthermore, the process of drafting the charter allows thought to be given to the objectives of the role, rather than allowing it to develop merely in response to short-term needs. This sentiment is supported by the following professional statements:

'The chief internal auditor should have a statement of purpose, authority and responsibility for the internal auditing department.' (IIA Standard 510)

'It is the responsibility of internal audit, to review, appraise and report upon:
(a) the soundness, adequacy and application of internal controls;
(b) the extent to which the organisation's assets and interests are accounted for and safeguarded from losses of all kinds arising from:
  (i) fraud and other offences;
  (ii) waste, extravagance and inefficient administration; poor value for money and other causes;
  (iii) the suitability and reliability of financial and other management data developed within the organisation.' (CIPFA 1979)

The planning process is illustrated on p 36:

An example from the public sector is as follows:

The principal duties of internal audit are to provide assurances to management:
1 that the policies, procedures and systems of internal control established by management ensure the efficient, economic and effective use of resources;
2 that those policies and procedures are being complied with and are effective in meeting the objectives of the Department;
3 that the assets and interests of the Department are properly controlled and safeguarded against losses of all kinds;
4 that the accounting and other records form a reliable basis for the preparation of appropriation and other accounts (including management and trading accounts);
5 that the financial and other data furnished to management in connection with decision-making processes is reliable;
6 that the business systems established should ensure the accomplishment of established objectives and goals.

2.1   Audit planning

'The internal auditor is responsible for planning and conducting the audit assignment subject to supervisory review and approval.' (IIA Guideline 410.01)

The planning process

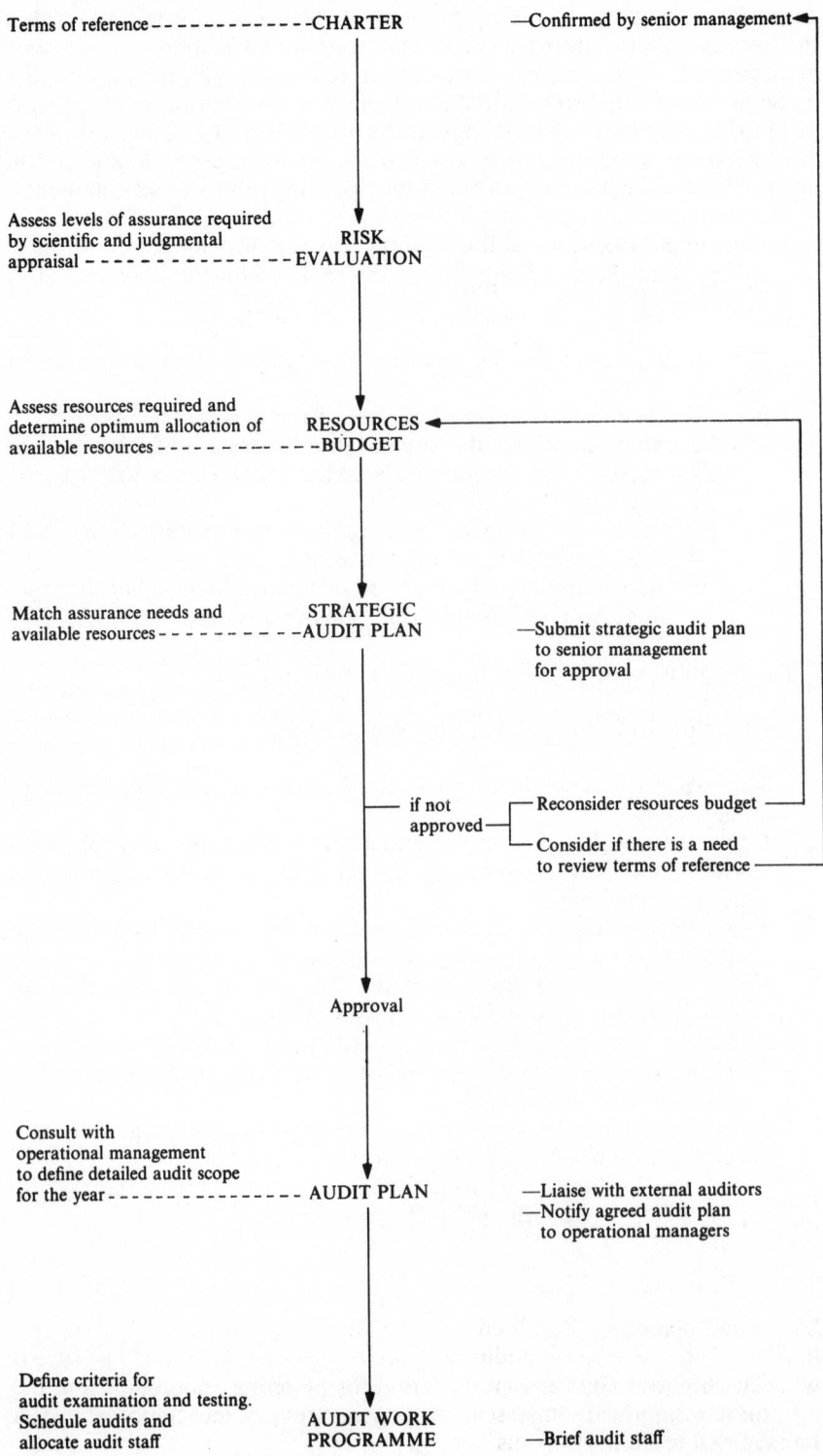

Within the audit department, the planning of audit activities must be undertaken to meet the objectives agreed in the terms of reference (charter).

The audit plan is of use to the following interested parties:

1 *Chief internal auditor*—for the purpose of:
Matching resources to output (staff to workload).
Motivation of staff by target setting.
Control via measuring performance.
Demonstration of efficient management to others.
Informing management of the areas to be examined.

2 *External auditors*—for the purpose of:
Identifying the areas to be subject to internal audit.
Avoiding duplication of work.
Encouraging a professional working relationship.

3 *Financial director*—for the purpose of:
Providing a means of checking financial security.

4 *Other senior managers*—for the purpose of:
Allowing for discussion of the audit role in order to maximise its usefulness to the organisation.

However, a plan, if too rigidly adhered to, may be counter-productive, the fulfilment of the plan rather than the meeting of audit objectives becoming the target. A plan should also contain reasonable provisions for illness, and contingencies such as investigations and urgent or unforeseen problems. It should also be remembered that a plan is a guide to a well controlled audit department; it does not guarantee the audit department's effectiveness.

2.2 Planning stages

The following steps are recommended by CIPFA:

'1 Define the audit objectives
   (a) character (regularity, probity, VFM)
   (b) confidence levels (frequency, depth)
2 Define the field of audit activity
3 Identify resources needed and the resources available.'

Such steps should take account of the role of internal auditing, eg safeguarding assets, reliability of records, internal control, prevention of fraud and waste, ensuring adherence to regulations, with the overall objective being to enhance organisational performance.

2.2.1 *Definition of a plan*

'A method or way of proceeding thought out in advance' (*Oxford Dictionary*). When applied to auditing a plan determines the nature and type of work to be undertaken in a given period, using given resources.

When considering the timescale three stages may be identified—strategic, tactical and operational plans.

STRATEGIC PLAN

A general exercise indicating the manner in which audit is to fulfil its terms of reference, and to review the changing environment under which audit operates. It is a policy statement indicating where audit emphasis will lie in the next two to five years.

TACTICAL PLAN

Used within the framework of the strategic plan, giving a programme of work to be undertaken over the ensuing year—the audit plan. This plan would indicate the audits to be made, the planned resources (audit days) and contingencies allowed for.

Audit plan 1992/93

1. *Available audit days*		
	Days per auditor	*Total team days*
Annual leave	25	250
Statutory hols	8	80
Sickness	3	30
Training	5	50
Research	4	40
Conferences	4	40
Administration	1	10
Audit days	210	2,100
	260	2,600

2. *Allocation of audit days*			
Unit ref no	*Audit days*	*Date*	*Auditor*
4,200	5	7/92	JB
4,201	7	2/93	ANO
4,202	10	9/92	JS
4,300	5	10/92	TMCA
4,301	10	10/92	MT
4,302	3	3/93	DR
4,303	10	10/	
Total	2,100		

OPERATIONAL PLAN

This plan describes the immediate operation of an individual audit. It would cover audit scope and tests to be applied.

In determining areas to be investigated, the chief internal auditor should consider the following criteria:

1 *Financial*—volume of transactions—value of assets.

2 *Internal control*—an evaluation—systems audit.

3 *Probity*—incidence of fraud—cash audit.

4 *Consequential loss*—protection against disaster—computer security.

5 *Nature of systems*—function and degree of reliance.

6 *Managerial ability*—implementation of policy and reporting procedures.

7 *Value for money*—elimination of waste.

8 *Special investigations*—requests from management.

2.3 Approval of plan

Once the objectives have been agreed the strategic plan should be approved by senior management maintaining audit confidentiality. The importance of gaining such approval is emphasised by the following reference to *the Chief Inspector of Audit's report for 1982*—Local Government:

> 'One fairly common criticism was the lack of an audit plan scanning all the various aspects of the local authorities' activities which ought to be examined, the necessary frequency of each examination and the work actually done. Such plans are essential to the effective management of internal audit. It is equally important that plans and their implications are submitted to appropriate Chief Officers. Any arrangement which fails to take this step is selling short the internal audit function.'

2.4 Working papers—assistance with planning

The operational plan can be assisted by reference to the previous year's working papers because they:

1 Provide a detailed description of the auditee's system in operation at the last audit.
2 Provide documentation of the financial system upon which management reports are based.
3 Provide data useful in assessing areas of significant weakness in the system.
4 Estimate the resources required to undertake the work.
5 Provide details concerning the auditee's work environment.

2.5 Nature of the plan

There are two types of plan format in common use:

1 On a departmental basis, whereby audit activity is allocated by service or department, eg production department, Social Services, R & D department.
2 On a functional basis, whereby audit activity is related to an area or type of audit, eg contract audit.

It is for the individual manager to determine the nature of his plan's format.

2.6   Problems of planning

Once a plan is devised and authorised, audit performance is measured against the completion of the plan, ie expected performance (target times for audit) is compared to actual performance, thus if the objectives of the plan are overambitious, the result can be 'mechanical' auditing in order to meet the target. Due professional care is not then the objective, being surpassed by 'getting the audit done and moving onto the next audit'.

2.7   Planning and audit risk

The determination of the audit plan needs to be based on the knowledge of the organisation's areas of vulnerability, the assessment of the chance of disaster and the consequent effect upon the organisation, together with the expertise and resources available to the chief internal auditor. A balance must be struck between risk, vulnerability and resources available.

2.7.1   *The evaluation of risk*

Because of restricted resources, modern internal audit has had to adopt a risk-based approach to the allocation of its resources, so allowing the auditor to concentrate on areas of organisational vulnerability. In this process five elements are identified:

1 *Identification* of the nature of the risk, eg value of cash handled.

2 *Measurement* of the risk, whereby an attempt is made to measure:
   (a) The probability of disaster occurring.
   (b) The severity of such a disaster.
   In practice there tends to be a trade off between these two elements, eg the consequence of a catastrophe from an earthquake may be severe, the probability of such an event being unlikely. Where this does not occur something practical must be done to prevent the catastrophe, eg construction of the Thames flood barrier to prevent flooding of London.

3 *Avoidance*—The establishment of procedures to avoid potential severe consequences, eg back-up computer facilities.

4 *Reduction*—The potential risk may be reduced by adopting certain procedures, eg the potential to defraud the organisation may be reduced through the enforcement of a system of internal control.

5 *Accommodation*—This element deals with the insurance aspect of a risk, whereby once all practical measures have been implemented, an organisation can only resort to an insurance policy by which to protect itself. Common practice is to insure against excessive risk externally while low risk may be provided for by an internal fund, or the organisation may decide to suffer the consequences and not insure. An example of this is 'fidelity' insurance for only those employees who are in a position to defraud.

2.8   Audit risk analysis

Once the risk has been evaluated, internal audit will need to maximise its resources in those areas of highest risk.

2.8.1 *Audit objective*

To produce a list of audit risks expressed in terms which will allow measurement and comparison of those risks to be made for the following purposes:

1 Allocating a priority ranking to certain audits.
2 Justifying the need for certain audits.
3 Calculating the resources (man days) required.
4 Allowing for relative consideration of the importance of audits.
5 Judging the effectiveness of internal controls.

2.8.2 *Risk analysis*

Intuitively the knowledgeable and experienced audit manager will rely upon judgement to determine areas of organisational vulnerability. However, such knowledge may be supported by a more scientific analysis which may expose areas of risk, allowing a priority for audit review to be determined. Such a ranking is achieved by attempting to quantify the change of an event occurring and the cost to the organisation of the potential catastrophe, ie the organisational vulnerability is the product of the chance of the risk materialising multiplied by the estimated cost of catastrophe. The audit objective of such an analysis is to produce a list of audit risks expressed in terms which will allow for measurement and comparison of those risks to be made for the following purposes:

1 Allocating a priority ranking to certain audits.
2 Justifying the need for certain audits.
3 Calculating the audit resources required.
4 Allowing consideration of the relative importance of audits.

2.8.3 *Elements used in risk indexing*

These elements can be identified over the following six areas:

1 *Financial*—Volume of transactions; nature of transactions; (cash) value of assets; importance to the organisation.

2 *Nature of management*—Ability to manage effectively; accountability and quality of internal controls; staff turnover; expertise and morale.

3 *Operational*—Complexity of operations and importance of such activity to organisational achievement.

4 *Impact on organisation*—The importance to the organisation of the system subject to failure.

5 *Internal controls*—Adequacy of internal control.

6 *External factors*—The effect of external factors upon the internal systems and the organisation.

2.8.4 *Determining the weighting factors*

Having determined the methodology for identifying areas of risk, the other element is to determine the chance of that risk occurring, and its impact upon the organisation. This depends upon:

1 Materiality—the cost of catastrophe.
2 Long- or medium-term effect upon the organisation.
3 Contingency arrangements made or available.
4 Adequacy of internal control.

2.9 Indexation of risk

The nature and type of index used can be divided into two areas; the financial audit and the operational audit.

FINANCIAL AUDIT INDEX

The following matters require consideration:

		Weight
A	Annual income divided into cash and credit	× 1
B	Annual credit income	× ·5
C	Annual expenditure	× ·1
D	Value of attractive and portable items	× 1
E	Cash (no income) on site permanently	× 1
F	Degree of internal check	× (1–4)
G	Extraordinary matters	× (0–3)
H	Need for assistance	× (0–5000)
	Total index	

These factors were considered by Berkshire CC (Local Government Finance Act 1973) and given weightings from which to produce an index based on a formula $(A + B + C + D + E) \times (F + G) + H$.

Factors	Small children's home	Surveyor's division	Technical college
A	230	1,200	42,000
B	—	3,500	40,000
C	215	7,000	6,000
D	380	10,000	10,000
E	400	180	3,000
Total	1,225	21,880	101,000
× (F + G)	(4 + 1)	(1 + 0)	(1½ + 0)
=	6,125	21,880	151,500
H	4,000	2,000	2,500
Risk index	10,125	23,880	154,000

Professor A D Chambers in *Internal Auditing* (1984) suggests H may not be sufficient and should be replaced by a multiplier, ie × (1–5). As previously mentioned, methods are arbitrary, but should be tailor-made for each organisation, giving quantitative support to the auditor's judgement.

The following, for the sake of comparison, is an alternative index:

A = No of staff (graded 1–10), eg 20 = 5
B = Complexity of operation (1–10), 10 = very complex
C = Level of security needed (1–10), 10 = very necessary
D = Amount of cash and other negotiable instruments handled (receipts and payments, eg £s converted onto a range 1–10)
E = Default level (1–10), 10 = high
F = Size of capital and revenue budget under the manager's control (1–10), where 10 is large
G = Extent of authority to commit the organisation (1–10)
H = Special factors (1–10)

Again, the auditor's judgement is an essential requirement, but if the formulae are applied consistently from year to year a benchmark for risk can be established so identifying the areas where catastrophe may occur.

OPERATIONAL AUDIT INDEX

A similar method is used to that for financial audit, however the approach is different, the emphasis being on managerial ability as follows:

A = Capital employed (an agreed definition is required together with consistent application)
B = Experience of management (no of years)
C = Technical expertise required (1–5)
D = Degree of internal control established (1–5)
E = Extent to which management can influence events (1–5)
F = Special factors (1–5)
G = Need for assistance (1–5)
H = Degree of risk to which organisation is exposed by management (1–5)
Formula $(A + 3B + 5E + 5F + 8G) \times (7C + 10D) \times 5H$

In order for both indexations to be effective a further weight should be entered—the time lapse since the last audit. The technique of risk indexation readily identifies with computerised techniques. The index should also be subject to regular review to take account of changing circumstances. Risk analysis is important to the internal auditor to ensure audit resources are concentrated on areas subject to greater risk.

2.9.1 Advantages and disadvantages of indexation

ADVANTAGES

1 An attempt at evaluation is better than no attempt.
2 Provision of a basis for planning the use of audit resources, through the provision of a notional risk index, allowing resources to be directed towards the highest ranking risk.

DISADVANTAGES

1 The auditor's judgement is a very heavy weighting factor and this ability will vary from auditor to auditor, so weakening the exercise of comparability.
2 The task of providing a suitable index will reduce time spent auditing.

In conclusion, audit resources should be concentrated on areas of greatest need, indexation being a scientific means of quantifying judgement.

2.10   Risk exposure analysis

This is a development of the risk analysis where the analysis is restricted to three elements:

1 Monetary value—Exposure (E);
2 Likelihood of loss—Vulnerability (V);
3 Effectiveness of internal control—Control assessment (C).

(a) *Exposure*—This element is assigned a monetary value based on, for instance, turnover, expenditure or net present value of asset or cashflows. These values are then ranked accordingly,

low	= 1 say under £0.5 million
medium	= 2 say £0.5–5.0 million
high	= 3 say over £5.0 million

(b) *Vulnerability*—This is of a less quantifiable nature, being dependent upon the auditor's judgement, ie based on a combination of the following factors: complexity and character of operations; employee or contractor involvement; adequacy of supervision; industrial relations; physical location; and communications and public image. Again this opinion is ranked over three strata: low (1), medium (2), high (3).

(c) *Control assessment*—This is again judgementally based, the auditor determining whether to state that control is either adequate (1) or weak (2). It is assumed that strong control is a result of overstaffing! Such an appraisal is based on the results of the last audit, the time since the last audit, the performance of the auditee against expected results and management concerns.

Audit ref	Exposure	Vulnerability	Control assessment	Sum	Product
1	High	High	Weak	8	18
2	High	Medium	Weak	7	12
3	Medium	High	Weak	7	12
4	High	High	Adequate	6	9
5	Medium	Medium	Weak	6	8
6	High	Medium	Adequate	6	6
7	Medium	High	Adequate	6	6
8	High	Low	Weak	6	6
9	Medium	High	Weak	6	6
10	Medium	Medium	Adequate	5	4
11	Medium	Low	Weak	5	4
12	Low	Medium	Weak	5	4
13	High	Low	Adequate	5	3
14	Low	High	Adequate	5	3
15	Medium	Low	Adequate	4	2
16	Low	Medium	Adequate	4	2
17	Low	Low	Weak	4	2
18	Low	Low	Adequate	3	1

Source: Risk Exposure Analysis Shell UK Exploration and Production

EXAMPLE

Audit: Goods in transit	Ref: Aud/123/456	
Exposure: £4 million bank value	Medium	2
Vulnerability: Established staff	Low	1
Control assessment: Previous audit–		
recommendations accepted implemented. 2 years		
since previous audit	Adequate	1
Procedures in place.		
Risk ranking = 2 + 1 + 1 = 4		

It is then possible to assist the audit plan by identifying a 'cut-off' point where resources allowed or available match the requirements of the plan. The advantage of this technique is its simplicity and ease of understanding compared to the more complex risk analyses. It is to be remembered that other factors such as requests by senior management also influence the determination of the audit plan. However, by using this technique audit can be ranked by risk.

2.11　Audit profile triggers (APTs)

This is a technique for developing a detailed internal audit examination programme designed to identify and address the specific risks and opportunities which apply to the area to be examined at the time of the audit. The technique is based upon reference to a digest of key topics for each main area of audit scope to be considered in the context of a range of fundamental audit questions.

APTs are not intended to be used as checklists but as a means of prompting constructive thought by the auditor when designing an objective audit programme which is most likely to lead to a highly effective internal audit service. Every topic relevant to the audit being planned must be considered against a general APT designed to prompt the principal basic audit questions to be addressed. These questions are fundamental to all audit work. For example:

General APT		
1 Organisation	6 Instructions	11 Efficiency
2 Objectives	7 Compliance	12 Security
3 Authority	8 Monitoring	13 Legality
4 Accountability	9 Control	14 Risks
5 Resources	10 Effectiveness	15 Opportunities

This General APT would be regarded as the framework for determining the audit programme. The areas of audit scope for each of which there should then be detailed APTs might be classified as set out in the table on p 46.

1 *Marketing*:
1.1 Pricing structure; 1.2 Quotations; 1.3 Order processing;
1.4 Sales administration; 1.5 Distribution; 1.6 Debtors.

2 *Material management*:
2.1 Purchasing; 2.2 Stock control; 2.3 Creditors.

3 *Fixed assets*:
3.1 Capital expenditure; 3.2 Fixed asset management.

4 *Data processing*:
4.1 D P operations; 4.2 D P security.

5 *Security*:
5.1 Site security; 5.2 Insurance; 5.3 Cash; 5.4 Payrolls.

6 *Production*:
6.1 Production records; 6.2 Production planning and control.

7 *Management accounting*:
7.1 Costing; 7.2 Period accounting; 7.3 Accounting records.

Examples of detailed APTs are given in a number of places in this book, normally at the end of those sections which deal with general coverage areas of internal audit examination.

When using APTs to develop a detailed internal audit programme the auditor may find it convenient to prepare matrices of the most relevant general and detailed APTs to enable the risks and opportunities to be compared and ranked in order of priority. This ranking is a matter for the auditor's judgement based upon experience and knowledge of the organisation and the activities to be audited. The use of computerised spreadsheet techniques can greatly assist in preparing matrices for these judgements.

Large complex organisations tend to comprise many management centres each specialising in a specific part of the overall objective of the total enterprise. This can involve different markets, different technologies and differences in management styles and cultures. Consequently the information needs and the control systems may vary significantly from unit to unit. The risks and opportunities can also be expected to vary in emphasis between one unit and another. Moreover all organisations must be adaptable and respond to a continuously changing environment.

Internal audit is a service to management which identifies control weaknesses and gives positive reassurance for the areas which are well controlled. Such a service is likely to be the more effective, the more closely it can relate to the particular circumstances of each separate unit and the environment in which it operates. By doing so the internal audit service will bcome a valuable management aid which can also focus on risks and opportunities from the perspective of an independent viewpoint.

APTs provide a useful audit management tool which enables an element of flexibility to be introduced in a controlled way into planning the detailed examination work for each separate audit. The audit programme is then designed to take into account the conditions and circumstances prevailing at the time of the audit.

When the APT technique is used, responsibility for detailed planning of the audit work may be delegated to competent experienced auditors who then bring to bear their detailed knowledge of the area under consideration. This enables the use of auditing time to be directed so as to penetrate into those areas which will result in recommendations likely to be of greatest benefit to the management.

3.0 ORGANISING

3.1 Provision of internal audit services

Management has three main choices in the provision of internal audit services: namely, in-house, consortia and external. In-house provision is tailor-made for the organisation, having the advantages of no conflict of loyalty, interest in the well-being of the organisation and familiarity with organisational goals and needs.

3.1.1 *Consortia, agency or shared audit*

This represents an arrangement whereby internal audit serves more than one organisation. Following the Salmon Report, such an arrangement is now to be found within the NHS.

Three forms of agreement are in use:

1 Where the major organisation services the needs of smaller organisations.
2 Where smaller organisations service the major organisation (sometimes known as 'backdoor' arrangements).
3 Where all users contribute to the provision of shared auditors.

3.1.2 *Audit service provided by major organisation*

NEED

1 Smaller organisations may not have sufficient finance to support their own audit department.
2 Smaller organisations may require specialist expertise (computer audit), which only a large organisation can provide.
3 Due to limited scale the smaller organisation may not be able to attract staff of the right calibre. Similarly the experience to be gained and the career prospects may be more restricted in a small organisation.
4 In the public sector close co-operation may be required to improve services and avoid duplication of work.
5 Pressure to improve internal audit standards (eg Salmon Report) applies mostly to the larger organisation.

An example of such an operation is Cambridgeshire County Council which services South Cambridgeshire District Council, East Cambridgeshire District Council and the East Anglia Regional Health Authority.

ADVANTAGES

1 Potential for training and obtaining skilled and specialist auditors.
2 Easier to attract staff by offering wider experience.

3 Staff cover not so critical in a larger organisation.
4 Independence of agency auditor.
5 Cross-fertilisation of ideas.

DISADVANTAGES

1 Potential conflict of loyalty.
2 Ensuring fair treatment in use of resources.

3.1.3   *Other organisations servicing a major organisation*

Although less common, the advantages of such an operation are largely the saving of expense through not having to audit establishments over a large geographical area. An example of such an operation is Fareham, Portsmouth and Southampton District Councils auditing Hampshire County Council services (prior to 1985).

DISADVANTAGES

1 Communications—The chief internal auditor will have to control several auditors from different agencies.
2 Potential conflict of loyalties.
3 Ensuring fair treatment in use of resources.
4 Confidentiality—This is of utmost importance in the private sector.

3.1.4   *Use of external auditors for internal audit*

This form of agency is unlikely to be satisfactory because the objectives of external audit are fundamentally different from those of internal audit. Conflicting interests could reduce the effectiveness of internal audit and prejudice the independence of extrnal audit.

However, in certain specialised areas, eg computer audit, the use of expertise offered by the external auditor may be welcome when compared with the cost of hiring a computer expert.

The Audit Commission does not allow the use of external auditors. Several district health authorities have employed private firms as 'internal auditors' but with the purpose of training an adequate internal audit service from their own employees.

3.2   Status of internal audit

'The organisational status of the internal auditing department should be sufficient to permit the accomplishment of its audit responsibilities.' (IIA Standard 110)

The status of internal audit is vitally important as it plays a major role in the ability of internal audit to achieve its objectives. There are three recognised forms as follows:

3.2.1   *Reporting directly to a chief executive or managing director*

This is considered to be the ideal situation. However, it has not always proved to be totally successful because:

1 Audit ideals may be pursued to the detriment of operational performance.

2 The auditor may be perceived as a restricting influence.
3 Difficulties may arise in liaising with other departments.

These difficulties may reflect a negative attitude about internal audit to the detriment of the decision-making capacity of line management, ie the organisation is not meeting its objectives because audit objectives are taking precedence over operational objectives.

3.2.2 *Reporting to a departmental manager or local manager*

The auditor is responsible to a departmental manager. This is probably the worst situation for both audit and the organisation. One advantage is that of specialised local knowledge. The main disadvantage is the tarnishing of audit independence, the auditor being too close to the management of one department. Secondly, professional audit experience gained in such a department is unlikely to compare with the promotion prospects offered within a centralised department, with the consequence that attracting qualified auditors is difficult and this may lead to poor auditing standards.

3.2.3 *Reporting to a director of finance*

This is the most common situation and has the following advantages:

1 The finance department has skilled accountants and already operates effective channels of communication.
2 The director of finance is concerned with financial control of the organisation as a whole, and acts in an unbiased manner as far as the departments are concerned. Indeed it may be the director of finance's statutory responsibility to maintain a current internal audit, eg as in local government.
3 The finance department will have the expertise and resources upon which both internal auditor and accountant can draw, leading to greater benefits for the organisation as a whole.

DISADVANTAGES

It may be considered by line managers subject to audit that they are exposed to criticism while the finance department may not be. The chief internal auditor must provide an impartial service which clearly demonstrates that this claim is unfounded. Additionally the finance department is subject to a rigorous independent external audit.

3.3 Determining a minimum level of internal audit

Having identified the strengths and weaknesses of internal audit, the chief internal auditor must form a judgement on not only the expertise of internal audit but the number of staff required to undertake the tasks given by senior management.

A report by the DSS/AHST audit working group gives an example of how this may be done:

Per		*Audit man days*
£1 million	Annual expenditure (excluding employee costs)	70
£1 million	Annual income	70
1,000	Employees	580
	Total	720

When compared to an auditor's working year, ie approximately 210 man days (after holidays and bank holidays, training etc) such a figure represents approximately 3 to 3½ (full time equivalent) auditors. Of course, such a method is very crude, taking no account of the systems being operated by the organisation. However, if applied with judgement to a consistent scale for measuring audit quality, it could lead to a more adequate means of determining a minimum internal audit provision. Thus, where the minimum level stated by the DSS is divided into the maximum score (1,500), this will give a maximum score per auditor. When the actual score is divided by the actual number of auditors this will give guidance as to the quality of work being undertaken. There is not much point in employing greater quantity when the problem is quality, eg:

		No of auditors	*Score*	*Score per auditor*
A	Actual:	5	500	100
	DSS minimum level:	6	1,500	250
B	Actual:	10	1,200	120
	DSS minimum level:	15	1,500	100

In A's case the quality of auditors is the 'real' problem, while in B's case a greater number of auditors would be of assistance.

3.4   Other measures of internal audit

It is to be remembered that one full-time equivalent employee represents approximately 210 man days (52 wks × 5 = 260 man days less 50 days for holidays, sickness, training, etc).

Indeed it might, with improved co-operation between internal auditors, be possible to establish an index of audit cost per £1,000 turnover per type of industry. It is interesting to note the following table compiled by Tim Shaw, *Accountancy* March 1984, regarding external auditors. The figures are merely intended to demonstrate the concept that if such data can be compiled for external auditors a similar technique could be used for internal audit.

Using the *Financial Times* categories to group companies in similar trades and ignoring the mixed bag of industries:

Trade	No of companies in the sample	Audit cost in pence per £ of shareholders' funds
Oil and gas	25	.097
Drapery and stores	39	.111
Beers, wines and spirits	25	.111
Chemicals and plastics	15	.129
Mines	3	.173
Hotels and caterers	8	.179
Building industry, timber, roads	46	.228
Food and groceries	29	.253
Shipping	6	.263
Electricals	43	.301
Newspapers and publishers	12	.309
Motors, aircraft trades	12	.323
Textiles	8	.337
Engineering	42	.415
Overseas traders	8	.469
Leisure	12	.532
Paper, printing, advertising	9	.555
	342	

The danger of not establishing a minimum level of audit provision is that in times of hardship an erosion of the internal audit workforce may occur, resulting in performance below the minimum acceptable level as stated by British Gas. The British Gas approach involves implications for both management and audit:

1 Management—The adoption of a minimum level of audit based on a review of internal control presupposes that every system's weakness is due to error or management inaction.
2 Internal audit—Given reasonable circumstances, standards of performance must be met.

It is of interest to note the following statistics provided by a small survey of UK multinationals undertaken by BP.

	External audit fees + internal audit fees, as a % of turnover	Number of employees per internal auditor	£ million turnover per internal auditor	£ million net assets per internal auditor
Average	0.14%	1057	79	36

This survey conducted in March 1984 can only be used as a 'rough indication' of internal audit provision as no attempt was made or intended to be made as to how representative the survey was. However, as a discussion point and guide it is of interest.

It is for the internal audit manager to determine whether the terms of reference (charter) offered correspond to the needs of the organisation and, if not, to persuade senior management to redress the situation. Organisations are administered by different individuals in differing environments functioning in different ways. Internal audit must acknowledge these differences, fully adopting the standards of independence and due professional care.

Once the minimum level of audit has been agreed, a plan of work should be compiled based on the resources available and the degree of risk ascertained. A cyclical pattern may be adopted for audit scoping, eg:

1 Annual audit visits to be scheduled for each operational area or management centre.
2 Larger units and high risk areas may be scheduled for more frequent visits.
3 Control areas for every unit should be classified to be subjected to audit examination on a cycle of one, two or three years according to the risk rating.

3.5   Structure and organisation of the audit department

Following agreements on the audit objectives the structure of the internal audit department should be established to allow the execution of a plan to meet the agreed objectives.

3.5.1   *Organisation of a department*

The chief internal auditor must decide the number and structure of personnel required for the efficient and effective functioning of internal audit. The following factors should be taken into account:

1 Geographical area to be covered—The larger the area the more non-productive time is required for travel.
2 The volume of the organisation's transactions—The larger the volume the greater the need for control.
3 The value of the organisation's transactions—The larger the value the greater the security needed.
4 The degree of specialist work required—Computer/contract audit.
5 The nature and quality of systems operated by the organisation.
6 The attitude of management to internal audit.

In an audit section there will be blends of skill and personality which can be further developed by a sound training programme. Once the number of staff and structure have been agreed, good channels of communication should be established together with provision for a recognised career structure.

3.5.2 *Job description of a chief internal auditor (manager)*

1 Responsibility to the senior management team for the provision of an internal audit function in accordance with internal auditing standards.
2 Preparation of, and monitoring of performance against, an audit plan.
3 Maintenance of adequate audit standards.
4 Liaison with external auditors
5 Continuous review of management instructions and all financial procedures.
6 Audit staff recruitment and provision of adequate training facilities.
7 Appraisal of the adequacy and operation of the management information and control systems.
8 Direction of investigations into fraud and misappropriations.
9 Maintenance of an adequate level of computer audit, where appropriate.

3.5.3 *Job description of an internal auditor*

1 Examining management control systems, organisations and operations.
2 Analysing effectiveness, efficiency and economy.
3 Making impartial judgements and offering feasible constructive recommendations for improvement.
4 Presenting conclusions to management on the significance of the findings.

3.5.4 *Job description of a contracts auditor (specialist)*

1 Responsibility to the audit manager for the audit of contract expenditure and income.
2 Maintenance of current contract files and performance of site visits on major schemes.
3 Review of audit programmes for all areas of contract audit.
4 Preparation of capital expenditure audit manual.
5 Assistance in preparation of the audit plan.
6 Consultation with other internal auditors on matters related to contract audit.
7 Supervision of staff as appropriate.
8 Identification of possible subjects for and participation in value for money studies.

3.5.5 *Job description of a computer auditor (specialist)*

1 Responsibility to the audit manager for audit of the computer facility in accordance with CIPFA computer audit guidelines.
2 Act as a deputy for the chief internal auditor as required.
3 Assist in the preparation, monitoring and review of the audit plan.
4 Consultation with other internal auditors on computer audit to ensure adequate coverage with minimum duplication of effort.
5 Supervision of senior auditors.
6 Identification of possible subjects for value for money studies.
7 Supervision of investigations.
8 Supervision of training.

3.6 The cost of internal audit

Cost is largely a function of size and is composed of the following elements:

1 Salaries and on cost (employer's NI and superannuation contributions).
2 Travel and subsistence expenses.
3 Office accommodation.
4 Administrative expenses, eg stationery.
5 Central administrative charges, eg fuel, light, heat, computer.

The burden of justifying the expense may be determined by allocating the costs of internal audit as a charge to operating units based on audit activity. This will allow the auditee (departmental manager/subsidiary) the opportunity to evaluate the service provided against the internal charge made. An alternative is an attempt to quantify the potential damage caused by poor systems, and failure to detect fraud and waste (such an attempt may not withstand close scrutiny) and to offset this guesstimate against the actual cost of audit.

3.7   Staffing requirements

'The Chief Internal Auditor should establish a programme for selecting and developing the staff of the internal auditing department.' (IIA Standard 540)

Personal qualities of a 'model' auditor:

1 *Integrity*—The knowledge of an auditor's integrity enhances the faith people have in his judgement and report.

2 *Independence*—His opinion is arrived at by himself, without duress.

3 *Objectivity*—To take the overall view with regard to the organisation as a whole rather than the narrower audit viewpoint is said to be objective. The use of the audit measure irrespective of whether people agree with it or not is said to be subjective.

4 *Tactfulness*—Skill in communicating with people without causing offence yet extracting information in the most efficient manner.

5 *Inquisitiveness*—A searching and enquiring mind.

6 *Method*—A methodical approach is essential to demonstrate 'due professional care' has been exercised.

7 *Practicality*—Recommendations must be feasible within the limitation of available resources.

8 *Communication*—Ability to listen and comprehend and to express ideas cogently.

9 *Assessment*—Ability to evaluate and analyse someone else's work.

10 *Reporting*—Ability to write concise and readable reports.

11 *Assistance*—To be seen to be working for the good of the organisation.

3.8   Personnel management and development

This aspect of audit management has been well summarised by the IIA:

'The chief internal auditor should establish a programme for selecting and developing the staff of the internal auditing department. The programme should provide for:
1 Developing written job descriptions for each level of the audit staff.
2 Selecting qualified and competent individuals.
3 Training and providing continuing educational opportunities for each internal auditor.
4 Appraising each internal auditor's performance at least annually.
5 Providing counsel to internal auditors on their performance and professional development.' (IIA Standard 540)

3.9 Training

Training can be provided in many ways, to name but a few:

1 Professional qualifications (including 'Continuing Professional Education').
2 Audit manuals and progressive practical experience.
3 Audit training packages (including the establishment of a technical library).
4 'In service' courses.
5 Audit bulletins and notes of technical guidance.
6 External courses.

Whatever the chosen method, it should cover the following major areas or skills, preferably leading to a recognised professional qualification.

1 Knowledge of systems adopted by the organisation.
2 Knowledge of structure adopted by the organisation.
3 Preparation and conduct of audits.
4 Auditing techniques.
5 Communications (eg verbal and written reports).
6 Behavioural aspects of auditing.

An example of a training programme follows:

3.9.1 *Audit training programme*

The objective of this training programme is to develop individuals with proven skills to become effective as internal auditors. Its purpose is:

1 To complete the experience requirements not satisfied in previous placements.
2 To develop skills in penetrating examination and meaningful analysis.
3 To develop a capacity for making relevant judgements.
4 To develop powers for effectively presenting an impartial case.

PHASE 1

Assisting on selected audits under direct instruction from the internal auditor responsible. This stage involves learning and applying the techniques of audit examination. Experience in this phase should include a reasonable sample of coverage areas.

PHASE 2

Supporting on selected audits under supervision from the lead auditor responsible for the audit. This stage involves taking responsibility for specific areas of coverage, making audit judgements and presenting your conclusions to management. Experience in this phase must include a reasonable sample of coverage areas including any omitted at Phase 1. We take special care to include studies of marketing, production and commercial operations.

PHASE 3

Taking full responsibility for small audits under guidance from the audit manager.

This stage involves selling your ideas for improved efficiency to management both verbally and in a formal written report.

The time required for each phase of training will vary from one individual to another, depending upon previous experience and training. Progress will be closely monitored by the audit manager and reviewed regularly with the trainee. Each phase must be fully mastered before moving on to the next.

4.0 DIRECTING

Of equal importance to the other factors comprising what is understood to be management, is the skill of directing the staff of the department so that the department's 'terms of reference' are achieved both efficiently and effectively. The importance of this aspect of management is summarised by IIA Standard 530:

> 'The chief internal auditor should provide written policies and procedures to guide the audit staff.'

This standard is further elaborated:

> 'The form and content of written policies and procedures should be appropriate to the size and structure of the internal auditing department and the complexity of its work. Formal administrative and technical audit manuals may not be needed by all internal auditing departments. A small internal auditing department may be managed informally. Its audit staff may be directed and controlled through daily close supervision and written memoranda. In a large auditing department, more formal and comprehensive policies and procedures are essential to guide the audit staff in the consistent compliance with the department's standards of performance.' (IIA Guideline 530.01)

4.1 Audit briefing

Prior to each audit, the auditor should be briefed as to the objectives and conduct of the audit, giving consideration to details such as: the auditee's environment, past audit problems, current audit objectives, the purpose of the audit and the resources allowed. An important objective is to motivate the audit staff, as well as to explain the approach to the audit.

4.1.1 *Example of an audit brief*

Confidential

Report to: Mr J Jones

Subject: Central Distribution Provision

Date

Audit reference: 09/1234/567

Audit coverage:

4.1.2 *Background*

A central warehouse has been provided at Greenfields for supplying regional distribution centres in order to improve customer service while at the same time reducing stock holding. Demand has rapidly outgrown the capacity of the warehouse and additional capital expenditure is planned which will more than double the capacity of the warehouse.

4.1.3 *Areas to be appraised*

Restricted warehouse capacity has contributed to stock management difficulties. The stockholding is above budget; the statutory auditors have expressed lack of confidence in the stock records; and staff are having to spend excessive time resolving queries from customers and suppliers.

Senior management have requested an appraisal of this area of activity.

4.2 Statement of internal audit's function

This is examined under **Essential requirements** (**3.0** in Chapter 2). The importance of such a statement is twofold: firstly for the use of auditors; and secondly as a means of promoting the usefulness of internal audit to the organisation, eg through ensuring sound controls and communications organisational performance is improved. Once senior management has agreed the objectives of the internal audit function, the audit manager is in a position to formulate policy and to compile a plan to meet the stated objectives: the internal audit department's terms of reference.

4.3 Audit policy

Audit policy must be based on the terms of reference. In the past, traditional audit has been restricted to financial and regularity auditing. Modern internal audit has been expanded to include value for money and management investigations. In order to meet objectives, the manager must determine the proportion of the types of audit to be undertaken, prior to submission of the plan to senior management for approval.

4.4 Approaches to audit work

4.4.1 *Financial audit (transactions audit)*

Sometimes called 'probity audit', this means a check of honesty or integrity, the emphasis being on 'financial security'. This type of audit tends to take the form of the transaction approach where a large sample of transactions are verified to supporting documentation, eg cash audit (see verification of assets). This approach is time consuming and typified by the substantive test. Included in this form of audit is the physical inspection of stock and other assets to safeguard and ensure their existence. (The protection of the organisation's asset base.)

4.4.2   *Regularity audit (systems-based)*

This type of audit involves the examination of internal control procedures to ensure compliance with the rules and regulations of the organisation. It is typified by compliance testing supported by substantive tests where weaknesses are detected to reassure management that the instructions complied with are leading towards the achievement of organisational objectives.

4.4.3   *Operational audit*

Operational audit and management audit have different meanings to different people: the following definitions are, however, preferred,

> 'A forward looking evaluation by internal auditors to identify areas in which economy, efficiency and effectiveness may be improved or to evaluate compliance with operational plans, policies and procedures.' (*Government Internal Audit Manual*)

> 'An objective and independent appraisal of the effectiveness of managers and the effectiveness of the corporate structure in the achievement of company objectives and policies.
>   Its aim is to identify existing and potential management weaknesses within an organisation and to recommend ways to rectify these weaknesses.' (CIMA Management Accounting *Official Terminology*)

Operational audit can also be defined more simply as the audit of non-financial activities or financial activities not involving probity, ie the efficiency of credit control would be considered to be both a financial activity but also an operational audit, the examination is one of management efficiency.

4.4.4   *Social audit*

This form of audit embraces social accountability and responsibility. Social audit has been defined as 'encompassing the economic, legal, ethical and discretionary expectations that society has of organisations at a given point in time'. (Albanese *Managing: Towards Accountability for Performance*)

Large organisations have a significant impact on the local community within which they operate. Although not mandatory in Britain, in France it is and includes the appraisal of the following areas of organisational activity:

> Employment levels; Remuneration and other benefits; Training programmes; Health and safety; Industrial relations; Living conditions of employees—housing and travel.

It has further been suggested that areas of activity such as environmental pollution, energy conservation and welfare programmes should also be included for consideration.

It is only a matter of time before internal audit departments in the more enlightened organisations undertake reviews in these areas; failure to do so could leave the organisation vulnerable to catastrophe of such magnitude that its very survival is threatened. Less dramatically, when companies attempt to establish industries, local organisations are inclined to request details of the product, associated dangers, and the expertise of the company in meeting such dangers. The reader can no doubt readily identify man-made catastrophes that have threatened the existence of organisations associated with the disaster. It is reasonable for an auditor to advise upon factors impairing the corporate image, and to monitor corrective action. Indeed the ability to resolve legal issues needs to be appraised, so that areas of vulnerability can be strengthened. It is important for the auditor to be able to appraise the effectiveness of the corporate image, thereby providing management with independent advice on sensitive issues.

4.5   The systems-based approach

4.5.1   *Definition*

'Under the systems based approach the nature, extent and timing of detailed audit procedures, including appropriate selective tests of the validity and integrity of transactions, are based on an organised study and evaluation of controls within a system to determine what reliance can be placed on the system to ensure effective planning and management of resources and to provide accurate information. Although some detailed testing of transactions (substantive tests) is necessary to ensure that the identified controls are effective, this approach enables the auditor to concentrate the audit effort in areas where controls to assist in the conduct of operations do not exist or are not operating properly. At the conclusion of the examination the auditor is in a position to point out the consequences of the weakness.' (Canadian Auditor General *Public Finance and Accountancy* 1981)

This long definition may be summarised as follows:

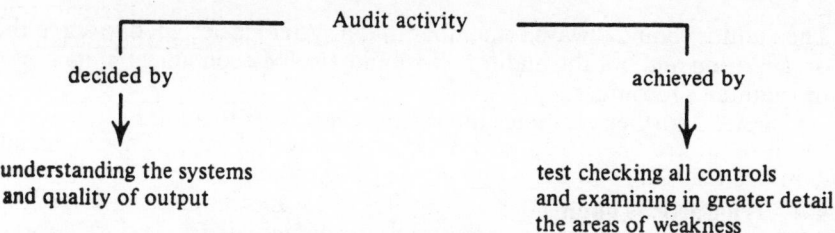

4.5.2   *Systems and controls*

Growth in the scale and complexity of organisations leads inevitably to increased delegation of responsibilities, senior management being ever further removed from the point of daily operational activity. Thus, the control of day-to-day operations relies on the existence of procedural and other controls which regulate activities, monitor operating systems and set standards. This expansion has also caused the auditor to change his technique from examination of every transaction—complete audit—to using a sample as a basis upon which evidence is gained so as to test the compliance with regulations. From such evidence the soundness of internal control can be assessed.

The *Oxford Dictionary* describes a system as 'an arrangement of many parts which work together with one purpose'. In order to examine a system, the parts comprising it—internal controls—must be examined so that the auditor can place a degree of reliance upon the whole.

4.5.3   *Examining the system*

THE EXISTING SYSTEM

The auditor's recommendations regarding any changes in procedures will be confined by the nature of the auditee organisation, eg the volume of transactions, the complexity of accounting systems and the resources allocated to accounting staff.

MANAGEMENT STYLE

It is important for the line manager to recognise the abilities of his staff. By way of anecdote I remember a chef good at cuisine but unable to match purchase order against invoice! The point is that recommendations must take account of the limitations of human nature, the quality and quantity of available staff.

REQUIREMENTS OF THE ACCOUNTING SYSTEM

These must be established at the outset because they determine the manner in which records are kept and the relative importance attached to certain sensitive areas. The minimum statutory requirement is for the accounting system to fulfil statutory disclosure requirements. However, it is important that management information is based on sound data. Thus, the level at which transactions are aggregated, analysed and funded are matters which the system needs to accommodate to allow for planning, targeting and decision making.

COST/BENEFIT RELATIONSHIP

The auditor should always remember that a system is designed to serve the organisation and not the auditor. It should also be economical in its use of the auditee's resources.

Chapter 5 further examines the systems approach to auditing.

4.6   Transactions audit

4.6.1   *Definition*

'The vouching or proving of a large proportion of transactions to documentary evidence.' (M J Pratt *Auditing*)

The use of this audit technique will be determined by the size and nature of the organisation, whether internal control exists in the systems, and the completeness and accuracy with which transactions have been recorded.

With smaller organisations the transaction audit approach is usually by means of matching transactions recorded to supporting documentation, eg purchaser records to invoices—'substantive testing'. In order to gain adequate evidence the auditor will need to test a large proportion of transactions.

In a larger organisation with a high volume of transactions and with accounting systems using soundly based controls the transactions approach may be neither practical (time restraints) nor necessary. Instead the auditor may adopt the system approach, thereby reducing the volume of transactions tested. An illustration of the use of this approach may occur in a payment system where a compliance test identifies a weakness in control, ie discounts received not being deducted from the total amount payable. A substantive test would then be applied to determine the materiality of the weakness of this control.

Whenever possible it is recommended the auditor adopts a systems approach as it allows for better use of audit resources, being a more efficient method of obtaining evidence—it is further supported by the Auditing Practices Committee (APC) Audit Standards.

4.7 Conclusion

Having determined plans, methods of control, direction and form of organisation, it is important for the audit manager to provide a good working environment, as the following quote demonstrates:

'. . . without an appropriate environment the work of any internal audit unit may be poorly directed, misunderstood by line management, conducted in an atmosphere of confrontation and generally fail to represent an efficient or effective use of internal audit resources.' (F D Booth 'A Good Working Environment for Internal Audit' *Internal Auditing* January 1984)

Reasons for systems-based audit (regularity)	*Reasons for transactions-based audit (financial/probity)*
1 Meets the growing demands of complexity and size of organisations through more efficient use of audit resources	1 Meets the need to know the accuracy or correctness of transactions
2 Due to shortage of audit resources auditor is required to be more selective in his approach	2 Forms the basis to probity checks
3 Allows an opinion to be expressed, based on a small representative sample	3 Provides a thorough examination of a large proportion of transactions
4 Where significant weaknesses are found the transactions approach may then be adopted, eg substantive testing of those critical areas	
5 Considered to be the more relevant approach for modern organisations	

The following five areas are identifed as being critical to a good working environment for internal audit:

1 Good channels of communication with senior management. In this context the use of audit committees, with periodic meetings, can be helpful.
2 An understanding of internal audit's role by both senior management and line management. In this area the disclosure of audit objectives is crucial.
3 The design of planning, controlling and reporting procedures for the benefit of the organisation and not solely for the use of internal audit. Audit works for the organisation, not vice versa.
4 Audits should be approached in a constructive and helpful manner with auditors acting as advisers rather than internal policemen. It is important for the auditor's training to be aimed not only at technical skill but also towards a facility for good communications with the auditee.
5 Audit reports should be supported by senior management thereby giving credibility to the auditor, and the auditor should reciprocate by acknowledging and supporting management action on recommendations which are imlemented—this represents the trust between internal audit and senior management.

5.0   CONTROLLING THE AUDIT DEPARTMENT

The chief internal auditor needs to implement a system of control to ensure the agreed annual plan is efficiently executed in accordance with the approved terms of reference. Deviations from the plan must be fully explained and documented.

As with many other management tasks the degree of success achieved depends upon effective delegation. Providing an effective audit service for a major organisation requires a staff of competent internal auditors who have suitable temperaments and who are adequately trained and well motivated. It is responsible work and each internal auditor must not only be skilled in collecting audit evidence but must also be capable of working on his or her own initiative and exercising mature judgement in the interpretation of the evidence collected.

The management task is to provide the framework in which the endeavours of each individual auditor will contribute fully to the successful achievement of corporate objectives in executing the agreed audit plan. This task involves recruiting the right people, guiding their development and training for the job, briefing them on the work assigned to them and motivating them to identify enthusiastically with the pursuit of clearly defined team objectives. It is then necessary to monitor performance and administer appropriate guidance and encouragement as well as regular recognition of good work and occasionally correction or even admonition. The most effective monitoring systems are those in which the individual auditors measure their own achievements against agreed benchmarks.

Directing the internal audit service for a major organisation involves:

1 *Recruitment of suitable staff*—internal auditors should have:
   (a) A well developed sense of responsibility—able to work on own initiative and having confidence in own judgement.
   (b) Intelligence to be able to grasp quickly the fundamentals of complex systems, methods and techniques.
   (c) Inquisitiveness—an eagerness to learn.

(d) Sensitivity to the views and attitudes of others.

(e) Interpersonal skills, especially the ability to communicate.

2 *Staff development*—Working with each individual internal auditor on plans specifically designed for each to achieve his or her full potential. These will involve planned work experience, specific training courses in professional skills and personal development and regular audit training conferences for the whole team.

3 *Monitoring performance*—Maintaining the departmental record of achievement by each internal auditor against agreed benchmarks and demonstrating the importance of progressing according to plan.

4 *Motivation*—This reflects the quality of management rather than representing a separate management function. It is achieved through the approach adopted for each of the other functions 1 to 3 above. Strong motivation will be based upon:

(a) Leadership—positive direction of the internal audit service with clear objectives giving sound guidance and encouragement and acknowledging good work.

(b) Team spirit—belonging to a successful team of competent internal auditors which demands high professional standards and commands respect for its services.

(c) Responsibility—individual accountability for audit judgements based upon own findings.

(d) Job satisfaction—interesting valuable work offering useful career experience with prospects.

5.1 Internal audit reports

'Activity reports should be submitted periodically to management and to the board. These reports should compare:

(a) performance for the department's goals and audit work schedules, and

(b) expenditures with financial budgets. They should explain the reasons for major variances and indicate any action taken or needed.' (IIA Guideline 520.06)

Audit reports are crucial to efficient managerial control: they constitute the authentic permanent record of the auditor's work and conclusions supported by detailed findings and recommendations. Reports should confirm the issues discussed with the responsible management at the end of the audit and serve as a checklist for action agreed and for subsequent auditors to follow up. Reports should also inform other interested parties, who often have some authority to influence the action to be taken by the responsible management. Audit reporting is dealt with in detail at **7.2** in Chapter 4.

5.2 Quality assurance

'Quality assurance is essential to maintaining an internal auditing department's capability to perform its functions in an efficient, effective manner. Quality assurance is also important in achieving and maintaining a high level of credibility with management, the audit committee, and others who rely on the work of the internal auditing department.' (IIA Statement of Internal Auditing Standards No 4)

'The Chief Internal Auditor should establish and maintain a quality assurance programme to evaluate the operation of the Internal Audit Department.' (IIA Standard 560)

The objectives of such a programme are to ensure adherence to the 'terms of reference' (charter) and compliance with professional standards, guidelines and recognised ethical conduct. As such the programme has three modes of operation.

5.2.1   *Supervision*

The auditor should be the subject of a continuous review of work undertaken embracing the following aspects of audit work:

1 Compliance with programme.
2 Adequacy of work performed.
3 Future training and career needs.
4 Behavioural skills.

An example of such work may be a file review, whereby the work is reviewed for the skill with which it was completed, the adequacy of documentation, validity of opinion reached, adequacy of evidence supporting that opinion and the clarity of findings reported. This form of review is commonly undertaken by an audit senior on a continuous basis.

5.2.2   *Internal reviews*

The chief internal auditor should review the performance of both the staff and the department. The review should embrace matters already described, but relate the review to departmental performance rather than individual performance.

Such a review should be undertaken on a periodic basis with similar techniques to those used on an audit. Indeed there should exist agreed review procedures and programmes to be used by the manager or person appraising performance.

It is particularly important that the internal auditor should report the findings of the review to the audit committee and senior management, thereby allowing internal audit to promote its useful role within the organisation.

5.2.3   *External review*

This form of review can be undertaken by management consultants or, indeed, an internal review body (eg HM Treasury undertakes a review of departmental audit units within central government) eg persons who are not only independent, but also qualified to undertake such a review.

The IIA recommended such a review be conducted every three years, with the emphasis being placed upon compliance with approved auditing standards.

5.3   The use of computers in audit management

Initially computers were used to improve secretarial and planning support to the manager through such facilities as word processing and spreadsheets. However, as awareness of the use to which computers can be put and availability of computers at a reasonable cost have increased, so the extent to which the audit manager makes use of computers has also increased. Clearly the technique of risk analysis readily lends itself to computing, as does unit costing and exception reporting. Such techniques assist the audit planning and control process. These are computer assisted audit techniques (CAAT).

Techniques already in use include general audit software packages which are pre-programmed software allowing for audit sampling. It assumes the auditor is familiar with the information subject to examination. Examples are CARS, Auditape and STRATA. For the audit manager it could mean that the auditor spends less time determining the sample to be taken and more time auditing. This results in more effective use of scarce resources.

Utility programmes are written by either computer manufacturers or software houses, specifically to meet the needs of users. Such uses may be the merging, sorting, editing and recording of certain files requested. Examples are as follows:

1 *Program comparison utilities*—Compares versions of program and reports variations, thereby allowing for verification of alterations.

2 *Logic path analysis programs*—This utility allows for the conversion of a source program into a flowchart or diagram.

3 *Tracing and mapping*—Both techniques involve logic paths, tracing where a path is used and mapping where an expected path is not used (eg illicit use).

4 *Tailor-made programs*—These programs are written for departmental use, eg a banking report, detailing the last banking amount.

5 *File dumps*—Seldom used due to volume data, all data being dumped onto hard copy.

6 *Logging aid*—Identifies activity on the computer-programs run, access to files, terminals used and attempts to gain entry to the system.

7 *Integrated audit monitors*—These are embedded or resident audit checks written into the application system. Invaluable for very large transaction volumes, otherwise cost makes its use prohibitive.

8 *Program auditing*—The auditor reads the program. Again this method is expensive in audit time and is used as a last resort.

Although not directly of use to management, the use of these techniques may make for more effective auditing. The use of the computer for monitoring adherence to audit plans is well documented, as is budgetary control, and manpower planning.

The ability to interrogate various operating systems allows auditors to undertake much of their work without the tedious process for sorting massive volumes of documentation and through the use of analytical techniques to gain representative samples or selective samples with rapidity.

5.4 Audit task analysis

This is a documentary aid to the chief internal auditor, developed at Kingston upon Thames Borough Council and used to assist in determining work that is complete and that which is outstanding. For each of the areas to be covered in the audit plan, a detailed task analysis is devised, thereby allowing for the identification of areas requiring future audit, ie gaps in the system subject to audit. It allows for the methodical documentation of a system and consequently the designing of an audit programme. Furthermore, compilation of the analysis reveals the frequency of audits of the particular areas, those requiring further appraisal and an assessment of internal control. Such an analysis provides for a checklist of key areas of audit coverage, frequency of areas subject to audit and the identification of areas requiring further attention, eg:

Audit task analysis

Master ref	Title	Audit interval (months)	84/ 85	85/ 86	86/ 87	87/ 88	88/ 89	89/ 90
8041	*Central wages system*							
(i)	Organisation and division of duties within payroll function							
(ii)	Establishment control							
(iii)	Control of master file, including (a) setting up of new employees; (b) rates of pay and amendments thereto; (c) statutory deductions; (d) input/output controls							
(iv)	Leavers							
(v)	Payments input and output control							
(vi)	Overtime claims							
(vii)	Payment of bonus							
(viii)	control over sundry additions and deductions							
(ix)	Unclaimed wages							
(x)	Payroll reconciliation (including control accounts)							
(xi)	Operation and reconciliation of wages bank account							
(xii)	Budgeting and budgetary control							
(xiii)	Efficiency and value for money issues Nb, See also File 9061—Audit of Computerised Systems and Applications (Wages) and Files 8042 to 8047 —Wages Feeder Systems							

Source: Nigel Jackman *Public Finance and Accountancy* 2 *February* 1987.

Audit assessment schedule

Subject	Code
Cash	
Income systems	
Ordering and payments	
Assets control	
Security	
Employees	
Budgetary control	
Accounting controls	
Contracts	
Computer systems	
Other	
Codes	
A = Sound control	
B = Some weakness in control	
C = Poor control	
D = Not examined	
E = Not applicable	

Source: *Public Finance and Accountancy* 20 February 1987

Further reading

Patton, J M, Evans, J H and Lewis, B *A framework for evaluating internal audit risk* Research report No 25 (1986) (IIA Inc).

Risk analysis for internal auditing (1987) (IIA–UK).

Woolf, E *Auditing today* (4th edn, 1990) (Prentice Hall).

CHAPTER 4 Audit skills and attitudes

Objectives	To describe the conditions which affect the auditor's environment and the skills needed to perform effectively
Contents	Auditee perceptions; factors which influence auditors; management perceptions; behavioural aspects; legal aspects Fact-finding interviews Reporting skills
Summary	Both management and auditors need to be aware of all the factors which may influence the quality of an auditor's work. Auditors need to have well developed inter-personal skills and communication skills in particular

1.0 SKILLS AND ATTITUDES

In undertaking audit tasks, the auditor is dependent upon inter-personal skills which affect the relationships established with both auditee and management. Of significant importance are report writing and interviewing those holding the information required to undertake an effective audit. The application of such skills is affected by the auditor's attitude to work; job satisfaction, itself being dependent upon the image projected by internal audit within the organisation: self esteem is important.

1.1 Auditee perceptions of the internal auditor

Behavioural research by F E Mints and others reveals that auditees tend to regard auditors as controllers or inspectors, while the auditor regards advice provided as being of an educational and supportive nature, facilitating the resolution of a particular problem. Such diversity of views is summarised in the table on p 69.

Indeed, at one extreme the auditee perceives the audit role as that of the policeman, while the auditor perceives the same situation as being that of a friendly adviser giving a positive solution to particular problems examined: advice which may be either accepted, or with good reason, rejected.

Possible solutions regarding the conflict in perceptions of the audit role lie with the chief internal auditor. Selective recruitment, gaining those temperamentally most suitable to internal audit, together with the active

Aspect of internal audit	Internal auditor's view	Auditee's view
Nature of work	Adviser (assists all levels of management)	Policeman (with backing of authority)
Authority	Informal (invited to examine)	Formal (power to examine)
Source of authority	Personal abilities (good relations)	Senior management (directed by)
Sanction	Suggestion (recommendation)	Coercion (report)

support of senior management for a positive approach to internal audit will help to promote a fairer perception of the role. It is important for the chief internal auditor to publicise the role and responsibilities of internal audit within the organisation. Perception of the role of internal audit depends upon the observer's background, which may not be financial. There can be an ability to conceptualise strategies without realising the need for an effective system of internal control to implement and support the strategy. However, practices already described in Chapter 3, such as an agreed audit charter, agreed annual plan and direct access to senior management, will assist the chief internal auditor to promote the role of the department.

1.2 Factors which influence the internal auditor

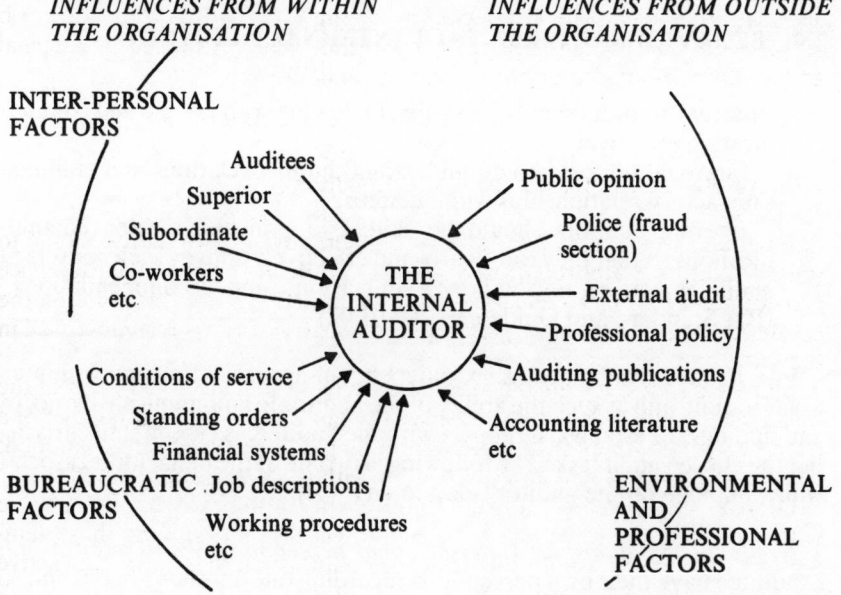

INFLUENCES FROM WITHIN THE ORGANISATION

INFLUENCES FROM OUTSIDE THE ORGANISATION

INTER-PERSONAL FACTORS

Auditees
Superior
Subordinate
Co-workers
etc

THE INTERNAL AUDITOR

Public opinion
Police (fraud section)
External audit
Professional policy
Auditing publications
Accounting literature
etc

Conditions of service
Standing orders
Financial systems
BUREAUCRATIC FACTORS Job descriptions
Working procedures
etc

ENVIRONMENTAL AND PROFESSIONAL FACTORS

The auditor needs to respond to many factors. These have been summarised by CIPFA in *Audit Management* by the diagram on p 69, which is based on research by Morgan and Patterson.

This diagram identifies three groups of factors which determine the internal auditor's role, namely:

1 *Inter-personal factors*—Personal relationships with auditees and others.

2 *Bureaucratic factors*—Regulations determining the work environment.

3 *Environmental and professional factors*—External influences and the means of achieving professional excellence.

Individual auditors identify these factors with their own personal situations in their work environment and this has a bearing on attitude to work and ability to maximise performance.

1.3   Management perceptions of internal audit

Internal audit has a supportive role to senior management, which may involve clarifying policy implications to operational managers where necessary. However, it is important that auditors do not usurp management authority. The auditor is an adviser, being a systems expert and responsible for appraising the efficiency and effectiveness of operational systems. Taking operational decisions would immediately destroy the auditor's independence. Where management has authorised such action, it is for the chief internal auditor to make senior management aware of the implications. Role conflict will occur if an internal auditor seeks to impose changes upon operational managers, rather than persuading them to accept the case for the changes recommended.

2.0   BEHAVIOURAL ASPECTS OF INTERNAL AUDITING

'Internal auditors should be skilled in dealing with people and communicating effectively.

Internal auditors should understand human relations and maintain satisfactory relationships with auditees.

Internal auditors should be skilled in oral and written communications so that they can clearly and effectively convey such matters as audit objectives, evaluations, conclusions and recommendations.' (IIA Standard and Guidelines 260.01/02)

Internal audit is defined as an 'independent appraisal function within an organisation' and as such the ability of the auditor to communicate his needs and findings, to establish a rapport with the auditee, is essential to carrying out the chosen audit task. The following are some of the behavioural aspects which impinge on the auditor's day-to-day work:

1 *Needs and relationships (inter-personal perception)*—Both auditor and auditee have their own perceptions regarding one another's needs and so

have an expectation as to the nature of their relationship. When the needs are not met, eg the auditor becomes part of internal check, doing basic parts of the auditee's job, then dissatisfaction arises, which if corrective action is not taken, can be damaging. Such dissatisfaction may motivate the auditor to seek work elsewhere.

2 *Formal and informal relationships*—Normally formal relationships are represented on the organisation chart or plan; however, human nature being what it is, informal relationships will not conform to such a convenient hierarchy and are dependent on the personal attitudes and qualities of the individuals involved, eg a manager may not in reality be capable of making decisions of importance, a subordinate may take over this role using unofficial discretion.

3 *Effective communication*—Where the auditor is seen to be not only unhelpful but also ineffective, this can only damage the relationship between auditor and auditee, management, external auditor or other departments. It is through effective communication that internal audit exists, by disseminating information, evaluating performance and reporting on work undertaken.

3.0 MOTIVATING THE AUDITOR

Over the years a variety of philosophies on the employer/employee relationship has evolved:

3.1 The paternalistic approach

This approach assumes people will be motivated to perform their tasks effectively to the extent to which their needs are satisfied in these jobs. The more the needs of employees are satisfied in the job, the greater the extent to which they will respond out of gratitude and loyalty. Such ideas, although applicable to Victorian conditions, have less relevance to today's working environment. However, that is not to say auditors do not appreciate comfortable working conditions, job security and predictable promotion patterns, but in times of great expectations and increasing demand for job satisfaction this is not the stuff of motivation.

3.2 The scientific approach: Taylor

This philosophy is based on the law of effect, eg that an auditor undertakes an audit and this action is followed by reward, then the probability is that good audits will be repeated. The problem is how to evaluate a 'good' audit:

1 Compliance with sound audit procedures?

2 Completion of audit within time allocated?

3 Detection of error and fraud?

4 Establishment of sound management procedures?

5 Promotion of value for money?

6 Effective communication?

However, without doubt, auditors are motivated by a known goal, eg being associated with a department which is respected for improving organisational performance or profit.

3.3   Participative management

This approach, developed by people such as Maslow, acknowledges that it is possible to motivate a worker by giving him identification with the organisation's objectives. Applied to auditors this means that an auditor, given audit objectives to achieve, will be better motivated if allowed to plan and conduct the audit using his own discretion, rather than by working to explicit instructions. To apply this approach to the auditor, Maslow's hierarchy of needs should be considered (see p 73).

Using this adaptation of Maslow's hierarchy of needs the auditor satisfies basic needs before higher needs emerge as a consequence of training and experience. To develop this approach further Herzberg's (1966) Hygenic Theory of Motivation should be mentioned. In his studies he interviewed 200 Pittsburg accountants and engineers about matters concerning job satisfaction and dissatisfaction. The conditions which led to job satisfaction called 'motivators' were as follows:

1 Advancement
2 Responsibility
3 Stimulating work
4 Recognition
5 Achievement

The first three were of greater importance.

The less motivating factors were found to be:

1 The environment
2 Company policy and administration
3 Supervision
4 Salary   known as 'Hygene' factors
5 Inter-personal relations
6 The loneliness of work.

Present thinking is that a mixture of all three approaches applies, dependent upon the individual auditor and organisation. The auditor's effort, performance and satisfaction are based on 'future expectations' (advancement, responsibility and interesting work), and that those expectations, when fulfilled, are judged by the auditor to be acceptable. The organisation similarly is satisfied with the auditor's work and thus is able to match ability to task, reward to performance, leading to mutual benefit and respect.

Rensis Likert, besides identifying participative management, also identifed three other management styles:

1 *Exploitive/authoritative*—Downward communication based on fear of authority.

2 *Benevolent/authoritative*—Upward communication, but main decisions being taken by senior management.

3 *Consultative*—Two-way communication—main decisions taken by senior management.

Maslow's Hierarchy of Needs

Progression to each higher level of needs will not be achieved until those at each lower level have been satisfied in turn.

Needs:

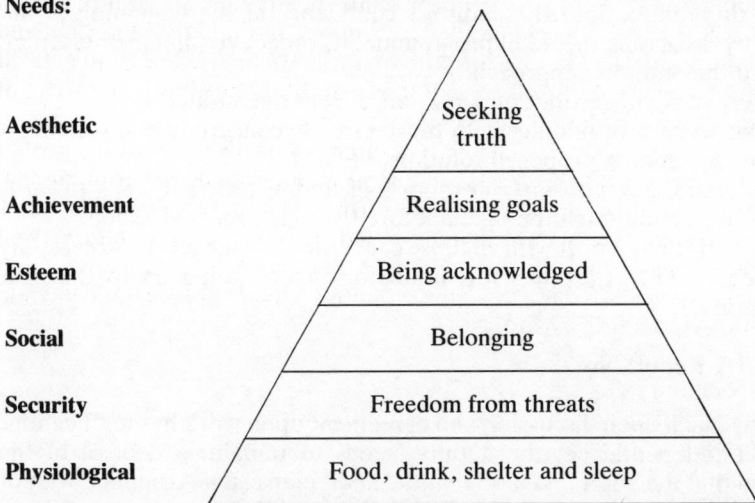

Aesthetic — Seeking truth

Achievement — Realising goals

Esteem — Being acknowledged

Social — Belonging

Security — Freedom from threats

Physiological — Food, drink, shelter and sleep

This may be translated for the role of internal auditor as follows:

Needs:

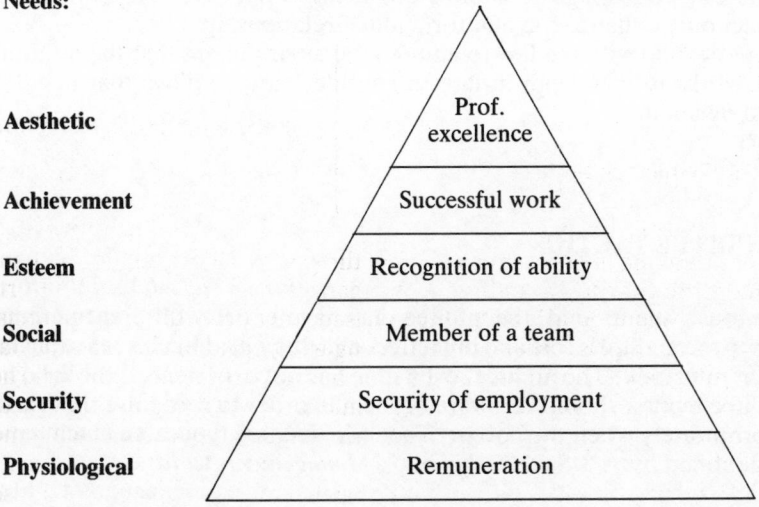

Aesthetic — Prof. excellence

Achievement — Successful work

Esteem — Recognition of ability

Social — Member of a team

Security — Security of employment

Physiological — Remuneration

Source: A H Maslow 'A theory of Human Motivation' Psychological Review 50 (July 1943)

3.4   Participative auditing

Frederick E Mints, IIA Research Report 17 entitled 'Behavioural Patterns in Internal Audit Relationships' (1972) first studied the participative approach to managing audit work. Following Likert's work, Mints examined the adaption of the participative management style to the work of internal audit, calling it the 'teamwork approach'. The purpose of this approach was to assist both auditor and auditee to achieve organisational goals and with this common purpose to improve auditor/auditee relationships. A major element in the participative approach is to allow auditees to take an interest in audit work and activities. To this end, Mints identified the following five elements of the 'teamwork approach'. The auditor should:

1 Take the auditee into the auditor's confidence at the beginning of the audit by discussing the audit programme, its objectives and the reasoning behind the auditor's approach.
2 Actively seek suggestions and assistance from the auditee.
3 Discuss all current findings with those directly concerned and seek their help in developing proposed solutions.
4 Provide auditees with interim reports of findings so that steps towards corrective action might be taken before the final report is issued.
5 Review the final report with all those concerned at each level and carefully consider their suggestions for modifying before going on to the next higher level.

Souce: IIA Report No 17

Clearly, such open discussion and agreement upon work has implications for audit independence; the auditor needs to remain in control of the direction that the audit takes, so that the audit plan can be complied with or changed where the auditor judges it to be necessary. It is important for the auditor to determine the areas subject to examination and the suitability of the various techniques to be applied. However, the need to explain the audit role, thereby educating the auditee about the supportive role of internal audit, can only enhance the auditor/auditee relationship.

Before dealing with the law relating to the environment that the internal auditor works in, it is appropriate to consider various ploys that may be adopted by auditees.

4.0   AUDITEE TACTICS

As previously mentioned, the auditee may have entirely different perceptions as to the auditor's role and objectives and this will affect his reactions to the audit interview. The auditor, even if he has not experienced the following auditee tactics, should be aware of them in order to recognise them and act appropriately when they occur. The following are typecasts which have been identified by A J Sayle in his book *Management Audit*:

1 *Timewasters*—Audit time being restricted, the longer an auditee wastes time the less time there is for audit work.

(a) *The waffler*—The auditee speaks at length and does not answer the question.
(b) *The 'dog and pony show'*—A long elaborate presentation and discussion used to impress the auditor—Key issues become submerged in insignificant detail. Auditor should courteously call an end to the proceedings.
(c) *Long lunch break*—The idea is to form a 'good working relationship' whereby auditee begins, 'I know a good pub, would you care to join me for a drink?' The pub is miles away, after many drinks auditor returns—unable to work.
(d) *Late arrival*—This tactic wastes limited audit time, aimed at preventing a detailed examination of auditee's work.
(e) *The long way round*—The system or factory, to consume auditor's time.
(f) *The forgotten document*—This brings proceedings to a halt and may break the auditor's line of questioning.
(g) *Interruptions*—These make interviewing difficult, if not impossible.
(h) *The 'clean' room*—Eg ensuring the auditor abides by complex hygiene and safety regulations which others in the organisation do not have to comply with—a delaying mechanism.
(i) *Lack of preparedness*—If personnel are not forwarned by management they may not be available for discussion with the auditor.

2 *The Cooks Tour*—Auditee attempts to determine the areas the auditor should investigate.

3 *Provocation*—Auditee attempts to provoke auditor into personal argument.

4 *Fixed ballot or loaded dice*—Auditee attempts to select auditor's sample.

5 *Special cases*—A device used to explain internal control lapses.

6 *Trial of strength*—Auditee attempts to reveal auditor's lack of knowledge of expertise.

7 *Insincerity*—Auditee attempts to flatter auditor with false admiration, so becoming over-familar and losing independence.

8 *'Poor me'*—Auditee tells tales of woe to make auditor pity him, so disregarding critical findings.

9 *Indispensible person*—Access to certain information is not available because this key individual is absent (sickness, holiday).

10 *Amnesia*—Auditee continually 'forgets' to provide data.

11 *Language barrier*—in foreign countries where auditee may pretend not to understand the auditor.

12 *Bribery*

13 *The quisling*—Auditee prepared to 'shop' other people in order to avoid investigation into his own work.

These are but a few tactics which may be adopted by an auditee and which the auditor must be experienced in overcoming in a polite and courteous way.

5.0   THE LAW AND THE INTERNAL AUDITOR

Compliance with professional guidance is not a statutory requirement; however, in conducting interviews and providing reports, the auditor needs to be aware of the legal position to which these activities may be subject.

5.1   The law of defamation

Defamation has been defined as follows:

'The publication (ie communication) of a statement which tends to lower a person in the estimation of right thinking members of society or tends to make them shun or avoid that person.' (Winfield and Jollowicz, *Tort*)

The test in a court of law is determined by what is taken to be meant by 'right thinking members of society': a reasonable person. It is for the court to decide on this in each case, as appropriate.

5.2   Libel and slander

1 *Definition of libel*—Publication of a statement in 'permanent form' (paper, radio/TV broadcast).
2 *Definition of slander*—A statement in non-permanent form, ie conversation.

The distinction is important because libel is actionable without the plaintiff having to prove he suffered any material damage other than intangible damage to his reputation. On the other hand, with slander the action may only be brought if he can show he has suffered some material damage. There are, however, four exceptions to the rule on slander:

1 If it is implied that a person has committed a criminal act punishable by imprisonment.
2 Imputation that person is diseased.
3 Imputation of unchastity. A suggestion that a school headmaster was committing adultery with a school cleaner would be actionable without proof of damage: *Jones v Jones*.
4 Allegation that person is unfit or incompetent in any office.
   This last exception is especially important for internal auditors, eg Hon Treasurer is fiddling the accounts of the badminton club!

5.3   Defences

A defendant cannot escape liability on the grounds that he was not aware that his statement was defamatory. However, the following defences are available:

1 *Justification*—If the statement complained of is substantially true, provided it was not made out of malice.

2 *Fair comment on matters of public interest*—May apply to the external auditor in the public sector provided what was said was 'fair'.

3 *Privilege*—The report of an auditor has the defence of 'qualified privilege' by reason of the auditor's duty to report to certain persons. So long as the auditor's report restricts itself to those matters which are properly the subject of an auditor's investigation there should be no liability for defamatory statements contained in them. Unfortunately this defence is not necessarily always upheld.

> 'A privileged occasion is, in relation to qualified privilege, an occasion where the person who makes a communication has an interest or duty, legal, social or moral, to make it to the person to whom it is made, and the person to whom it is made has a corresponding interest to receive it'

The internal auditor is only protected as regards persons entitled to receive his report, eg elected members/officer in a local authority, who are directly concerned with the matter, or the appropriate directors of an organisation.

However, should that report be passed on to another who is not entitled to receive it, the defence is not available, the person passing on the report will be liable for defamation—the auditor has not committed the act of defamation, eg *De Buse v McCarthy* where a clerk sent a committee report for public display in a library.

It is important to note that the defence of qualified privilege will be defeated if the internal auditor can be proved to have had malice of forethought. Malice may also be shown by publication to persons with no interest in the statement (dictation to a secretary or discussion with a professional colleague are considered to be excluded from such malice). It is important for auditors to know their legal position when making statements rather than risk costly litigation.

5.4 'Spent' offences

Under the Rehabilitation of Offenders Act 1974 s 9 it is an offence (with a fine of £200) to disclose that an employee or identifiable person has been convicted of a crime once that person has been rehabilitated: after a certain time span all offences are removed from the record, eg:

Penalty:	*Time:*
Conditional discharge or probation	After 12 months
Imprisonment up to 6 months	After 7 years
Lengthier sentences	After 10 years

The offence of disclosing a 'spent' conviction cannot be committed in the course of official duties.

Exemptions to compliance with 'spent' offences legislation:

1 Questions re entry into a profession (eg doctors).

2 Questions re employment in certain work (eg social workers, teachers, magistrates' clerks, policemen, etc).

3 Questions re miscellaneous work (eg manager of a casino, investment fund manager, etc).

5.5   When an internal auditor may be guilty of an offence

An offence may be committed by an internal auditor who:

1 Advises the auditee to commit a criminal offence.
2 Assists the auditee to plan or undertake a criminal offence.
3 Agrees to conceal or destroy evidence or mislead.
4 Knows or believes the auditee to have committed an arrestable offence and deliberately impedes the arrest or prosecution of the auditee.
5 Accepts a bribe to conceal information of use in the prosecution of the auditee.

6.0   FACT-FINDING INTERVIEWS

6.1   Some definitions

Interview—'A meeting of persons face to face specially for the purpose of formal conference on some point' (*Oxford Dictionary*).
Listen—'Make effort to hear something, hear with attention' (*Oxford Dictionary*).
Empathy—'The power of projecting oneself into the object (and so fully comprehending), of contemplation' (*Oxford Dictionary*), ie the establishment of a rapport between interviewer and interviewee.

A major facet of the auditor's work is fact-finding. Such work requires the skill of interviewing in order to determine where information required is to be found in a manner that is efficient and effective, and gaining knowledge concerning the organisation other than through reading. Accountants Digest No 90 introduces this aspect of audit work as follows:

> 'Conducting a fact-finding interview calls for considerably more skill than many people who conduct such interviews possess or even realise they should possess. It usually involves getting the interviewee to recall and bring out facts that are not in the forefront of his mind. This involves getting him to consider each question and its implications and then to search his mind for the appropriate information. It particularly calls for unobtrusive skill in producing a relaxed conversational atmosphere in which the interviewee gives the desired information freely and with personal satisfaction and without any feeling of being on the receiving end of a battery of questions.'

6.2   Planning and preparation prior to the interview

Successful interviewing is dependent upon the establishment of a rapport between interviewer and interviewee. The gaining of such a rapport requires tact and skill from the auditor. This allows the interviewee to relax and to be placed in a co-operative frame of mind that allows for a positive response to questions asked. Only sufficient notes should be taken to enable the auditor to recall information provided afterwards, over-elaborate note-taking may well destroy the rapport gained, the interviewee fearing that the information taken down may be subsequently held against him. Failure to provide the correct environment and to gain the confidence of the interviewee is likely to lead to delay in or failure to elicit information. When planning the interview the auditor should take account of the following matters:

1 Arrange the room to allow for a relaxed environment, ie type and positioning of furniture is important to encourage interviewee to talk.
2 Prepare a planned outline of subject area to be examined.
3 Ensure supporting documentation, if necessary, is readily available.
4 Prepare to have notes taken to record interview.
5 If fraud is suspected, be prepared to introduce the code of conduct (Police and Criminal Evidence Act 1984).
6 Arrange convenient time and place and notify manager of intention to conduct an interview. Ask manager if he wishes to attend.

6.3   Creating the appropriate environment

The auditor is in a powerful position, being in control of the direction that discussions may take. Such a situation is likely to cause the interviewee to be apprehensive and thus for an element of tension to exist. Besides providing the appropriate environmental conditions, location and time, the auditor needs to be aware of his own personal conduct. The following advice is provided by Accountants' Digest No 90:

> 'They (auditors) overlook the fact that they are guests of the interviewee—and that, like all guests, their behaviour should be both circumspect and impeccable.'

The Digest provides guidance, which we have summarised as follows:

1 Arrive at the appointment on time, no more than five minutes early.
2 Respond to shaken or offered hand—some people regard the offering of a hand as over-familiarity.
3 Only sit down or remove a jacket upon invitation.
4 Place briefcase on the floor and do not dislodge the interviewee's papers.
5 Do not give the appearance of attempting to read the interviewee's papers.
6 Be attentive and interested.
7 Do not appear to be interested in interruptions that may occur that do not affect your purposes.

In addition, the auditor should be aware of the importance of non-verbal communication and take advantage of it by observing the interviewee's actions, eg nodding signifies understanding or acceptance; frowning indicates a lack of understanding or confusion; a set expression may indicate disagreement, flickering of the eyes may indicate uncertainty or unwillingness to respond.

The auditor can similarly assist by demonstrating interest, understanding and encouragement to the interviewee. The auditor should not let the auditee think that interest is lost.

6.4   Questioning

Questions can be identified in two ways:

1 *Open-ended questions* allow for a wide variety of responses, eg what control do you exercise over the system? Such questions may be used to relax an inhibited interviewee because they are of a general nature.

2 *Closed questions* give limited response, eg is internal control over the cash office adequate? Such questions are useful for definitive responses, but a series of them may discourage the interviewee from providing further responses.

It is important that questions are asked to elicit information in such a manner that the interviewee is not placed under duress, but rather a discussion of a problem is occurring.

Asking the appropriate questions allows interviewees to demonstrate their knowledge and understanding of their work environment in a positive and helpful manner, while at the same time allowing the auditor to gain both evidence and information.

6.5   Gathering the information

Gathering information takes two forms: listening and recording. To quote:

'Listening effectively in fact-finding interviewing means listening attentively whilst at the same time encouraging the other man to express himself as well as possible. Here are some points of guidance:

(*a*) *Look at the other man all the time whilst he is talking*
This is important for three reasons. First, it helps the interviewer concentrate on the other man and what he is saying. Second, it encourages and flatters the other man. Third, it enables the interviewer to get the full benefit from what the other man is saying because it is supplemented by non-verbal communication.

(*b*) *Sit up alertly*
Sitting up physically helps one 'sit up' mentally. If the interviewer adopts too relaxed a position he is likely to relax mentally—away from the interviewee.

(*c*) *Listen to understand*
The interviewer should listen with full attention in order to understand what the interviewee is saying. This involves not only absorbing and interpreting the information but also trying to interpret the non-verbal communication.

(*d*) *Avoid being diverted easily*
The interviewer should avoid allowing himself to be diverted by the environmental conditions or circumstances. He should also avoid diverting himself (for example, by 'doodling', or reading, or looking around).' (Accountants' Digest No 90 (ICAEW))

6.6　After the interview

Following the interview the auditor should thank the interviewee for his co-operation and file the notes recorded during the interview.

7.0　AUDIT REPORTS

The internal auditor should ensure that findings, conclusions and recommendations arising from each internal audit assignment are communicated promptly to management.

7.1　Objectives

1　To provide reassurance to management concerning operations as soon as possible following the audit.
2　To provide useful advice to management regarding the adequacy of controls and the efficiency of operational performance.
3　To provide a formal record of audit activity and the response from management.

7.2　Audit reporting

Reporting takes two forms, namely verbal and written. The verbal report, which is presented at the end of the audit, is used by the auditor to discuss with operational management the findings of the audit, identifying all matters and making particular reference to matters of significance, which are to be included in the written report. The auditor should be able to provide constructive advice, taking into account the environment and resources available to the operational manager. Similarly, the operational manager is able to state whether he considers the auditor's findings reasonable and of assistance. It must be remembered that internal audit has a supportive role to management, providing them with reassurance regarding the adequacy and effectiveness of controls within the operations for which management has responsibility. The auditor should inform the operational manager what the written report will contain as to audit findings and the agreed action to be taken by the operational manager. It is important that operational managers are not surprised by the written audit report, as this may cause the forfeiture of audit credibility at operational level. The investigation of fraudulent activity could provide an exception to this rule.

7.2.1　*Some guidance on verbal reporting*

Verbal communication is an essential feature of effective day-to-day management. For much of it, written confirmation is neither necessary nor feasible.

　　Misunderstandings do occur but normally get rectified before damage results. This is because:

1　Continuous rapport provides for repeated review and monitoring.

2 The management network provides internal checks.

The internal auditor's communication does not have either of these safeguards. The auditor departs from the scene immediately after the end of audit meeting, leaving the management to act on their own interpretation of what was said. It is therefore especially important that auditors take maximum care to avoid every possibility for misunderstanding from the close of audit verbal communication.

The written report must be equally clear in confirming the same meaning. When appropriate care is exercised, the draft written report, when submitted, will convey to the management precisely the same interpretation as that which they had understood from the verbal communication. To fail to achieve this objective is a very serious failure.

1 The management may perceive the differences as a change of attitude or a revised opinion and interpret such a change as a credibility gap.
2 Further time and effort will have to be spent by both the management and the audit team in identifying and resolving the differences.
3 The professional reputation of the internal audit department will have been damaged.

ADVANTAGES OF VERBAL REPORTS

1 Speed—Speech comes easier than writing.
2 Amplification—Words can be augmented by body language.
3 Reception—The listener can ask for clarification.
4 The listener's comprehension can be verified.

DISADVANTAGES OF VERBAL REPORTS

1 Misunderstanding—Unintentional ambiguity is common.
2 Impermanance—Memories tend to be fugitive.
3 Drift—Subsequent events colour recollections.
4 Distortion—Opportunities for deliberate misinterpretation.
5 Control—It is difficult to monitor progress on unrecorded decisions.

7.2.2   *Written audit reports*

A written report is an essential feature of every audit:

1 It constitutes the authentic and permanent record of what the auditor examined, the findings obtained and recommendations made.
2 It confirms the issues discussed with the responsible management at the end of the audit and serves as a checklist for action that has been agreed and for the next auditor to follow up.
3 It informs other interested parties who often have some authority to influence the action taken by responsible management.

FORMAT

Each organisation adopts a format suitable to senior management. Although the format may differ, the contents should be similar, ie:

1 *Coverage*—The areas examined as listed in the audit plan.

2 *Findings*—Statements of fact as identified under each area of coverage.

3 *Conclusions*—A brief statement of professional opinion and expert advice arising from the audit examination of each area of coverage.

4 *Recommendations*—Practical courses of action arising from findings under each area of coverage.

Where an audit report is a lengthy document, a synopsis should be prepared and appended to the report. It should list the coverage areas examined with a succinct note on the outcome for each, preferably expressed as a one-line sentence.

7.2.3 *Guidance notes for audit reports*

1 Audit reports have an important purpose to give reassurance on areas found to be well managed. The auditor must look beyond perceived failings and concentrate on opportunities for improvement. This means using positive statements wherever possible. The report then takes on a constructive character.
2 The audit report must be clearly seen to be a direct personal communication from the auditor to the responsible manager. This demands active rather than passive forms of language.
3 It must use ordinary language which is readily understood by all recipients: jargon is inappropriate.
4 The language must be unambiguous. This means that it must be capable of one interpretation only; the one the auditor meant.
5 The language must be clear. Clarity depends firstly on presenting the ideas so that they lead on in a logical sequence and secondly on using simple words and short sentences wherever possible.
6 The presentation of audit reports must be of the highest professional standard to do justice to the quality of the audit work. These reports are intended to be used by busy executives: only the best presentations earn a right to serious consideration.
7 Auditors must acknowledge the amount of effort necessary to produce a good report and plan sufficient time for it.

7.2.4 *Audit conclusions*

These should be statements of audit judgements on each area of coverage listed in sequence. It is helpful to adopt discrete forms for expressing audit judgements distinguished by the opening words for the statement. The form to be used should reflect the nature of the judgement.

1 *Security judgements:* 'We consider . . .'—This is appropriate for audit judgements about the adequacy of specific systems and procedures for financial control or security. Internal auditors are the acknowledged experts in this area and audit judgements must be stated with authority.
   Examples:
   (a) 'We consider your cash receipts are at risk because they are not always banked promptly.'
   (b) 'We consider your sales invoicing system is not adequate to ensure that all despatches get invoiced.'
   (c) 'We consider your site security arrangements provide adequate protection.'

2 *Risk judgements:* 'We believe . . .'—This is appropriate for audit judgements on lapses in compliance with the established procedures of the business. The lapse itself should not be in dispute but the auditor is offering a view on its effect.

Examples:

(a) 'We believe your management accounts may be distorted and could mislead due to the practice of withholding disputed purchase invoices from the system.'

(b) 'We believe that lapses in your personnel records system could result in paying for non-existent staff.'

(c) 'We believe your stock records may be unreliable and your customer service is at risk due to stock recording omissions.'

3 *Expert opinion:* 'In our opinion . . .'—This is appropriate for expressing an expert audit judgement on general areas of activity where the auditor is expected to be an expert.

Examples:

(a) 'In our opinion your monthly management accounts are properly prepared and fairly reflect the activities of your business.'

(b) 'In our opinion your procedures provide an adequate basis for effective control and they are being properly applied.'

(c) 'In our opinion your costing system does not provide an adequate basis for assessing profitability when making judgements about selling prices.'

Judgements which are truly matters of expert opinion must always be clearly labelled as such by using the words 'In our opinion'. Without this the statement is an assertion and has no place in an audit report.

4 *Lay judgements:* 'In our view . . .' This is appropriate for observations on operational efficiency. It implies a lay judgement based upon carefully analysed detailed evidence.

Examples:

(a) 'In our view you could improve customer service by re-organising your stores layout to take account of the volume and frequency of demand for different products in your range.'

(b) 'In our view this is a well run branch.'

(c) 'In our view you could improve your material yields by extending your quality control activity to the receipt of raw materials.'

Similar comments to those about clearly labelling expert opinions apply to lay judgements. The words 'In our view' should not be omitted.

5 *Value judgements:* Audit conclusions often contain value judgements. These may occur in any one of the main forms dealt with above. Value judgements are usually expressed by words which imply a threshold of acceptability such as:

adequate or inadequate;
satisfactory or unsatisfactory;
competent or incompetent;
reliable or unreliable;
sound or unsound.

When these words are used it is important to define the standard adopted for making the judgement.

Examples:

Adequate as a basis for effective control or for achieving specified objectives.

Satisfactory as a means of pursuing specified objectives.

Competent to discharge specified duties.

Reliable as a basis for specified management decisions.

Sound in terms of generally accepted principles for accounting or management control, etc.

6 *Recommended changes:* Effective operational audit is about promoting change to achieve improved efficiency and effectiveness. Consequently there will be cases when the changes recommended will be so significant and far-reaching that it is necessary to summarise them in the body of the report as well as stating them in detail in an appendix.

It is not appropriate and could even mislead to present recommended changes among the audit judgements expressed under the heading 'Conclusions'. When necessary, a separate section headed either 'Summary of recommendations' or 'Main recommendations', as appropriate, should be presented to follow the 'Conclusions'. This sequence establishes first the context in which the recommended changes are perceived to be advisable enabling them to be stated succinctly and with clarity.

7.3 Jargon

Use of jargon in internal audit reports can turn them into models of obscurity for many recipients.

Jargon is a communication aid between experts in a particular body of knowledge. It allows them to condense the verbiage necessary to convey specific complex ideas. If jargon is adopted as a substitute for clear thinking it debases the language and results in meaningless statements. Using jargon when endeavouring to communicate with non-experts in the subject is likely to confuse and may be judged arrogant use of specialist terms. It can also be misleading to use jargon which has adopted restricted meanings for words commonly used with a much wider range of meaning. Many terms used by accountants come into this category. It is important to remember that the recipients of audit reports are not all accounting experts and so care must be taken in employing such terms as:

'reconciliation'
'accrual'
'provision'
'control'
'to depreciate'

Link words can be helpful in arranging ideas in a logical sequence. For example:

POSITIVE LINK WORDS

'also'
'thus'
'therefore'

NEGATIVE LINK WORDS

'whereas'
'however'
'nevertheless'
'even so'

It is important to be very careful about using such words as 'neither' which can imply double admonition. All admonition when appropriate must be expressed in direct terms, never implied.

Long adverbial or adjectival clauses can effectively obliterate the real meaning and purpose of a sentence. Better, if at all possible, to put them in a separate sentence following the main sentence.

Starting a sentence with a qualification introduced by a phrase such as:

'in view of the fact that',
'since'
'due to'
'because of'
'owing to'
etc

is a sure formula for a long sentence, which may become almost incomprehensible (like this one!).

Experienced auditors will read over their drafts after writing them for the specific purpose of eliminating barriers to clarity. They should also study the editorial amendments to their drafts. Each will soon become aware of their own particular forms of expression which may inhibit clarity or could be prone to misinterpretation.

7.4   Follow-up audit work

Internal audit is a service to management. It must be seen to be independent and impartial:

1 Auditors have no authority to make changes.
2 Auditors observe and make recommendations.
3 Auditors frequently have to exercise powers of persuasion.

Accountable managements must be free to judge priorities between the action auditors recommend and other perceived needs of the organisation.

Internal audit is a continuous service to management. The joint consideration of risks and opportunities for improved economy, efficiency and effectiveness becomes progressive.

Audits normally occur at annual intervals and there is often a change of auditor each time round. The formally-written audit report and response are therefore, essential continuity documents.

7.5 Conclusion

To conclude, it is appropriate to quote from the IIA Guidelines on communicating results.

'Reports should be objective, clear, concise, constructive and timely.

.1 Objective reports are factual, unbiased and free from distortion. Findings, conclusions and recommendations should be included without prejudice.

.2 Clear reports are easily understood and logical. Clarity can be improved by avoiding unnecessary technical language and providing sufficient supportive information.

.3 Concise reports are to the point and avoid unnecessary detail. They express thoughts completely in the fewest possible words.

.4 Constructive reports are those which as a result of their content and tone, help the auditee and the organisation and lead to improvements where needed.

.5 Timely reports are those issued without undue delay and enable prompt effective action.' (IIA Guideline 430.03)

Further reading

Bromage, Mary C *Writing audit reports* (2nd edn, 1979) (McGraw Hill).

Gowers, Sir E, Greenbaum, S and Whitcut, J *The complete plain words* (3rd edn, 1986) (HMSO).

Heeschen, P and Sawyer, L B *Internal auditor's handbook* (1984) (IIA Inc).

Matthew, H W *Fact finding interviews* Accountants digest No 90 (ICAEW).

Mints, F E *Behavioural patterns in internal audit relationships* Report No 17 (IIA Inc).

CHAPTER 5   Systems evaluation

Objectives	To explain the techniques used by internal auditors in the context of the internal auditing standards
Contents	Planning, controlling and recording; pre-audit work; audit working papers
	Ascertaining and recording the system; internal control memoranda; internal control evaluation questionnaires; flowcharts; audit programmes
	Testing the system; compliance and substantive tests; sampling techniques
	Evaluation of internal control systems
	Reviewing and reporting
Summary	The audit should be conducted in a methodical manner using accepted audit techniques which are supported by adequate documentation, logically filed

1.0   PLANNING, CONTROLLING AND RECORDING

Internal auditing standards require that the auditor should adequately plan, control and record his work. This is to allow the audit to be undertaken in both an efficient and effective manner. A diagram based on the internal auditing standards demonstrates the audit process (p 89):

1.1   Planning

Upon allocation of an audit the senior auditor should make adequate plans to:

1 Establish the manner in which the audit objectives will be achieved.
2 Allow the audit to be directed and controlled properly.
3 Ensure the concentration of audit resources in key areas.
4 Allow for the completion of the audit in an efficient and timely manner.

In order to be able to plan the work properly the auditor requires an understanding of the nature of the auditee's financial affairs, the structure of the organisation and methods of operation. From such an understanding the effect of events and transactions on the organisation can be assessed. This may be achieved by comparing the reality of the situation with what was

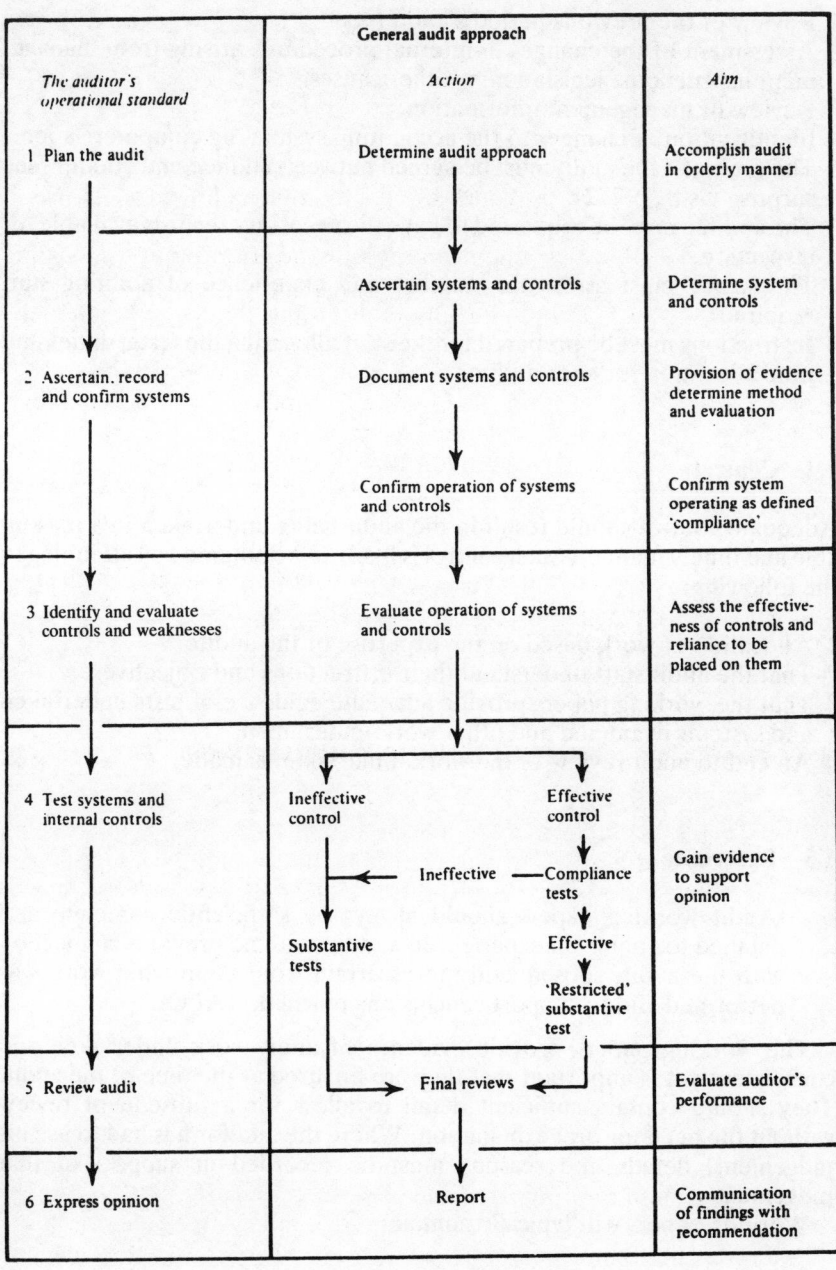

The auditor's operational standard	General audit approach	
	Action	*Aim*
1 Plan the audit	Determine audit approach	Accomplish audit in orderly manner
2 Ascertain, record and confirm systems	Ascertain systems and controls	Determine system and controls
	Document systems and controls	Provision of evidence determine method and evaluation
	Confirm operation of systems and controls	Confirm system operating as defined 'compliance'
3 Identify and evaluate controls and weaknesses	Evaluate operation of systems and controls	Assess the effectiveness of controls and reliance to be placed on them
4 Test systems and internal controls	Ineffective control Effective control	
	Ineffective —Compliance tests	Gain evidence to support opinion
	Substantive tests Effective 'Restricted' substantive test	
5 Review audit	Final reviews	Evaluate auditor's performance
6 Express opinion	Report	Communication of findings with recommendation

reported to senior management. In drafting the plan the auditor will need to take account of the following matters:

1 Review of the previous period's audit file.
2 Assessment of the changes in internal procedures arising from management instructions, legislation or other causes.
3 Review of management information.
4 Identification of changes to the accounting system, eg computerisation.
5 The timing of the audit must be agreed between auditee and auditor (see surprise visits, p 272).
6 The auditee must be requested to have the necessary records available for inspection.
7 The senior must assess the number and experience of auditing staff required.
8 Instructions must be prepared for the staff allocating the tests, duties and time allocation for each auditor.

1.2   Control

Adequate control should result in the audit being undertaken in a reasonable and timely manner. Such control is likely to be obtained by attending to the following:

1 Allocation of work based on the expertise of the auditor.
2 That the audit staff understand their instructions and objectives.
3 That the working papers provide adequate evidence of tests undertaken and systems examined and other work undertaken.
4 An end to audit review of the work undertaken is made.

1.3   Recording

'Audit working papers should always be sufficiently complete and detailed to enable an experienced auditor with no previous connection with the audit, subsequently to ascertain from them what work was performed and to support conclusions reached.' (APC)

The working papers provide evidence of audit work undertaken and consequently it is important that they are finalised at the time of the audit. They should contain sufficient detail to allow for a subsequent review without the need for oral explanation. Where the auditor has had to use his judgement, details and reasons must be recorded in support of that judgement.

Working papers will typically contain:

1 Information of importance to the audit, eg management instructions, and memoranda.
2 Audit planning information.
3 The auditor's assessment of the organisation's control systems and the effectiveness of internal controls.
4 Details of the previous audit report, work undertaken and outstanding.
5 Evidence that the audit work previously undertaken has been reviewed.

6 Copies of management statements.
7 Details of statistical data re income, expenditure, number of employees and organisational structure.
8 A summary of significant matters reported and action taken.
9 Copies of relevant correspondence.

It is difficult to be precise about such details because each chief internal auditor will have his own views about the records to be maintained on file. The matters referred to above are therefore of a general nature—the objective being to gain cumulative auditing knowledge and experience.

1.3.1 *Cumulative auditing knowledge and experience (CAKE)*

In planning, recording, ascertaining, evaluating and testing, the auditor is seeking knowledge from which to form an opinion. As the audit is repeated so knowledge is accumulated, allowing the audit to be concentrated on areas of materiality. 'CAKE' is thus of use in identifying material items, and similarly areas where audit risk is low and audit testing can be minimised.

'The main ingredients of CAKE are likely to include knowledge of:
—the business;
—the control environment and the flow of transactions;
—the accounting policies adopted by the enterprise;
—previous occurrence of errors;
—Accounting matters that require estimates on the part of the directors.' (APC True & Fair Bulletin No 28, Autumn 1984)

Note: In planning the audit, the auditor must ensure knowledge is updated so that CAKE is relevant and its use maximised.

1.3.2 *Pre-audit work*

Much of this work can be done centrally, at the office, prior to visiting the auditee. Pre-audit work should cover the following areas:

1.3.3 *Working papers*

These should include:

1 The programme of the audit work.
2 The summary of material figures and relationships for the current period.
3 A summary of comparisons with budgets and with the results of the previous year.
4 Details of material variations (including details of the results of investigations into such variations).
5 Audit conclusions reached, identifying those included in the report.
6 Information considered necessary for assisting in the planning of the audit.

1.3.4 *Analytical review techniques*

Such techniques are designed to ensure that the various items making up the financial statements are consistent with:

1 Each other (eg the relationship between creditors and purchase).

2 Known trends (eg the likely effect of relaxing controls over hire-puchase agreements).
3 The auditor's knowledge of the organisation.

These techniques may be summarised as follows:

Types of data, ratios, etc	*Comparison with:*
Financial data (eg items in annual statements, management accounts, budgets, account balances)	(i) corresponding period (ii) budgets and forecasts
Non-financial data (eg production and employment statistics)	(i) entries in accounting records (ii) other financial data
Performance indicators	(i) CIPFA/Extel, etc
Ratios and percentages	(i) preceding period (ii) budgets and forecasts (iii) industry statistics

When interpreting the results of analytical techniques the auditor should be mindful that there may be 'simple' explanations for variations, for example:

1 Inflation (as summarised by the appropriate index).
2 Specific price changes (goods and services used by the organisation).
3 Seasonal factors (eg winter or summer).
4 Industrial disputes including those affecting essential suppliers.
5 Macro-economic activity—UK economy.
6 Technological changes making products or services obsolete or uncompetitive.
7 Changes in management policy (directors' minutes).
8 The effect of government action (eg changes in taxation and legislation).
9 Social changes (ageing population—public sector).
10 Environmental change (climatic factors).

In considering variations, two factors must be fully considered:

1 Changes occurring which materially differ from those expected.
2 Changes normally expected which do not occur.

1.3.5　*The value of standardisation of working papers*

1 Increases the efficiency of the review of working papers.
2 Maintains quality control of documentation.
3 Makes delegation of audit tasks easier.
4 Provides a checklist for work to be undertaken.

All documentation in audit files should be allocated an appropriate section and cross-referenced to the audit programme and flowchart. Where evidence is supporting opinion in the audit report it should also be referenced to the report for ease of retrieval of data supporting the auditor's opinion.

As an example of standardisation, Scottish Gas in the 1970s introduced seven standard working papers:

1 Audit objectives.
2 Details of systems.
3 System changes and meetings held.
4 Actual proof of system.
5 Basis of tests and audit checks.
6 Results of audit checks.
7 Conclusions and review of efficiency of system.

1.3.6 *Audit files and working papers*

Filing methods will vary in detail from organisation to organisation, however the following system is reasonably representative—the objective being to assist the auditor to gain cumulative auditing knowledge and experience (CAKE).

PERMANENT FILE

This should contain matters of continuing importance (ie beyond the period of audit), eg:

1 Rules and regulations (standing orders, financial regulations, management instructions, company memorandum and articles of association).
2 Extracts from minutes.
3 Address and description of location.
4 Organisational chart
5 Name, position and telephone number of contact(s).
6 Previous reports and correspondence.
7 Statistical data.
8 Details of relevant legislation (eg health and safety legislation).

CURRENT FILE

This should relate to the current audit and normally contains:

1 Copies of management reports since last audit.
2 An index of all working papers.
3 Copies of ICQ and ICEQ (key control questionnaire) and audit programme.
4 Other audit documentation—flowcharts, etc.
5 Outstanding work.
6 Outstanding work from previous audit.
7 Weaknesses found and corrected without being reported to senior management.
8 Significant weaknesses reported.
9 Action to be taken by management concerning weaknesses.
10 Analytical review records.
11 Any other documentation which may be required as evidence, eg copies of correspondence or auditee records.

SYSTEMS FILE

Some organisations prefer to maintain a separate systems file for all documentation relating to systems, though many maintain such documentation on a permanent file.

Example of permanent file index

	File: Ref:
Auditee's name	

Section A	Location, telephone number and contact
Section B	Documents and correspondence of a permanent nature
Section C	Statutory matters
Section D	Management policy
Section E	Management instructions

Review details:

Year to:	Prepared by:	Date:	Reviewed by:	Date:
xx xx xx	Z	xx xx xx	JS	xx xx xx

2.0   EVALUATING SYSTEMS CONTROL

Before we consider evaluating systems, it is important to define a system and the auditor's objectives with regard to the examination and appraisal of a system.

A system may be defined as a series of inter-related procedures, composed of processes and controls designed to operate together to achieve a planned objective. Processes are those activities which aim to progress data or transactions through a system. Controls ensure that processes accord with the system's objectives.

2.1   Audit objectives

The objectives of controls within a system are to:

1 Ensure adherence to management policies.
2 Enable the efficient and orderly conduct of the affairs of the organisation.
3 Protect assets and to prevent wastage occurring.
4 Secure the completeness and accuracy of records.
5 Ensure compliance with legislation.

To provide assurance that the objectives are met, the auditor needs to understand the operation of the system as designed and as applied in practice. Before any tests can be undertaken, the auditor will have to record the system and gather copies of documentation currently in use. This enables appropriate tests to be designed to establish whether the procedures prescribed by management are being complied with. Thus the auditor is matching the assessment of the adequacy of controls, based on past experience, and what has been recorded with the system being applied in practice. It is through this process of matching the auditor's expectations with the results of tests that the auditor is able to give assurance that the findings presented are reasonable. It is of major importance for internal audit to be able to reassure senior management that their policies are being adhered to and to provide advice to management where certain policies or systems need review. Management is responsible for maintaining an adequate and effective system of internal control.

2.2 Understanding and recording the system

Some common approaches are:

1 Reliance upon the auditor's expertise, experience and judgement.
2 Internal control questionnaire (ICQ).
3 Key questions (or internal control evaluation questionnaire (ICEQ)).
4 Flowcharts (F/C) and systems documentation.

These four points are considered in more detail below.

2.3 Reliance on the auditor's experience and judgement

This commonly happens in practice but raises a number of problems:

1 Such judgement is subjective and makes objective standards difficult to apply.
2 Different auditors will reach different conclusions about the same situation.
3 Judgement is influenced by the auditor's background and training.

2.4 Systems documentation

It is necessary for the auditor to record the system to be audited for both current and future use. Accepted procedure is to ask pertinent questions and to take notes. In this manner a general impression is gained of the system. The next stage is to present the system in a diagrammatic form—a flowchart. Again this may be done in a rough form—more often than not to visualise the system. It is often at this stage that the auditor sees the gaps in his knowledge of the system. Having gained some knowledge, though not entirely complete, the auditor will be in a position to draft an internal control questionnaire (ICQ). It is part of the process of gaining cumulative auditing knowledge and experience (CAKE).

The diagram on p 96 shows the steps in the audit approach.

2.4.1 *Internal control memorandum*

This is where the auditor following questions and observation of the systems describes them in narrative form. Such a method is generally only suitable for simple systems as set out below. It can easily be seen how in more complex organisations this technique would be too cumbersome to use and that other techniques (ICQs, ICEQ flowcharts) are preferable.

	Audit ref:
Client:	ABC plc
Year:	to 31 December 1980
Prepared by:	J Snooks
Control reviewed:	Opening of mail procedures with reference to cash and cheque remittances

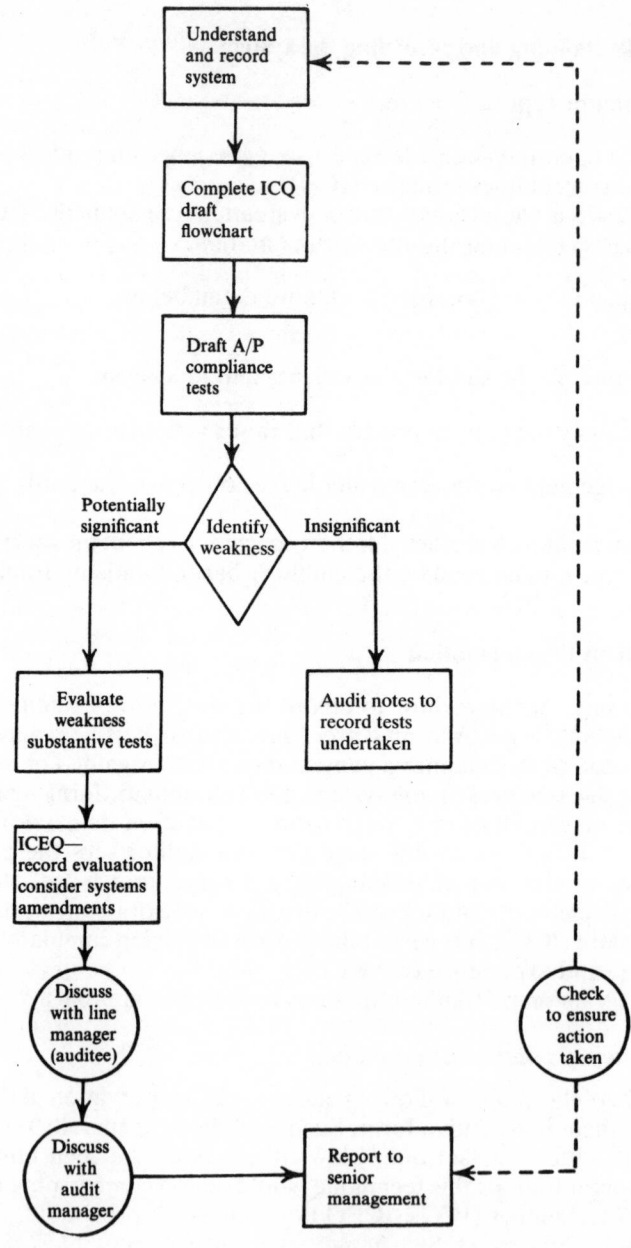

1 Mail is received and opened each morning supervised by either of the following senior executives of the company: company secretary or chief accountant. This duty is done on a weekly rotation basis by these persons.
2 Details of the cash and cheque remittances received are dictated to a member of the secretarial staff, and the cheques and postal orders are crossed 'account payee only'.
3 A typist then types a detailed list of the remittances, taking three copies to be distributed for filing, the sales ledger department for maintaining debtors' records, and, with the remittances, to the bank.
4 The list is added, and totals recorded by the office clerk.
5 The executive then checks and initials the list, as does the clerk.
6 The executive opening the mail completes a bank paying-in slip and sends it, a copy of the remittances list and the remittances to the bank by messenger.
7 Total figures relating to the banking and the types of remittances received are sent by the executive to the cashier to enter in the cash book.

2.4.2 *Internal control questionnaires (ICQs)*

DEFINITION

An interrogation package designed to give the auditor an overview of the controls operating in a system and allowing the identification of weaknesses therein.

The questionnaire is designed to determine the existence of internal controls, and to record the manner in which those controls operate. The questionnaire is so formulated that the answer 'no' indicates a weakness. A cross-referencing system is used to link the control to a visual diagram of the system in use—and to the audit programme (tests undertaken).

OBJECTIVE OF ICQS

To assess the internal controls in operation and to state who is responsible for them and how they function prior to performance of audit tests. Some general considerations are:

1 ICQs must be reviewed and updated periodically and the questions should be listed under operational subsections.
2 Assisted by an ICQ the auditor is able quickly to gain an understanding of the operational systems and the relevant parts of the auditee's organisation. Appraisal of the questionnaire enables the auditor to assess the weaker and the more reliable parts of the system of internal control.
3 The auditor will then be in a position to advise the auditee where the system requires modification and also to plan his audit programme. The programme will test those areas which the questionnaire shows to be weak in matters of control.

2.4.3 *Internal control evaluation questionnaires (or key control questions)*

ICQs tend to be very detailed and require time by senior audit management to extract critical information. To ensure that senior management time is used to its maximum advantage the various ICQs are co-ordinated by use of the internal control evaluation question.

This summarises vital points to be covered in the form of key questions. The questions obviously vary according to the assessment of internal control, but unlike ICQs the questions are so phrased that a 'yes' response indicates a weakness. See example on p 100.

ICQS

Auditors have differing views about the role and method of completion of ICQs. Some believe it is a good idea for the auditee's staff to complete ICQs. Others strongly oppose this view. The argument may be summarised:

Arguments for auditee's staff completing ICQ	*Arguments against auditee's staff completing ICQ*
1 Saves audit time.	1 Auditee learns about audit methods.
2 Auditee's staff do not give unconsidered responses.	2 The questions may indicate where the organisation is open to fraud.
3 Auditee's staff become aware of the importance of internal control.	3 Some questions will be meaningless to the auditee without explanation.
4 Auditee's staff are uninfluenced by the auditor.	4 Questions may be given the responses it is thought the auditor wants to hear.

The more orthodox practice however is for the auditor to complete the ICQ.

Some advantages and disadvantages of ICQs

Advantages	*Disadvantages*
1 A well designed ICQ will cover most typical weaknesses in a system.	1 The questions do not differentiate between major and minor weaknesses.
2 Provides a checklist for the auditor.	2 The auditor must still use judgement in reaching conclusions in the system of internal control.
3 Can be used in conjunction with flowcharting and audit tests.	3 ICQs are by their nature general—they may not suit the specific situation of an organisation.
4 Useful for review purposes to have data in standard format.	4 They may encourage 'mechanical' replies.
5 Quality control is facilitated.	

Disadvantage 4 has given increased importance to ICEQs, where fewer but more important questions are asked.

ICQs are commonly designed according to either of the two following formats:

Example 1

Internal control questionnaire

Auditee ....   Prepared by ....

Reviewed by ....   Date ....
Purchases

	YES	NO	N/A	A/P	F/C	Comment
Ordering						
1 Are all orders made by numbered and printed order forms!						
2 Are all orders signed by a responsible officer?						
3 Are tenders from alternative suppliers regularly solicited?						
Invoices/credit notes						
1 Are invoices checked with goods inwards notes?						
2 Does the accounts department receive a copy of every invoice prepared?						
3 Etc						
Ledger/statements						
1 Are statements received regularly every month?						
2 Are statements checked with ledger accounts as soon as received?						
3 Etc						

Example 2

Sales ICQ

Auditee ....   Prepared by ....

Reviewed by ....   Date ....

Question	F/C	Answer	Systems test	Assessment
1 What record is kept of sales orders received?				
2 Are customers' credit limits checked before orders are accepted?				
3 Etc				

Note: ICQs can lead to a 'mechanistic' approach, hence the introduction and use of ICEQs (Key Control Questions).

PURCHASE AND TRADE CREDITORS

1 Can goods or services be ordered without authorisation?
2 Can liabilities for goods or services received be incurred without being recorded?
3 Can liabilities be omitted, wrongly recorded, or wrongly charged?
4 Can goods or services be paid for without being received?

The difference between ICQs and ICEQs is that ICQs concentrate on desirable internal controls being present and ICEQs evaluate the possible types of misstatement in management information due to fraud, error or misrepresentation. The auditor must make a preliminary assessment of the system, including operation of internal controls, before the nature and extent of testing (compliance and substantive) can be determined. The most important methods of evaluation are by a combination of ICQs and ICEQs.

A further type of questionnaire which supports the ICQ and ICEQ is the segregation of duties appraisal form, of which the following is an example:

	Cash control	
Operation	*Person responsible*	*Weakness*
Operation of cash till	Mrs Jones	x/
Reconciliation of till record	Mrs Jones	x/
Banking of till monies	Mrs Jones	x/

2.5   Flowcharting

Flowchart—a diagrammatic presentation of a system.

A flowchart may be described as 'a map of inter-related operations specially arranged to indicate the sequence and type of these operations as part of a larger unit'. Detailed narrative is replaced by standardised symbols and inter-connected lines indicating the flow of documentation.

2.5.1   *Collection of information*

In order for the flowchart to portray the system operating it is important to discuss that system with the manager responsible for it. It is also important to discuss with each employee responsible for internal checks how they operate the system—this may be totally different from management's perception of the system. During an interview with an employee notes should be taken and a rough diagram prepared, using flowchart symbols. The following facts should be gained from this interview:

1 Title of the person.
2 Department in which the person works and his duties and the person to whom he is responsible.
3 What document is used.
4 Where each document comes from.
5 What operations are carried out with the document and why.
6 How many transactions are dealt with during the course of a week or month.
7 Any time limits by which the work must be completed.
8 What information is added to or taken from the documents.

9 What happens to documents after each operation.
10 Who receives each document.
11 What controls and checks are present and how often they are carried out.

Additional information regarding the system should also be obtained, eg:

1 Lists of samples of all forms and reports used.
2 Lists and functions of machines.
3 Procedures during holiday and sickness
4 Unusual or abnormal duties that seldom occur.

From such 'rough' work the flowchart may be prepared using symbols as follows. It is to be noted that different organisations have adopted different symbols, hence a 'grid' explaining the symbols used is required:

2.5.2 *Flowcharts, symbols and their meaning*

The authors are grateful to the ICAEW for allowing the reproduction of Accountants' Digest No 32, written by Paul J Rutteman BSc (Econ), FCA, Ernst and Young (formerly Arthur Young MClelland Moores & Co). This digest, written in 1976 is widely acknowledged as being the basic guidance to flowcharting for auditors.

THE SYMBOLS

The template. A template is supplied with this digest. It contains a number of symbols which fall into two categories:

 (i) basic symbols—described in bold type in Figure 1;
(ii) computer symbols—described in italics in Figure 1.

Figure 1

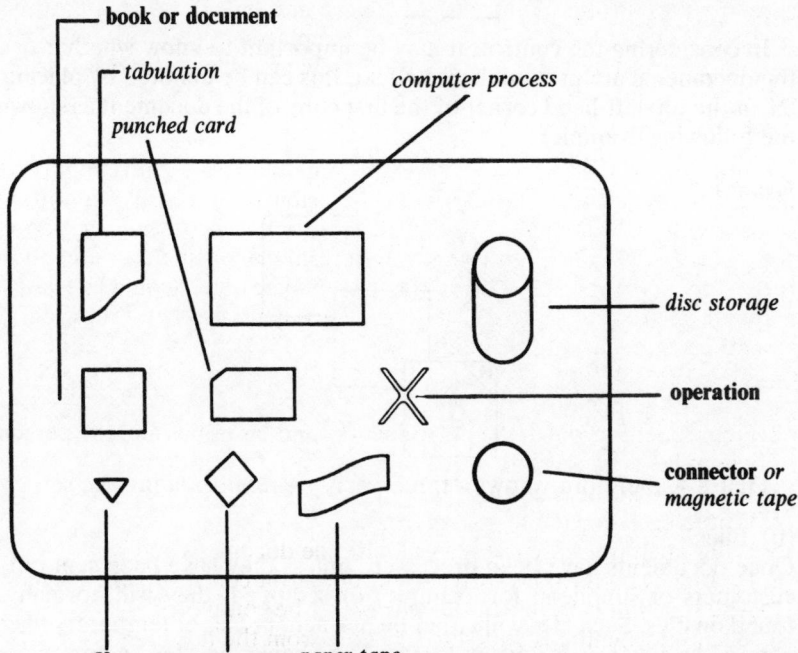

Basic/computer symbols.   The basic symbols are used in all systems and the computer symbols are used to supplement the basic symbols for systems which rely on mechanised processing. The basic symbols are used as follows:

(a) The book or document

The book/document symbol is used to denote an accounting document or book of account as shown in Figure 2 below.

Figure 2

A book of account is distinguished from a document by a vertical margin representing a book's spine. Note that each document or book of account should be clearly labelled.

An auditor may be interested in the various copies of a document such as an invoice and to identify the individual copies on the flowchart it is useful to number them thus:

Figure 3

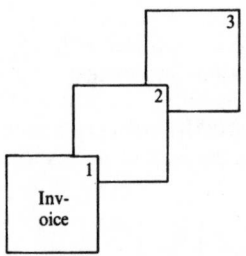

In considering the controls it may be important to know whether or not the documents are pre-numbered. If so, this can be denoted by placing an 'N' at the top left-hand corner of the first copy of the document as shown in the following example:

Figure 4

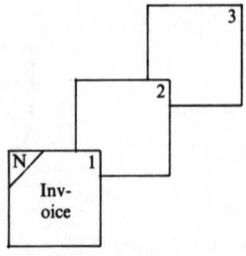

Figure 4, therefore, shows a three-part, *pre-numbered* invoice set.

(b) Files

Once documents have been processed, unless they have been sent out (to customers or suppliers, for example) or scrapped, they will normally be found on files. Such files will either be permanent files or temporary files. A copy of an invoice, for example, would normally be filed as a permanent record, while an order for goods which are temporarily out of stock may be placed on a temporary file until the goods are delivered. The two sorts of file are denoted by the same symbol, but temporary files are marked with a 'T'.

Figure 5

Frequently, however, it will be useful to show whether the documents are filed in alphabetical order, numerical order or in date order. This can be done by marking the file with the appropriate initial as shown below:

Figure 6

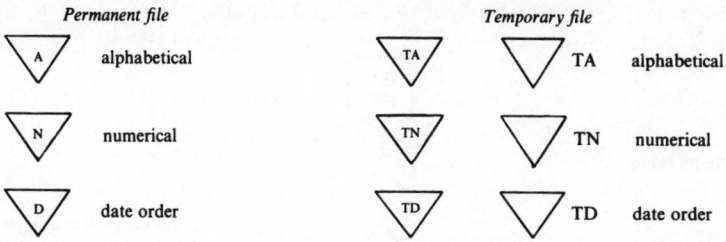

(c) Operation
One symbol is used to represent any operation (except a check function) on a document or a book of account. It follows that the operation must be described in narrative against the operation as in the following examples:

Figure 7

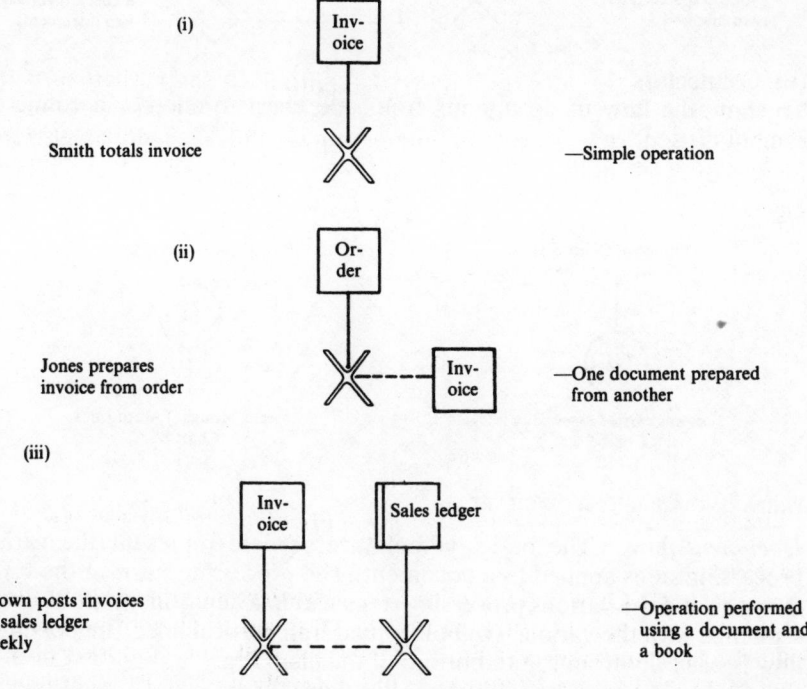

Example (iii) above demonstrates that the operation is considered to relate to the document so that a posting process may result in more than one operation symbol.

The scrapping of a document and the mailing of a document to a customer would normally also be represented by an operation symbol with appropriate narrative.

(d) Check functions

Check functions are of particular interest to the auditor because they represent controls in the system and a separate symbol therefore has been adopted to enable these functions to be immediately recognisable. Many such checks are also operations, but if an operation is also a control function the check symbol should generally be used in preference. Figure 8 shows examples of check functions.

Figure 8

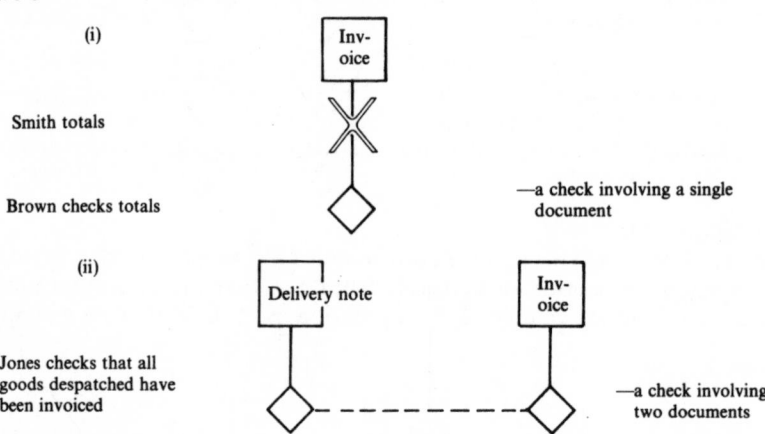

(e) Connectors

To show the flow of documents from one chart to another a connector symbol is used, eg

Figure 9

PREPARING A BASIC FLOWCHART

Document flow. The basic symbols are used to represent the various processing steps applied to a document. The processing starts at the top of the page and the various processing steps within a department are shown in sequence with the various symbols joined by a vertical line. The document flow is basically from top to bottom of the chart, eg:

Figure 10

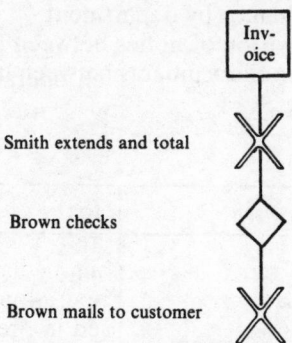

A separate vertical line will be needed for each copy of a document except that where the copies remain attached and are therefore processed together, the vertical document flowlines can be brought together (see Figure 11).

Information flow. Frequently information is transferred from one document to another. This may happen, for example, when a document is prepared, when a document is posted to a book of account or when two documents are compared. The information flow is represented by a broken horizontal line.

Figure 11

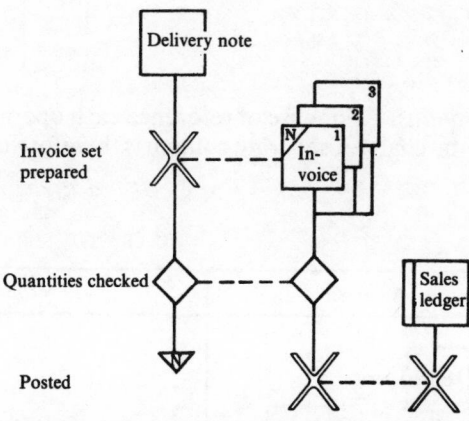

Note that the processing history of each document can be followed individually by reading the processing steps down the appropriate vertical line. The information flows shown above arise when details are entered on a new invoice set from a delivery note, when quantities on the invoice are checked against the delivery note and when the invoice is posted to the sales ledger.

Division of duties. The primary function of a flowchart is the recording of the controls operating within a system and a key feature of good internal control is an adequate division of duties. This is represented on the flowchart by vertical columns indicating how the duties are segregated. In smaller organisations the vertical columns will be division of duties between individuals; in larger organisations the division may be between departments because several individuals perform similar functions. In each case it is important that the vertical columns set out clearly the segregation of functions, whether by individual or by department.

Figure 12 shows the division of duties between Mr Smith and Mr Jones. Note also that the transfer of documents between individuals is represented by a horizontal flow line.

Figure 12

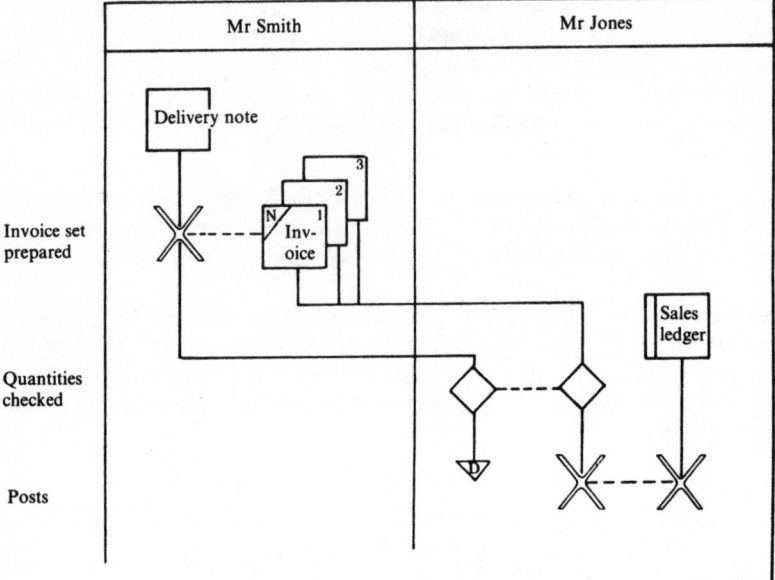

Sequence of operations.　For ease of reference each operation is numbered in a sequence on the chart. A separate column is therefore included as shown below:

Figure 13

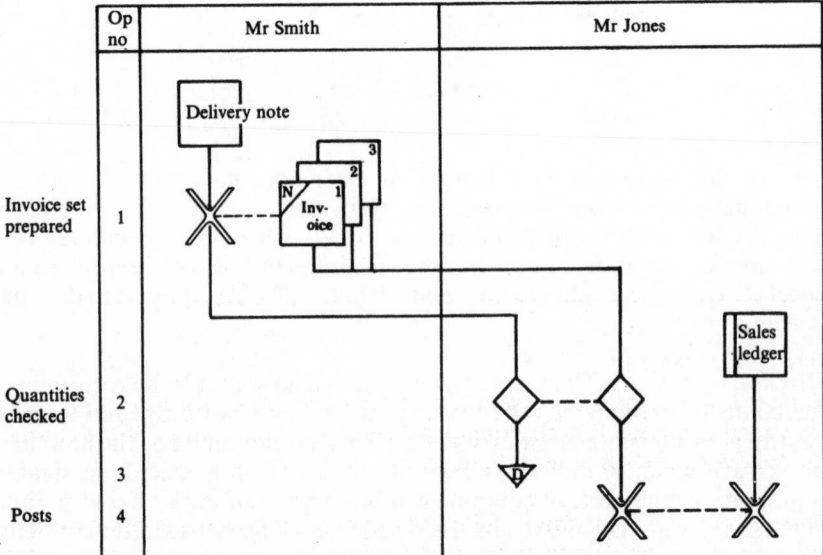

The operation number is set horizontally against the symbol representing the process being described. Each operation, check function and file (permanent or temporary) should be given an operation number.

Care must be taken when drawing the chart to see that no two operations appear on the same horizontal line, for it would cause confusion if two operation numbers were to appear horizontally adjacent to one another in the reference column.

When several charts are used to describe a particular system, each chart should be given an identifying number. For example, a sales system might be described on Charts S.1 to S.4. It may then be convenient to number operations from say 1 to 15 on each chart and to use the chart number in an operation reference, eg an operation may be described as Operation Number 10 on chart S.2.

Description of operation. The chart is completed by the addition of a narrative column describing key operations. Such narrative should be kept to a minimum necessary for the understanding of the system of controls. Files, for example, rarely require any narrative description at all—the symbol is complete in itself. In a check function, on the other hand, the extent of the information checked may require explanation in the narrative column. A simple chart can now be drawn as follows:

Figure 14

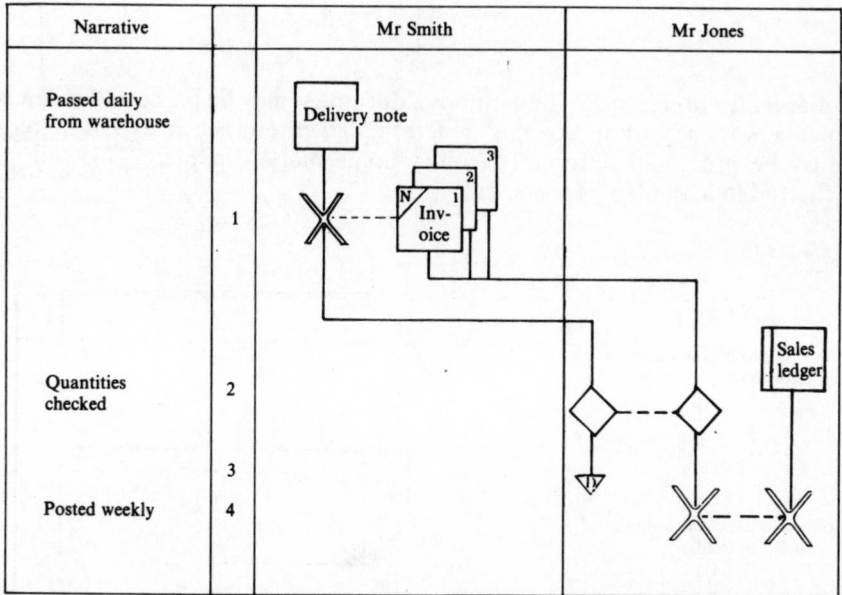

CHART ORGANISATION

While a flowchart consists essentially of the basic symbols already desribed, a key factor in good flowcharting practice is the organisation of the charts. The following are some useful guidelines.

Charting the document flow. Chart the document flow from top to bottom and generally from left to right. By convention the flow can never return upwards. The flow may be from right to left of a page, but if the reverse flow is too frequent a chart becomes difficult to read.

Avoidance of diagnonal lines.   Avoid using diagonal lines. The eye can follow vertical and horizontal lines more easily. Moreover, there is a convention that vertical lines represent the passage of time, horizontal solid lines the transfer of documents between departments or individuals, and horizontal broken lines the transfer of information concerning two or more documents. Documents can therefore only be processed on a vertical line, never on a horizontal line. While horizontal solid lines will only normally be between departments because they represent the transfer of documents, the broken horizontal lines will only be within a department because information flow represents transfer of information between two documents which would normally be carried out within one department.

Intersection of lines.   Where lines cross, make clear which way the flow continues. This is most easily achieved by showing a 'hump' in the crossing lines, eg:

Figure 15

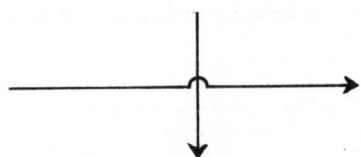

Alternative processing.   Sometimes a document may be processed in alternative ways according to some predetermined criteria, eg an export invoice may be processed differently from a home market invoice. This can be charted in a number of ways, eg:

Figure 16

(i) both procedures shown on
    same chart.

(ii) procedures dealt with on
     different charts.

(iii) by narrative:—
      if goods for export, invoice is passed
      to bankers for payment, otherwise
      mailed direct to customer.

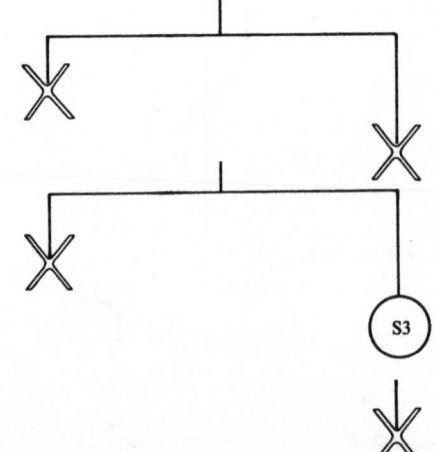

Avoidance of excessive detail.   The purpose of a flowchart is to provide an understanding of the controls operating in a system and this must always be borne in mind. It is not, therefore, necessary to show operations that are irrelevant to such an understanding.

Avoidance of too many notes. Avoid too many notes on the face of the chart. The operation description column is the best place for notes, and even there they should be kept as brief as possible.

Avoidance of too many columns. Too many columns can make a chart difficult to follow. When documents are sent for counter-signature, for example, rather than have a special column for the person countersigning, a simple alternative device is shown below. Note that the two lines (an interrupted flow) are intended to indicate that the document has temporarily left the department.

Figure 17

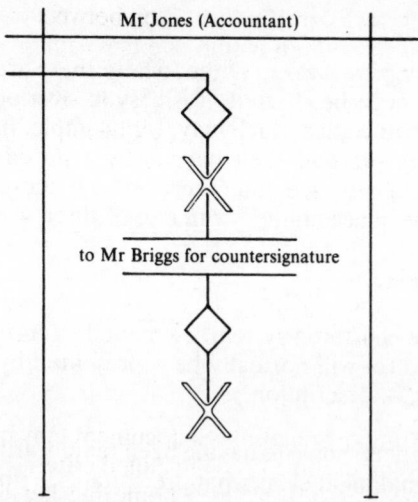

Splitting the system into sections. Split a system into logical sections that can be charted separately. For example, a sales system may be split into sections as follows:

(a) order processing;
(b) invoicing;
(c) sales ledger recording;
(d) cash collection.

Avoidance of unusual abbreviations. When a document is first shown it should be named in full if an abbreviation is likely to cause confusion. In a purchasing system the abbreviation PO for purchase order is reasonably obvious, as in GRN for goods received note, but GIN for goods inwards note may distract the reader!

'Ghosting'. When documents are first shown in a system they are shown by 'boxes' drawn in solid lines. Normally there is no need to show the document symbol again, but when a document is carried forward to another chart, or when copies which have previously been processed together are ultimately split up, it is often useful to 'restate' the documents by means of symbols drawn in broken lines, eg:

Figure 18

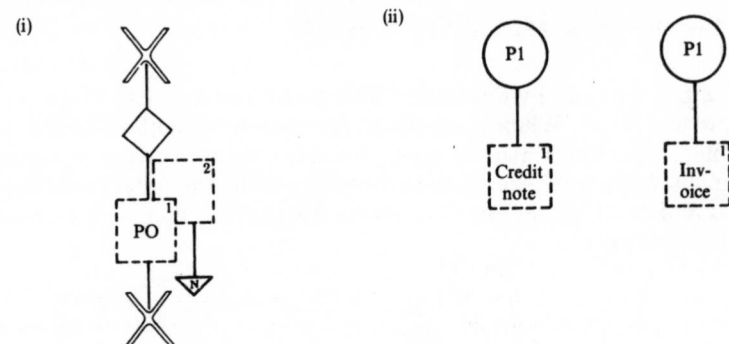

Avoidance of incomplete trails.   Often, where there are a number of documents whose flow must be charted, it is easy to overlook what happens to some quite important copies which may, for example, have been charted as far as a temporary file and then have been ignored. The chart should therefore be checked to see that there are no loose ends and that all documents have been accounted for in one of three ways:

(a) permanently filed;
(b) destroyed;
(c) having left the chartered system, eg mailed to customer.
   (Items (b) and (c) will normally be represented by operation symbols with appropriate description.)

   When a document is shown as having been temporarily filed, there should also be narrative making it clear what precipitates action to remove it from that file. For example, where a customer order is filed temporarily in an 'out of stock' file, the order will be released on information that the goods are once more in stock.

Correct papersize.   Use A3 or double foolscap size paper to provide ample room for working. Rather than try to chart a whole system on one page, it is often clearer if the system is spread onto a number of charts. In this case the documents should be shown as carried forward to the next chart using properly referenced connector symbols.

WHAT TO INCLUDE IN THE CHART

If a flowchart is to be used in connection with the evaluation of internal control, it is important that the chart should indicate clearly the key control features. Other factors are of lesser importance to the auditor and there is no need to chart in great detail procedures of minor importance. When drawing a chart it is useful to have in mind the controls one would expect to find in a system. The following guidelines indicate the points the auditor would expect to find included in a flowchart.

Sales system.   A sales system is taken to encompass all processing from the receipt of an order, to proceed through the despatching of goods, invoicing the customer and on to the collection of payment.

Sales system questions

(a) How are customers' orders received (mail, telephone, sales, etc)?
(b) Are these transcribed onto standard order forms for internal use?
(c) How is the customer's credit standing checked?
(d) What documentation is used to organise delivery of the goods?
(e) How is it ensured that all goods shipped are invoiced?
(f) What check procedures are in force to see that the invoice is correct as regards:
  (i) pricing;
  (ii) extensions and totals?
(g) How is it ensured that all invoices are entered in the books?
(h) How is the sales analysis carried out and does this also embrace cost of sales information?
(i) How are credit notes raised and authorised?
(j) What procedures are there for:
  (i) reconciling debtor balances with total accounts;
  (ii) preparing and mailing customers' statements;
  (iii) following up queried statements;
  (iv) preparing an aged analysis of debtor accounts;
  (v) following up overdue accounts;
  (vi) providing for doubtful accounts?
(k) What procedures are there to ensure all cash receipts from debtors are properly entered up and banked promptly?
(l) How are cash sales dealt with?
(m) Is there a proper segregation of duties?

Purchasing system.   A purchasing system is taken to encompass all processing from the request for purchase to the final payment of the supplier's invoices.

Purchasing system questions

(a) What triggers off the ordering of goods (re-order levels reached, specific purchase requisitions, etc)?
(b) How are purchase orders authorised and placed?
(c) What system is there for recording receipt of incoming goods?
(d) Is there a system of inspection of those goods to ensure:
  (i) correct quantity;
  (ii) adequate quality?
(e) Is there a system of matching suppliers' invoices with goods received notes and purchase orders prior to payment?
(f) How is unmatched documentation dealt with?
(g) What checks are made on invoices received?
(h) What procedures are used to raise debit notes?
(i) What controls are there to see that all invoices are entered in the books?
(j) How are invoices analysed to the proper charge account and what check is there on the analysis?
(k) Is the purchase ledger regularly balanced and reconciled with supplier statements?
(l) What procedures are there for ensuring that cheques are drawn only for invoices properly approved for payment and for ensuring that they are then sent direct to suppliers?

(m) Are documents cancelled to prevent re-use?

(n) Are there separate procedures for processing invoices with cash discounts?

(o) Are bank accounts regularly reconciled?

(p) Is there adequate segregation of duties?

SOME PITFALLS

Convention has dictated that the following five features should not be allowed to occur—they cause confusion and poor presentation.

1 *Diagonal lines*—Vertical and horizontal lines can be followed more easily than diagonal lines, and the latter should not be used.

2 *Excessive detail*—It is unnecessary to show procedures, books, etc which are not relevant to the understanding of the system.

3 *Excessive narrative*—Writing on the face of the chart should be avoided, any required explanations being written in the narrative column to the side of the chart.

4 *Incomplete trails*—All documents should be accounted for in one of the following ways:

   (a) permanently filed

   (b) destroyed   see appropriate symbol

   (c) sent to customer or supplier

The chart should be checked to ensure that no documents are left unaccounted for. Where a document has been filed temporarily there should be an explanation of what has to happen before it is removed from the file.

5 *Crowding*—Rather than trying to chart a whole system on one page, it is often better to use several charts and split a system into logical sections that can be drawn separately. For example, a sales system could be split into the following sections:

(a) Ordering

(b) Assembling goods for customer

(c) Delivery of goods and documentation

(d) Sales ledger recording

(e) Cash payments/debtor system

TESTING THE FLOWCHART

Having drawn the flowchart it is necessary to test its accuracy. This is necessary even when last year's flowchart is carried forward unchanged. It is always possible that the flowchart has been incorrectly drawn or that the information received does not reflect what actually happens in practice. If this is the case, the flowchart should be altered accordingly. To avoid the possibility of basing the audit approach on incorrect information, a simple test is carried out on the accuracy of the flowchart. This test is often referred to as a 'walk-through check'—actually following several documents through the system. In practice a useful technique is to draw a chart in pencil, then photocopy it and initial and date the photocopy. Such a technique allows for future amendment to the original without the time consuming effort of redrawing.

2.5.3 *Examples of flowcharts*

Example 1 (p 115)

Cashiers system—banking monies from till
Narrative (memorandum)
At 4.00 pm each day the supervisor together with the cashier agree the monies received to the till roll. Upon agreement the cashier enters a takings form and the supervisor completes a reconciliation form. Both sign both forms as agreed.

The monies are then made up for banking, and put in the safe. Meanwhile the supervisor takes the reconciliation form to the income clerk who completes a paying-in slip before entering the sum received in the cash book. Once agreed by the supervisor, monies and paying-in book are placed in a sealed envelope awaiting collection for banking by a messenger from a security firm. This messenger gives a receipt upon collection of the sealed package. All documentation is filed in date order.

Example 2 (p 116)

Rotary Engine plc assemble rotary engines for vehicles and consequently supply complete engines and spare parts to the trade. In assembling the engines a spare part re-ordering system is operated.

The system:

1 Orders are placed with the supplier when stocks reach a minimum order level which is entered on the 'bin' card for each type of part.
2 Bin cards are updated daily.
3 Requisition notes are initiated by the stores clerk and checked by the stores manager prior to being sent to the buying office.
4 The purchase clerk completes a four-part carbonised purchase order set which is distributed in the following manner:
   (a) Top (white) copy to supplier.
   (b) Second (blue) copy to the warehouse receiving bay.
   (c) Third (pink) copy to the incoming goods warehouse.
   (d) Fourth (green) copy placed in orders pending file.

When goods are received they are checked for quantity and quality, and any queries are discussed with the supplier. If the goods are satisfactory a three-part carbonised goods received note is originated by the warehouse and distributed as follows:

1 Top (gold) copy is attached to the blue copy of purchase order and sent to the purchase invoice section in the accounts office.
2 Second (purple) copy is sent to the buying office where it is used as authority to transfer the green order copy from 'orders pending' file to 'orders delivered' where it is attached to the green order.
3 Third (yellow) copy is filed in the warehouse section.

When invoices are received from suppliers each invoice is matched to the gold GRN for comparison of details. If agreed, the invoice is passed for payment with purchase order and GRN attached.

COMMENTS ON FLOWCHART 2

1 No start points.
2 Bin cards not entered.
3 Assumptions made re filing systems.
4 Order of sections incorrect—should be stores/warehouse/buying/accounts.
5 Requisition note became order?
6 Volume of system not entered.

There is little, if any, internal check in the system, eg the manager does not initial or sign order, copy orders are not checked.

Example 3 (p 117)

Now read the flowchart for ABC plc and enter the narrative as you understand the system to be.

NARRATIVE FOR FLOWCHART 3

1 Order received.
2 Sales order ($\times$ 4) raised.
3 Checked by clerk.
4 Checked by supervisor.
5 Top copy to customer.
6 No 2 to credit controller. No 3 and 4 to DC.
7 Checked by credit controller and returned.
8 Filed by clerk.
9 Attached to order from customer.
10 Order made up by clerk.
11 Checked by supervisor.
12 Copy No 4 to invoice clerk.
13 Copy No 3 attached to GDN to customer.
14 SO4 checked.
15 SO4 filed.

ADVANTAGES OF FLOWCHARTS

1 Clear and concise to read.
2 Weakness easily identified.
3 Display of disciplined approach to understanding the system.
4 Gain thorough knowledge of system—if you can draw it, you must understand it.
5 Understood by other auditors.
6 May be understood by computer staff (computerised system) being a technique applied by computer staff to describe system procedures.

DISADVANTAGES

These really amount to limitations in the technique:

1 Intelligibility often dependent on accompanying narrative.
2 Complications in a system may be best described in narrative.
3 Requires skill in drawing.
4 Time consuming
5 Difficult to update
6 Only accurate at one point in time (time of drawing).

Flowchart 1

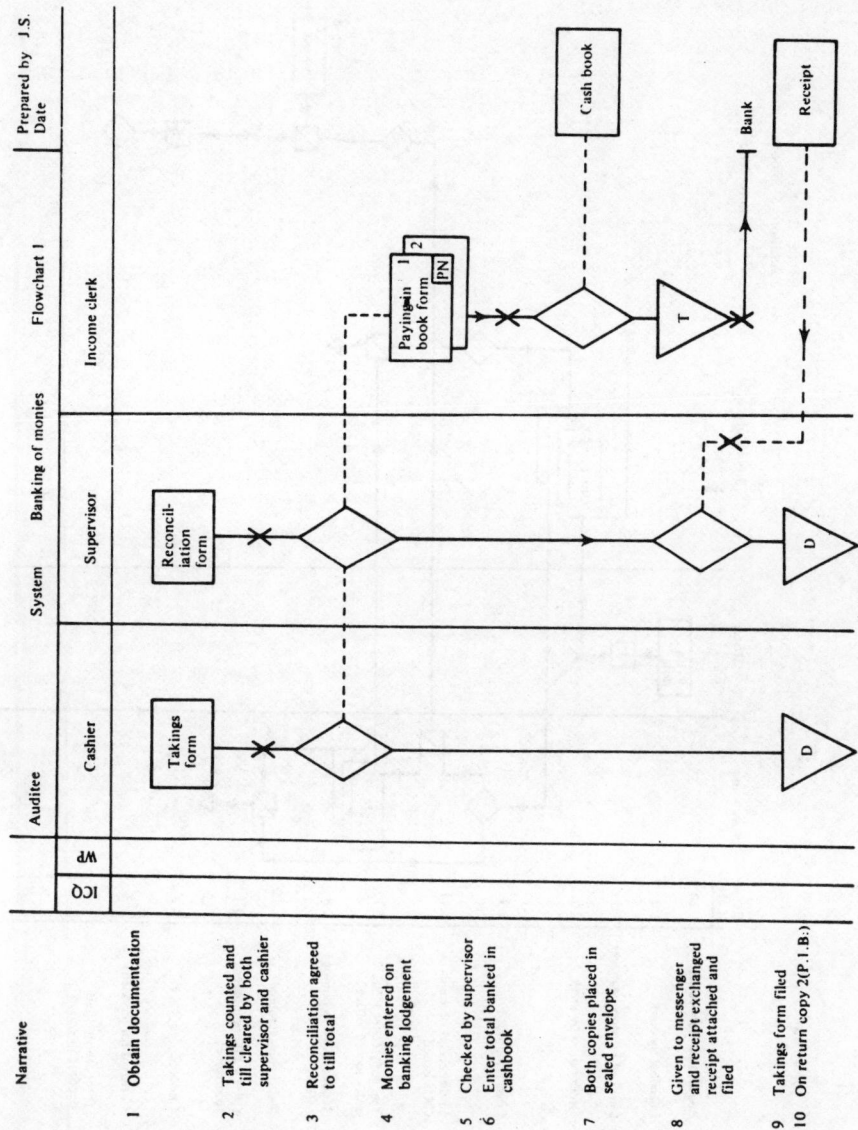

Flowchart 2

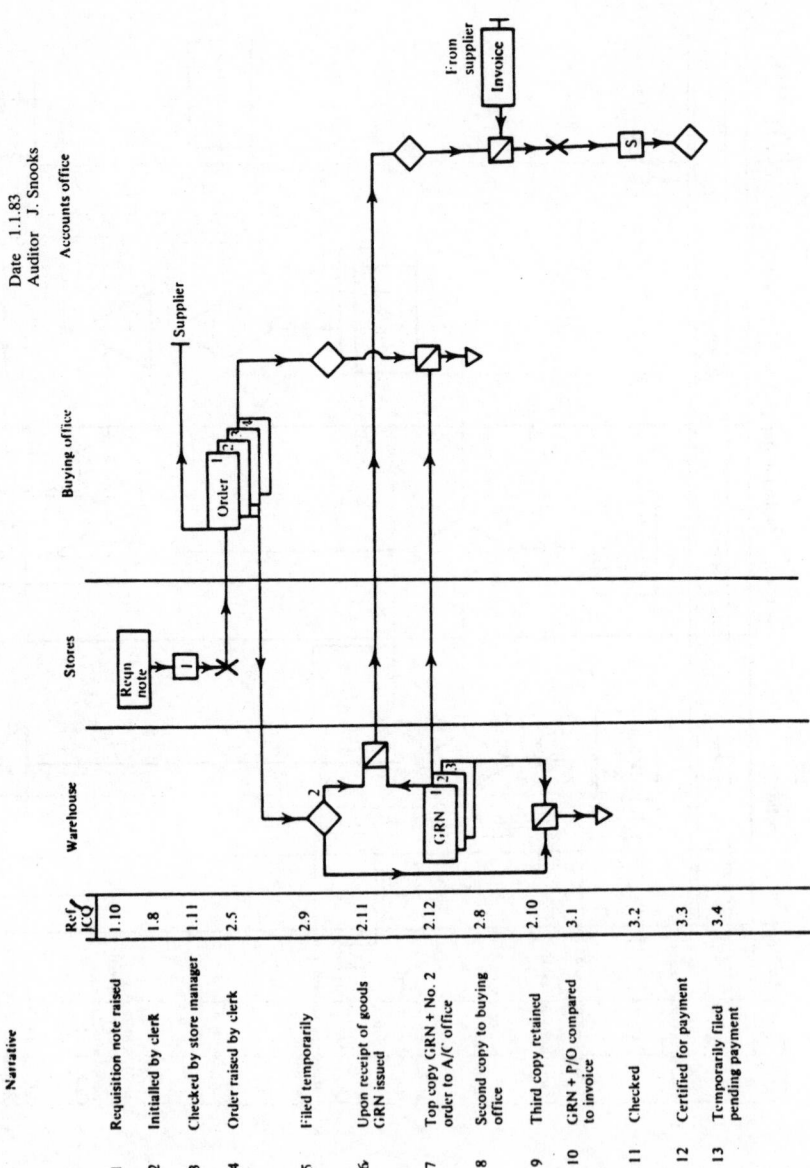

Flowchart 3

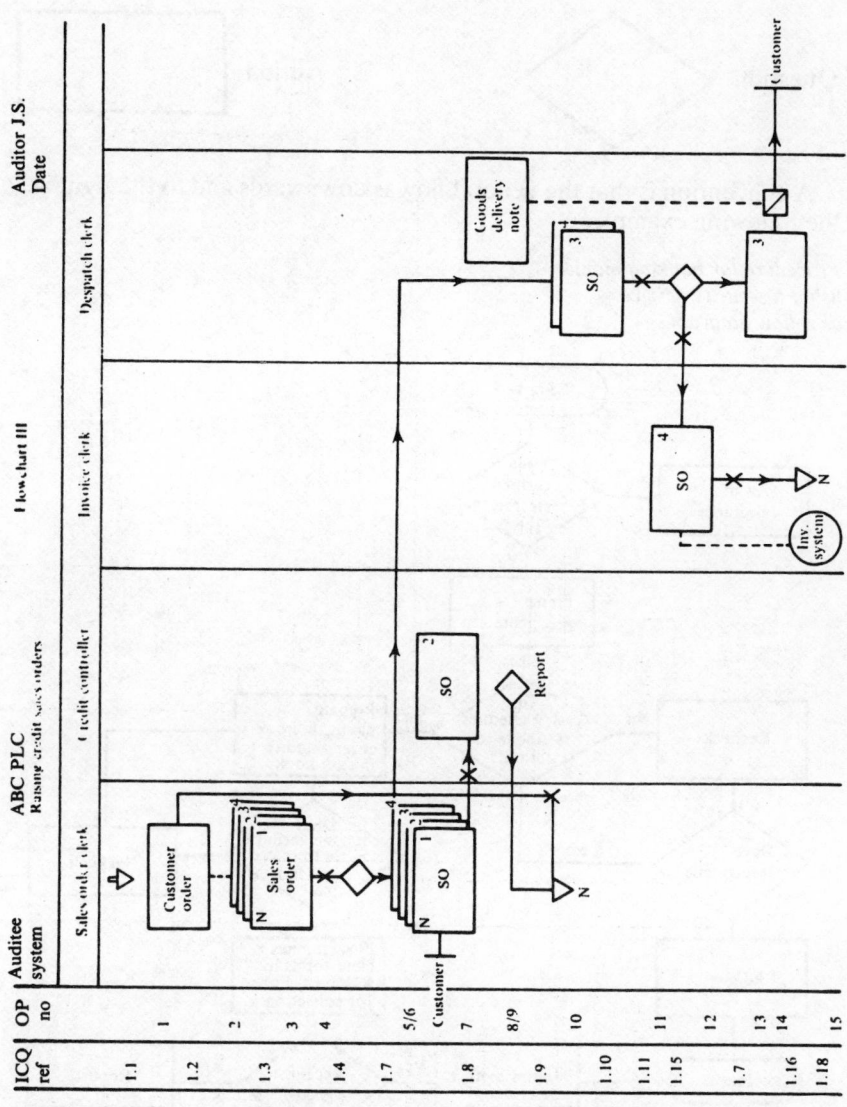

2.5.4   *Other methods*

FLOW DIAGRAMS

A flow diagram is used to display the system in a logical sequence, based on a question and action response.

Question   Action

A convention is that the general flow is downwards and to the right as in the following example.

Procedure for banking monies using a security service as a flow diagram

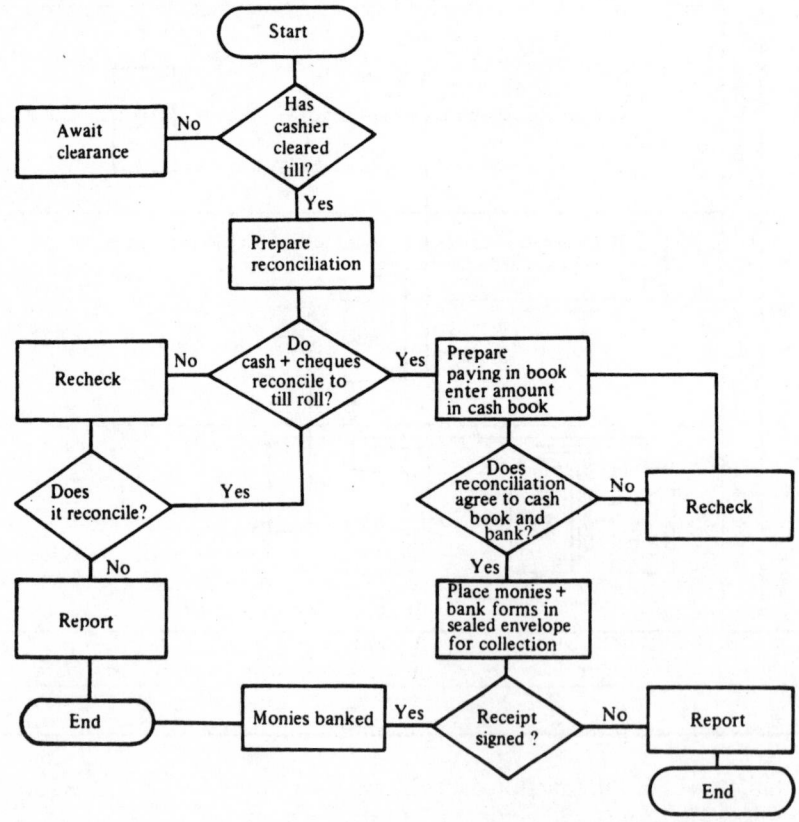

PROCESS CHARTS

This is a form of description using a diagram of various stages in a system which distinguishes between activity and non-activity. Generally such a chart takes one of two forms:

1 The processes carried out in undertaking a particular task.
2 The activities of an employee in doing a task.

SYMBOLS GENERALLY USED

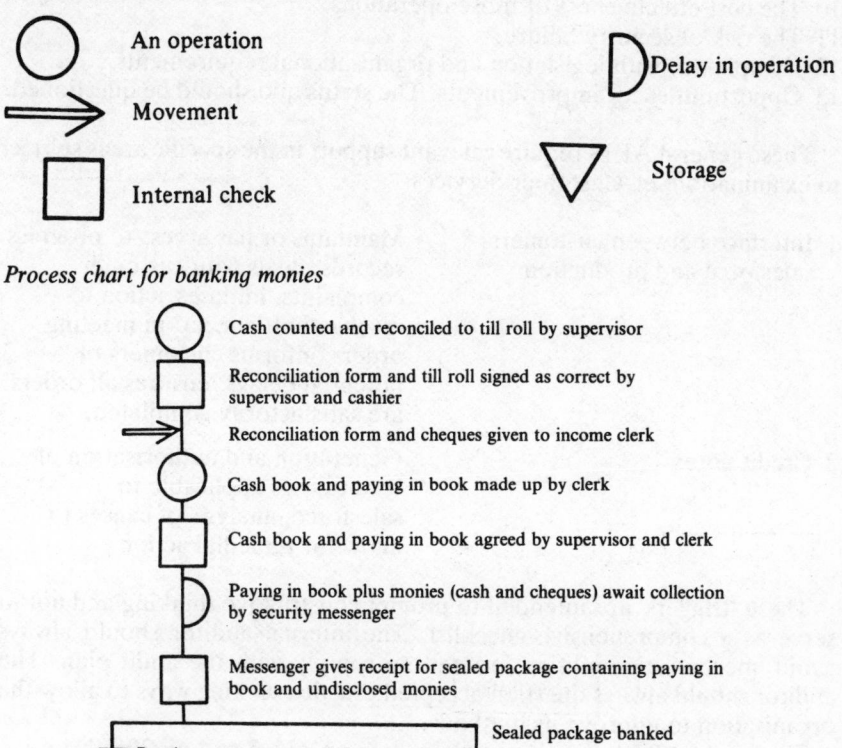

Process chart for banking monies

2.6 Audit profile triggers (APTs)

This is a useful technique whereby auditors are able to plan coverage of the audit through the use of 'triggers' to alert them to possible areas of investigation. They are not meant to replace the detailed steps and checks to be planned and undertaken at each audit. They are a thought provoking device to enable the auditor to undertake a positive approach.

As such, APTs take two forms, the general form and the detailed form: The general form is applicable to all audits. The objective is to provide a list which covers the principal areas for examination, ie:

1 Objectives of the function to be examined.
2 The organisation and resources of that function.
3 The authority and accountability of that function.
4 Operating instructions, manuals, directives and procedural notes applicable to that function.
5 Changes that have occurred since the last audit and since the instructions were issued.
6 Compliance with procedures.

7 Effectiveness with which objectives have been achieved.
8 The manner in which control over the function has been monitored and reviewed.
9 The overall efficiency of that function in its day-to-day operations.
10 The cost effectiveness of those operations.
11 The risk of security failure.
12 Compliance with legislation and organisational requirements.
13 Opportunities for improvements. The status quo should be questioned.

These general APTs require relevant support in the specific areas subject to examination, eg Customer Services:

1 Interface between customers, salesforce and production	Maintains or has access to progress records; deals with customer complaints, initiates action to resolve 'bottlenecks' in meeting orders; informs customers of potential delays; ensures all orders are satisfactorily completed.
2 Credit notes	Generation and authorisation of credit notes applicable to salesforce; analysis of causes to allow for remedial action.

These 'triggers' are intended to prompt constructive thinking and not to serve as a comprehensive checklist. The internal auditor should always avoid 'mechanistic auditing', merely to comply with the audit plan. The auditor should always question accepted practice seeking ways to allow the organisation to improve its methods.

The use of APTs is further explained on pp 45–47 and pp 305–306.

2.7 Audit programmes

2.7.1 *Definition*

An audit programme may be defined as written instructions containing the basic tests and examinations that the auditor should carry out in order to complete the audit.

2.7.2 *Function*

The programme is a written record of work undertaken. Such work will include the tests undertaken.

2.7.3 *Objectives*

1 To record work undertaken for review by the audit manager or senior audit staff.
2 To provide evidence of work undertaken.
3 To identify the auditor responsible for the work.
4 To ensure a methodical approach to the audit.
5 To give instructions to new staff . . . providing assistance.
6 To aid the planning of future audits.

Audit programmes should be carefully constructed so that initiative should not be stifled (the auditor, if not satisfied, should probe the matter to the bottom). The work specified should be regarded as a minimum, allowing the auditor to examine further until satisfied.

2.7.4 *Format*

This will vary according to departmental policy, but the following layout may act as guidance.

PART A

1 *Introduction*—Giving brief details of the audit to be undertaken and instructions on completion of the programme.

2 *Audit preparation*—Details of information required, commonly known as 'prep' pre-audit work. An analytical review should be undertaken and copies of documentation obtained, eg wage sheets, etc.

3 *Audit documentation*—Files and correspondence from previous audits.

4 *Details of visit*—Location and contact points.

PART B

5 *Audit programme*—A schedule of work to be undertaken.

Once the system has been understood and documented, an audit programme can be devised allowing the audit to be completed in an orderly and timely manner. See p 122 for an example of an audit programme.

2.7.5 *Advantages of an audit programme*

1 Provides a clear and concise set of instructions to be followed.
2 Provides a record of work to be undertaken, ie evidence.
3 Prevents duplication of work.
4 Acts as a checklist to ensure all areas are audited in a methodical manner.
5 Demonstrates the exercise of 'due professional care'.
6 Assists in the planning of future audits.
7 Identifies the auditor responsible for work delegated and undertaken.

2.7.6 *Disadvantages of an audit programme*

1 Encourages 'mechanical' auditing, the auditor seeing the completion of the programme as the objective, rather than the examination of the auditee's work. The auditor must examine the evidence supporting the reports to both line and senior management.
2 Because the individual auditor is given a programme for a part of the audit, that the auditor may not realise the overall implications to the audit of these examinations.
3 Initiative may be curtailed, ie work 'restricted' to audit programme.
4 The auditee may become aware of the tests and circumvent the system undetected by the tests applied periodically by the auditor.

It is recommended that an audit programme should comprise the following:

1 Basic audit instructions.
2 Amount of detailed checking recommended.

3 Actual amount of checking undertaken.
4 Name(s) of auditor(s) responsible for tests.
5 Time planned for each test.
6 Cross-referencing to ICQ or ICEQ.
7 Extent of tests noted, initialled and dated by the auditor.
8 Both compliance and substantive tests should be shown.
9 The pre-audit work used, in conjunction with ICQs, as a base when deciding tests.

An example of an audit programme appears below:

Auditee: Period: Prepared by:					Audit file Ref:
Instructions	*Volume to be checked*	*Volume checked*	*Checked by*	*Time taken*	*Comment*
Wages preparation Check time records to wages sheets Check other payment records (bonus) to wage sheets Check appropriate rates applied to wages sheets Check calculations of gross pay Check amendments					

2.8   Audit trail

This term refers to the ability to pursue a transaction from its inception together with its supporting documentation through to its inclusion in the accounts and the final filing of the documentation. A trail, to be complete, must be capable of being followed in a given direction from a given stage in the system. The maintenance of a satisfactory 'audit trail' must be considered essential to any accounting system so that the auditors can place reliance upon the records examined. However, in many computerised systems the audit trail is seldom readily apparent. In spite of such problems auditors should always satisfy themselves that whenever possible an audit trail exists.

2.9 Conclusion

The use of these methods will vary from internal audit department to department depending on the needs of the individual organisation and the objectives of internal audit within the organisation. A further factor is the ability of the staff, their expertise and experience and resources available to monitor and supervise those staff. Clearly, the better the techniques used, the more effective the internal audit, that is, the more positive the contribution and the greater the benefit to management.

3.0 AUDIT SAMPLING

3.1 Selection techniques

3.1.1 *Random selection*

Using random number tables to identify the items to be examined. This method is simple to apply, provided the items being examined are similar in both type and value.

3.1.2 *Stratified selection*

This method involves dividing the population in strata, taking a selection from each level. This allows the auditor to ensure all areas are examined with particular reference to items having material value, eg:

£	Examination
4,000–4,999	All
3,000–3,999	50%
2,000–2,999	25%
1,000–1,999	10%
0– 999	5%

ie the higher value items having more emphasis placed on them by weighting them or using judgement.

3.1.3 *Cluster selection*

This method involves dividing the population into groups (clusters) and the cluster is then randomly selected for checking, eg:

Invoice population: 5,000 per numbered
Cluster randomly selected: Nos 500–550

3.2 Assurance and risk

The term audit assurance applies to the confidence that the auditor has in the auditee (organisation's) systems. By way of example, a 95% confidence level indicates a 5% risk of arriving at an incorrect conclusion. Audit risk can be separated into non-sampling risk and sampling risk.

3.2.1 *Non-sampling risk*

Despite the most advanced techniques an auditor may jeopardise an audit due to many factors: for instance, inability to do the work properly or to conduct the audit with due professional care, ie audit evidence obtained to support an opinion is not satisfactory.

3.2.2 *Sampling risk*

This risk arises from the chance that a conclusion based on a sample of a population is different from one given if the whole population were examined, ie the sample is not representative. The auditor must be aware that the sample he chooses is critical—an unrepresentative sample can endanger the validity of an auditor's opinion, thereby undermining the whole audit.

3.3 Assessment of sampling risk

Large and complex organisations, together with limited audit resources, have meant reduced amounts of testing based on the auditor's confidence regarding the auditee's systems. Thus, where the acceptable risk is 5%, the appropriate confidence level is 95% analysed between reliance on internal control, say 9%, and substantive testing, say 86%, to detect errors. Because the confidence level has been reduced due to the reliance placed on internal control, so the reliability factor has similarly been reduced, eg:

	%	%	%	%
Audit risk	5	5	5	5
Reliance on internal control	32	17	9	0
Substantive testing	63	78	86	95
Total percentage	100	100	100	100
*Reliability factor (R)	1.0	1.5	2.0	3.0
Extent of reliance on internal control	v high	high	medium	none
*per reliability tables				

The reliance on internal control can be assessed from the initial compliance test. It should be noted that no control, however well designed and implemented, can totally prevent material error, human nature being what it is. Consequently auditors seldom exceed a maximum confidence level of 78% in a control to prevent or cause the detection of a material error.

Prior to further examining sampling techniques, it would be of use to illustrate a sampling decision method.

Sampling decision tree

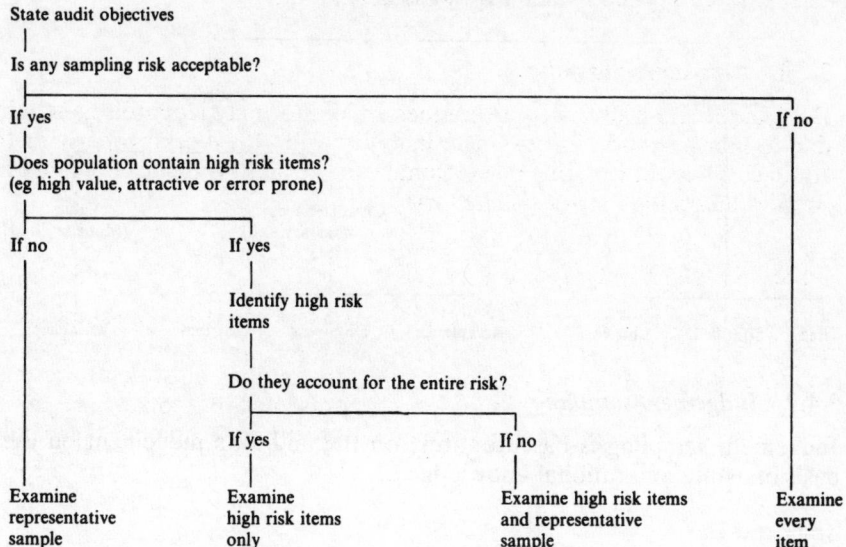

State audit objectives
|
Is any sampling risk acceptable?
|_____
If yes   If no
|
Does population contain high risk items?
(eg high value, attractive or error prone)
|_____
If no   If yes
| |
| Identify high risk
| items
| |
| Do they account for the entire risk?
| |_____
| If yes   If no
| | |
Examine   Examine   Examine high risk items   Examine
representative   high risk items   and representative   every
sample   only   sample   item

3.4   The sampling plan

In order to allow for the successful completion with the minimal use of resources a sample plan should be devised. When referring to sampling techniques the following questions need answering:

1 What knowledge of the population to be sampled is required?
   (a) Estimation of the volume of occurrence of a certain event—attribute sample.
   (b) Estimation of the value of the occurrence of that event—variable sample.
   (c) To find through a sample one occurrence of each characteristic—discovery sample.
2 What are the parameters of the population to be sampled? Does it require stratification.
3 How is a random sample to be obtained? Is it representative?
4 What size of sample should be used to allow for a reasonable evaluation?
5 How should the sample results be interpreted?
6 What additional work is needed?
7 What are the audit objectives?

The objectives of sampling methods are to ensure:

1 *Reliability*—Degree of prudence essential to audit.
2 *Consistency*—Known level of prudence applied.
3 *Usefulness*—Arriving at a meaningful result.
4 *Economy*—Ability to use technique within available resources.

3.4.1   *Sampling methods*

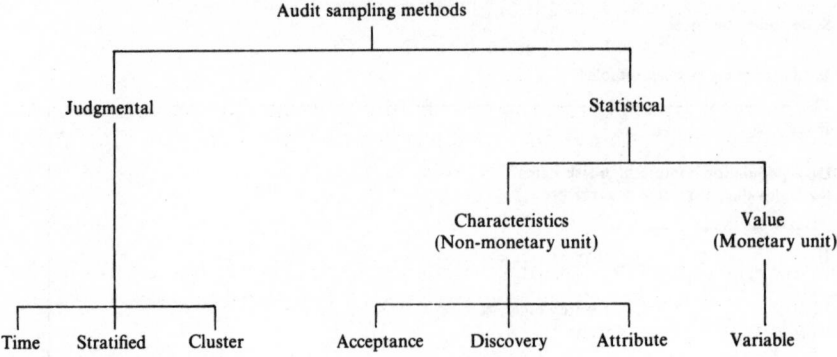

3.4.2   *Judgement sampling*

Judgement sampling is based entirely on the auditor's judgement on the basis of astute and rational knowledge.

ADVANTAGES

1 It is well understood and allows the auditor to exercise his experience.
2 Specialised knowledge of statistics is not needed.
3 Allows more time to be spent auditing.

DISADVANTAGES

1 No quantitative results are obtained.
2 Wasteful—often sample sizes are too large.

Judgemental sampling is unable to give assurance that the sample chosen is representative, leaving the auditor's findings open to question on grounds of bias. In practice, with judgemental sampling, a certain period is chosen together with the end of period to establish cut-off procedures. The transactions of these periods are then proved, to establish the correctness and reliability of systems.

3.4.3   *Statistical sampling*

Prior to discussing the use of statistical techniques in determining an audit sample, the following terms should be defined:

POPULATION

Items of a similar nature (eg sales invoices) about which the same knowledge/evidence is required.

PRECISION LIMIT

This means the range within which an error lies, ie less than 5% errors in a given population.

CONFIDENCE LEVEL

This means the probability that the given characteristic (error rate) is within the chosen precision limit, ie 95% confident that 19 out of 20 entries are correct (5% precision), ie one incorrect. Auditors regard a 75% confidence level as representing reasonable internal control.

ATTRIBUTE

This means a given characteristic, ie failure to deduct discounts receivable. The auditor tests a population to determine how many correct transactions there are, thereby giving an error rate.

FREQUENCY

In order to determine sampling size a judgement is needed regarding frequency of error based on audit experience. If this proves incorrect, a larger sample will be needed.

3.4.4 *Relationship between confidence level and precision limits*

To have more confidence in a sampling result, a larger sample is necessary. However, instead of a larger sample it is possible to widen the precision limits. It can be said that while an auditor may be 90% sure that the error rate is not more than 10% in a population, he can be even more sure that it is not more than 20%.

3.4.5 *Population size and sample size*

The accuracy of the statement depends on the absolute size and validity of the sample, not on the proportion of the population included in the sample. It has been said that this point is the most important contribution made by statistics to auditing. It is the opposite of what might be expected by auditors accustomed to selecting one month's invoices or one week's wages or 10% of the stock calculation (block testing).

For an audit situation it has been found that population increases require increased sample sizes as follows:

Population	Sample size
1,000	210
10,000	260
100,000	270
500,000	270

What matters is the size of the sample, not the proportion of the population, allowing for saving of audit time while maintaining the same reliability.

3.5 Statistical sampling in practice

Much of the compliance and substantive testing undertaken by internal audit is of a routine nature involving the checking of a large number of similar items. Because audit resources do not allow for a 100% check, a representative sample has to be chosen and one method of arriving at a representative sample is the use of statistical techniques. This technique involves the following separate stages in order to ascertain the level of error in the system being examined:

1 Specifying audit objective to which test is being directed, eg accuracy of balance on personal account.
2 Designing a suitable sample. This involves:
   (a) Determining by judgement the maximum acceptable error in a population (precision limit).
   (b) Determining by judgement the degree of data reliability required to stay within the precision limit, ie the probability that errors in the population will not exceed the precision limit (confidence level).
3 Selecting a sample—The basic principle is that the selection procedure should allow each item in the population an equal chance of selection.
4 Examination of sample items—Here normal auditing procedures are adopted—vouching and verification.
5 Evaluating results of sample tested—The auditor arrives at a reasoned opinion.

3.5.1   Designing a sample

When designing a sample the auditor must make initial judgements based on experience, and from such judgements a 'scientific approach' can be adopted, using the following stages:

1   DECIDE ON ACCEPTABLE ERROR OR DEVIATION

This may be either a volume (numerical—NP) or value (monetary—MP) precision limit.

2   ASSESS THE RELIABILITY OF SAMPLE (DEGREE OF CONFIDENCE IN THE STRENGTH OF INTERNAL CONTROL IN THE SYSTEM)

For example, a 95% confidence level with 1% precision states that in samples drawn from a population there is a 5% chance that errors exceeding 1% of the population will not be revealed. The auditor accepts this risk.

Before examining the techniques used, it should be mentioned that these techniques can be used either to identify given characteristics or to assess the value of a characteristic.

3   DETERMINE THE SAMPLE SIZE

Sample size may be affected by four factors:

Audit risk	— The chance that an invalid conclusion will be drawn from the sample taken.
Tolerable error or deviation rate	— Maximum acceptable error or deviation rate, allowing the auditor to conclude that the audit objective has been achieved.
Expected error or deviation rate	— Needs to be accounted for when determining sample size.
Stratification	— The division of the population into sub-populations, allowing for greater weighting to be given to those sub-populations considered by the auditor to be potentially vulnerable.

3.6 Some techniques

MONETARY UNIT SAMPLING (MUS)

This technique was developed specifically with the auditor in mind. The major difference from other statistical techniques is that the standard deviation of the population need not be known. Because it is a monetary unit sample the size of the sample is based on value rather than the number of transactions. Every £1 value has an equal chance of selection.

Using judgement, the auditor must decide on:

Minimum acceptable error value—monetary precision (MP)
Confidence level (%)
Sampling interval (f)
Sample size (n)

Example

Population size (g)	£100,000
Monetary precision (MP)	£5,000
Confidence level	95%
Reliability factor (R) based on the	
Poisson distribution ($1 = 63\%, 2 = 86\%, 3 = 95\%$)	3

$$\text{Sampling interval (f)} = \frac{MP}{R} = \frac{£5,000}{3} = £1,667$$

$$\text{Sample size (n)} = \frac{g}{f} = \frac{£100,000}{£1,667} = 60$$

Thus transactions examined might be:

Transaction no	Cumulative value
10	£1,667 +
22	£3,334 +
23	£5,001 + etc for 60 items.

Advantages and disadvantages of monetary unit sampling

Advantages	Disadvantages
1 Understandable and easy to apply.	1 Small values may conceal understatements which have little chance of selection. Zero is never selected.
2 Technique has stood the test of time.	2 Errors forming a cyclical pattern which is similar to the sample interval are less likely to be detected.
3 Appropriate for critical materiality judgements.	3 Concentrates on error detection rather than system weaknesses.

NON-MONETARY UNIT SAMPLING (INTERVAL SAMPLING)

This technique can be used to determine which item by number should be examined.

Non-monetary precision (NP) is calculated as follows:

$$NP = \frac{\text{Monetary precision (MP)}}{\text{Total value of population (g)}} = \frac{£5,000}{£100,000} = 0.02$$

Number of items in the population (N) = 5,000

$$\text{Sampling interval (f)} = \frac{NP \times N}{R} = \frac{0.02 \times 5,000}{3} = 33.3$$

$$\text{Sample size (n)} = \frac{\text{Number of items in population (N)}}{\text{Sampling interval (f)}} = \frac{5,000}{33.3} = 150$$

Thus every 33rd item would be examined until the total sample taken reached 150 items.

Note: Reliability factor R = 3 as in previous example.

3.6.1 *Acceptance sampling*

The auditor specifies a given error rate (characteristic), and if this is exceeded will reject the population. The technique is of limited value because the answer is numeric (not financial), the auditor having applied judgement to determine an acceptable rate. It is of use in compliance testing where a particular type of error may occur frequently—the frequency of the error being significant (systems failure) rather than the materiality of the value.

3.6.2 *Discovery sampling*

This technique is used where evidence of a single error necessitates further examination, eg fraud. A sample is chosen to determine how many times a certain weakness occurs, ie erosion of control. This technique is useful in compliance testing to determine the proportion of failures of a given characteristic in a system, ie if the error rate exceeds one, there could be a fraud caused by that characteristic, eg teeming and lading. Very similar to attribute sampling, but instead of measuring a given characteristic, discovery sampling is used to determine if that characteristic exceeds a given rate.

3.6.3 *Attribute sampling (estimation sampling)*

This technique attempts to measure the actual proportion of the population having a given characteristic, eg miscodings, arithmetical errors. The auditor is trying to establish a given characteristic. Methodology:

1 Determine five factors.
2 Determine sample size.
3 Select random sample of that size.
4 Test.
5 Interpret result.

If the result causes concern another sample should be chosen. The auditor's interpretation is likely to be 'I am 90% certain that the error is less than 10%'. It is a matter for the auditor to exercise judgement concerning the acceptability of such a result.

3.6.4 *Estimation sampling programme (ESP)*

This is based on the random selection of sample items. In order to be useful it is necessary to stratify the population, compiling the chosen sample from each strata level. It is sometimes called variable sampling.

The level having the highest value would attract the most audit attention from the point of view of materiality, ie the higher strata would be allocated a larger number of items to be checked.

This technique is more suitable to computer applications due to the knowledge of statistics required, ie using a program which automatically computes the sample size when provided with both precision and confidence levels. It is essential that the auditor using this technique has a good understanding of statistical techniques.

Uses of estimation sampling are:

1 To verify that stated book values are correct.
2 To ensure adjustments made are significant ones.
3 To estimate book values from unvalued records.

A conclusion reached by the auditor using estimation sampling might read 'I am 95% confident that the true value of debtors is between £500,000 and £520,000'.

The advantage of estimation sampling is that it provides quantifiable evidence, a disadvantage being its complexity. For example, use could be made of this technique in a company with, say, 150,000 lines valued collectively at £35 million. By counting only 6,000 lines which represented 70% of the total stock value, it was possible to establish that 95% of the estimate fell within the precision limits. The auditor therefore being 95% confident of the total value placed on the stock. A larger number of lines counted would present a higher confidence level.

Steps used in adopting such a technique would be:

1 Obtain a copy of stock (inventory) master file at stocktake date.
2 The estimation sampling programme (ESP) should be applied to the master file by making use of statistical methods based on confidence and precision levels specified by the auditor to produce the number of lines or items to be checked.
3 Specify the strata level in monetary terms and identify those items that are of an attractive and portable nature, so that areas subject to audit risk are covered.
4 The ESP programme will then extract a sample of items for checking from each strata level, the most valuable items usually being subjected to a 100% check.
5 The sample items are checked, the data from the check being used to update the master file, and any differences found are reported by quantity and value.
6 The ESP then evaluates the sample and produces an estimate of the value of stock based on that sample and the precision level achieved.
7 Provided the precision level achieved is acceptable, the valuation based

on this is taken, unknown differences being allocated to a suspense account and treated as being immaterial for reporting purposes.

This technique is not always considered to be appropriate, although it is widely used. The benefits are the saving in resources due to:

1 Lack of disruption to auditee during the stock check.
2 Saving of audit time allowing audit resources to be released for tasks elsewhere.

3.7　Use of the computer

Computerised systems lend themselves to the use of statistical sampling techniques as far as the auditor is concerned to:

1 Select samples—randomly or by interval.
2 Provide random numbers.
3 Exception report items as requested.

Prior to concluding this section, it is perhaps wise to consider the decision chart regarding the use of statistics in compiling acceptable evidence from which an opinion may be drawn and reported:

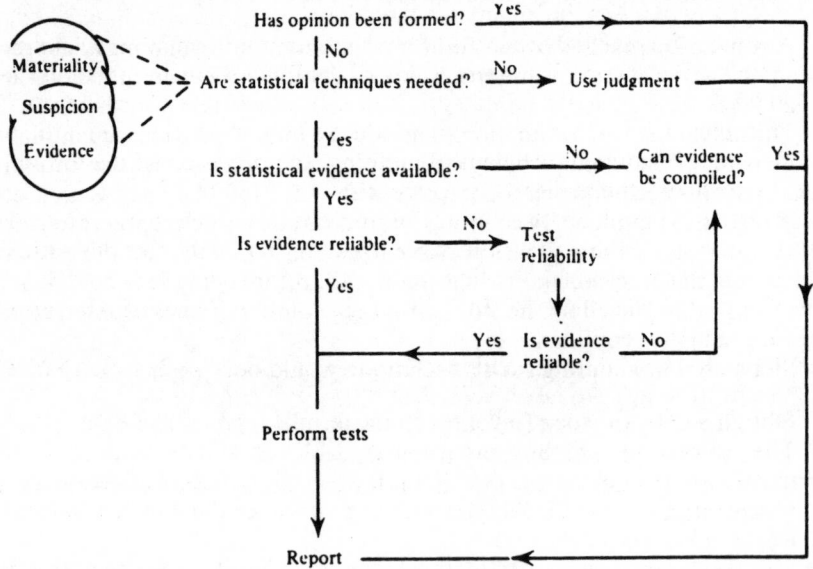

3.8　Advantages of statistical sampling

'Audit sampling is defined in the exposure draft as "the application of a compliance or substantive test to less than 100% of the items within an account balance, class of transactions or other population, as representative of that population . . .". The emphasis is on being *representative* as the basis for all sampling. This would not be achieved if items were selected for their particular significance (eg large or unusual items).' (APC True and Fair Bulletin No 33)

1 A total check is not necessarily reliable because of the tedium of examining large numbers of items.
2 If techniques are employed correctly, the sample will be unbiased.
3 The auditor may determine sample reliability (precision) and the risk inherent in relying on the sample (confidence level).
4 The auditor has to plan audit testing more systematically than is usually the case with judgement sampling.
5 Interpretation of the results of the test is more objective and is expressed in quantitative terms.
6 It avoids the auditor using a larger sample than is necessary.
7 Items selected are more criticlly appraised due to more time being made available.
8 The auditor is able to give precise information to management in reports.
9 The sample result is objective and defensible (eg in a court of law). The technique is recognised in American and Canadian courts of law.
10 More information can be obtained than is possible with test checks.

3.9 Disadvantages of statistical sampling

1 The population may not be sequentially numbered making random samples difficult to extract.
2 Risks are inevitable in any form of checking where less than the whole of the data is examined, though this risk can, of course, be quantified.
3 In attribute sampling, more than one attribute is commonly examined.
4 Lack of knowledge of statistics can cause incorrect conclusions to be drawn.
5 It may encourage mechanical auditing, the precision of the technique overriding the auditor's judgement.
6 Time is spent on the audit carrying out work which is not directly relevant to the audit objective. This tends to occur when statistical sampling is used for the first time.
7 Some factors may be difficult to quantify in the statistical sample selected.
8 Small values may conceal understatements which have little chance of selection, ie zero never selected.
* 9 Errors forming a cyclical pattern (every electricity bill) which is similar to the sample interval may never be detected.
*10 Errors frequently occurring in lower values are less likely to be detected.

*Associated with Monetary Unit Sample

3.10 Examples of statistical sampling in auditing

1 In all situations where errors may be present.
2 Auditees' stock counts.
3 Stock prices.
4 Stock extensions
5 Debtors' age analysis.
6 Recording of employees' hours worked in payroll calculations.
7 Classification of expenses in the nominal ledger.

8 Trade creditors verification.
9 In any situation in which information is required about a large population
   of items by examining only a sample of them.

3.11   Conclusion

It is helpful to quote Professor Bird—'Accountancy Age' 1973:

> 'Statistical sampling has a place in modern auditing. But there is dis-
> agreement between auditors whether it is a central technique in raising
> audit to the status of a science or whether it is an incidental aid in a few
> specific areas of some audits. The importance of statistical inference in
> auditing depends upon the importance of sampling the quality of large
> collections of similar data; this will depend in turn upon the audit
> approach which dominates the scene. Statistical sampling is likely to be
> of only limited value in a future where systems review is the primary
> approach with a balance sheet approach in supporting role.'

With regard to internal auditing statistical sampling is of value in the
examination of a large population. Judgement by the auditor is still required
with regard to level of confidence and the desired precision. With the
increasing presence of computers and the use of computers by auditors, the
computer can select the sample and indeed prevent much unnecessary audit
work through exception reports, eg capital posted to revenue expenditure.

3.12   Glossary of terms

Audit risk: the risk accepted by the auditor that an invalid conclusion will be
drawn after completion of all audit procedures.

Audit sampling: the application of a compliance or substantive test to less
than 100% of the items within an account balance, class of transactions or
other population, as representative of that population, to enable the auditor
to obtain and evaluate evidence of some characteristic of that population
and to assist informing a conclusion concerning that characteristic.

Detection risk: the risk that material errors occurring in a population will not
be detected by the auditor's substantive tests.

Error: in this document the term 'error' is used in the context of substantive
tests to include both 'errors' and 'irregularities', that is misstatements arising
both unintentionally and intentionally.

Non-sampling risk: all those risks of drawing an incorrect conclusion from an
audit test that are not due specifically to sampling. This includes, for
example, the risk that the auditor will draw an incorrect conclusion about an
individual item in the sample tested.

Non-statistical sampling: any approach to sampling which does not fulfil all
the conditions set out below for statistical sampling.

Population: the entire set of data, such as account balances or specified
transactions, from which the sample is selected and about which the auditor
wishes to draw a conclusion.

Sampling risk: the risk that the conclusion drawn by the auditor from the results of testing a particular characteristic(s) of a sample of items differs from the conclusion which he would have drawn had he tested the entire population in like fashion.

Sampling units: the individual items making up the population.

Statistical sampling: an approach to sampling which requires the use of random sample selection and uses probability theory to determine the sample size, to evaluate quantitatively the sample results and to measure the sampling risk.

Tolerable error/deviation rate: the maximum error (for substantive tests) or deviation rate (for compliance tests) that the auditor is prepared to accept in the population and still conclude that his audit objective has been achieved.

Source: Audit sampling (Draft APC Auditing Guidelines 1987)

4.0 TESTING THE SYSTEM

The internal auditor is primarily concerned with the adequacy of internal control within the systems of the organisation. Thus the main objectives of audit tests are to provide assurace to the auditor:

1 That controls have been adhered to.
2 That the controls apply to the current system in operation.
3 That the controls have been approved and authorised by management.
4 That the controls are cost effective.
5 That the controls support the accuracy and reliability of financial and other information.

Many transactions of an organisation can be classified into one of two types, the revenue (sales, debtors, income) cycle and the expenditure cycle (purchases, creditors, expenditure). To meet the control objectives auditors use two forms of testing: namely, compliance and substantive testing.

4.1 Compliance tests

The Auditing Practices Committee have defined compliance tests as follows:

'Those tests which seek to provide audit evidence that internal control procedures are being applied as prescribed.'

The purpose of such tests is to ensure that the controls are operating as intended. It is the control that is being evaluated, not the value of the transaction. A weakness in the system may be of insignificant value per transaction, but of considerable value in total or in effect upon the performance of the organisation. Thus, once a weakness has been identified, the materiality of that weakness needs to be assessed upon the organisation as a whole. Indeed, the Auditing Practices Committee have stated:

'If compliance tests disclose no exceptions, the auditor's preliminary evaluation is confirmed and he may reasonably place reliance on the effective functioning of the internal control tested. He can therefore limit his substantive tests to relevant information in the accounting records.'

The procedure to be adopted where compliance tests disclose exceptions is illustrated below.

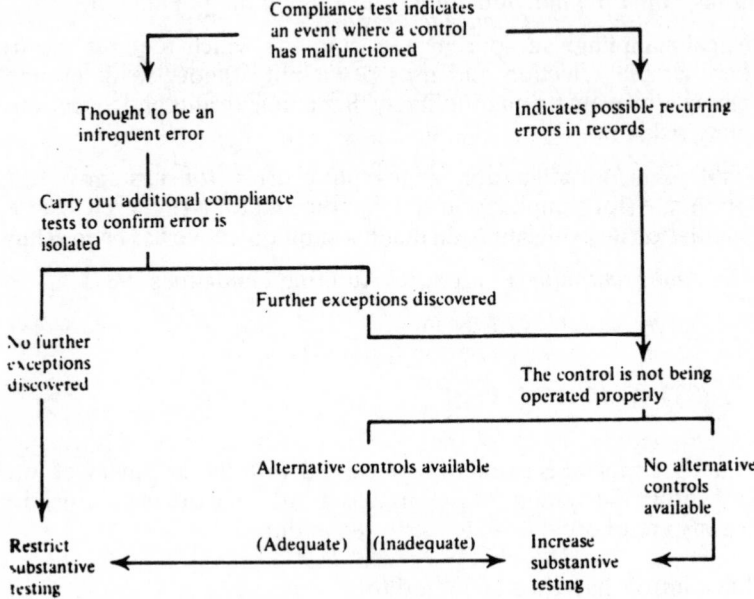

4.1.1   Compliance test design

The compliance test should provide evidence regarding the adequacy of internal control within the operation system. The system, and not the transaction, is evaluated, hence value is not being assessed, but controls are. Consequently all deviations from the defined system must be considered when evaluating whether or not such breaches warrant further investigation. Internal control comprises the following features:

Features	*Objectives*
Segretation of duties	— One person to check the work of another so allowing for earlier detection of error and fraud.
Organisation	— Identification of responsibility.
Authorisation and approval	— All transactions should be authorised by persons of the appropriate level of responsibility.
Personnel	— Staff are competent to undertake their responsibilities.
Management	— Review the adequacy of internal controls.
Arithmetic	— Review for accuracy.
Protection	— Safeguarding the asset base.
Supervision	— Internal checks should be supervised by competent staff.

An example of a compliance check is the pursuit of a transaction, eg creditor payment, through the records, examining supporting documentation and internal checks. A failing to adjust the payment for a discount receivable would be seen to be a weakness warranting further investigation.

4.1.2 *Analysis of compliance test results*

Following a compliance test the results must be analysed. Prior to analysis a distinction must be made between errors and exceptions:

> 'An exception is an example of non-compliance with the control (ie a deviation from the system). An error is a substantive error (ie monetary) error.' (Thornton Baker *Audit Manual*)

Once this distinction has been made, both exceptions and errors should be analysed to determine:

1 The cause—Whether it was intentional or not, eg lack of staff cover.
2 The effect—Material or not on resultant events.
3 The potential effect if not corrected, and the effect on other areas, eg error on sales list would affect invoicing, profitability and cash flow.
4 The implication regarding the compliance test sample and its relationship to the population examined, ie

$$\text{error in sample} \times \frac{\text{population size}}{\text{sample size}}$$

4.2 Substantive tests

The Auditing Practices Committee have defined such tests as:

> '. . . those tests of transactions and balances, and other procedures such as analytical review, which seek to provide audit evidence as to the completeness, accuracy and validity of information contained in the accounting records or in the financial statement.'

Such tests take two forms, namely, tests of detail and analytical review.

TESTS OF DETAIL

With this method, procedural checks are retraced, evaluated and confirmed. From the sample an error rating can be established, and where significant, further testing will be required. This is a very laborious process, heavily consuming audit resources and as such is used to evaluate the materiality of a weakness in the system of controls or the extent of damage as a result of fraudulent activity.

ANALYTICAL REVIEW

Using this method the auditor is trying to determine whether there is an acceptable reason for unusual trends revealed by a review of the financial reports, ie worsening credit control, or delays in raising sales invoices etc. In addition, the auditor is trying to obtain reasonable evidence that particular items are substantially correct.

For the internal auditor these tests are used to provide evidence concerning the materiality of control weaknesses identified by substantive tests used to determine the effect of the breach or potential breach. However, where the auditor is satisfactorily reassured as to the adequacy of controls subject to review, the amount of substantive testing can be reduced, but not eliminated. Substantive testing commonly involves the testing of large volumes of transactions and hence is a heavy consumer of audit resources.

Prior to further examining the use of compliance and substantive tests, it is necessary to distinguish between the two tests. Compliance tests are used to evaluate controls, while substantive tests are used to determine the completeness, accuracy and validity of the recorded transaction. The auditor may, however, use the same sample to undertake both compliance and substantive testing, referring to the same documentation for different objectives, but undertaking the examination simultaneously. Such a testing technique is referred to as dual purpose testing.

Other tests are described on pp 140–141.

4.3   Example of compliance and substantive testing

THE SYSTEM

The objective of the internal control of a 'wages' system is to ensure that payment is made only to employees:

1 For work done.
2 At the properly authorised rate.

To achieve an adequate system of internal control, the following four functions should be separated to reduce the possibility of fraud and to strengthen internal check:

1 The personnel department should be concerned only with the 'hiring and firing' of employees and the fixing of rates of pay. Proper records must be maintained, covering names and addresses, ages, references and skills, to mention but a few.
2 Proper authority. An authorised person should record all time and piece work. Duties should include approving overtime and lay-off and redundancy payments.
3 Preparation of the payroll, which should be done only against properly authorised documents with separate persons preparing, checking and approving the payroll.
4 Payment of wages which must always be performed by persons independent of the payroll preparation section. Adequate security should be provided for cash collection and the payout itself. For wages and salaries paid by cheque, controls are necessary to ensure that, in addition to the above, employee signatures should be examined to ensure that the employee receives the cheque. All documents should be evidenced by an authorised signature throughout. Rotation of duties within the wages and salaries department will reinforce internal control.

AUDIT OF WAGES AND SALARIES

The auditor will concern himself not only with verification of the gross and net wages, but also with the payroll deductions. From the records the auditor should confirm that:

1 There are no 'ghost' employees on the payroll.
2 Employees are paid the correct wages.
3 The right employee is paid.
4 Unclaimed wages are properly dealt with, ie rebanked after being temporarily kept in a safe.
5 Statutory deductions made from wages are correctly calculated and paid over.
6 There is proper employee authorisation for all non-statutory deductions and that they are duly paid over and accounted for. Use may be made of control accounts for all wage deductions.
7 The amount drawn from the bank is the net wages as appears on the payroll.
8 Persons receiving ex gratia payments, eg pensions, are still alive.
9 All the wages sheets are properly totalled and the additions and cross costs are verified.

THE COMPLIANCE TEST

Compliance tests should ensure that the following key controls are working efficiently:

1 Employees can be paid only for work done.
2 Employees are paid at the correct rate at the time agreed (ie current rates for current work).
3 Errors do not occur in the calculation of the payroll or the deductions from gross pay.

The programme of compliance tests suggested would be:

1 Test sample of time records for:
   (a) approval by responsible official;
   (b) check of casts and calculations.
2 Test the authority for payment of casual labour.
3 Observation of wages distribution for compliance with written procedures.
4 Test authorisations for payroll amendments.
5 Test control over payroll alterations.
6 Examine evidence of checking of payroll calculations.
7 Examine evidence of approval of payrolls by a responsible official.
8 Examine evidence of independent checks on payrolls.
9 Check a sample of payroll reconciliations.
10 Examine explanations for payroll expense variations.
11 Test authorities for payroll deductions.
12 Examine personnel records for conditions of service/entry/exit records etc.

All the above tests are concerned with the checking of controls.

THE SUBSTANTIVE TEST

As previously mentioned, a substantive test is defined as:

'those transactions and balances, and other procedures such as analytical review, which seek to provide audit evidence as to the completeness, accuracy and validity of the information contained in the accounting records or in the financial statements.' (APC)

Once the compliance tests have been completed, the level of substantive testing can be determined. Suggested substantive tests to be carried out are:

1 Take sample of time records and test casts and calculations.
2 Test sample of personal records for:
   (a) rates of pay
   (b) authorisation of changes in rates of pay
   (c) exit and entry details.
3 From samples of payrolls:
   (a) check to time records etc
   (b) test to personnel records
   (c) test casts and calculations
   (d) vouch deductions.
4 Vouch sample of payroll reconciliations.
5 Test totals of cheques drawn to net pay due.
6 Test controls over unclaimed wages and vouch signatures for receipt to personnel records.
7 Test posting of payrolls to nominal ledger accounts.
8 Tax paid to Inland Revenue at correct date.

Bear in mind that the objective of substantive testing is to give direct evidence on the accuracy of information contained in the records, ie to test that the amount recorded can be substantiated.

4.4 Other tests

DIRECTIONAL TESTING

Depth testing can result in duplication of effort between compliance testing and transaction testing. Quite clearly in a double entry book keeping statement an error in one section must inevitably mean a corresponding error in another (provided the books balance!). It must mean:

1 The asset balance is understated or the liability overstated, or
2 The income account overstated or expense balance understated.

Using this principle of directional testing, audit work can be minimised, but caution is required, because of dependence on the trial balance, and such a technique is not universally accepted, eg creditor's account debited with payment of £1,000 when it should have been £100—thus creditor's balances are understated and expenditure overstated by £900.

This technique is used to validate the balance sheet and as such is the final stage of an external audit prior to the report. It is also a relevant technique used by internal auditors when examining accounting systems.

DUAL PURPOSE TEST

This is an audit procedure designed to provide both compliance and substantive evidence. In practice this normally applies to the same items being examined on which both substantive and compliance testing takes place.

SEQUENCE TEST

This is examining documentation to ensure copies are not missing, ie to ensure all data is accessible and that cancelled items are retained, eg cheque numbers, invoice numbers, etc.

DEPTH TESTING

This test is the pursuit of a representative sample of transactions from inception to final recording and vice versa. Such a test forms a major part of compliance and walk through tests.

WALK THROUGH TESTING

This is a preliminary test to allow the auditor to understand the system, covering, for instance, one example of each type of transaction. It is not intended to be a representative sample, unlike depth testing.

BLOCK TEST

This is an extensive depth test.

Numerous other tests exist, many of which may be categorised into either compliance or substantive testing.

In most cases a compliance test is used to identify weaknesses and the substantive test used to evaluate damage caused by such a weakness. One such example used in local government is the 'Cardiff check'—a depth test where the sample taken is chosen independently by members of the authority.

4.5 Audit testing summary

Test	Objective	Technique	Sample selection
Walk through	Evaluation of internal control ensuring system functioning as described	Depth test Inspection Observation Enquiry Computation	Judgemental
Compliance	Confirmation that internal control procedures comply with system described	Depth test Inspection Observation Enquiry Computation	Judgemental Statistical
Substantive (test of detail)	Substantiation of transactions and balances underlying financial statements	Depth/directional test Inspection Observation Enquiry Computation	Judgemental Statistical
Analytical review	Substantiation of transactions and balances underlying financial statements	Corroboration of relationships between accounts using ratio analysis	Comparative data

4.6   Evaluating the results of tests

Once testing has been completed, the auditor needs to analyse the results. Confirmation should be sought that the actual results compare favourably with the expected error or deviation rates. Failure to achieve this may necessitate further testing in order to establish the reason for such failure.

Secondly, the auditor needs to project the result from the representative sample to the whole population from which the sample or stratification was taken. The overall result will then either meet or fail to meet the auditor's expectations: cumulative auditing knowledge and experience.

Thirdly, the auditor needs to assess the risk of drawing the incorrect conclusions from the results of tests. Where the auditor cannot obtain the degree of assurance required, ie within the tolerable error, the auditor should undertake the following action:

1 Audit procedures and tests will need to be extended.
2 Adopt alternative procedures to provide for cumulative assurance from evidence gained.
3 Seek reasons from the auditee for such an unexpected result.

5.0   EVALUATING THE SYSTEM

With a sole trader or small organisation controls are normally entrusted to the owner, which presents few problems. With larger organisations where management is more remote from the trading operations, internal control becomes critical to the successful operating of the business.

5.1   Systems creation

'Rome was not built in a day.'

1 *Existing system*—Almost always, even though it may be unwritten, a system or method exists, thus the first rule is to define the system that exists no matter how rudimentary it may be.

2 *Future requirements*—The new system must not only correct past failings, but must also be sufficiently flexible to allow for growth of the enterprise.

3 *Parameters*—The system must necessarily be contained by the resources available to operate it and the scale of the operation.

4 *Management's role*—Management may be remote from the day-to-day operation of the system. Management should, however, control the system, and not vice versa. The auditor should provide management with positive reassurances that the controls are operating to achieve organis-ational objectives.

5 *Accounting system*—The well designed accounting system will provide information for planning, decision making, co-ordination, control, motivation and leadership.

5.2 The systems approach

5.2.1 *Auditing the system*

Primarily, the responsibility of internal audit is to examine systems of control. Nevertheless, the auditor should look beyond controls to the relationship of the controls to the objectives of the organisation, eg cost effectiveness, efficiency, utilisation of resources. Three questions concern the auditor:

1 What is the approved system and is it recorded?
2 Is it operating correctly or as originally intended?
3 Is it adequate to achieve effective internal control?

In answering these questions the internal auditor must pay attention to the following matters:

1 Financial regulations (rules and instructions) and controls devised by senior management.
2 Aims and objectives of the organisation.
3 The management structure of the organisation.
4 Legislation affecting the organisation.
5 Maintenance of professional audit standards.
6 Whether or not the control leads to duplication or wasteful bureaucracy.

In undertaking an examination of a system, the following four steps have been identified:

1 Recording the system.
2 Analysing the system.
3 Criticism of the system.
4 Recommendations for improving the system.

Once the system has been recorded and tested the importance of weaknesses found should be assessed prior to beginning the review procedure.

5.2.2 *Assessing internal control*

When assessing the importance of controls, both accounting and administrative, four levels should be adopted:

1 Not material.
2 Significant control.
3 Major control.
4 Critical control.

The following diagram illustrates how each may be assessed:

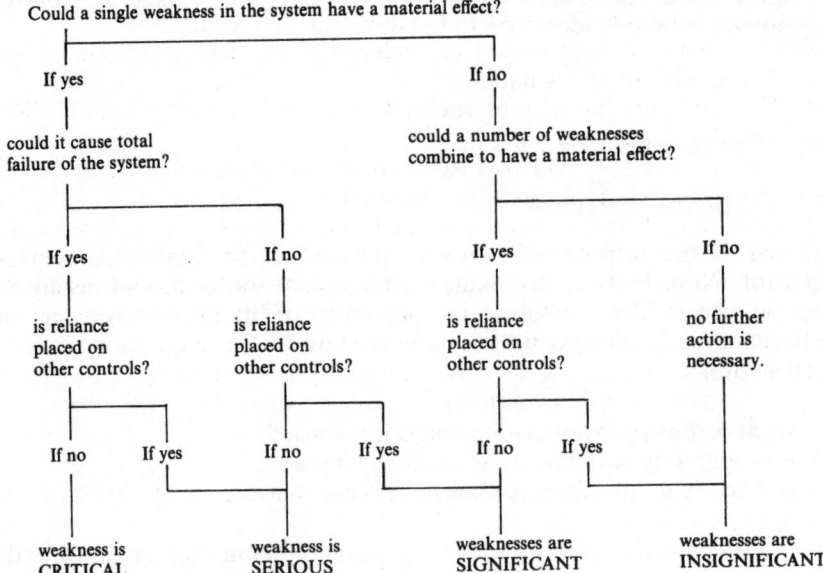

5.2.3 *Internal control review*

The internal control review evaluates the above steps in a logical order, ie:

Internal control review stages	Audit documentation
A Initial study of the internal control system	Memorandum and ICQ
B Draft flowchart	F/C
C Documentation of the observed system	F/C
D Compliance testing of documented system	AP
E Review and evaluation of compliances tests of the documented system	Working papers
F Review flowchart	F/C
G Determination of the nature, quantity and scope of substantive tests	AP
H Application of substantive tests	Working papers
I Comparison of the results of the substantive tests with the previous compliance evaluation	ICQ/ICEQ
J Extend reviews and substantive tests if dissatisfied with the results of the first tests	AP/working papers
K Use results of the compliance and substantive tests to help to formulate the audit opinion	ICEQ
L Reporting to management of any weakness in the system	Report

The following comments elaborate on some of these steps:

A This early information stage involves the auditor in questioning, observing, examining and investigating to determine the controls in a system.

B Once an opinion is formed this should be reproduced on paper in draft form and agreed with line management. The next stage is to obtain documentation of the system to allow tests to be designed.

C Compliance testing should be undertaken to identify weaknesses and divergences from regulations.

F The flowchart can then be reviwed to compare the operation in theory with that in practice.

G The weakness should be evaluated to determine whether or not the damage is material or has the potential to be material.

I Once the substantive tests have been completed they can be compared to the initial expectations of the system established by the compliance test.

J If the substantive tests provide unsatisfactory results, further testing may need to be made, while if satisfactory, such information provides evidence on which an opinion can be formed.

L All weaknesses once identified should be reported to line management with material and potentially material weaknesses being reported to senior management.

By adopting such an approach the auditor is trying to determine whether there is in existence:

1 An adequately planned, controlled and supervised control system, producing reliable information.
2 An adequate level of internal check and separation of duties to minimise the possibility of fraud and error.
3 A reliable system of controls and accountability to protect the organisation's assets.

5.2.4 *Internal control*

As with systems creation, the first task of an auditor is to identify the purpose of the activity under review. Special emphasis should be directed towards the control procedures, which should have the following characteristics:

SEPARATION OF DUTIES

Responsibilities are clearly defined.
This means separating responsibilities for:

1 Certification and initiation of transactions.
2 Protection of assets.
3 Raising adequate documentation.
4 Recording of transactions.

Duties should be so divided that these functions are performed by different personnel.

WRITTEN MANUAL OF INSTRUCTION

This ensures the correct performance of tasks and that adequate staff cover and training needs are met. Such manuals require periodic review.

ORGANISATIONAL STRUCTURE

This establishes clear channels of command and a system which allows for selection, promotion, training and allocation of duties to staff. Again, periodic review should take place.

CERTIFICATION PROCEDURES

A system allowing for an individual to initial the procedures making up the system. Such methods may make use of rubber stamps and grid stamps. Similarly audit staff should initial the audit programme on completion of a test.

SECURITY DEVICES

These ensure the physical protection of assets (including records), eg a keys procedure, till to be visible, audit till roll locked and released by a supervisor. It should be noted that the possibility of collusion (two or more people operating together) is difficult to eliminate.

ADEQUATE DOCUMENTATION

This is necessary to support the transfer of goods and assets, eg triplicate stores request (one for storeman, one for originator, one for stock manager). However, a cautionary note should be added, documentation should support the system, not vice versa, the purpose being to perform an operation, not pass paper in a circular manner!

AUTHORISATION PROCEDURES

Transactions should be adequately authorised by responsible staff with defined responsibilities.

INTERNAL AUDIT

Internal audit should monitor and review the systems in operation.

REVIEW OF SYSTEM

All internal control systems should be flexible to allow for amendments and to enable an assessment to be made of the system's continued adequacy and reliability.

MANAGEMENT CONTROLS

Overall supervision including budgetary control.

5.2.5   *Criticism of the system*

Most criticism falls into four main categories, namely:

DEVIATIONS

Breach of official instructions, which may have harmful consequences in the areas of internal control and security.

EFFICACY OF RECORDS

Such a review concentrates on duplication of record keeping and poorly designed or labour intensive document flow, all of which cause wastage of scarce resources.

CHANGED ENVIRONMENT

Developments caused by technology, new operations and regulations should lead to amended systems adapting to the changed environment. The auditor should ensure that the amended systems represent an improvement to the functioning of the system.

RECOMMENDATIONS

Recommendations by auditors should be discussed with the accountable management and it should be confirmed that the proposed changes are practical to operate within the given resources. Indeed such recommendations should always constitute an improvement to the system already in operation.

An example of some errors and accompanying possible controls now follow. With reference to the transactions cycle the following are examples of errors that may occur and the controls required to prevent their reoccurrence. This is only an example and the recommendations may need adjustment to meet each organisation's needs. By way of example the 'Purchase cycle' is considered:

5.2.6 *Purchase cycle*

ERROR 1

A liability can be recorded but goods or services are not received.

Controls

1 Suppliers' invoices are matched with goods received notes and purchase orders for type, quantity and price.
2 Goods are examined on receipt for quantity and quality.
3 Control exists over goods or services delivered direct to sub-contractors or customers.
4 Purchase invoices are cancelled to prevent duplication.
5 Proper authorisation procedures exist for services.

ERROR 2

A liability for goods or services can be incurred but not recorded in the books of account.

Controls

1 Goods are received at a central receiving point.
2 Pre-numbered goods received notes are made out immediately on receipt.
3 Goods received notes are periodically agreed to purchase orders.
4 Regular independent reconciliations of suppliers' statements are carried out.

ERROR 3

Liabilities for goods or services are wrongly recorded or classified.

Controls

1 Regular independent reconciliations of suppliers' statements are carried out.
2 Suppliers' invoices are checked for prices, calculations and correct accounting classification.
3 Adequate cut-off procedures exist at year end.
4 Invoices are matched with goods received notes prior to processing in the accounting records.

ERROR 4

Goods or services can be ordered without authorisation.

Controls

1 Purchase orders are authorised by a responsible official.
2 Formal ordering limits exist.
3 Pre-numbered purchase orders are used for all purchases of goods and services.
4 A list of approved suppliers is maintained.
5 Control exists over goods or services delivered direct to sub-contractors or customers.

An alternative approach is the use of APTs, allowing the auditor to identify and recommend corrective action to areas of concern. For comparative purposes the APT for purchasing procedures is shown on pp 341–342. Similarly, to demonstrate the use of APTs referring to other operational cycles the APTs for payroll and sales orders are also listed on pp 275–276 and pp 336–337 respectively:

Further reading

Rutteman, P J *Flowcharting for auditors* Accountants' digest No 32 (1976) (ICAEW).

CHAPTER 6   Information management

Objectives	To describe the methods available to the auditor to determine whether the systems which process information adequately maintain the validity and security of the data
Contents	Information management; need to comprehend information technology; audit role; application controls; security and confidentiality of data; risk identification; audit techniques; concurrent auditing
Summary	Inaccurate or false information can mislead and puts the credibility of the information service at risk. Collecting, processing and communicating information all involve cost. This has to be carefully weighed against its usefulness in judging the degree of accuracy required for sound decision making and accountability

1.0   INTRODUCTION

The management of information systems is continually evolving to meet demands imposed by modern technology for ever greater speed and accuracy of information. However, the management of information is similar to that of other management activities, the raw material or data is collected and manipulated or processed into an understandable form. As with any standard industrial process, the end product is distributed in a secure, timely and orderly manner. Nevertheless, there are differences, mainly due to the supportive rather than operational nature of the product. These differences are summarised by Willson and Root in *Internal Auditing Manual*:

'It is a business within a business.
It is service orientated.
It operates in a dynamic, fast-changing environment.
Despite seemingly large and ever-growing budgets, it often faces resource shortages.
The users of the service are often unfamiliar with the technology and may be unaware of their responsibilities.'

A proliferation of mini and micro-computer systems for which the software is now user friendly, allows those with little expertise to extract, manipulate and store critical information with minimal controls and consequently places the organisation in a vulnerable position. Resolution of problems posed by this situation will be described later. For the internal auditor the appraisal of manual and computerised systems presents similar problems which require different methods of analysis.

	Manual systems	*Computer systems*
Controls over:	*Individual items*	*Batches of items*
Computations	Individual calculations	Systems and programs
Amendments	Individual authorisation	Individual authorisation
Program controls	Individual instructions	Correctly authorised and recorded
Recording	Verified manually	Verified by computer, rejections verified manually
Audit trail	Can be visually examined	May not be obvious

Audit examinations should be frequent in the computer environment which is subject to the rapid technological change and information may be prone to corruption or loss; eg disk storage may be over-written or hard copy destroyed. It is important that audit trails can be followed while they exist. The auditor needs to come to terms with the following:

1 The complexity of the system.
2 The computer 'jargon' used.
3 Computer concepts, eg program controls.
4 Frequent amendments to programs.
5 Maintenance of the programs and the computer system.
6 Documentation which may be inadequate or excessive.

If the words computer or computer terminology are removed the problems are similar to those faced by an auditor examining aspects of organisational activity for the first time. It is important for the auditor to overcome the myth attached to the audit of computerised systems and to apply basic audit principles before advancing to the examination of the process.

Throughout the next two chapters the protection of computerised systems is recognised as being of significant importance to the survival of the modern organisation. Computerisation has brought significant benefits to industry and public sector organisations, but it has also placed organisations at risk. To quote: 'In the US 80% of companies that have a computer disaster go to the wall despite all their insurance policies'. David Davies 'Insuring against computer disaster' *Risk Assesor, IT/User*, January 1986.

It is with this sobering thought in mind that management needs internal audit support to ensure that systems are adequately protected. Computerised information systems not only contain vast quantities of sensitive information but are also a major consumer of resources: hardware, software, staff and accommodation. Indeed when mainframes are involved, it is an organisation within an organisation, having its own disciplines, working hours and esprit de corps which is often identified with a hardware supplier. Management's demand for more information more rapidly is insatiable.

To quote:

'It is not unusual for the information management function to have experienced some or all of the following, during a given two or three year interval:
A major mainframe acquisition
At least one operating system conversion
Facilities expansion and/or move
Organisational and reporting realignment
Quadrupling of demand for direct access storage
Developing and installing several major new applications
Numerous modifications of existing systems
At least one major system development
Vast improvements in software and programming aids
Significant increase in the number of mini- and micro-computers, many of which are in the custody of and controlled by users
A doubling of technical staff (eg, progammers, analysts)
A tenfold increase in the number of terminals
High turnover in professional and technical DP positions
Constant user complaints and criticism
Many revisions to purchased utilities
Several interruptions that narrowly averted becoming major catastrophes.' (Willson and Root *Internal Auditing Manual* (Warren Gorham & Lamont, 1984))

Systems have to match ever increasing demands from operational activities for:

1 Collection, transmission, storage, processing and retrieval of data.
2 Timely, orderly and secure distribution of information.
3 Continuity of operations without interruption.
4 Assistance towards achieving management objectives.

2.0 THE AUDIT APPROACH

The main audit objective is to provide management with reassurance concerning the reliability and validity of information, processed in an orderly manner with timely distribution while maintaining security. To achieve this the auditor needs to be alert to the following potential problems, prior to determining the audit approach:

2.1 Audit trail problems

With the more advanced computers audit trail difficulties can occur due to one or more of the following reasons:

1 *Deletion of data*—Some organisations delete transaction records after a certain period of time in order to make better use of the limited storage space on magnetic disk, ie only current data is held. Unless all the data is requested by report (hard copy), the auditor may be unable to pursue transactions: 'dumping' to a back-up tape may provide a limited trail.

2 *Use of magnetic storage files*—Data stored on magnetic disks or tapes cannot be directly inspected, unlike permanent visual copy.

3 *Sorting*—Prime documents are frequently not sorted, the data being sorted by computer, causing difficulty in the tracing of such documentation.

4 *Reports*—The computer may generate reports showing totals, analyses and balances but without disclosing the information leading to them. The audit trail will be lost unless a report, isolating changes from source data can be produced, either following transactions or for the action that has taken place between two points in time. Unfortunately this problem can be exacerbated when it is advantageous from the point of view of storage to program a computer not to report certain information separately. For example when the total VAT reconciles to the 'batch total', the individual items making up the batch are not identified.

To overcome such problems the following techniques are available:

1 Special reports for auditors.
2 Computer assisted auditing techniques (CAATS).
3 Clerical recreation—Very tedious and impossible or impractical for large organisations.
4 Total testing—With other data and previous periods.
5 Physical checks—Stocktakes.
6 Use of test packs.

2.2 Systems design

A well designed computer system will provide for self audit tests. It is wise to consult internal audit about the tests to be incorporated in the programs at the design stage of every new computer system. Once the system is operating it is too late to program in audit checks. Internal auditors should ensure that this is understood both by management and systems designers.

2.3 Visual inspection

Data may be directed via routines, which may not allow for visual inspection, necessitating the auditor to use different techniques. However, in large organisations the auditors may be able to examine such data where it is held in program libraries.

2.4 Data entry by VDU

Modern computer systems rely on direct entry via keyboards, with storage of data on magnetic disk. It is then the usual practice to confirm the accuracy of the information entered via a Yes/No response on the visual display unit, ie there may be no report or hard copy supporting documentation. This is a real time system.

2.5   Centalised information

Large organisations often have a policy for centralised information processing as a service to user departments using mainframe computers and standardised or integrated systems. Such systems are necessarily complex and
sometimes not fully understood by the managements who depend upon
them or by their staff who have to work with these systems. This can lead to a
feeling that control is being influenced by the computer. The organisation
may, as a result of centralised data processing, be exposed to major risks
from computer failure or fraud. If fraud does occur the complexity of the
systems may make it difficult to discover. Conversely, a complex system
could also deter a potential fraudster without a detailed knowledge of the
system and all its controls.

2.6   Terminology

Computer systems are likely to be much more complex than manual and
machine accounting systems. Indeed a specialist 'language' has evolved to
describe the systems and, to be effective, a computer auditor must understand this language and its audit implications. A lack of understanding may
well lead to an inability to evaluate the system and thereby to ensure that the
installation is adequately protected.

2.7   Computer dependence

Business development in a competitive climate has made computer dependence unavoidable and many organisations would not be capable of functioning without access to computers. Risk of failure increases with the
complexity of operations. To reduce the chance of the organisation suffering
catastrophe, internal audit can offer management assistance by:

1 Testing back-up procedures.
2 Reviewing the disaster recovery plan.
3 Checking the terms of insurance cover—Consequential loss.
4 Reviewing the extent of dispersed processes, thereby avoiding depen-
    dence upon one computer.

3.0   COMPUTER AUDITORS

3.1   Need for computer auditors

A computer represents a significant investment of resources. It is also a
very important management tool. The concentration of critical information
for computer processing makes the organisation vulnerable from loss, corruption or fraudulent misuse of this information.

Thus there is a need for assurance that adequate protection has been provided against such risks, that data is being managed efficiently and that the information being provided for operational management is valid and reliable. This is the role of the computer auditor; it involves:

1 Independent appraisal of the computer installation and its environment.
2 Evaluating and reporting to the appropriate operational management on the systems in use for processing information needed for operational control.
3 Contributing to the development of computer systems with expert advice on essential control features and provision for audit trails.

It was usual for most manual systems to have been evolved step by step over a long period with frequent updating to improve efficiency in use and to reflect changes in requirements as they arose: flexibility was an important characteristic. Computer technology makes possible the integration of a range of information needs with advantages in efficiency of processing; eg:

1 Several aspects of a transaction may be simultaneously processed from a single entry of input data.
2 Electronic transfer of data between processes can be instantaneous and should be error proof.
3 All departments will be using information from common source data so eliminating a need to reconcile and the risk of conflicting interpretation.

However, integrating information requirements for several departments inevitably involves an increase in complexity and a loss of flexibility. Strict disciplines are necessary to ensure data input and processing are valid and accurate to satisfy the requirements of all users.

Because of these characteristics, computer systems have to be designed with scrupulous attention to the requirements of all users and implementation must be planned with great care. This is time consuming and it absorbs costly resources; consequently, once the system is in operation it may not easily be changed.

To reiterate, the importance of the internal auditor being fully involved with all computer developments from the earliest opportunity cannot be over emphasised. This involvement should preferably start from the feasibility study stage but at the very latest at the design stage of any system. This is extremely important because at this point essential audit controls may be incorporated, which would be very expensive to introduce later on, and probably totally impractical once the system was in operation.

3.2   Terms of reference

The computer auditor's role is to provide an overall review of the operations and management of the computer services department and the efficiency, security and effectiveness of computer application systems acting as an adviser to internal audit generally regarding the computer methods employed by the organisation.

3.3 Expertise of computer auditor

Auditor trained in computer skills	*Computer staff trained as auditor*
For: 1 Overall perspective of business systems and how control is maintained 2 Understands audit procedures	1 Understands computer better 2 Better relationship with computer staff
Against: 1 Limited knowledge of computers 2 Auditor unproductive during training 3 Other auditors may not understand problems faced	1 May not fully appreciate audit role 2 Divided loyalties 3 May require training in both audit and computer development

4.0 INTERNAL AUDIT ROLE

It is the responsibility of management to ensure that management information systems are sound and reliable, and this includes information via the computer facility. It is for internal audit to reassure management as to how well this responsibility is fulfilled. Although basic audit principles such as establishing internal control require application, they may need to be modified for the computer environment. Because most of the controls are concentrated in the computer department together with data files and the programs processing the data, effective disciplines and adequate separation of duties are essential. Whereas administrative procedures apply to the overall operation, audit techniques must be adapted to protect each stage of operation, be it normal processing, amendment or development.

4.1 Objectives of the internal auditor

The internal auditor's terms of reference are determined by senior management, however internal audit has a positive role to play in providing management with reassurance in the following areas:

1 *Economy*—An examination of the use of the computer system to ensure this costly resource is utilised to its full potential for the benefit of the organisation at minimum cost.

2 *Effectiveness*—An examination of the controls adopted, the purpose of those controls and the computer objectives of such controls to ensure adequate standards of internal control exist over all stages of the system and its operation.

3 *Efficiency*—That provision is made to determine that requirements most beneficial to the whole organisation are developed on the computer in preference to lesser needs.

4 *Security*—That the installation is adequately protected, that risks are insured against and that errors in connection with the system are not weaknesses of principle.

4.2   Internal v external audit approach

Different emphasis to be placed on computerised accounting systems is adopted by internal and external audit, due to their different terms of reference. External audit is primarily concerned with the accuracy of data and the manner in which it is reported, while internal audit, although concerned with this, adopts a wider viewpoint embracing:

1 Adequate protection of systems, equipment and data.
2 Sound procedures to ensure value for money is gained from an expensive resource.
3 Contingency provisions in case of disaster.
4 Prevention and detection of fraud.
5 Sound internal control.

This reflects the fact that internal audit is part of management, while external audit places its emphasis on the reliability of information for the statutory accounts.

5.0   EXAMINING THE SYSTEM

The Auditing Practices Committee in the Auditing Guideline *Auditing in a Computer Environment*, identified two forms of control: application and general. General controls are discussed in the next chapter.

5.1   Application controls

5.1.1   *Definition*

'These controls relate to the transactions and standing data appertaining to each computer based accounting system and therefore specific to each application. The objectives of application controls which may be manual or programmed are to ensure the completeness and accuracy of the accounting records and the validity of the entries made therein resulting from both manual or programmed processing.'
(APC Guideline *Auditing in a Computer Environment* (1984))

INTERNAL CONTROL

'If the auditor wishes to place reliance on any internal controls he should ascertain and evaluate those controls and perform compliance tests on their operation.' (Auditor's Operational Standard (APC))

With regard to computer operations such controls take two forms as mentioned above—application controls and general controls (which include systems development controls). Application controls are concerned with the reliability of data and general controls ensure the continuity of operations. The total security concept unites this analysis into one comprehensive control—the system only being as strong as its weakest control.

Such controls are summarised by six essential objectives namely: economy, efficiency, effectiveness, security and privacy, accuracy, completeness.

CONTROL PRINCIPLES

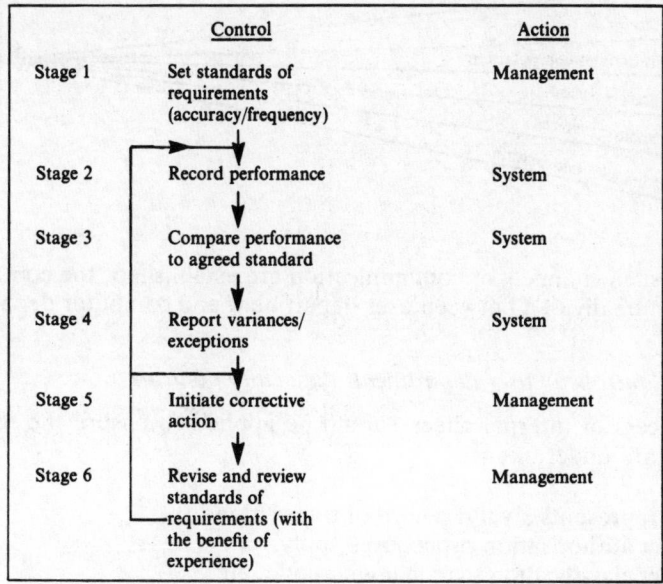

Within the application system the following data flow controls exist:

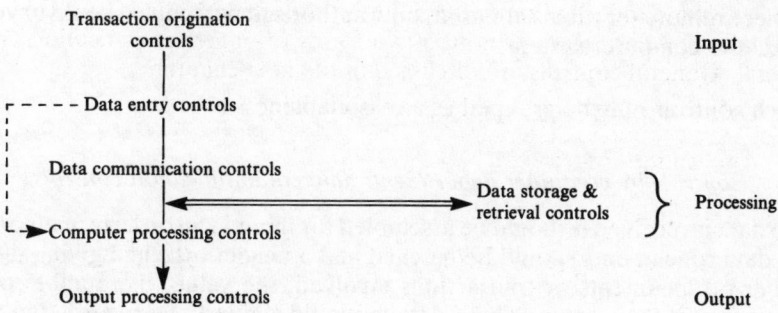

(Based on B J Travis *Auditing the development of computer systems.*)

5.1.2 *Input controls*

AUDIT OBJECTIVES

1 To ensure the timely and orderly processing of data.
2 To ensure the completeness and accuracy of data input.
3 To ensure that proper authorisation procedures have been adhered to.
4 To ensure security and privacy of data.

In order for data to reach the computer various channels of communication must be established so that not only are internal controls maintained but also data remains uncorrupted. It is important that particular attention is paid to document design and authorisation procedures so that the correct data arrives in the correct place at the correct time.

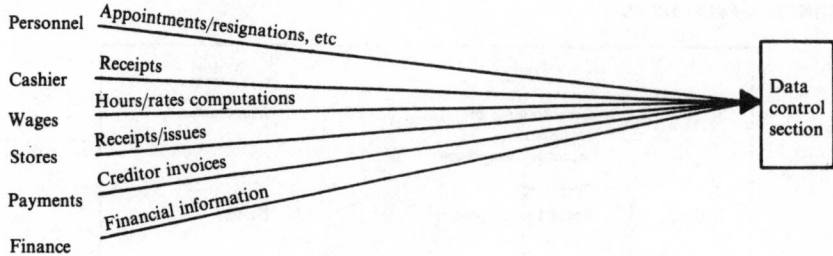

Once such channels of communication are established, the control over input can be divided between user department and computer department.

5.1.3   *Controls by user department: data entry controls*

The process of internal check should be applied to ensure the following controls are undertaken:

1 Input represents a valid record of transactions.
2 Correct authorisation procedures apply.
3 Correct classification by document, code, etc.
4 Accurate compliance with standards of input documentation, ie acceptable to those who input the data.
5 Where remote terminals are used, only authorised personnel should have access to computer system.

Such controls may be grouped as a reasonableness check.

5.1.4   *Controls by computer department: data communication controls*

Once data is received it should be assembled for input in an orderly manner. Like data, documents should be batched and a header attached giving the number of documents or transactions involved, the value, the number of rejections and their value. These details should similarly be recorded in a 'control' log so that input data can be reconciled in total to that successfully processed. In addition to ensuring codes are correctly entered, a 'hash' total may be used to verify correctness of entry (a total of all codes processed being recorded on batch header and in control log) against the total produced by the computer. These controls should take place in the data preparation room and access should be denied to computer operators and programmers. In practice, where difficulty in tracing a particular error is experienced, it may be necessary for the programmer to examine the original documents.

The following controls are likely to be undertaken by the control section who review program produced exception reports. These act as an internal check between data preparation and the computer operators.

CHECK DIGIT

This is where one of the characters of a field represents a mathematical function of all others—usually used for key reference fields, eg payroll number.

COMPATABILITY

This is used where an account's validity may be verified to computer using a check digit as an integral part of a code, eg orders on department 1 can only have a location subsection of code designated 100 upwards to 199; department 2 being 200 to 299. Thus orders with sequential numbering beginning at 100 can be matched against department 1.

PARITY CHECK

A check that the last character in a field (not part of the data itself) makes up that field to an odd or even total value. This is usually a check used during processing or data transfer.

FORMAT CHECK

Where a code would not be recognised by the computer, eg 7 characters recorded when 9 are required. Such a check is useful because it ensures that the data to be entered is in a standardised form, allowing the computer to 'read' it. A format check also verifies alphanumeric characters.

MASTER FILE CHECKS

Such checks prove the existence and state of records held on the master file before such records are subject to amendment. Included in such a check may be a 'header' code to identify that the correct file has been entered thereby preventing overwriting.

RECORD COUNTS

This is a check whereby the computer agrees the totals received to the summary (batch header) input. It also includes 'hash' totals, document counts, line counts, the sequence counts, etc.

5.2 Controls over processing

These controls exist to ensure all data is processed correctly and masterfiles appropriately updated. Output reports should be complete and accurate. It is obviously important for all data to be validated independently at each stage of operation.

5.2.1 *Mechanical checks*

Where control features are internally installed:

1 Internal checks to ensure correct reading of input.

2 Duplicate circuits to separately check calculations.
3 Test programs used by engineers to locate faulty circuits.

5.2.2   *Programmed controls*

The auditor should have ensured that adequate controls already operate in a system to ensure:

1 Only data relevant to application is processed.
2 Data is complete and accurate with regard to the following areas:

   (a) Reasonableness check—parameters which if exceeded the computer will exception report, eg wages increased by 100% over previous week.
   (b) Sequence check—built into system to ensure that input data is processed in same sequence as master file is updated. It is also used to exception report gaps in critical sequences, eg cheques.
   (c) Hash totals and check digits—as mentioned previously.
   (d) Matching check—matching input data against that held on masterfile or pipeline files. Where a mismatch occurs, the item should be rejected and reported via an exception report.
   (e) Check points—used where data is copied over a long period of time, to sections that run into smaller segments, thereby reducing chance of total loss of data.

5.2.3   *Operational controls*

The operators should have total control over processing and to this end the following should be considered:

1 Their work should be controlled by an operational manual covering:
   (a) Operating instructions.
   (b) Console log comparison with the log prepared by the operators, though in larger installations such logs are considered too large to be meaningful, especially with virtual storage operating systems.
   (c) Minimum number of operators per shift (usually two).
   (d) Effective supervision—solo operation must be regarded as a risk.
   (e) Rotation of duties, so that operators do not always run the same jobs.
   (f) Job scheduling.
   (g)) Job assembly.
2 They are prevented from amending input data, either transaction or standing data.
3 There are adequate controls on all shifts (including night shifts).
4 An operating schedule should be drawn up and a copy given to audit.

COMPUTER SEQUENCE

It is now appropriate to illustrate by way of a diagram a batch system for computer processing.

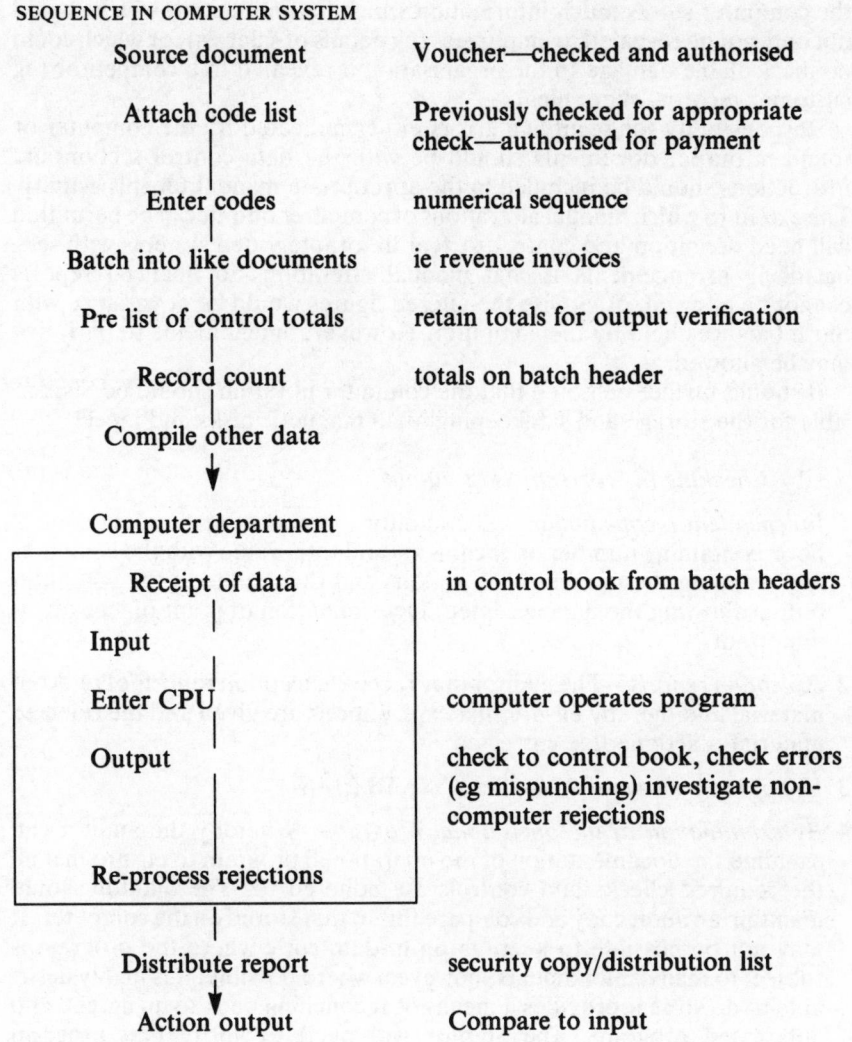

SEQUENCE IN COMPUTER SYSTEM

Source document	Voucher—checked and authorised
Attach code list	Previously checked for appropriate check—authorised for payment
Enter codes	numerical sequence
Batch into like documents	ie revenue invoices
Pre list of control totals	retain totals for output verification
Record count	totals on batch header
Compile other data	

Computer department

Receipt of data	in control book from batch headers
Input	
Enter CPU	computer operates program
Output	check to control book, check errors (eg mispunching) investigate non-computer rejections
Re-process rejections	

Distribute report	security copy/distribution list
Action output	Compare to input

(Based on E Wolfe *Auditing Today*.)

CONTROLS OVER DATA STORAGE AND RETRIEVAL

Such controls embrace file security and back-up procedures examined in Chapter 7.

5.3   Controls over output

The output of a computer consists of printed reports from the line printer and updated magnetic tapes and disks. It is vitally important that only the 'right' people receive the 'right' information. Consequently a distribution list should be drafted to show who receives what information, when and where. It is also sound audit practice to ask 'why' because critical examination of distribution lists can increase efficiency by reducing the amount of needless information senior management may have to sift through. Secondly, the computer stores much information which is confidential, which should not only not be revealed to employees (eg details of salaries), or which could do incalculable damage to the organisation if revealed to a competitor (eg customer records, client files).

Responsibility for rectifying errors either indicated by the computer or found in output documents should be with the data control section and instructions should be included in the appropriate manual for this activity. The extent to which manual alterations of computer output can be permitted will need definition and control. A feature of integrated systems with self-balancing arrangements is that manual alterations to financial reports cannot be allowed, otherwise the altered figures would be at variance with those balances held by the computer. However, amendments to narrative may be allowed.

It should further be noted that the computer librarian should be responsible for the storage and safekeeping of all magnetic disks and tapes.

5.3.1   *Checking the correctness of output*

1 *Independent reconciliation*—The auditor can reconcile the data control book containing number of documents and total value with the computer log revealing the number of rejections and their value to the computer output showing the data accepted. Determination of point of 'cut-off' is important.

2 *Exception reports*—The auditor may receive exception reports of rejected material and thereby ensure that explanations are given and the rejected material is actioned, ie corrected.

3 *Use of test packs and data*—See CAATS (p 167).

4 *By examination of the operational program*—Whereby the auditor can examine the documentation of the operational program to ensure that all the required checks and controls are adhered to. The auditor should maintain an audit copy and compare this to that stored on the computer. It may not be possible to keep an up-to-date copy where the program is subject to many amendments; however, where possible, it is highly desirable to do so as it provides a means of reconciling back to an agreed and authorised program. The auditor will need to verify that program amendments are adequately controlled.

6.0   SECURITY AND CONFIDENTIALITY OF DATA

The following sections **6.1** to **6.6** inclusive, comprise a summary of Information Technology Statement No 1 (ICAEW 1985).

6.1   Consequences of failing to protect data

Within the context of data is included word processing, which clearly embraces the storage of confidential data. Due to the reliance placed by organisations upon computerised information systems, organisations are vulnerable to:

1 Failure of the organisation due to lack of management control.
2 Losses incurred due to incomplete or inaccurate data.
3 Loss of confidential data caused by the deliberate removal of sensitive data and possibly being sold to competitors (client files).
4 Breach of security of personal and other confidential information, causing severe embarrassment and loss of credibility to management.
5 Increase in fraudulent activity due to lack of control.

6.2 Management commitment

'Management commitment is essential if an organisation is to develop and maintain a successful data security programme. This commitment is also an example to other staff: without it staff are likely to apply security measures ineffectively. Such measures are only effective if they are applied systematically and consistently. To be fully effective they must be applied and reviewed imaginatively, not mechanically.' (IT Statement No 1 ICAEW)

6.3 Responsibility for data security

Management should develop a policy for data security and nominate an individual to be responsible for monitoring the operation of security procedures. It is recognised that where shared use of computer facilities exists, physical security is eroded. To overcome such a difficulty, it is necessary to identify a person responsible for each activity involving the sharing of the facility.

6.4 Risk to data

Management need to identify and to analyse potential risks such as:

1 Human error—An area containing the greatest incidence of risk.
2 Technical error—The cause of many malfunctions.
3 Natural disaster—See hazard management (Chapter 7).
4 Deliberate action—Fraud, espionage, malicious damage, industrial action.

6.5 Evaluating the risk

As with all risks, the chance of the event occurring and the consequences to the organisation of that occurrence need to be evaluated, so that the best mix of counter-measures are adopted.

6.6 Meeting the risk

Once identified and appraised the risk is contained by two methods:

1 Data security program—To ensure the continuity of processing, protection against breach of the law (Data Protection Act) and against physical damage.
2 Counter-measures—Application controls and general controls.

This summary demonstrates the wide ranging nature of the internal audit role, which must be to support management to protect the organisation. However, 'the whole programme should be animated by the commitment of senior management and the will to implement it effectively'. (IT Information Statement No 1 (ICAEW))

7.0   RISK IDENTIFICATION AND MEASUREMENT

It is recommended that the auditor identifies all potential catastrophes and then compiles a list of risks categorised into the various groups as described previously. Against each risk can be entered a probability of the event occurring together with an estimate of the amount of damage due to the disaster, thereby producing a crude index.

Having identified the risks the auditor can then use auditing techniques to evaluate the consequences of disaster prior to recommending improved controls. It is in this context that the various auditing techniques are now examined.

7.1   Description of the system

In line with audit techniques, before testing can take place the system must be described through the use of ICQs and flowcharts. Particular attention will need to be paid to the following:

1 Standards of discipline and procedures maintained.
2 Documentation of systems.
3 Separation of duties between computer personnel.
4 Capability for file reconstruction.   Internal
5 Stand-by arrangements (back-up facilities).   control
6 Safeguarding of master file and programs.   (A)
7 Controls over amendments to programs.
8 Controls over access to the computers.
9 Corrective action on all failing.

Similarly, audit working papers should be well ordered and cross-referenced, containing:

1 A narrative description of the system.
2 Flowcharts describing the system, computer
  program operations.
3 Copies of all documentation in use.   Working
4 Details of manufacturers of all types of hardware in use.   papers
5 Copies of all output documentation.   (B)
6 Internal audit programme.
7 Previous report.

Once these procedures have been undertaken, the system needs evaluation. This may be undertaken by the use of ICQs and flowcharts.

7.2 Control point identification

Transactions are the basic element of internal control, and it is on such entries that the auditor must concentrate. Indeed, the auditor's review should be:

'. . . designed to provide an understanding of the flow of transactions through the accounting system. . . . Within a computer system compliance with this statement may be difficult. To ease this difficulty, one approach is to concentrate on the examination of "specific system control points".' (Statement on Auditing Standards 3 ('The Effects of EDP on the Auditor's Sudy', AICPA 1974))

A means of identifying such controls is the use of computer flowcharts, eg:

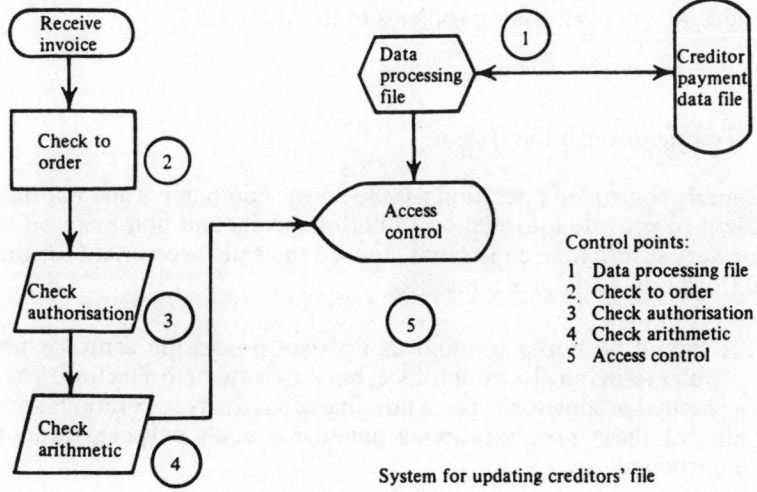

Control points:
1 Data processing file
2 Check to order
3 Check authorisation
4 Check arithmetic
5 Access control

System for updating creditors' file

8.0 TECHNIQUES USED IN AUDITING COMPUTER SYSTEMS

There are two common methods in current use:

8.1 Auditing 'round' the machine: checking input to output

This is sometimes referred to as the 'black-box approach'. Modern computers present auditors with problems regarding the maintenance of 'audit trail'.

With earlier computers it used to be possible to ignore the machine, merely comparing input to output—auditing 'round' the machine.

With developments in all aspects of computer technology, processing speeds are now so rapid it is uneconomic to produce reports (hard copy) at each stage of the system—the printer being mechanically slow and producing excessive volumes of paper. Due to the slowness of the printer, modern systems rely on 'exception reports' to inform managers of malfunctions or significant variances. Such procedures allow for rapid processing. Audit resources could also be concentrated on significant areas—providing the system for exception reports is trustworthy. The auditor cannot make such an assumption and has to test that the exception report system operates to ensure that:

1 Exception report programs are functioning accurately.
2 All exceptions occurring are reported.
3 Only authorised programs are actioned.
4 Programmed control parameters exist which meet the organisation's internal control requirements.

Due to the system of exception reports audit trail has vanished, the auditor relies upon 'tests through the machine' to ensure the exception report system exists in a satisfactory state. Printouts of data input and amendments, may alleviate problems of lost audit trail.

8.2   Testing through the system

A properly controlled operational cycle for the computer is all important to enable it to provide information to both financial and non-financial users within very severe time constraints. Indeed the chief accountant for British Coal (formerly NCB) has remarked:

> 'It should be borne in mind that a data processing centre is not in popular terms an electronic office, but is more akin to a factory. There is a planned production cycle, a flow line of successive operations and any idea of these processes being halted for audit purposes cannot be entertained.'

As auditors have increasingly recognised the need to test while the machine is operating, testing through the machine has become the generally accepted practice. In undertaking such a test, two audit objectives are present:

1 The system for input must be proven to be accurate, ie batch header totals, hash totals, control totals, etc.
2 The processing system must ensure that:
   (a) All input received is entered or reported.
   (b) Rare conditions do not cause systems failure.
   (c) Neither operator nor computer can make undetected changes to the report.
   (d) Exception reports alert both operator and auditor to potential problems.
   (e) A log is maintained by the computer, accounting for all user time and indicating any attempted interference. Sight of such a log reading should be restricted to manager and auditor only.

8.2.1 *Techniques of auditing through the system*

The following techniques require discussion:

COMPUTER ASSISTED AUDITING TECHNIQUES (CAATS)

Such techniques make use of audit software packages which consist of one or more programs designed to perform data processing functions called Generalised Audit Software Packages (GASP). A second form makes use of test data (test packs).

Reasons for using CAATS—Reasons will vary from organisation to organisation and may be summarised as follows:

1 The volume of data to be examined makes it impractical to adopt manual techniques.
2 Audit trail may have been lost either due to lack of input listings or the processing function itself (the integration of processing functions).
3 The scope of the tests can easily be extended to take account of changing judgement regarding the reliability of internal control.
4 Once established and tested, the gathering of audit evidence is much more rapid than by manual operations.

CAATS may be divided into two methods: computer audit programs and test packs, as follows.

Computer assisted audit techniques	
Computer audit programs The computer is used to assist the auditor with the verification of data on file	*Test packs* To test program controls and procedures

Computer audit programs (CAPS) = *interrogation software*—Such programs are specially designed for audit purposes and have the following advantages and disadvantages:

Advantages	Disadvantages
1 Speed of interrogation.	1 Technical skill required in developing program.
2 Practical method of examining large volumes of data.	2 Greater knowledge of the system is needed than for conventional tests.
3 Use may be repeated until systems changes occur.	3 Frequent systems changes mean changed program.
4 Offer of economy in use of audit resources.	4 Difficulty may be had in gaining adequate access to the computer.

In most cases the advantages heavily outweigh the disadvantages. Such programs can be divided into two categories:

1 *Parameter driven*—Which consists of report printing programs specifically written for the system, the contents of the report being restricted by the parameters determined by the auditor at the time of writing the programs.

2 *Program generator*—This requires the auditor to present the requirements in a format that is acceptable to the 'generator software', this software then interprets the specification to create a program. This program enables the auditor to include analytical and sampling techniques. It is a more flexible approach though it demands greater technical skill from the auditor.

Examples of some commonly used packages:

Auditape 2	Coopers & Lybrand Deloitte	Wide range of IBM, ICL, Honeywell, Burroughs, Univac, Hewlett Packard machines
Filetab and Usertab	National Computing Centre	IBM, 4300 Series, 3030 Series; ICL 2900; Univac 90; Honeywell 66
Mark IV Auditor	Informatics	IBM 370, 4300 Series, 3030 Series
Panaudit	Pansophic	Many IBM, Univac
Strata	Touche Ross	IBM 370, 4300 Series: Large Burroughs machines
System 2190	KPMG	IBM 370, 3030 series, 4300 Series; Medium and large Burroughs machines, Hewlett Packard 3000; ICL 2900 (VME)

There are many others—Easytrieve, CARS—to name two more. An approach to the 'computer user group' relating to the hardware used by the organisation to seek further advice is to be recommended, so that access to the latest techniques is gained.

Test packs—This technique makes use of simulated data created to test the systems control. Although unable to provide assurance on 'live' data processed and stored in the system, it does test controls within the system by executing the system to provide results which are already known.

Where 'live' data is mixed with test data during input and processing procedures it is sometimes referred to as the 'integrated test facility' or 'extended test data'. Where the whole system is subject to testing this is sometimes referred to as the 'base case system evaluation', as opposed to the 'extended test data', when only certain aspects are subject to examination.

The use of 'test data' is of great value during the development of a system. However there are problems for auditors in the use of test packs, namely:

1 The difficulty in determining that the program tested is the one currently in operation.

2 It is argued that unless 'live' data is used, actual transactions and live recovery procedures cannot be tested. The computer department may view this as the auditor attempting to 'break' the system, causing it to crash, with the resultant delays to the computer operating schedule— hardly a popular move!

3 Following the above limitations, the security risks involved make it impractical to use test packs on live files. Consequently test packs are used in conjunction with audit tests on actual data, tests on organisational controls and tests on the controls over amendments and updating of programs and files.

The advantages and disadvantages of test packs can be summarised as follows:

Advantages	*Disadvantages*
1 Assurance that controls are operating as intended.	1 Difficulty in knowing the total outcome on the whole system.
2 Use can be repeated until program changed.	2 Difficulty in obtaining computer time.
3 Considered to be inexpensive to develop.	3 Processing delays often occur due to the artificial type and small volume of data used.
4 Once operational, packs are inexpensive to use.	4 Danger to the system by causing a crash at a critical time for other users.
5 Packs can be added to and the tests extended	5 Only tests for known conditions.

8.3 Concurrent auditing

Traditionally, auditors examine historic data; however, the speed of the information system requires concurrent auditing. Ron Weber in his book *EDP Auditing, Conceptual Foundations and Practice* has suggested that with modern computer facilities, it is becoming difficult to gain assurance about applications by the pursuit of walk through tests: logic paths are becoming increasingly complex to follow. To meet this challenge, auditors have developed the 'integrated test facility'. This technique, described in *Systems Auditability and control study—Data Processing Practices Report* (p 119), allows test transactions to be processed at the same time as normal activity on the current system in use. Such data is at a later date corrected!

In addition, the following techniques are used to support such test facilities:

EMBEDDED AUDIT DATA COLLECTION (AUDITOR'S RESIDENT MODULE)

Using this method the auditor places coded data collection modules in strategic positions within the system to select, gather and record data transactions that meet the auditor's predetermined criteria for examination and review. Such criteria trigger an 'audit control'. The advantage of such a device is that it provides the auditor with the capability to monitor and review all input and to 'exception report' the alarm signals, which were previously identified. It is an invaluable technique used in the audit of 'On-line' systems, which for reasons of rapid performance or cost may leave inadequate 'audit trails' in the processing of transactions. To overcome such problems 'extended records' are created. Such a technique is undertaken by collecting throughput (data) related to the relevant transaction, the extended record then being used to re-create 'visible audit trails' where none existed previously. A further development of this technique is called sample control audit review file (SCARF), whereby transactions are collected on a sampling basis and stored for later analytical review. An advantage of this technique is that it allows for some of the audit work to be undertaken while the data is being processed.

SNAPSHOT/EXTENDED RECORD

The audit objective is similar to that of a 'compliance test', whereby instead of the auditor pursuing a transaction through the system, the computer reports upon the actions taken—the transaction is 'tagged'. As the 'tagged' transaction is pursued so an audit trail is created. Thus this technique provides the auditor with a degree of reassurance on internal controls within the system. It further assists in 'de-bugging' a new system, identifying errors and weaknesses. It is called the snapshot technique because as the transaction proceeds through the system it is identified at various checkpoints. This is illustrated by the diagrams on pp 171–172:

8.4   Other techniques

UTILITY PROGRAMS

These programs are similar to generalised audit software packages and are also known as 'system software'. Their use is as follows:

1 To generate data.
2 To allow the performance of tracing and mapping routines (see pp 172–173).
3 To assist with program development.
4 To make comparisons of separate versions of software programs.

Utility programs were used by programmers, but an appropriately trained auditor may find them useful to identify unauthorised amendments to programs. To ensure that the auditor's own program is not corrupted, the program should be obtained direct from the supplier and stored under the control of audit.

PROGRAM VERIFICATIONS

Such verifications necessitate the listing and reading of the source code, normally undertaken automatically, so that a comparison can be made between the original program and that currently in operational use. In this manner unauthorised amendments can be detected.

Flowchart of the snapshot audit technique

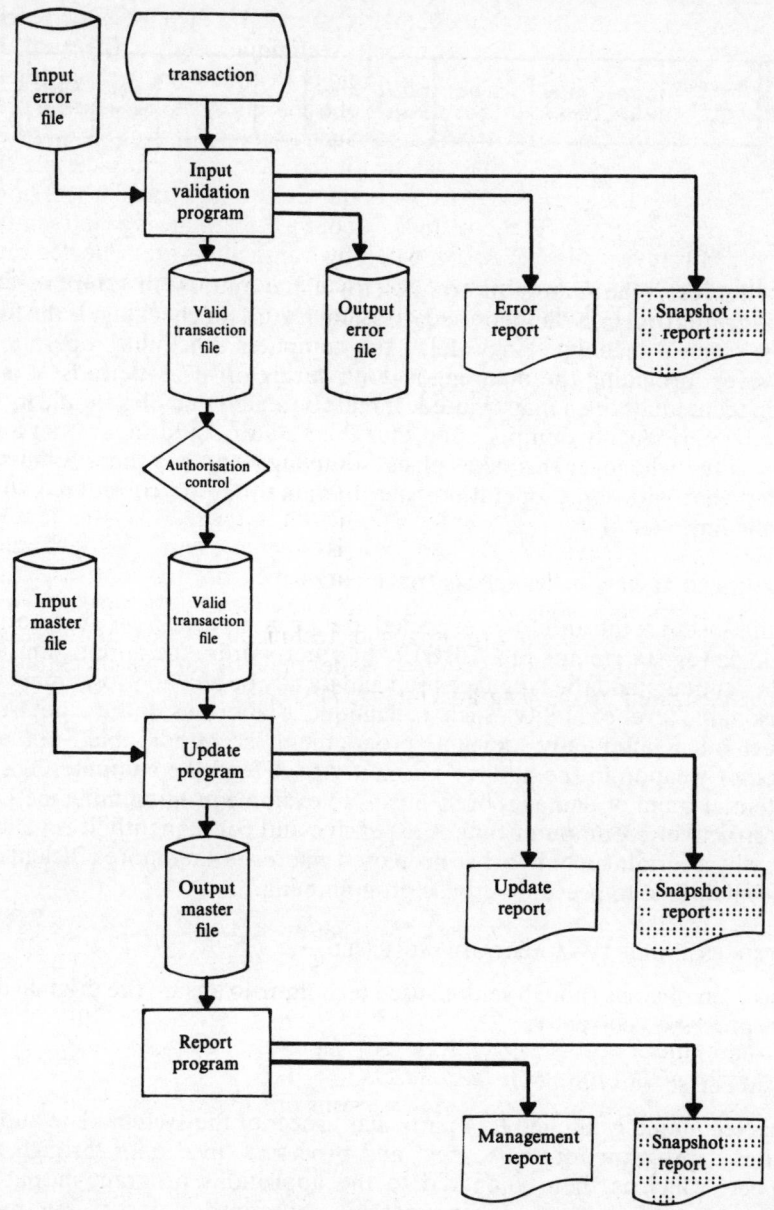

Source: Weber, R EDP Auditing, Conceptual Foundations and Practice (McGraw Hill Book Co.)

Depiction of the extended record technique

	Snapshot point 1	Before-image	After-image	Snapshot 2	Before-image	After-image	...	Snapshot point *n*	Before-image	After-image	

FILE DUMPS

As a last resort the auditor may request for all the contents of a computer file to be printed out in order to provide a visible record for checking. If the file is large, such a technique may delay the computer scheduling operations, however, providing the dumping is done during off-peak periods, it is an audit technique which may be used. It must be stated that files should in any case be periodically dumped, and thus the auditor could request an audit copy is run whenever this takes place, so saving computer time. It must be stated that with large operations file dumping may be considered to be totally impractical.

A DETAILED REVIEW OF PROGRAMS (DESK CHECKS)

In this instance the auditor is expected to read at his desk a program testing its logic (eg statements in COBOL). In other words, the auditor must be able to understand the language used and ideally be able to programme at a reasonable level of ability. Such a technique is laborious, but the deterrent effect on a potentially 'deviant' programmer is considerable—not only another weapon in the auditor's armoury to defend the computer against potential fraud or damage, but a means to examine programming methods constructively. Computer time is expensive and consequently it is valid to ask why a certain technique has been used where another more efficient one is available, ie to prevent verbose programming.

REPROCESSING OF DATA ALREADY PROCESSED

This is an obvious though seldom used technique to ensure the original data was processed correctly.

PARALLEL SIMULATION

This technique is applied to a particular aspect of the system. The auditor writes a program for that aspect and processes 'live' data through that aspect, which is then compared to the applictions program output for variances and analysis. Unfortunately, both time and cost are major deterrents to the use of this technique.

MAPPING

This technique is used in addition to others and is used to identify hidden routines which may only operate under certain given circumstances: 'logic bombs'. Using this technique software is used to allow a count to be kept of 'program code execution' thereby identifying a program sequence (logic) which has not been tested, and then either notifying audit or locking out the system.

TRACING

This is a device built into the application program with the purpose of reporting the actual logic path executed. It is the opposite of 'mapping', which involves identifying a deviation from the tested logic path.

CODE COMPARISON PROGRAM

The audit objective is to ensure that the programs reviewed by the auditors are the ones actually used in 'live' operations. The program operates by comparing the audit 'file' with that in use to identify variances.

NORMATIVE TESTING

Tests are designed to examine 'control norms' prescribed in the system in order to provide a basis for the evaluation of internal control. The method used resembles 'file integrity', where balances of sub accounts are aggregated to reconcile to the control account balance in the general ledger.

THE 'CUSUM' (CUMULATIVE SUMS) TECHNIQUE

Such a technique is used to identify lapses in internal control, ie the number of errors of a certain type, the number of entries made, etc. It is ideally suited to identify the number of 'rejections' made. Totals may be accumulated or be subject to a moving average for reporting purposes. Certain of these techniques are for use on specific occasions. However, together they provide an attempt to gain reassurance as to the operations of the applications system.

Audit profile trigger (Defined at **2.11** in Chapter 3)

DATA PROCESSING—OPERATIONS

The increasing extent of computerisation has made data processing operations a part of all aspects of audit coverage. The APTs for this coverage provide triggers which apply whether a system is manual, mechanical or computerised. This APT applies to the operation of data processing department or function. Portions of it can also be applied to specific applications.

Where technical involvement is necessary there should be collaboration/liaison with the relevant corporate/operating group data processing management.

HARDWARE
Owned or leased
Cost
Age
Contracts
Configuration
Existing power
Ability to extend/upgrade
Interface with other equipment
Current utilisation
Application

Timetable
Log books
Planned utilisation
Maintenance
Planned
Emergency
Back-up facilities
Future plans
New/additional/upgraded   equipment,   Programme—sanction/authority,
acquisition, installation, conversion/operation Steering committee—decision
making, monitoring/control

SOFTWARE
Own programmers
Package(s)
Modified package(s)
Software house special design
Corporate DP special design
How maintained
Register of software

Authority to modify:
    Routine modifications
    Enhancements
    Major changes
    Contracts
    Other corporate users
    Languages
    Compatability/interface with other applications
    Testing/dummy running arrangements

Developments:
    Timetable
    Reviewing procedures

SYSTEMS SPECIFICATIONS
Feasibility study
Description of each facet of each procedure
Flow diagrams
Decision trees
Documents

User manual:
    Procedures
    Timetable
    Documents
    Audit trail
    Controls
    Up-dating arrangements

STAFFING
User staff
Systems analysis
Programmers
Operations staff

Adequacy of numbers, calibre, succession, back-up
Adequacy for routine work
For development
For future requirements
Education and training arrangements
Organisation
Plans
Job specifications

QUALITY CONTROL
Data collection
Data preparation
Batch/run control
File maintenance
EDP standards
Output schedules/read outs
User satisfaction
Application achievement
Post-implementation review

COSTS
Control on revenue expenditure
Effective use of hardware/software/staff resource
Control on capital expenditure
Accountability
Charging arrangements

DATA PROCESSING—SECURITY

PREMISES
Building security—Day and night
Authority for access
Means of access
Enforcement measures
Fire security

HARDWARE
Persons authorised to access equipment:
   Directly
   Through VDUs
   Through communication links

Password arrangements:
   Allocation
   Logging
   Revision

FILES
Protection of files
In operation
Off line
Back-up

SOFTWARE
Persons authorised to access software:
　Directly
　Through VDUs
　Through communication links

Password arrangements:
　Allocation
　Logging
　Revision

Persons authorised to modify software:
　Logging
　Control

INSURANCE
Building
Equipment
Consequential loss

Further reading

Doswell, R and Simons, G L *Fraud and abuse of IT systems* (1986) (NCC Publications).

Tricker, R I *Effective information management* (1982) (Beaumont Executive Press).

CHAPTER 7   Computer security

Objectives	To describe audit techniques designed to assess the adequacy of protection for continuity of service from computerised information systems
Contents	Hazards: environmental; hardware; software; data; staff, systems development and installation Disaster planning; total computer security concept Procurement of computer facilities Computer fraud; data protection and privacy
Summary	Most organisations place considerable reliance on computer-processed information for continuing their day-to-day operations. In many cases failure or corruption of the information system would be disastrous. Consequently there is a crucial management need to analyse these risks very carefully and to ensure adequate protection is provided

1.0   INTRODUCTION

In the previous chapter application controls were examined. This examination involved the appraisal of the security of the process for generating information by computer. This chapter examines the security of the computer system, its hardware, software and staff who operate the system. It is therefore appropriate to define 'general controls':

> 'Controls, other than application controls, which relate to the environment in which computer based accounting systems are developed, maintained and operated, and which are therefore applicable to all applications. The objectives of general controls are to ensure the proper development and implementation of applications, and the integrity of program and data files, and of computer operations. Like application controls, general controls may be either manual or programmed.'
> ('Auditing in a Computer Environment' APC Audit Guideline July 1984)

The technique of hazard management is adopted to examine these controls. For the purposes of this technique hazards are identified over the following five resource groups:

1 Environment
2 Hardware
3 Software   Systems developed and installation are
4 Data   dealt with within these five groups.
5 Staff

For each of these areas a general evaluation is made followed by 'hazard assessment schedules'. These schedules are not intended to be exhaustive but to act as a catalyst to thought and action. Readers should add further items where appropriate. Each resource group has a subsection embracing six parts:

1 Possible source of hazard.
2 Prevention of its occurrence.
3 Insurance cover if it occurs.
4 Monitoring for early detection.
5 Corrective action during and after.
6 Disaster planning points for survival and recovery from the consequences.

Please note that there is a strong emphasis upon prevention. Many preventative measures are repetitive; protection of one resource may, however, be beneficial to others.

When determining the possible measures to counter hazards, factors such as cost effectiveness and the relevance of the measures to the circumstances of each installation should be considered. Indeed, the following diagram illustrates a suggested review process.

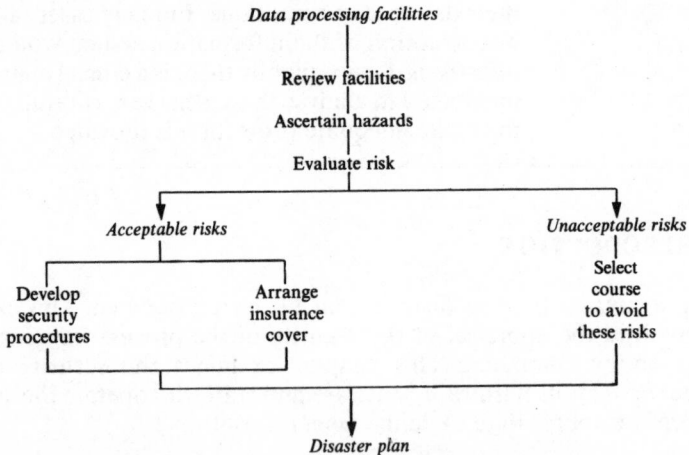

The technique of using 'audit profile triggers' which is explained at 2.11 in Chapter 3 can be applied to the examination of data processing security including the assessement and evaluation of the risks and the adequacy and effectiveness of plans for dealing with them. The examples used to illustrate each of the paragraphs which follow are taken from a Reed International internal handbook designed to be used by management as a self-audit tool for computer security. They also provide the audit profile triggers in this key area.

2.0   ENVIRONMENTAL HAZARDS

The traditional data processing environment is a closed, air conditioned room, staffed by specialists, containing environmental sensors and alarm systems. This can provide a high degree of protection to the data processing facilities. It is probably costly to install and service and would take some time to replace after a disaster. Much modern hardware can now be sited in ordinary offices and is used by non-specialist staff. This increases its exposure to potential hazards.

2.1 The physical environment

THE BUILDING

Whenever a computer site is chosen the choice should be based on minimum risk, eg in areas not subject to flood, earthquake, subsidence or other natural disaster. As well as a good site, adequate provision should be made to prevent harm to the installation, eg intruder alarms.

FIRE AND ARSON

In America half of all fire losses are due to arson. To counteract this, intruder detection devices can be used. Computer room fire extinguishers are normally gas filled with halon which does not damage the equipment, but is lethal to human beings so there must be time before they are activated for personnel to be evacuated. Water must not be used for fire protection of the computer environment which should be well out of the range of automatic sprinklers. Magnetic disks are vulnerable to fire damage and should be stored in a fireproof safe. If damage does occur there are companies which specialise in retrieving fire damaged disks.

ACCESS CONTROLS

Only authorised personnel should gain access to computer rooms. The means used to separate the authorised from the unauthorised may be keys, or card, voice or fingerprint identification. However, whatever the method adopted, it should not inconvenience the authorised persons or else the system will be subject to abuse. In designing a security system, account must be taken of the level of discipline required from the authorised users.

INTERRUPTION OF SUPPLIES

The computer installation is dependent on electricity, for the operation of the computer, of air conditioning, warning devices and telecommunication equipment. Similarly it is dependent on maintenance and the availability of spare parts together with the personnel to operate it. It is common practice to provide cover for interruption of power supplies by the use of stand-by generators which operate from the moment power fluctuates—the shortest interruption can be disastrous to the functioning of a computer.

Similarly, an organisation which is wholly dependent on a sole supplier of spare parts is unduly at risk—the supplier may become unable or unwilling to continue supplies, or could go bankrupt. Also an interruption of international telecommunications could prevent transmission of essential input data and output information.

2.2   Insurance

Adequate insurance cover may be taken out to provide against loss due to accidental and deliberate actions. It may also cover losses due to industrial action and failure of critical components or ancillary equipment. Vandalism should also be insured against.

2.3   Environmental hazard management

Environment—fire

HAZARD ASSESSMENT

Possible sources

> Fire may originate within the environment or surrounding areas; above, below the same level
> DP hardware faults
> Other faulty equipment
> Faulty electrical cables
> Consequence of explosion, etc
> Accidents
> Malicious acts by employees or others
> Cigarette ends or matches

COUNTER-MEASURES

Prevention

> Regular maintenance of hardware and services equipment
> Regular inspection of electrical wiring
> Local environment away from known fire hazards
> Keep environment and surrounding areas clear of combustible materials
> Fireproof construction surrounding the environment
> Flame retarding materials within environment
> Smoking prohibitions
> Controlled access to the environment
> Visible security may deter vandalism and malicious acts
> Regular audits and safety inspections may reveal sources of hazard and possible remedies

Insurance cover

> Cost of new environment
> Consequential loss

Monitoring

> Smoke and heat detectors:
> — within environment
> — in surrounding areas
> — in false floors, ceilings and service ducts
> Automatic alarms and links to fire services
> Staff vigilance
> Security patrols
> Surveillance equipment

Corrective action

Automatic extinguishing equipment
Halon gas not sprinklers (see flooding)
Automatic shut down of equipment
Fire drill
Manual fire alarms
Suitable hand extinguishers (not water or CO_2)

Ascertain extent of damage and repair if feasible
Assess effects of damage and duration
Activate disaster plan as necessary
Discover source of hazard if possible

Disaster planning

Alternative location for environment:
— on site
— elsewhere
Contract to provide an emergency environment
Alternative data processing methods
Alternative facilities:
— own processing sub-divided into separate locations
— other users off site
— specialist companies

Environment—flooding and liquids

HAZARD ASSESSMENT

Possible sources

River flooding, etc
Heavy rainfall
Burst water mains
Burst pipes caused by freezing conditions
Faulty equipment in surrounding areas:
— pipes
— water tanks
— WC and bathroom facilities
— kitchens
— heating systems
Sprinkler systems and fire extinguishers
Fire brigade hoses
Pipes, etc ruptured due to fire or explosion
Spilt drinks and cleaning fluids
Accidents
Malicious acts by employees or others

COUNTER-MEASURES

Prevention

Locate environment away from known flood hazards (NB basements
    and ground floors)
Keep roofs in good repair
Protect the building against frost

Regular inspection and servicing of:
— air conditioning
— other plumbing
Prohibition of drinks and other liquids in the environment
Drainage in the floors of the environment and surrounding areas
False floors may give some protection from minor floods
Regular audits and safety inspections may reveal sources of hazard and
   possible remedies.

Insurance cover

Cost of new environment
Consequential loss

Monitoring

Flood detectors
Staff vigilance
Security patrols
Surveillance equipment

Corrective action

Automatic pumps
Automatic shut down of equipment
Automatic power shut down
Flood alarms
Flood drill

Ascertain extent of damage and repair if feasible
Assess effects of damage and duration
Activate disaster plan as necessary
Discover sources of hazard if possible

Disaster planning (See disaster planning for fire p 181)

Environment—explosions

HAZARD ASSESSMENT

Possible sources

Boiler faults
Hazardous chemicals
Gas
Explosions
Fracture of services as a consequence of fire or structural weakness
Electrical faults
Emergency power supply battery faults
Accidents
Malicious acts by employees or others
Hazards are more likely to arise in surrounding areas than in the
   environment

COUNTER-MEASURES

Prevention

Locate environment away from known explosive hazards
Regular inspection and servicing of:
— boilers

— gas supplies
— other equipment
See fire prevention (p 180)
Adequate site security
Controlled access to environment
Regular audits and safety inspections may reveal sources of hazard and
  possible remedies

Insurance cover

Cost of replacement environment
Consequential loss

Monitoring

See monitoring of fire (p 180)
Gas detection equipment
Vapour detecting equipment in chemical stores
Operator vigilance for suspicious objects

Corrective action

Explosion drill
Ascertain extent of damage and repair if feasible
Assess effects of damage and duration
Activate disaster plan as necessary
Discover source of hazard if possible
Call police to deal with suspicious objects

Disaster planning (See disaster planning for fire p 181)

Environment—projectiles

HAZARD ASSESSMENT

Possible sources

Aircraft (in whole or part)
Motor vehicles
Railway trains
Fragments of buildings (see structural weakness p 185)
Falling trees
Other (see human interference p 184)

COUNTER-MEASURES

Prevention

Locate environment away from known hazards:
— busy roads
— lorry turning areas
— airport runways
— railway embankments and bridges
— dilapidated structures
— large or old trees
— top floors of buildings

Install protective barriers around environment:
— window screens

— walls
— ditches
— fences
— bollards
See prevention of human interference (below)
Shut down facilities in severe weather
Regular audits and safety inspections may reveal sources of hazard and
    possible remedies

Insurance cover

Cost of new environment
Consequential loss

Monitoring

Limited to detection after the event;
    security patrols and surveillance equipment might help

Corrective action

Ascertain extent of damage and repair if feasible
Assess effects of damage and duration
Activate disaster plan as necessary
Discover source of hazard if possible

Disaster planning (See disaster planning for fire p 181)

Environment—human interference

HAZARD ASSESSMENT

Possible sources

Upset staff—leavers or redundant
Industrial action
Vandalism
Burglary
Sabotage—internal or external
Riots
Terrorism
Warfare

COUNTER-MEASURES

Prevention

Management vigilance
Do not make environment obvious to the outside world
Environment entrance should not be on a main street
Ensure site security is adequate
Control access to the environment:
— security locks, various types available
— identification passes
— manned entrances, etc
Local environment outside areas manned by non-clerical unions
Locate safes away from the environment
See prevention for projectiles (p 183)

See prevention of staff hazards to operations (p 230)
Regular audits and safety inspections may reveal sources of hazard and
   possible remedies

Insurance cover

Cost of new environment
Consequential loss
(Insurance may not be available or cost effective against some sources)

Monitoring

Management and operator vigilance
Intruder alarms
Security patrols
Inspection and logging of passes—manual or automatic
Surveillance equipment
See fire monitoring (p 180)

Corrective action

Close down environment as necessary
Active defence of environment may be feasible in some circumstances:
— own security staff
— police
Ascertain extent of damage and repair if feasible
Assess effects of damage and duration
Activate disaster plan as necessary
Discover source of hazard if possible

Disaster planning (See disaster planning for fire p 181)

Environment—structural weakness

HAZARD ASSESSMENT

Possible sources

Faulty construction, building or nearby
Earthquakes
Landslips
Extreme weather (eg hurricanes)
Building damaged by other hazards:
— fire
— flooding
— explosion
— projectiles
— human inference

COUNTER-MEASURES

Prevention

Locate environment away from known hazards:
— earthquake zones
— steep hillsides and cliffs
— valleys below dams
— spoilage tips

Survey of buildings intended to contain environments

Environment buildings or surrounding constructions designed to withstand hazards

Regular audits and safety inspections may reveal sources of hazard and possible remedies

Insurance cover

Cost of new environment

Consequential loss

Monitoring

Regular inspection of buildings and protective constructions by qualified surveyors

Management vigilance

Corrective action

Ascertain extent of damage and repair if feasible

Assess effects of damage and duration

Activate disaster plan as necessary

Discover source of hazard if possible

Disaster planning (See disaster planning for fire p 181)

3.0   HARDWARE

Hardware can be a desk top micro-computer or a large mainframe installation sited in a protected environment, with all categories of peripheral equipment. Hardware is increasingly linked in networks.

A micro-computer is more at risk from theft or damage but is relatively cheap and easy to replace. Very large computers justify elaborate environment protection. The choice of appropriate security for intermediate equipment is a matter of critical judgement.

Current hardware is very reliable. However, it requires expensive software to ensure that it is working correctly. Error-detecting circuits and software giving a complete log of intermittent faults are now in daily use. An embedded data and time clock allows for the recording of all use made of all computer time, and the use of critical codes ensures that only certain operations can occur when all the circumstances match the requirements. The main memory may be divided into sectors within each of which reading and writing can only occur with the authorised program. The hardware can also restrict alterations to the operating system to one specific controlled input device. On all occasions there should be contingency plans for systems failure and adequate supervision of users and programs. With large systems 'survivability' and 'graceful degradation' are the objectives to ensure that a failure is not a catastrophe, but that a lower standard of service, concentrating on the priorities, is provided for the duration of the failure. The computer facility survives by providing a restricted service.

However, like any other process equipment, hardware is subject to obsolescence and depreciation and a planned replacement programme is essential.

A PERSPECTIVE ON COMPUTER SECURITY

When computer security is mentioned the layman tends to think of the dramatic computer fraud. To put security into perspective, it is interesting to note the following occurrences involving computer installations:

1 *Saboteurs*—Government installations have been bombed in Northern Ireland, Spain, Italy, France and the USA.

2 *Industrial action*—The Ministry of Defence alone is estimated to have lost £22m. Other organisations have also suffered, though damage caused has not been published.

3 *Earthquakes*—Three installations in Greece have been damaged.

4 *Flood*—Damage suffered because of flood represents 13% of computer insurance claims.

5 *Theft*—This represents 17% of insurance claims.

6 *Human error*—Accounts for approximately half the damage caused to computers.

7 *Malicious damage*—Accounts for a further 15%.

8 *Power failure*—Such an event is normally caused by circumstances outside the organisation's control.

Based on an article by Magdalena Gardner-Braun *Accountancy* March 83.

To protect the computer installation against these risks, three possibilities may be considered:

1 *Dispersion*—To minimise loss in the event of deliberate or accidental damage.

2 *Duplication*—Back-up copies of all files stored off site and arrangements to use compatible back-up hardware elsewhere should enable service to be continued.

3 *Defence in depth*—In order to harm the installation a series of failsafe devices must be overcome.

In discussing these three approaches, dispersion is seen as an effective defence provided the system will still function if one part fails. However, it is more difficult and more expensive to protect a dispersed system. Duplication, is a basic method used for the detection of error and as a means of providing back-up for components of the installation which might fail. The provision of back-up hardware is referred to as 'duplexing', eg a pair of identical processors and printers. If duplexing is not available, it may be necessary to fall back on manual systems, eg a computer failure in one organisation meant that management had to write cheques for 2,000 staff manually to ensure employees received some form of payment, which was adjusted when the system was retrieved. Defence in depth can be likened to the medieval castle with the keep being the data base, and the various walls, ramparts, moats and sentries being the checks which have to fail for the installation to become vulnerable. It is now appropriate to examine hardware security for each aspect of the computer department's operations.

3.1   Hardware hazard management

Hardware—damage to environment

HAZARD ASSESSMENT

Possible sources

Hazards to environment from:
— fire
— flooding
— explosions
— projectiles
— human interference
— structural weaknesses
are highly likely to cause damage to hardware

COUNTER-MEASURES

Prevention

Management vigilance
See prevention of environment hazards, (pp 178–186) particularly care
   in siting the environment and controlled access to it
Subdivision of processing facilities into separate locations will spread
   the risk
Regular audits and safety inspections may reveal sources of hazard and
   possible remedies

Insurance cover

Refurbishment of hardware
Replacement hardware
Installation costs
Consequential loss

Monitoring

Monitoring of environment hazards
Temperature and humidity sensors

Corrective action

Flood and fire drill
Ascertain extent of damage
Assess effects of damage and duration
Salvage serviceable hardware
Repair or replace hardware as necessary
Activate disaster plan as necessary
Discover source of hazard if possible

Disaster planning

Identity essential applications
Formulate alternative processing methods
Arrange alternative processing facilities:
— own processing sub-divided into separate locations
— other users off-site
— specialist companies

Ensure that data transmission/transfer facilities are available
Determine sources of replacement hardware:
— manufacturer
— suppliers
— contract for emergency supply of hardware
Determine supply lead times and installation times (including repair of
data transmission facilities)

Hardware—operating parameters exceeded

HAZARD ASSESSMENT

Possible sources

Heat
Cold
Humidity
Dust
Smoke
Vibration
Radiation
Power cuts
Power fluctuations
Static electricity
Lightning

These are more likely to cause temporary interruptions to processing than
permanent damage

COUNTER-MEASURES

Prevention

Air conditioning—properly maintained
Locate environments away from known sources of hazard (pp 178–186)
Firm supports for hardware
Air filters
Faraday screens for electrostatic radiation
Power supply regulators
Emergency power supplies and generators
Anti-static mats
Food, drink and smoking prohibitions in environments
Regular audits on expert inspections may reveal sources of hazard and
possible remedies

Insurance cover

Loss of working
Repair or replacement of hardware in extreme cases

Monitoring

Monitoring systems built into hardware and operating software should
reveal the existence of some problems
Temperature sensors
Power fluctuation sensors
Smoke detectors
Operator vigilance

Management review of:
— console log printouts
— operating reports
'Bug' reporting procedures

Corrective action

Automatic switch over to emergency power supplies
— batteries
— generators
Automatic shut down if parameters are exceeded
Ascertain cause of hazard
Access effects and possible duration
Maintenance contracts with fast call out
Activate disaster plan as necessary

Disaster planning (See disaster planning for hardware affected by damage to environment p 188)

Hardware—breakdowns

HAZARD ASSESSMENT

Possible sources

Equipment faults
Normal wear and tear
Software problems
Data overload
Consequence of operating parameters being exceeded
See also direct damage to hardware, (p 192) and age and obsolescence
  (p 193)

COUNTER-MEASURES

Prevention

Regular preventative maintenance
Planned replacement of hardware
Software maintenance contracts
Regular rationalisation of data stored 'on line'
Management review of:
— console log printouts
— operating reports
— bug reports
Regular audit may reveal sources of hazard and possible remedies

Insurance cover

Loss of working
Repair or replacement of hardware in extreme cases

Monitoring

Operator vigilance
Management review of operations
'Bug' reporting procedures

Corrective action

Fast call out contracts for:
— hardware repairs

— software maintenance
Assess effects and probable duration of breakdown
Activate disaster plan as necessary

Disaster planning (See disaster planning for hardware affected by damage to environment p 188)

Hardware—theft

HAZARD ASSESSMENT

Possible sources

Unauthorised use of DP facilities
Removal of:
— hardware
— parts
— vital spares
In the main environment or at remote locations, by employees or others

COUNTER-MEASURES

Prevention

Management vigilance
Controlled access to environment
Adequate site security
Operating timetables
Operation reports
Rotation of operator duties
Joint staffing of environment outside normal office hours
Asset records and regular inspection of remote equipment
Parts and spares stockchecks
See also prevention of theft of software (p 207), and data (p 215)
Regular audit may reveal sources of hazard and possible remedies

Insurance cover

Cost of replacement hardware and its installation
Loss of working

Monitoring

Monitoring system built into hardware and operating software
Intruder alarms
Surveillance equipment
Security patrols
Management and operator vigilance
Management review of operating reports

Corrective action

Automatic shutdown of CPU ports to terminals disconnected before
   'log out'
Ascertain extent of loss and probable method of theft
Assess effects of theft and duration of any down time
Activate disaster plan as necessary
Inform the police

Disaster planning

Applicable to removal of hardware
(See disaster planning for hardware affected by damage to environment p 188)

Hardware—direct damage

HAZARD ASSESSMENT

Possible sources

Accidental or malicious by employees or others
Damage could occur:
— within the main environment
— to remote hardware
— to data links
See sources of human inference in environment (p 184)

COUNTER-MEASURES

Prevention

Adequate site security
Controlled access to environment
Management vigilance
See prevention of hazards to staff from operations (p 228), and hazards
    to operations from staff (p 230)
See prevention of human interference in environment (p 184)
Environment sufficiently large for hardware and operators
False floors and ducts for cables
Equipment cabinets closed and locked
Regular audits may reveal sources of hazard and possible remedies

Insurance cover

Cost of hardware repair, replacement and installation
Loss of working

Monitoring

Management and operator vigilance
Intruder alarms
Surveillance equipment
Security patrols
Monitoring system built into hardware and operating software to report
    terminal and data link problems

Corrective action

Automatic shut down of CPU ports to severed data links or damaged
    terminals
Fast call out repair contracts
Ascertain extent of damage and cause
Assess effects of damage and duration of down time
Activate disaster plan as necessary

Disaster planning (See disaster planning for hardware affected by damage to
the environment p 188)

Hardware—age and obsolescence

HAZARD ASSESSMENT

Possible sources

Supplier defunct
Manufacturer defunct
Hardware no longer manfactured
Spares not easily available
Excessive maintenance required
Maintenance company defunct or unable/unwilling to renew repair contract
Inadequate capacity for current requirements or anticipated developments

COUNTER-MEASURES

Prevention

Choose a reliable supplier
Choose a reputable manufacturer
Planned regular replacement of hardware
Regular maintenance of hardware
Find alternative suppliers
Find alternative maintenance contract
Regular audits of operations may reveal sources of hazards and possible remedies

Insurance cover (Unlikely)

Monitoring

Management review of maintenance pattern
Review of trade and technical journals
Management awareness of the age and state of hardware
Supplier notification of refusal/unwillingness to renew contracts

Corrective action

Stock key spare parts or complete secondhand machines as necessary
Plan for early replacement of hardware at risk
Assess probable remaining active life; (this could be an opportunity to upgrade DP systems)
Activate disaster plan as necessary

Disaster planning

Hardware obsolete
Identify essential applications and formulate alternative processing methods
Hardware old
See disaster planning for damage to the environment (p 188)

4.0   ADVANCED TECHNIQUES

4.1   Database management systems

Generally defined as a repository for stored data which is both integrated and shared: duplication is eliminated. It is not a file. It is a large accumulation of data crossed-referenced and controlled by a software package. It allows management to receive inter-related information in a single report. One entry updates the system, thereby saving time. It also provides a level of control between application programs and data being used. It may be used to cross-reference financial information to non-financial information, eg wages to personnel records.

DBMS allow increased efficiency by eliminating duplication of data input as the following diagram shows:

Stock data files using individual application packages

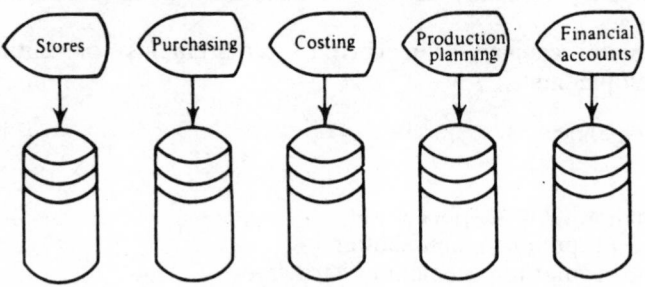

Stock data files using data-based management systems (DBMS)

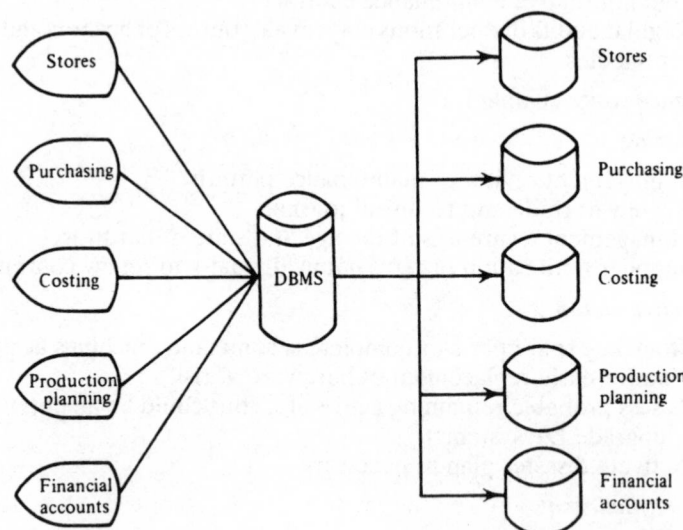

(Based on an article by A and E Birchall 'Management Accounting', March 1984).

However, any lack of integrity or any loss of data would be damaging. Database mangement systems require large computers and sophisticated programming. This results in increased computing costs and software risks. Strict control of data storage volumes, storage periods, access frequencies and methods is essential to contain costs.

ADVANTAGES

1 Updates/deletions need only be made once, eg a new entry does not require all files to be amended, hence less chance of error.

2 Programs can be restricted to certain data, again reducing the risk of corruption of data.

DISADVANTAGES

1 Increased cost of computing requiring powerful hardware and sophisticated software.
2 All information is in one place and therefore vulnerable, when compared to a system using individual packages.

4.2   Internal control re DBMS

General internal control problems associated with computer operations apply; however, special emphasis should be given to the following areas of potential weakness:

1 *Access*—Should be restricted by programs giving access to certain files only for the purposes of reading, updating, adding or deleting data.
2 *Back-up and recovery*—This is particularly important in DBMS because:
   (a) DBMS is normally used to support real time systems upon which the organisation's operations rely.
   (b) A large concentration of data is at risk and could be a major loss.
   (c) Due to cross-referencing and large numbers of operations, corruption can occur over a larger area of data.
   Elements of back-up:
   (a) Before and after copies should be retained.
   (b) Updating transaction copies should be retained.
   (c) Database or segments thereof should be periodically 'dumped', ie printed out onto hard copy.
   (d) Creation of 'checkpoint' records, ie a record showing the state of the computer system prior to change—record counts and names of all financial files held; all active programs identified; all active terminals identified.
3 *Dual updating protection*—Problems occur when two different programs update the same file (change of data) at the same time. The computer becomes confused and may reject both good and corrupted data—'lock out'. A system should exist whereby a high priority program 'locks out' a low priority program, ie the high priority program gains access—'queuing'.
4 *Integrity of the database*—Data is cross-referenced and linked by a system of 'chains'. If the chain is broken by a 'bug' or error while the system is being updated by an application program, it will cause failure of the system. In order to prevent such an occurrence an integrity checking program should operate to ensure chains are not broken. This program would check the application program before the up-dating takes place.
5 *General security*—DBMS is vulnerable because it contains so much information centrally. Personnel involved in such operations must be technically competent, have identifiable responsibilities: they should be covered by fidelity insurance. Adherence to safety precautions must be strictly enforced—as mentioned for computer systems. Losses in DBMS

can be very high in the event of systems failure and consequently adherence to back-up, recovery and security procedures is important.

4.3   On line systems

4.3.1   *Definition*

'A real time system is one designed to produce results in a timescale which enables it to be used to control the environment producing the input.' (NCC Computer Audit)

Usually a number of terminals are located where transactions take place and are linked to a central computer installation.

Difference between on line and real time—'On line systems have direct access at a given time, real time has direct access without a time constraint.' The advantage of a real time system is that it enables the user to be in immediate contact with the system, giving:

1 Direct access to data.
2 A sense of control and responsibility.
3 A reduction in the records other than computer files required.

However, there are special problems for the auditor, namely:

1 Control over the volume and value of input documentation cannot be confirmed in the same way as is possible with batch processing. Indeed there may be no input documentation.
2 Control over access to the terminals is critical. Access to files and terminals may be restricted to authorised personnel.

4.3.2   *Valid data input*

More sophisticated terminals allow for a buffer store, enabling input to be validated by program checks before live files are accessed. Such a store could also be dumped before processing, facilitating reconstruction if required.

Where the terminal is directly on line, files can be instantly updated, permitting the operator total control over input and its validity. In such circumstances there may be no audit trail. Where such events occur a system of regular back-up and security procedures must be strictly enforced to prevent corruption of master files.

4.3.3   *Control over access*

1 When terminals are introduced at distant locations, examination must be made of user needs, restricting the number of terminals with input access but allowing sufficient terminals with 'read only' or 'interrogation' access to meet the perceived need.
2 Key control or password—Keys, codes, cards or other devices can be used to restrict access, further reinforced by a 'rotating' password system. Other devices such as voice, fingerprint or palm recognition may be used, as too can a time device allowing entry only during operational times, eg 9.30 am—3.30 pm.

3 The terminal and central computer should record on a log who is operating which screen when, and for how long, and which file is being examined or updated.
4 Only authorised users should gain access.
5 A confidential area should be reserved for the terminal to which access can only be gained by authorised staff.
6 A manual record of transactions should be kept.

Needless to say, point 5 may be difficult to enforce where the terminal is seen as a user friendly device providing information to the office as a whole and point 6 may not be appropriate to all operations. An illustration of access control now follows:

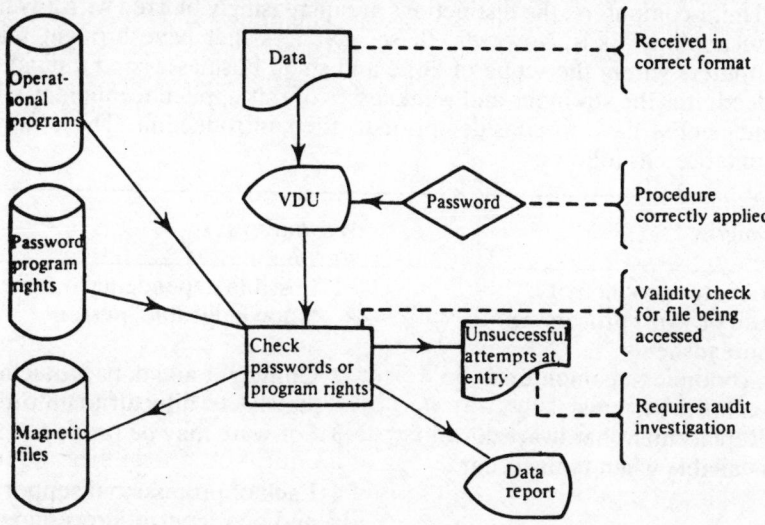

4.4   Distributed and network systems

DEFINITIONS

'A collection of computers and terminals connected by a communications system.'

'A centralised network is characterised by a centralised computer system, a communications system and several terminal devices.'

'A distributed network is characterised by several computer systems that are connected via a communications system in a distributed network, users may interact with one of the computer complexes via local communications facilities or may be connected to the communications system directly.' (D D Spencer *Data Processing—An Introduction*)

Network systems permit efficient access to data processing facilities by remote users, and in some cases enable dispersal of those processing facilities. The general consequences of a disaster in any one processing centre can be reduced as a result of dispersal. User departments (originators) can be identified as being responsible for input of their own data. There is, however, an increased risk of unauthorised access to the facilities through penetration of the network. It is for management, supported by internal audit, to ensure that adequate disciplines and compliance with operational manuals, are maintained, not only for the purposes of security, but also for economic and effective operation.

5.0 MICRO-COMPUTERS

An increasing risk area for orgnisations is the proliferation of personal computers. We shall not attempt to identify the differences between micro- and mini-computers; the distinctions are increasingly blurred with advances in technology. It is, however, these advances that have brought micro-computers within the scope of large and small businesses and individuals. Indeed, it is the strengths and weaknesses of this applied technology which management have to consider prior to their introduction. These may be summarised as follows:

Strengths	*Weaknesses*
1 Greater productivity: use of word processing/ spreadsheets	1 Possible dependency on one 'knowledgeable' person
2 Economic to computerise complex systems	2 Copyright and data protection legislation difficult to enforce
3 Replacement hardware is available when faults occur	3 Software may be prone to error
	4 Lack of professional support and poor control procedures
	5 User department may not have the discipline to process data accurately
	6 Need for training may not be appreciated by management
	7 Hardware is portable and attractive — subject to theft
	8 Prompt and effective maintenance may be difficult to obtain
	9 Software compatability problems may occur
	10 Difficulty in restricting access to terminals
	11 Proper environment may be difficult to achieve

On the basis of these strengths and weaknesses the internal auditor can evaluate the balance between the costs of the control and the potential risk of damage to the organisation from a control failure.

5.1 Lack of audit trail

A casual operating environment may lead to the loss of audit trail. These computer systems are popular because of their 'user friendly' nature: enabling those with limited expertise to operate them. It is important that the application controls already discussed are applied to the environment of personal computers, ie controls over access, program changes, testing, back-up and recovery. Further problems are created by the ease with which data can be modified without the production of an adequate audit trail. Such a deficiency can be remedied by the maintenance of a log of transactions processed together with transaction counts for each terminal or user. Items entered should be documented so that where errors of failures occur, a trail exists to support the activity that has taken place.

Those inputting or manipulating data should be identified within the computer (eg by a password) so that they are made accountable for their actions.

The transactions log should be periodically reviewed by supervisors and exception reports produced for management. It should report variations from the expected and overall volume of activity. It must be remembered that personal computers may hold non-financial information which may be as sensitive as financial information: client listings, supplier details and employee details.

5.2 Erasure of transaction details

Due to limited storage space, it is not uncommon for details of previous activity to be replaced by a mere summary of activity when current data is input. This has the effect of removing the audit trail unless hard copy is made prior to erasure.

5.3 Informal library procedures

The indexing, labelling and copying of files may be lax due to the 'amateurish' approach to the computer environment. It is essential that proper back-up procedures are maintained. To quote:

> 'An improper amount of static electricity, careless use of the computer by an untrained user, or something as simple as spilling a cup of coffee on diskette can wipe out a month's work of processing activity' *Micro Computers—Their Use and Misuse in your Business* (Price Waterhouse & Co).

A person needs to be responsible for maintaining up-to-date copies of diskettes and for maintaining an adequate system of filing and distribution: a library. This person should also be made responsible for the issue of sensitive material, only releasing such information upon authorisation. The risk is not only the loss of valuable information but also other risks such as corruption of data, sabotage and selling that data to competitors.

5.4   Processing controls

Application controls have previously been centred on the 'moat and castle' effect, segregating the work of the user department from that of the computer department. Use of micro-computers places the control of the inputting and output process within the scope of user department activity, thereby making management dependent upon the accuracy with which non-specialist staff process data.

5.5   Control of output

Normal output controls, as previously mentioned, need to be applied.

5.6   Introduction of new software

New software needs to be tested on test files prior to introduction in order to assess the effect of such software upon the whole operational system.

5.7   Internal label checking

Files may be loaded incorrectly causing over-writing or corruption of standing data. Risk of such events can be reduced by proper training and discipline, use of security devices and use of proper back-up procedures.

5.8   Documentation and training

Management may perceive advantages in delegating responsibility for computer operations to one person; the organisation is then, however, vulnerable. It is important to ensure that others are trained and practised to support that person and where possible, internal checks and controls should be introduced. It is similarly important to have adequate documentation, supporting both systems and data.

5.9   Abuse of the mainframe

Controls established for mainframe operations could be eroded by use of micro-computers. This situation may arise where data is down loaded from the mainframe onto diskettes and modified on the micro-computer to be replaced in the mainframe system.

The risk of damage can be reduced by:

1 Ensuring all such access is authorised and supervised.
2 Preventing the 'down loading' of sensitive information by providing read only facilities.
3 Determining levels of authorisation required to gain access to certain levels of sensitive information.
4 Prevention of access to the mainframe outside certain restricted hours. This can be achieved by the use of time clocks linked to certain files. It also inhibits unsupervised work on the system.

5.10 Housekeeping controls

These are simple office rules designed to provide the appropriate environment for operations:

1 *No smoking zone*—Smoke can damage both hardware and diskettes.
2 *Delete old or extinct files*—Such files consume space that is restricted and may slow down activity as more records have to be searched.
3 *Controlled temperature*—Free circulation of air.
4 *Ban food and drink*—Accidents can damage the system.
5 *Select known or proven systems*—Prevents corruption of existing systems.
6 *Licensed products*—Ensure copyright is properly acquired.
7 *Data Protection Act*—Ensure appropriate registration.

5.11 Some general controls

1 RESTRICTION OF ACCESS

Access to the computer should be restricted to authorised and trained personnel. Fixed discs should not be used for storage of sensitive data. Such data should be securely stored on removable disks.

2 PASSWORD CONTROL

Third parties, such as maintenance engineers, should be properly vetted and all users should have passwords periodically reviewed. Further controls should be made on the number of attempts at gaining entry and restrictions placed on the time taken to gain entry. Similarly, where a terminal is left switched on, the system should automatically log off and clear the screen of information after an agreed period of inactivity.

3 PREVENTION OF EAVESDROPPING

Relatively inexpensive data collection devices can be used by unauthorised persons to transfer information displayed on the screen onto the device. Consequently where terminals display sensitive information, they should be adequately screened.

4 DISASTER PLANNING

Arrangements should be made for the secure storage of software and data files and for the replacement of equipment in the event of failure.

5 EQUIPMENT COMPATIBILITY

As new facilities are introduced so tests should be made to provide assurance that this introduction will not cause the system to fail.

6 THEFT

Both hardware and software are attractive and portable and thus vulnerable to theft. Both insurance cover and inventory control needs to be adequate. Similarly buildings need to be made secure.

5.12   Mini-computers

With the continuing increase in power of mini-computers, at the same time as they become more user friendly, problems of security increase. The signficance of procedures for restricted access, physical security, secrecy of output, program change authorisation, file management and general security may not be fully appreciated by the layman. Nevertheless similar protection to that given to a large mainframe is essential.

INTERNAL CONTROL

Rules:

1 Those in positions of responsibility should not become involved in executing their decisions.
2 Those responsible for recording functions should not have control over or access to assets whose movements they record.
3 Internal check must apply at all times for authorisation, accuracy, completeness and procedural adherence—one employee checking another's ˙work.

These rules may be applied in the following manner:

1 Only operations staff and maintenance engineers should have access to the computer room.
2 The manager should take no part in day-to-day operations.
3 Programmers should be segregated from systems analysts.
4 Log should record all computer operations (wherever possible).
5 Library should record all file movements, amendments and authority.
6 All program changes should be recorded.
7 Testing should not occur during live operation.
8 Terminal access should be restricted to authorised users.

6.0   COMPUTER BUREAUX

The services provided by bureaux vary from installation to installation depending on client needs and the expertise of the bureau operators. With regard to audit related problems the following quotation is taken from the APC guideline 'Auditing in a computer environment—1984'.

> 'Where an enterprise uses a third party service organisation such as a computer service bureau . . . the auditor may encounter practical obstacles as the enterprise may be placing some reliance on the proper operation of internal controls exercised by the third party. Consequently, where the auditor finds it impracticable to obtain all the information and explanation that he requires from the enterprise itself because the enterprise may not be maintaining sufficient controls to minimise that reliance, he should perform other procedures. These may include . . . carrying out procedures at the premises of the third party.'

In practice, the principal method of processing is likely to be the batch method. Clerical controls should be strictly enforced with particular attention being paid to the movement of data. When data processing is undertaken, copies of the data sent for processing should be retained. In particular, the auditor should ensure the following matters are adequately considered:

1 *Data*—Submitted to the bureau is returned to the organisation.
2 *Movement*—Of data should be secure.
3 *Internal control*—At the bureau must be adequate.
4 *Clearly defined liaison procedures*—The organisation should have a manager with liaison responsibilities.
5 *Contract terms*—This determines the working relationship between the organisation and bureau determining where the responsibility for certain operations lies. An amicable relationship with 'give and take' allows for successful operations. The contract documents are unlikely to resolve problems but they should help to prevent many arising.
6 *Periodical review*—The liaison manager and senior management should regularly review the service being provided by the bureau.
7 *Insurance cover*—The organisation should have access to the bureau's insurance records to make sure adequate protection is maintained against catastrophe.

Prior to signing a bureau service contract, or when renewing it, internal audit should examine the following matters concerning the bureau:

1 *Financial strength*—To maintain operations. In this area the following should be considered: expertise of the owners (members of British Computer Society); credit rating (per bank reference and Dun & Bradstreet); duration the bureau has been in operation (examine references from other clients); membership of trade associations (eg computer Service Bureau Association); the names of the other clients and the nature of their business (competitors); and expertise of the employees (MBCS).
2 *Location*—The accessibility of the bureau is important to ensuring uninterrupted processing as and when required.
3 *Operating capacity*—It is important to establish what degree of priority will be attached to the organisation's work in relation to that of other clients of the bureau. A high machine loading may result in delivery delays due to slow turnover of work caused by the volume being undertaken by the bureau.
4 *Liability*—The bureau should have adequate insurance cover to mitigate loss suffered by its clients as a result of deliberate and accidental events at the bureau.
5 *Back-up*—The stand-by arrangements should be adequate.
6 *Controls*—Internal control should be adequate and be regularly reviewed and evaluated. Similarly systems should be adequately documented and staff properly trained.
7 *Packages*—The packages in use should be evaluated for their suitability to the organisation's needs. The minimum of disruption should be caused to the organisation.
8 *Ownership*—It should be clearly stated in the contract where ownership of the programs and files rests. If with the bureau, provision should be made to take account of bankruptcy of the bureau, ie to ensure that in the event of bankruptcy the organisation's interests are protected.

7.0   SOFTWARE

7.1   Introduction

Software can be bought in ready-made packages or developed specifically for the user. Development can be by an outside contractor or by the user's own staff. As the user's environment and awareness of the capability of computerised systems change, so increasing demands for modifications occur. Able software designers have a tendency to be very mobile in their employment. Consequently it is essential that all systems are properly documented from first implementation. Large installations normally require specifically written software and may justify the expense and management effort necessary to employ and motivate an in-house systems department. Micro-computers are frequently operated using packaged software. This is likely to be properly documented and easily replaced if lost or corrupted. It is again a matter of critical judgement to decide on appropriate levels of security for intermediate systems.

Protection of software media is not difficult, the continued ability to service, modify and develop software can cause problems to the organisation. Adequate documentation and controls will minimise these problems.

The hazard schedules provide an analysis of potential problems and various solutions (see pp 206–209).

7.2   Unauthorised amendments to programs

Controls in this area are designed to prevent both accidental and deliberate corruption of program logic during either maintenance or operation. The following list of controls contains an element of repetition from those already quoted for computer hardware. This is because they are standard internal control procedures and techniques applied to the environment of programming.

CONTROLS APPLYING DURING MAINTENANCE OF PROGRAMS

1 Segregation of duties to prevent one person being responsible for all the operations.
2 Adequate training and supervision.
3 Rotation of passwords—Names of staff and children's names are not good passwords as they are easily detected.
4 It is vitally important during these operations that the integrity of the back-up copy file is maintained or else all is lost.
5 The programs should be adequately protected from physical danger.
6 A computer should record which files are being maintained and a schedule should be kept of those due for overhaul.
7 The auditor should carry out random checks on current programs comparing them to the originals to verify that all amendments are authorised.

CONTROLS APPLYING TO THE OPERATION OF PROGRAMS

1 Compliance with a procedures manual.
2 Access by operators restricted to programs in use.
3 Restricted access to computer installation.
4 Protection of the processor from unauthorised access, eg by passwords.
5 Investigation of delays reported via the operator's log.
6 Rotation of operator's duties.
7 Adequate training and supervision.
8 The minimum number of operators present should be two.

7.3 Controls to ensure program changes are adequately tested and documented

An instruction manual should state procedures to be used for testing, eg parallel running and when satisfactorily completed the successful program should be authorised for operational use. Internal control procedures should be adopted together with notification to both internal audit and line management that testing is taking place. It is appropriate to examine the diagram below showing the stages in program control amendment. Stage 1 represents the authorised change or amendment which is tested for compatibility or amendment to program in Stage II before parallel running and testing in Stage III. Stage IV would be live operation.

Program amendment controls

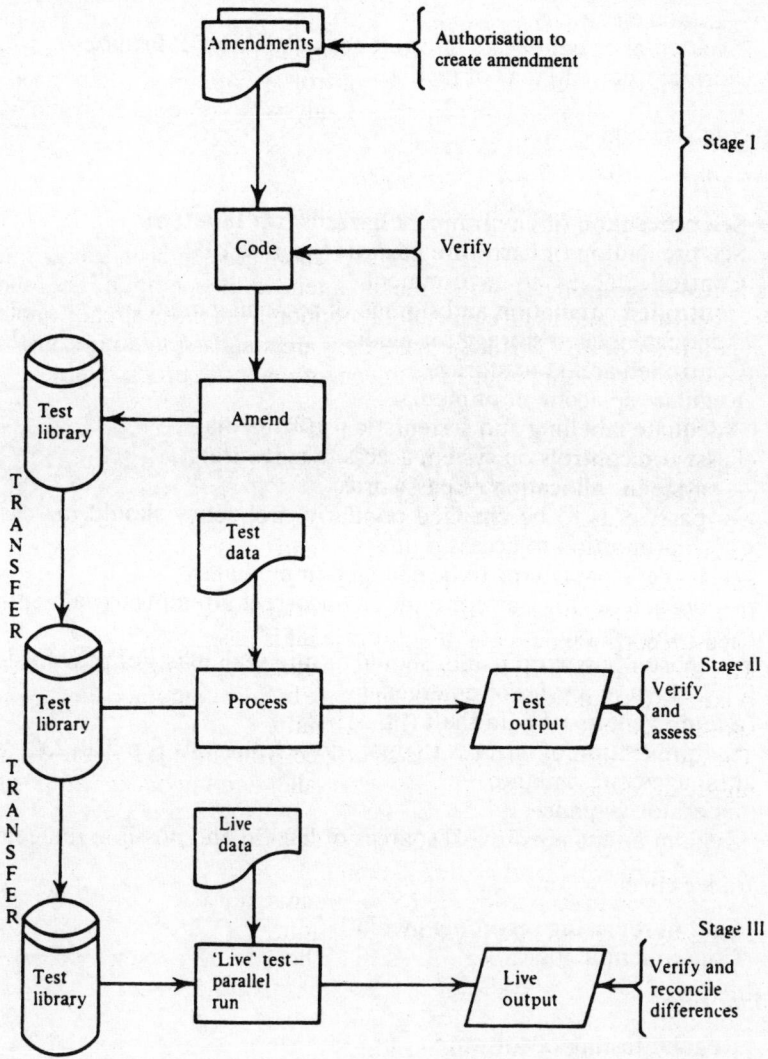

7.4   Software hazard management

Software—corruption or erasure

HAZARD ASSESSMENT

Possible sources

Damage or destruction of recording media by:
— environment hazards
— hardware hazards and faults
— careless handling
— accidents
Media susceptible to:
— heat
— humidity
— magnetic fields
— static electricity
Accidental or deliberate interference using the DP facilities
Normal wear and tear of media.

COUNTER-MEASURES

Prevention

See prevention of environment hazards (pp 180–186)
See prevention of hardware hazards (pp 188–193)
Controlled access to environment
Controlled circulation and storage of recording media
Adequate locked storage for media
Controlled access to storage
Regular replacement of media
Adequate labelling and systematic use of media
Password controls on system access to software:
— systemic allocation of passwords
— passwords to be changed regularly, frequency should increase in
    proportion to access rights
— leavers' passwords to be changed immediately
— automatic 'log out' for multiple incorrect attempts to gain entry to
    the system
— master password holder should ensure sealed lists of passwords are
    kept in a safe for emergencies
See prevention of data theft (pp 213–216)
See prevention of hazards to operations from staff (pp 230–232)
Management vigilance
Operator vigilance
Regular audits may reveal sources of hazard and possible remedies

Insurance cover

Cost of replacing recording media
Consequential loss?

Monitoring

Regular testing of software
Monitoring system built into hardware and operating software

Operator attention to console displays
Review of 'bug' sheets and operating reports by management
Surveillance of media storage areas
Environmental monitoring of media storage areas

Corrective action

Corrective action for environment hazards
Corrective action for hardware hazards
Ascertain source of hazard
Test hardware for processing faults before using back-up software
Retrieve copy software from immediate back-up storage
Activate disaster plan as necessary

Disaster planning

Ineffective unless other DP resources are covered by disaster planning
Store some back-up media copies of software remote from environment
    in locked, fireproof storage
Ensure copy software is at supplier (if applicable)
Ensure that software developed 'in-house' is fully documented
Documentation to be stored in a locked, fireproof cabinet or safe.

Software—theft

HAZARD ASSESSMENT

Possible sources

Unauthorised copying of software from:
— documentation
— media, using the DP facilities
Removal of media or documentation
Unauthorised use of the DP facilities
By employees or others

COUNTER-MEASURES

Prevention

Adequate site security
Controlled access to environment
Adequate locked storage for recording media
Controlled access to storage
See prevention of hardware theft (p 191)
Password controls on system access to software
Automatic 'log out' on multiple attempts to gain access to the system
See prevention of hazards from staff (p 231)
Management vigilance
Operator vigilance
Regular audits may reveal sources of hazards and possible remedies

Insurance cover

Cost of replacing recording media
Consequential loss?

Monitoring

> Monitoring system built into hardware and operating software should report irregular use of facilities
> Operator vigilance and attention to console displays
> Surveillance of media storage areas
> Security patrols
> Regular checks of records to media stored
> Management review of console logs and operating reports

Corrective action

> Ascertain method of theft
> Assess effects of theft and duration of any down time
> Retrieve copy software from back-up storage if necessary
> Activate disaster plan as necessary
> Inform the police

Disaster planning (See disaster planning for software corruption p 207)

> If software has been developed 'in-house' more than one copy of documentation should be made
> Copies should be stored in separate places

Software—lack of support

HAZARD ASSESSMENT

Possible sources

> Supplier defunct
> Departure of programmers:
> — at supplier
> — own staff
> No documentation of software:
> — in use
> — in development
> Supplier no longer willing to support current software

COUNTER-MEASURES

Prevention

> Planned replacement of software
> Purchase properly documented software
> Seek support warranties in contracts with software suppliers
> No phase of 'in-house' software development to last more than say 18–24 months
> More than one person should have detailed knowledge of software developments
> Proper documentation of software developed 'in house', including all amendments
> Ensure project teams are adequately motivated and remunerated
> Adequate notice periods for key staff
> Develop 'in-house' skills at maintenance of purchased software
> Regular audits may reveal sources of hazards and possible remedies

Insurance cover (None known)

Monitoring

> Regular contact with supplier
> Review of trade and technical journals for:
> — software developments
> — status of suppliers
> — market levels of remuneration
> Management vigilance

Corrective action

> Ascertain availability of any compatible alternatives
> Give priority to documenting software and amendments
> Assess probable remaining useful life; this could be an opportunity to upgrade DP systems
> Assess consequences of lack of support
> Activate disaster plan as necessary
> Take advice on legal action against the software supplier

Disaster planning

> Ineffective unless other DP resources are covered by disaster planning
> Identify essential information and formulate alternative data processing methods
> Keep back-up media copies of software and documentation, if available
> Find an alternative software maintenance contractor, if possible

8.0 DATA SECURITY

8.1 Introduction

With the exception of the security of staff this is the most important element of any data processing system. Measures to protect data are relatively simple, requiring a disciplined approach.

8.2 Security of files

The records of the organisation which are held on magnetic media are at risk through:

1 Operator mishandling, eg over-writing or deletion.
2 Machine malfunction, eg disk head crash.
3 Imperfect environmental conditions—dust, temperature, humidity.
4 Fire, flood or other natural disaster.
5 Theft or sabotage.

In the event of such occurrences retrieval of the system is vital and in the case of files this takes the form of file reconstruction, by use of back-up files. Files in the computer's own memory are described as on line and are subject to the problems described in 'Hardware' (pp 186–193).

Off line files are those located on separate disks/tapes stored in a library, access to the library being restricted to a librarian. Of course, from the time a disk/tape is linked to a central processor it becomes on line. Off line files generally hold the following information:

1 *Programs*—A set of sequential instructions in machine code to the central processor.
2 *Transaction data*—Data to update master files.
3 *Standing data*—Permanent data, eg salary scales, employee codes, sales price list, production routings, etc.
4 *Master files*—Files in continuous use of lasting importance, eg inventory, plant register, insurance listing, and legal terrier.

Due to the possibility of corruption or destruction of data the prime form of security is adequate supporting files, called 'back-up' files. Thus in the event of disaster, providing a master file is regularly updated, only a minimum amount of information will be lost and retrieval eased.

Forms of security applying to the two types of magnetic record are now discussed:

8.3 Tape security

Three generation file security (otherwise known as grandfather, father, son) is a technique which ensures data is retained until the third processing after its own, so that a facility for recreating of file exists. This system is best illustrated by the following diagram:

Tape security

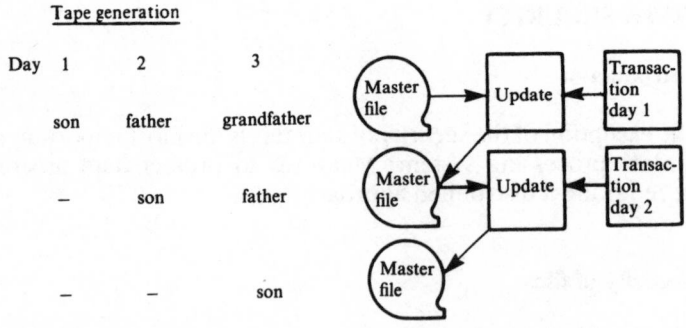

On day 4 tape 1 which has in turn been son, father and grandfather can be erased leaving tape 2 to be grandfather. Such security only applies to magnetic tape based records for which gaining direct access to a particular address (eg item or code) is very slow. This is because each address includes the one to be amended. In order to update such a file it is necessary to:

1 Read the contents into the computer memory.
2 Apply programed instructions to the transaction data.
3 Write current information onto a new 'clean' tape, which then becomes the new 'updated' master file.

As the renewal process uses two tapes—original master and updated master—the third tape should, for security purposes, be securely located elsewhere. In the diagram tape 1 (father) updates tape 2 (son); tape 2 (son) becoming the father to tape 3 (now son) and tape 1 (father) then becoming grandfather. In using such an updating procedure, the grandfather is in final 'back-up' in the event of the data on the previous two files being destroyed at the same time.

8.4 Disk storage control

In contrast to tape based systems, disk storage allows direct access to the address (item or code)—previous data does not require reading. Disks allow almost simultaneous reading and writing. Consequently, once the disk is 'on line' to the Central Processing Unit, immediate and direct updating is possible—making no requirement for the out-of-date file to be read prior to updating. Similarly, no additional files are created after each updating process. The duplicate is then the security file, should the need arise. In practice a third copy on tape is often used, all the data being dumped periodically, weekly or monthly, in the case of the unlikely event that while one disk is updating another catastrophe occurs. An event which might destroy a disk (dropping it!) is unlikely to destroy a tape . . . the objective being to minimise the chance of loss of data occurring.

Such techniques apply to both master files (similar to ledgers in a manual accounting system) and to 'pipeline' files (similar to suspense accounts, eg outstanding orders).

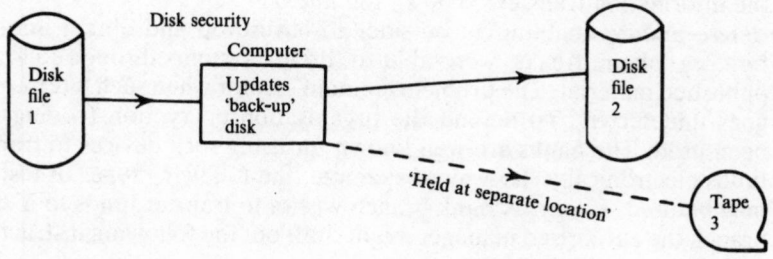

8.5 Other file security

MASTER FILE CONTROL

This control is vitally important because the reliability of processed data is dependent on the validity of the master file. To ensure validity of the master file, the contents of each master file should be periodically printed out ('dumped'). This is because each master file contains three types of data:

1 Static data—Eg customer's name, employee's name, creditor's name.
2 Reference data—Rate which may require periodic updating, eg customer discount scale.
3 Transaction data—Current information.

} Standing data

The printout of static and reference data allows for manual verificaion that such data is up-to-date, giving assurance on data controls. This tends to be a time consuming process and exception reporting using 'embedded' controls by a computer auditor will provide a more efficient means of making use of scarce resources.

8.6   Security of storage

FILE LIBRARY

It is important that all files are properly identified or marked and catalogued, with records showing when files were requested for operation, by whom and for what purpose. Thus the controls should be similar to those covering the computer equipment, ie access restricted to particular staff and precautions taken against catastrophe.

8.7   Telecommunications

Conventional batch processing ensures that only legitimate users can make use of the system and also makes it easy to restrict access to the installation to authorised personnel. However, telecommunication links between terminals and installation allows the physical access controls to be evaded. Such controls are referred to as authentication controls, ie the recognising of authentic users and operators.

However, before discussing such controls the reader should be aware of the two principal threats to telecommunications security, namely:

1 *'Noise'*—meaning electrical interference, which destroys the meaning of the information transferred down the line.
2 *'Interception'*—enabling an outsider to eavesdrop and obtain information, eg 'phone freaks' were able to 'break' systems through following published material. The problems remain greater when such interference goes undetected. To defend the organisation encryption (coding) has been used. The banks are well known for using such devices to transfer funds electronically. By way of example, the following types of test key may be used. If, say, X bank branch wishes to transfer funds to Y bank branch the authorised manager might draft out the following instruction:

From X		
To Y		
Please credit account no 111111		ABP CP plc with £1,250,000
Unique code X to Y		101
Date: December 20	60	
	111	
Currency—sterling	21	192
		293
Amount £		
1,000,000	93	
200,000	66	
50,000	75	234
Today's sequence no		33
Total:		560

The authorised manager would then use the test key or code 560 when sending the message.

8.8 Authentication

Test keys, as described above, can be used for authentication procedures as well as for encryption. However, tricking the authentication procedure is a common method of evading systems protection. Passwords are commonly used and unfortunately users are lax about their security, either using easily guessed words, eg their children's names, or not changing the password regularly. Some users keep a note of the password in their diary or wallet, even on a note stuck to the terminal! Below are listed some measures to prevent intentional unauthorised access:

1 Sufficient password length to reduce exhaustive search attempts.
2 Assignment of randomly generated passwords to prohibit sequence analysis.
3 Invisible input of passwords to avoid observation or 'scavenging'.
4 Frequent briefing of password holders concerning safekeeping of passwords.
5 Encryption of 'on-line' system password files.
6 Limiting guessing attempts at password through time restricted entry procedure.
7 Frequent random and visible audits to inhibit potential perpetrators and to ensure integrity is safeguarded.
8 Analysis of patterns of password use and failed access attempts.
9 Frequent testing of all protective mechanisms and preparation and implementation of contingency plans to avoid attack during systems or operations failure. (Based on 'Computer Security Defence for Accidentally and Intentionally Caused Losses', D B Parker in *Proceedings of the National Computer Conference 1978.*)

8.9 Data security hazard management

Data—corruption or erasure

HAZARD ASSESSMENT

Possible sources

Damage or destruction of recording media by hazards listed under software corruption and erasure (pp 206–207)
Hardware data storage capacity overloaded
Input errors;
— inaccurate
— incomplete
— duplicated
Loss of input documents

COUNTER-MEASURES

Prevention

Prevention of environment hazards
Prevention of hardware hazards
See prevention of corruption or erasure of software (p 206)
Users responsible for their own data;

— control of input
— review of output
Controls on entry of data:
— program
— administrative and clerical
Time limits for 'on line' storage of data
Housekeeping procedures to:
— summarise older data kept 'on line'
— store details 'off line'
— erase unwanted data
Frequent and systematic copying of data to back-up media and secure
   storage
See prevention of hazards from staff (p 231)
Management vigilance
Operator vigilance
Regular audits may reveal sources of hazard and possible solution

Insurance cover

Cost of replacing recording media
Consequential loss?
Costs of reconstituting data?

Monitoring

Monitoring systems built into hardware and operating software should
   report irregular use of facilities; operator vigilance is necessary.
Generation and review of reports
— amendments to master file data
— input of transaction data
— other printouts of file contents
Surveillance of media storage areas
Environmental monitoring of media storage areas

Corrective action

Corrective action for environment hazards (p 180–186)
Corrective action for hardware hazards (pp 188–193)
Discover source of hazards
Ascertain extent of loss
Assess effects of loss and duration of any downtime
Procedures to re-input data and correct errors
Retrieve data from back-up media stored nearby
Activate disaster plan as necessary

Disaster planning

Ineffective unless other DP resources are covered by disaster planning
Systematically store media containing back-up data in secure, fireproof
   locations:
— nearby, at least daily
— and in remote storage, less frequently
Ensure that users file source documentation and input reports systematically
Devise and test procedures to input back-up data and intermediate data
   from source documentation or input reports.

Data—theft

Possible sources

Unauthorised copying
Unauthorised access by:
— terminal enquiry
— printout
Removal of media
Theft could be by, or on behalf of:
— staff
— commercial rivals
— customers
— suppliers
— trade unions
— pressure groups
— journalists
— hackers, etc
Loss could occur on theft of hardware

COUNTER-MEASURES

Prevention

Vigilance by:
— management
— operators
— users
Controlled access to:
— site
— environment
— storage of recording media
Frequent and systematic recording of data on back-up media
Store sensitive or valuable data 'off line'
User responsibility for safe storage of 'off line' data
Encryption of data:
— on DP files
— in transmission to remote terminals
Segregate different applications
Control distribution of printouts
Program controls on system access to data distinguishing rights to:
— view
— amend
— erase
Automatic limits on access to system by:
— time
— application
— terminal
— user
Password controls on access to software
See prevention of hazards to operations from staff (p 231)
Regular audits may reveal sources of hazard and possible remedies

Insurance cover

> Cost of replacing recording media
> Consequential loss?
> Costs of reconstituting data?

Monitoring

> Monitoring system built into hardware and operating software should
>   report irregular use of facilities; operator vigilance is necessary
> Console log printouts should detail activities by:
> — terminals
> — user identification
> — application
> Review of console printouts by management
> Surveillance of media storage areas

Corrective action

> Discover method of theft
> Ascertain extent of loss
> Assess effects of loss and duration of any downtime
> Retrieve back-up media if necessary
> Change passwords if necessary to prevent further loss
> Activate disaster plan as necessary
> Inform the police

Disaster planning (See disaster planning for data corruption p 214)

> Damage to the commercial viability of the company is more likely than
>   disruption of data processing operations

9.0   SYSTEMS DEVELOPMENT

9.1   Optimising the use of computer resources

The implementation of a new or changed system is a major source of risk,
thus it is reckless to implement systems without adequate testing. Test
methods include the use of test data or some form of parallel operation. The
latter is preferable because it exposes many problems of practical working.
If carried out properly it is inexpensive compared to systems failure; extra
staff and resources will be temporarily required to support two systems and
to appraise results. Similarly a programme of staff training will be required.
The volume of work and unfamiliarity of much of it will increase pressures
upon staff. Normal controls and security procedures may lapse. Ideally,
implementation should be carried out in stages and parallel running should
be done in pilot areas.

Since the computer is a valuable resource with many demands being made
upon it, it is sensible to ensure it is used efficiently and with maximum benefit
for the whole organisation. Many organisations achieve this through a
computer development board or a committee with top management
involvement charged with responsibility for controlling the development of
computer systems. There should be a formal procedure for all development
proposals, each supported by a feasibility study, to be submitted to the

committee for priority ranking and eventual approval to proceed. The committee would rank proposals according to value to the organisation having regard to feasibility. There should also be a procedure for regular monitoring by the committee of progress on approved development projects. There should be no investment of development effort or commitment of resoures beyond the feasibility study stage for any computer development project until it is given formal approval to proceed.

Formal proposals for development of computer systems should cover:

1 Principal objective of the proposed development.
2 Description of the current system.
3 Description of the proposed system.
4 Proposed system structure, flowcharts and coding system.
5 Information proposed to be provided and to whom.
6 Data collection and validation proposals.
7 Data proposed to be held on file.
8 Software requirements.
9 Data processing capacity requirements.
10 Peripheral equipment requirements.
11 Work schedules and staffing requirements.
12 Training requirements.
13 Development programme and project control schedule.
14 Implementation programme and control schedule.
15 Justification statements—commercial, technical and financial.

A computer systems development committee is likely to be most effective when it has just three top management participants representing general management, financial and technical viewpoints respectively. A committee so constituted could be expected to allocate priorities in a way which best served the needs of the business of the organisation while at the same time being both financially and technically sound.

9.2   Ranking computer development projects

9.2.1   *Business need*

This is the most important of the criteria to be considered. The primary objective of every computerised information must always be to serve a business need or corresponding organisational goal in non-business organisations.

Judgements about the business needs will have regard to the degree of dependence of the business on the information to be generated by the proposed system. The benefits and risks may not always be readily measurable. They will often be related to a primary business need to be constantly seeking opportunities to gain or maintain competitive edge in the marketplace. These opportunities emerge as practical goals such as brand image and market share, customer service, premium quality products, competitive costs and so on. The table which follows shows by way of example the specific business needs which are served by some of the more common computerised information systems:

Information system	Business need
1 Market information analysis	To assist in determining action to be taken to optimise market exploitation.
2 Sales order processing	To facilitate efficient customer service.
3 Production planning and control	To facilitate efficient production.
4 Standard costing	To assist management decision making.
5 Budgetary control	To assist in the pursuit of value for money.
6 Fixed asset register	To provide a basis for accounting control and protection of assets.
7 Payroll	To discharge the obligation to reward employees for their labours in a cost effective way.
8 Material management	To provide an information base for cost effective procurement and to match production requirements for materials.
9 Perpetual inventory records	To assist stock management in providing appropriate services to production or to customers and in controlling working capital.
10 Product quality test analyses	To assist the pursuit of efficient quality control.

9.2.2   *Technical feasibility*

Computer technology continues to develop explosively leaving a trail of obsolescence. This means there is a high degree of risk involved in every major decision to proceed with a computer system development. It means the hardware and software being contemplated are likely to be overtaken by more efficient technology, possibly even before the investment has paid for itself.

This again is an area for judgement although in many cases there may be no reasonable alternative to proceeding and having to use the technology that is currently available. Nevertheless it is important that such judgements are as well informed technically as is possible. They should take account of the best available technical advice on the suitability of the technical choices being considered and on the state of the art at the time.

It may sometimes be necessary to weight the risk of choosing unproven technology against investing in established technology which is likely to be more prone to obsolescence. This judgement will of necessity be influenced by a vulnerability factor for the business need. For some applications, the risk of disruption caused by teething troubles with new technology may be totally unacceptable. For example, an organisation serving a highly competitive market would not readily put customer service at risk in the process of developing an improved sales order processing system.

Rapid advances in computer technology will give rise to a need for general enhancement of computer facilities from time to time. These enhancements will absorb resources and will need to be ranked for priority. In many cases there will be no easily identifiable commercial need other than to improve the efficiency or the service potential of data processing facilities. Conversion of operating systems and development of data base systems and networking arrangements would come into this category. For these proposals the technical evaluation would provide the primary criteria for priority ranking.

9.2.3 *Financial criteria*

Developing computer systems absorbs resources which have to be measured and allocated in competition with all other demands for resources. There are various criteria which may be used for the allocation of resources: these are discussed in Chapter 11. Application of resources for developing data processing services represents investment which is expected to contribute to the achievement of corporate objectives in the future. The possibility of obsolescence due to rapid advances in technology may reduce the future time span for effective contribution: for this reason many organisations adopt a prudent accounting policy to write off expenditure on computer developments and particularly on software, as it is incurred. Nevertheless the resources expended on these developments are often substantial and there is a need for this expenditure to be properly controlled.

The project proposal should provide an assessment of resources required for the project in terms of development staff time and the costs of bought in services and equipment. This assessment should be compiled carefully and in some detail with the full commitment of the management submitting the proposal. Once approved, the resource assessment then becomes the budget for controlling the project.

For many major systems development projects, neither the benefits expected nor those achieved will be readily assessable in financial terms. Evaluation may then be a matter of subjective judgement. However there should be operational criteria which can be clearly defined in the project proposal and used as benchmarks for monitoring progress.

9.3 Systems development controls

The main reasons for computerising a system are either the volume of transactions is considered to be too large for the human resources available or the calculations required are so complex that human error would be a problem. As a result the accuracy and reliability of records is dependent on the controls within the computer system. It is important that such controls are initiated at the development stage and also enforced throughout the operation of the computer system. Systems development controls embrace the following objectives: security and privacy, accuracy, completeness, effectiveness, efficiency and economy.

9.3.1   *Documentation*

To ensure adequate details of the knowledge of the systems and programs remains within the organisation, full documentation on the workings of the system should be maintained. Such provision will benefit the following:

1 Management
2 Internal and external auditors
3 The systems development section
4 New employees to the section

Such documentation should be regularly reviewed and updated. It is important to provide documentation for both the systems and the programs supporting those systems. The following chart will act as a checklist:

SYSTEMS AND PROGRAM DOCUMENTATION

	System	*Program*
1 Narrative statement defining objectives		
2 Systems proposal statements		
3 Specification statement		
4 Flowcharts		
5 Input forms		
6 Output records		
7 File record layouts		
8 Computer and audit controls		
9 Program listing		
10 Test data		
11 Evaluation report		
12 Manual giving operating instructions		
13 Output distribution list		
14 Schedule of programs		
15 Amendments		
16 Other documentation etc		

Systems development documentation: planning and control—During the development cycle continuous monitoring and review procedures should operate. Such procedures need to be reported upon:

Technical reports	*Managerial reports*
1 Project initiation report	Report on management
2 Feasibility report	decisions
3 Systems proposal	Reports of a technical
4 Specification report	nature
5 Technical design report	'Commissioning'
6 Construction report	package
7 Implementation report	Report evaluating the
8 Systems review report	success of the operation

Such reports should be identified with a schedule of planning and control (see the example below).

Such a schedule should be agreed and provide for standards against which performance can be realistically monitored and reported upon.

Systems development method and delivery: control areas—B J Travis, in *Auditing and Development of Computer Systems*, identifies the following eight methods:

1 *Identification of objectives*—Goals and performance measures—To establish targets against which to measure performance.
2 *Constraint identification*—To identify constraints or parameters (finance, technical feasibility, etc).
3 *Problem analysis*—To analyse the various problems requiring solution so that underlying causes are clarified.

Schedule planning and control

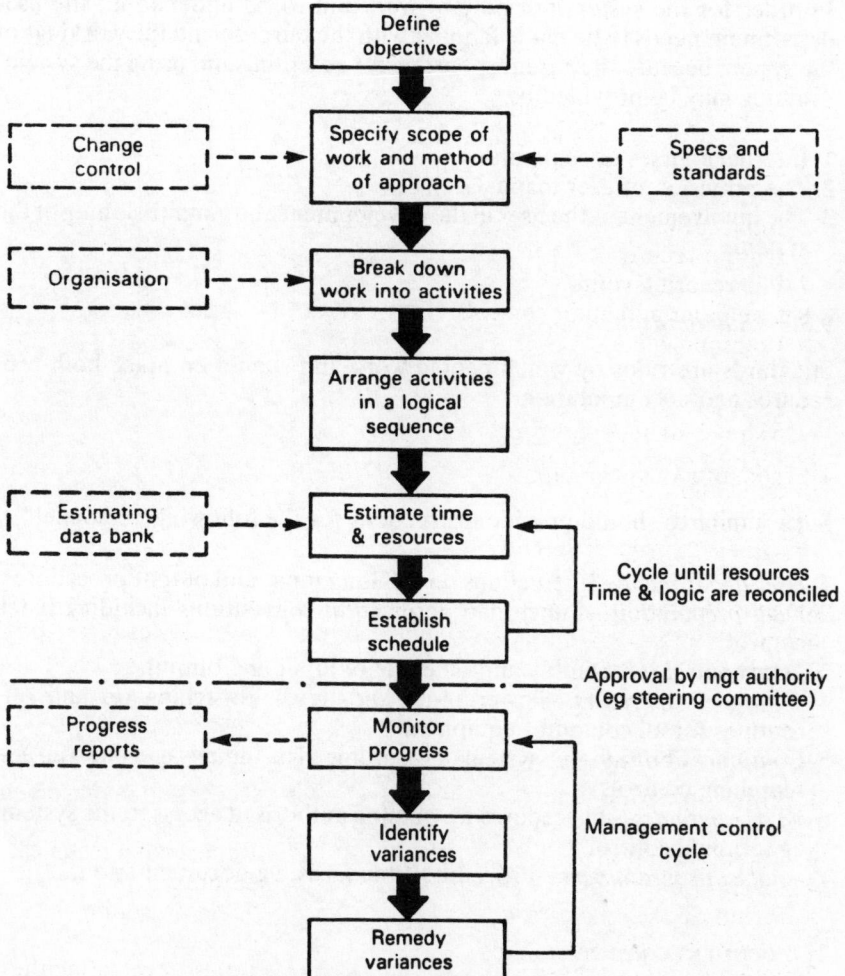

(*Source:* B J Travis *Auditing the Development of Computer Systems*.)

4 *Data analysis*—To allow for the documentation of data resources, thereby providing for the understanding of the operation and inter-relationships within the system.
5 *Functional analysis*—To identify 'what the business does now, or may want to do . . . functional analysis is a top down method which aims to break down the activities of a business in a progressive way from very broad generalisation to the most detailed elementary activity.'
6 *Access path analysis*—To provide a logic path (mapping) to ensure that the logic data model is complete, and that accesses can be quantified.
7 *Solution evaluation*—To ensure that decisions are based on adequate information, eg cost/benefit analysis, social factor table.
8 *Specification*—Documentation supporting systems design detailing relationships within the system, eg computer and clerical data models, transaction user matrix.

9.3.2 User training

In order for the system not only to work but to be understood, the user department needs to be made familiar with the purpose and the workings of the system because they are responsible for accepting and using the system. Training may be provided by:

1 Internal courses or seminars.
2 The provision of user manuals.
3 The involvement of the user in the development and commissioning of the system.

9.3.3 Standards

Standards are rules by which people work and should embrace both procedures and documentation.

1 PROCEDURAL STANDARDS

Such standards should provide instructions for the following personnel:

1 *User department*—Instructions on fulfilling input and output procedures.
2 *Data preparation*—Punch and verification conventions including batch control.
3 *Data control*—Assembly and schedule of input and output.
4 *Computer operators*—Powering-up and down (switching on and off) routines for all computer equipment.
5 *Computer librarian*—A system of recording files, their usage, back-up and searching controls.
6 *VDU operators*—Procedures for gaining authorised access to the system, eg terminal control.
7 *Analyst/programmers*—Procedural standards, eg documentation.

2 DOCUMENTATION STANDARDS

All documentation should be compiled in an agreed format that is understood by all that may use it.

9.3.4 *Testing*

To have confidence in the output of the systems and programs these should be tested to ensure they are working correctly. The following development tests may be used:

1 *Desk checking*—The programmer checks the logic of the program at his desk (sometimes this is called a 'walk through' test). Such a technique can be assisted by the use of a 'cross-referencing list' obtained from the manufacturers.
2 *Test data*—'Dummy' data is sent to the operators with instructions for testing the program on the computer.
3 *Siphoned data*—Live input extracted from live system for testing.
4 *Suite test*—'Dummy' data is run through the entire system to examine the effect that the new development will have on the system as a whole.

Once tested, an evaluation report should be produced explaining how and why the test was run. Pilot and parallel runnings are also used for proving the system. It should be noted that where a new format has been established, records from the old system should be accurately transferred to the new system (format), eg comparison of balances brought forward on a new system with those carried forward from the old system.

9.3.5 *Approval*

All developments should be authorised at each stage by the appropriate committee or senior manager. This is best undertaken by a steering committee on which are represented:

1 Senior management—To give approval.
2 Systems development personnel—To plan the project.
3 Members of the user department—To specify systems requirements.
4 Internal audit—To provide service advice.

9.3.6 *Conversion*

Systems or files undergoing conversion to a new system should be controlled by:

1 Reconciliation between old and new systems.
2 Sample checking between systems.
3 Sequence testing.

Prior to conversion taking place it is prudent either to parallel run (both systems operating simultaneously until the new one is finally approved) or pilot run (where a section of the new system runs simultaneously with the old system). It is not advisable to undertake a direct changeover (direct take-on).

9.3.7 *Amendments*

Detection and correction of errors together with other improvements should be controlled to ensure that the resultant amendments are:

1 Authorised.

2 Recorded.
3 Tested prior to entry on the live system.

By way of example the following diagram illustrates the various computer personnel associated with systems development control:

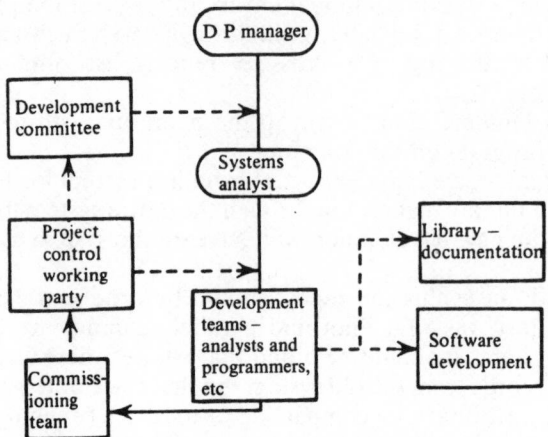

9.3.8 *Conclusion*

The internal auditor needs firstly to provide management with reassurance that systems development and associated procedures are functioning efficiently and effectively. Secondly, to ensure that controls introduced are adequate and that the system is appropriate to the user's purposes. Thirdly, to provide management with advice concerning any devices required to enhance auditability. The introduction of concurrent auditing by the auditor allows for advice that may resolve current problems and thus assist in determining present strategy.

9.4 Systems development hazard management

Systems development and implementation

HAZARD ASSESSMENT

> User requirements not met
> Continuity of operations not achieved
> Poor value for money provided
> Unauthorised changes to system
> Incomplete processing

COUNTER-MEASURES

> User committee
> Policy to rank priorities
> Adequate documentation
> User training
> Compliance with programming standards
> Proper testing
> Authorisation controls

Commissioning and formal acceptance by user
Written specification
Budgetary control

Insurance cover

Cost of replacement
Consequential loss

Monitoring

Periodic progress reports
Matching specificiation to actual performance
Staff changes
Preparation of operational manuals

Corrective action

Determine programme for rescheduling
Discover reasons for variation from agreed plan
Ascertain consequence of delay or inadequacy
Formally record concern
Notify contractor or employee(s)
Set date to review progress

Disaster planning

Reschedule work
Inform those affected
Maintain current system
Minimise loss

10.0 STAFF HAZARDS

10.1 Introduction

HAZARDS TO STAFF

These hazards are highly unpredictable, mostly being external to the organisation and thus beyond management control. Due to the cost of employing
staff, there is a tendency to maintain staff at the minimum level necessary for
operations resulting in increased vulnerability when key staff leave. Loss of
any staff can seriously weaken data processing operations and software
development capabilities. Staff availability should be key elements in any
disaster plan.

HAZARDS FROM STAFF

These hazards are as likely to occur in data processing operations as in any
other activity. Computer facilities can be abused to cause considerable
damage to data very rapidly. User organisations need to protect themselves
using normal management techniques as well as technical controls. However, it must be stressed that total reliance cannot be placed upon technical
controls alone. Proper monitoring and motivation of staff is a more secure
control than a lock on a computer-room door or written instructions.

In order for the internal auditor to evaluate staffing controls, an understanding of the environment and a rapport with the manager are necessary. Thus, we have summarised job descriptions of the various staff that are likely to work in this environment. Modern computer practice encourages work being undertaken in teams, thereby overriding the segregation of duties control. Such a system is believed to be more efficient and effective in achieving results. The auditor needs to be aware of both custom and practice as well as the cost of implementing audit recommendations.

10.2   Relationship with audit manager

The audit manager should ensure that in computer audit the same professional standards are applied as other audit matters, ie adequate documentation, regular reporting and sound auditing techniques. However, as with any other specialism, the computer auditor should be prepared to educate other auditors in the skill and use of his knowledge for the general benefit of all auditors.

10.3   Relationship with computer manager

'To maintain a co-operative and professional understanding of computer techniques ensuring that the computer is used to assist audit work and not to work for audit.' (CIPFA Computer Audit Guidelines)

It is now appropriate to develop this line of thought towards the computer department and the role of the personnel in it. Mention has been made of the relationship with the computer manager, and the auditor must be aware of his role, and that of the computer department, in the organisation. Most computer departments have two main areas of activity: the design of systems; and the operation of those systems. An organisation chart is set out below, together with a list of duties typically found in a computer department:

Typical computer department organisation

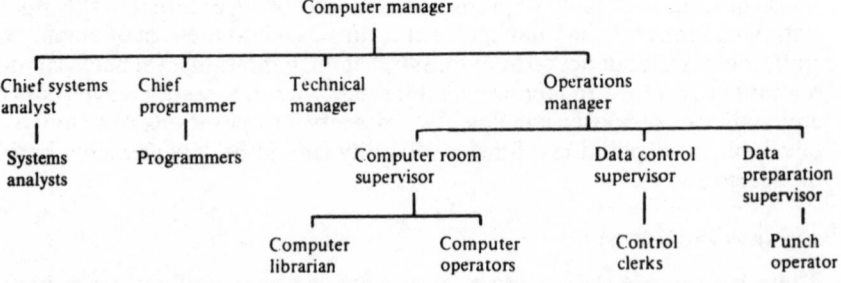

10.4   List of typical duties

COMPUTER MANAGER

1 To plan and undertake all activities necessary to provide an effective data processing service to the organisation.

2 To be responsible for the department's budgetary process.
3 To attend the computer users' and development committees.
4 To recruit, select and train staff.
5 To advise on the selection of necessary equipment to maintain efficient operations.
6 To establish and enforce agreed standards and procedures.
7 To liaise with internal audit where appropriate.
8 To maintain technical advisory services to user departments.
9 To review and report progress regarding project schedules and cost budgets to the computer users' and development committees.

SYSTEMS ANALYST

1 To carry out feasibility studies for proposed systems to determine the resources required.
2 To prepare outline systems specifications to demonstrate how systems would operate.
3 To perform fact-finding operations on current systems. Assess workloads being undertaken.
4 To design input/output files and processes for new computer applications.
5 To compile procedure manuals for use by computer staff.
6 To co-ordinate systems design work.
7 To provide test data and to supervise all program and systems testing.
8 To make periodic checks to ensure operational systems comply with stated objectives.
9 To attend the computer users' and development committees.

PROGRAMMER

1 To interpret the analyst's specifications into program specifications.
2 The chief programmer is to produce work schedules of work undertaken and work to be undertaken, giving 'target' times.
3 Test programs using data supplied by analyst.
4 Ensure adequate computer operating instructions exist.
5 Produce all necessary program documentation.
6 Perform maintenance or updating of programs as required.

COMPUTER OPERATOR

1 Assemble all required input data for each operation.
2 Ensure adequate stationery available.
3 Operate all equipment in compliance with programmer's instructions.
4 Monitor output and record rejected data, program failures and other interruptions.
5 Record machine utilisation.
6 Assist programmer during testing operations.

As can be seen, with regard to the organisation of a computer section, separation of duties is an important feature of internal control.

10.5 Procedures and discipline

It is important that manuals of instruction are adhered to and that operating procedures are strictly enforced. Where it is not possible to adhere to procedures because of staff shortages, illness etc there should be a procedure for increased controls and checks on the data being processed to be applied.

10.6   Computer personnel: audit reports

Although usually beyond the auditor's brief a report should be made upon the competence of computer staff—without computer staff internal controls will be difficult to establish. The following matters should be examined:

1 Staff should be adequately qualified (MBCS).
2 Staff should have proven experience.
3 Staff should be loyal, interested and co-operative.

Item 3 presents problems because promotion for computer staff may well not exist within the organisation but rather by moving to another organisation, ie to another similar computer system, thus corporate objectives may be of secondary importance to acquiring new technical expertise.

Rapid turnover can easily lead to poor morale and lack of efficiency, leading to a vulnerable system. It is most important to maintain the pay of computer personnel on a par with others in the field.

10.7   Staff hazard management

Staff—hazards from operations

HAZARD ASSESSMENT

Possible sources

Discomfort, illness, injury or death caused by:
environmental hazards
— hardware hazards
— electrocution
— noise
— VDU glare
— poor ventilation
— excessive heat or cold
— air conditioning faults
— fire extinguisher systems
— loose cables
— open hardware cabinets
— improper storage of printouts
— disputes
— overwork
— boredom, etc

COUNTER-MEASURES

Prevention

Management vigilance
Prevention of environment hazards (see pp 180–186)

Prevention of hardware hazards (see pp 188–193)
Keep the environment tidy
Ensure the environment is large enough for equipment and operators
Control access to the environment
Prohibit food, drink and smoking in the environment
False floors and ducts for cables
Keep equipment cabinets locked shut
Adequate lighting
Adequate ventilation
Adequate seating
Acousting damping of hardware and other sources of noise
Manual overrides to automatic fire extinguisher systems
Time limits on VDU use
Enforce rest breaks
Ensure staff take full holiday entitlements
Control the level of overtime worked
Train staff in safety awareness
Adequate motivation and remuneration of staff
Regular audits and safety inspections may reveal sources of hazard and
   possible remedies

Insurance cover

Public liability
Life insurance for key staff
Health insurance for key staff

Monitoring

Management vigilance and judgement
Joint staffing of environment outside normal business hours
Holiday planning
Review of attendance and sickness records
Health and safety meetings
Company medical service

Corrective action

Train staff in dealing with hazards:
— fire
— electrocution
— first aid
Discover source of hazard
Assess effect of hazard and duration of any downtime
Activate disaster plan as necessary

Disaster planning (More effective if there is disaster planning for other DP
resources)

Nominate and train potential replacements for key staff

Staff—external hazards

HAZARD ASSESSMENT

Possible sources

Numerous including:
— accidents

— ill health
— absenteeism
— alcoholism and drug abuse
— domestic problems
— mental problems
— financial problems
— violence
— death
— imprisonment, etc
Some may be a consequence of adverse working conditions

COUNTER-MEASURES

Prevention

Management vigilance
Medical checks before employment
Careful staff selection and promotion procedures
Prohibit all key staff from travelling together
Prevent hazards from operations (see pp 228–229)
Promote a happy working environment
Ensure that staff are adequately motivated and remunerated
Ensure staff take full holiday entitlements
Ensure staff take rest breaks
Control the level of overtime worked
Many hazards are beyond management control and necessitate disaster
   planning
Regular audit of operations and safety inspections may reveal sources
   of hazard and possible solutions

Insurance cover

Life insurance for key staff
Health insurance for key staff

Monitoring

Management vigilance
Performance assessment
Regular appraisal interviews
Review of attendance and sickness records

Corrective action

Management judgement
Interviews and counselling
Grievance procedures
Discover source of hazard
Assess effect of hazard and duration of any downtime
Activate disaster plan as necessary

Disaster planning (See disaster planning for hazards from operations p 229)

Staff—hazards to operation

HAZARD ASSESSMENT

Possible sources

Disruption or reduced efficiency caused by:
— ignorance

— carelessness
— accidents
— grievances
— disputes
— industrial action
— fraud
— sabotage
— theft of computer time
— malicious activities, etc

COUNTER-MEASURES

Prevention

Management vigilance
Particular care is necessary in cases of dismissal and redundancy
Careful definition of recruitment requirements:
— DP qualifications
— DP experience
— DP training
— satisfactory references, which should be taken up
Procedural manuals
Regular training and retraining of staff
Adequate grievance procedures
Planned use of computer time
Rotation of duties
Adequate password procedures
Division of responsibilities
Joint staffing of DP facilities beyond normal office hours
Prevent hazards from operations
Regular audits of operations may reveal sources of hazards and possible
   remedies

Insurance cover

Cover as described under:
— environment (pp 180–186)
— hardware (p 188–193)
— software (pp 206–209)
— data (pp 213–216)
Public liability
Life insurance for key staff
Health insurance for key staff

Monitoring

Management vigilance
Operator vigilance
Performance monitoring
Appraisal interviews
Management review of operating reports
Regular audit of operations

Corrective action

Management judgement
Grievance procedures

Negotiation and arbitration
Disciplinary procedures
Safety drill for emergencies
Discover source of hazard
Ascertain extent of damage
Assess effect of damage and duration of any downtime
Activate disaster plan as necessary
Inform the police as necessary

Disaster planning

Disaster planning for hazards to:
— environment (pp 180–186)
— hardware (pp 188–193)
— software (pp 206–209)
— data (pp 213–216)
— staff (pp 228–233)

Staff—probable events

HAZARD ASSESSMENT

Possible sources

Illness, employee or family
Holidays
Pregnancy
Retirement
Staff turnover:
— joiners
— promotions
— transfers
— leavers
These events should be accommodated in routine planning but can
cause disruption or reduced efficiency.

COUNTER-MEASURES

Prevention

Management vigilance
Available actions can reduce effects of hazards on operations rather
than their incidence
Holiday notification and planning
Nominate and train staff to cover for absentees
Use holidays to give cover staff practical experience
Planned recruitment of new staff
Training and induction of new staff
Adequate motivation and remuneration of staff
Adequate notice periods
Healthy working environment
Regular audits of operations may reveal sources of hazard and possible
remedies

Insurance cover (Not applicable)

Monitoring

Management vigilance
Review of attendance and sickness records
Review of intended holiday periods
Regular audit of operations

Corrective action

Management judgement
Change system passwords when key staff leave
Change individual passwords of all leavers
Assess effects of staff absence and duration of any disruption
Employ temporary staff if necessary
Activate disaster plan as necessary

Disaster planning (Should not be applicable)

See disaster planning for hazards to staff from operations (p 229)

11.0 DISASTER PLANNING

11.1 Objective

The objective of disaster planning is to survive and recover, at any time, when normal security procedures have been insufficient to prevent a disaster. For the purposes of computer operations, a disaster may be considered to be substantial operating delays or damage to, or complete destruction of, normal data processing facilities. The effort and resources directed to disaster planning should be proportionate to the organisation's dependence upon the facilities and the data at risk.

11.2 Damage assessment

Plans should include procedures and responsibilities for rapidly ascertaining the extent of any loss of resource and assessing the consequences, including the likely duration of the disruption to continuity of operations. In major disasters, priority should be given to continued generation of essential information over recreation of previous data processing facilities. The irony of a disaster is that it may provide the organisation with the opportunity to upgrade its computer facilities.

11.3 Essential information

Plans should be made identifying essential information, and the limits of delay and frequency of provision that can be tolerated by the organisation. During any disaster the user can concentrate upon preserving only essential data; unnecessary dissipation of effort may terminate an otherwise retrievable operation.

OTHER INFORMATION

1 *Timescale for recovery*—Plans should detail: what is to be done; when; frequency and duration.

2 *Details should include*—Immediate action; medium-term action; retrieval of the normal situation; prevention of future disaster.

3 *Responsibilities*—Provisions should be made for: temporary staff; release of key staff; liaison with staff in user departments.

11.4   Alternative arrangements

It is important that arrangements are made to allow for survival. Such arrangements should include the provision of alternative facilities—location; capacity; times available; period available; probable costs; limitations.

It is to be expected that owners of such facilities will allow their own work to have preferential treatment, giving the victim of disaster a lower priority. It is thus important that the status allocated to the victim's work is previously agreed in writing. It is too late to establish the victim's rights once the crisis has occurred.

Use of alternative facilities will require the transfer of information: consequently arrangements must be made for hard copy; handling procedures; controls; telecommunication lines; transmission equipment and use of terminals.

11.5   Internal audit review

Internal audit should regularly appraise and update disaster plans to ensure that they remain based upon valid assumptions. Other alternative arrangements may since have been developed, or changed, or the current system in use may invalidate the plan.

11.6   Testing the plan

In practice, management often decides that the cost of testing the complete plan is prohibitive. However, the plan can be segmented to allow for the testing of each segment individually, without incurring cessation of current operations. Tests should be as realistic as possible and should be carefully monitored and evaluated for future updating of the plan.

11.7   Gathering information

As with all audit techniques, documentation of evidence is essential to the ongoing appraisal of the plan. To achieve this the following assessment schedule is useful.

ESSENTIAL INFORMATION ASSESSMENT SCHEDULE

APPLICATION—

Details of information

Purpose of information

Potential consequences of loss:

Production method

Time taken

Frequency of generation:
(a) normal
(b) tolerable
Alternative production methods:

Probable times taken

Priority ranking

11.8   Total computer security concept (TSC)

The traditional approach identifying the various security aspects of computers individually is considered an outmoded concept. Current thinking is towards treating security as one concept enveloping all aspects, thereby taking account of the inter-relationship of all computer activity. This concept is called the total computer security concept (TSC). TSC, developed by Leonard H Fine in his book *Computer Security—a Handbook for Management*, has taken a new approach to an old problem. This concept has adopted a broad approach identifying two areas:

1 Management problems.
2 Technical and procedural problems.

These areas may be summarised as follows:

Management	*Technical*
1 Defined security policy	6 Equipment and data security
2 Organisational structure	7 File security
3 Physical security	8 Systems standards
4 Insurance protection	9 Internal audit role
5 Personnel practices	10 Catastrophe planning, testing and accommodation

Examination of the composition of these two areas reveals that there is not one element which, in its own right, is of supreme importance.

In order to apply the total security concept it is recommended that a computer security committee or working group is established with responsibilities to:

1 Devise and implement a written security policy.
2 Agree the assignment of responsibilities for security.
3 Implement controls and remedial measures.
4 Review and test the adequacy of computer security.

Members of such a group should be drawn from:

1 Senior management.
2 Computer management.
3 Internal audit.
4 External audit.
5 Insurance advisers.

The primary objective of any computer operation is to maintain continuity of service. Similarly, the auditor, when examining computer systems and related equipment, is attempting to ensure that the installation and its operations are protected against catastrophe. The approach to examining the provision should be undertaken in a methodical manner, eg the use of a checklist.

11.9 Internal control and computer systems

In many organisations the computer department is part of the responsibility of the director of finance. It exists to provide information for users as a whole, based on data submitted.

With regard to internal control, the computer department should not be the originators of input, nor should they act upon output.

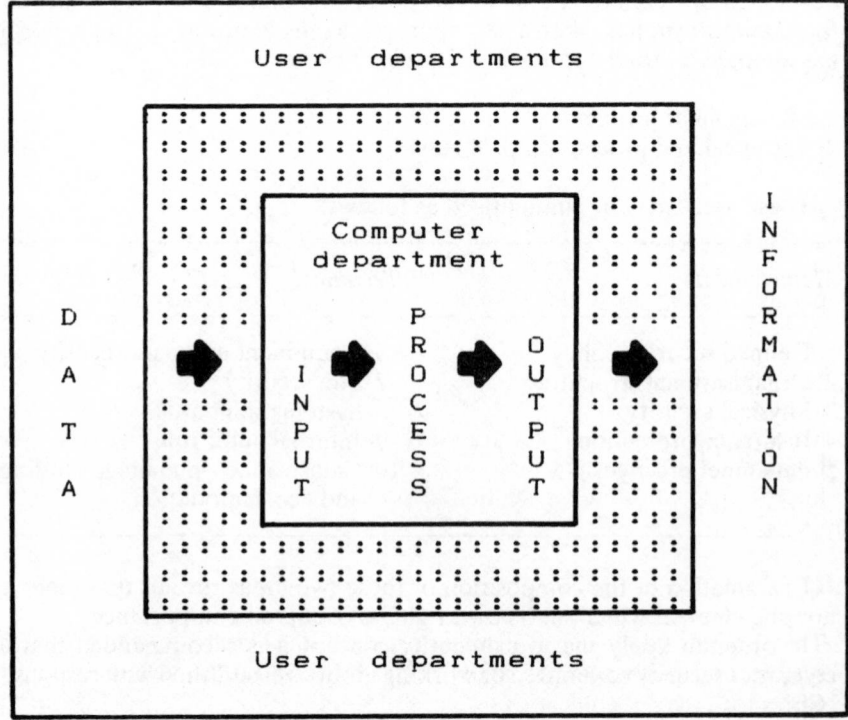

This diagram illustrates the major control—the segregation of duties—keeping the computer department isolated from user functions: the 'moat and castle effect'.

12.0 ACQUISITION OF COMPUTER FACILITIES

12.1 Objectives of audit

'To assess the adequacy of the procedures employed by an organisation when acquiring computer facilities.' (*Acquisition of Computer Facilities—An Audit Methodology* (DOE))

When examining the decision-making procedures leading up to the purchase decision the auditor should examine whether the following factors have been taken into account:

12.2 Cost

The computer market is fiercely competitive, making it difficult for the layman to evaluate equipment based on cost alone. Cost is obviously important but so too is the provision of servicing facilities, compatibility with existing hardware/software, manufacturer's product strategy and the life of the machine before it becomes obsolete. As with any item of major expenditure the organisation's procedures should be adopted.

12.3 Financial appraisal

A clear indication of costs and quantifiable benefits, properly appraised and capable of being measured after commissioning, should be stated.

12.4 Internal controls

As with systems development, the internal auditor should be acting as adviser during the appraisal stage. This should not be perceived as tarnishing the auditor's independence. The auditor must take care to avoid active participation in the decision so as not to compromise independence.

12.5 Flexibility

Modern equipment is 'user friendly' and becoming increasingly flexible, being able to undertake many varied tasks at one time. The flexibility is likely to provide some protection against obsolescence.

12.6 Impact

The computer may involve major organisational changes affecting staff, systems and daily operation of the organisation. An attempt should be made to evaluate such changes.

Once the auditor has examined whether or not sufficient information has been gathered, to ensure adequate discussion and to arrive at a reasonable decision, the following areas should be examined:

1 Decision-making structure—A multi-discipline working party with union representation should be established with the responsibility to oversee the purchase of computer equipment.
2 A feasibility study should take place to determine the likelihood of success of the proposed solution.
3 A specification should be drafted to meet the need so that competing suppliers can submit their proposals.
4 Such proposals should be evaluated in a methodical manner, with regard to costs, technical ability, delivery, reliability, maintenance and ease of commissioning.
5 Contractual documents and administration of the contract—see Chapter 9.
6 Post commissioning review to examine whether or not the installation is meeting the specification laid down in the original contract.

The auditor should maintain adequate documentation and provide regular review reports on the progress of all activity to evaluate the purchase of computer facilities.

13.0 COMPUTER FRAUD

The expression computer fraud is used to describe any fraud connected with a computer, however remotely. Many such frauds are not attributable to computer technology but are due to clerical control failures. Auditors have classified fraudulent practices where computers may be involved into three categories:

1 *Computer related fraud*—This occurs when computer processing is involved but no specific computer technology is applied in perpetrating or concealing the fraud. Standard internal control procedures will reduce this risk.
2 *Computer assisted fraud*—This occurs when computer system procedures are misused in order to conceal a fraudulent practice. Sound computer system controls applied with the necessary discipline will reduce this risk.
3 *Computer dependent fraud*—This occurs when computer technology is applied in the fraudulent manipulation of transaction data.

13.1 Computer fraud methods

1 *Data input*—Fraudulent data added or authentic data replaced by fraudulent data. Granting unauthorised discounts. Charging for fictitious services.
2 *File creation*—Creating unauthorised accounts in which the movement of misappropriated funds may be concealed and to which access can be gained. Creating bogus supplier accounts. Creating ghost employees.

3 *File amendment*—Error correction procedures used to make fraudulent changes. Unauthorised amendments to records.
4 *Irregular transfer*—Misappropriation by unauthorised transfer of funds to a legitimate account to which access can be gained.
5 *Program amendment*—Unauthorised amendments ('patches') made for fraudulent purposes.
6 *Faulty program*—A computer program with a capability written into it by which unauthorised transfer of funds may occur and be concealed so becoming available for misappropriation. This is more likely to occur as a sin of omission than of commission on the part of the programmer. When it is intentional it is 'programmed embezzlement'. Because of the ability of programmers to conceal what they are doing, programmed frauds can remain undetected without the use of advanced computer audit technology including computer assisted audit techniques (CAAT).
7 *Programmed sabotage*—Computer programs may contain instructions to be triggered by defined events such as dates, transaction parameters, specific transactions or transactions involving recourse to specified files. It is thus feasible for an erring programmer, probably motivated by revenge rather than greed, to write into a program, a devasting course of events to be invoked at some future time ('time bomb'). The results could include irreversible erasure or corruption of critical files or release of confidential information.
8 *Hackers*—Networked computer systems using public communications services are vulnerable to unauthorised interception. This also applies to any computer systems which are connected by public telephone lines to remote locations for on line data collection or access. Hackers will have well developed skills in computer technology and time and patience. The motivation could be greed, revenge or technological challenge. The results could be serious damage from theft to misdirection of funds, irreversible erasure or corruption of files or theft of confidential information.

Hacking is a criminal offence under the Computer Misuse Act 1990 where it is defined as including:

1 unauthorised electronic intrusion;
2 intervention to facilitate further crime such as blackmail; and
3 unauthorised modification of computer material; for example a computer virus.

13.2 Categories of computer fraud

Michael Cowen listed eight categories of computer fraud in *Professional Administration* June 1979. These are cases where a computer might be used to perpetuate or to conceal fraudulent activity; they are shown here starting with the most probable and ending with the least probable.

COMPUTER AIDED FRAUDS

1 Input of false data or code for transactions or communication transfers.
2 Failures, errors or delays in reconciling listings and balances.
3 False amendments to master files.

4 Manipulation of data into suspense accounts, exceptions and errors.
5 Manipulation, diversion or destruction of output.

COMPUTER DEPENDENT FRAUDS

6 Diversion of processing to a false program or false data source by using irregular instructions.
7 Unauthorised amendment to an application program.
8 Unauthorised amendment to computer operating system or hardware.

13.3   Preventive measures

1 *Management policy*—It is a management responsibility to maintain effective internal control. This responsibility is unlikely to be fulfilled unless there is a climate of honesty. The management must nevertheless, be alert to the opportunities for fraudulent practices to occur. It is necessary to cultivate conditions which encourage loyalty to the organisation and respect for its control procedures and also for the law. Two conditions are crucial: firstly, the example set by management throughout the organisation must be at all times beyond reproach; and secondly, any wrongdoing discovered must be seen to be dealt with fairly but firmly.
2 *Internal control*—Formal systems of internal control are an essential feature of every effectively managed organisation. Their purpose is to ensure that management policy and directives will be properly implemented as intended. They should also ensure that the endeavours of all employees contribute towards achieving the established objectives of the organisation. Thus the internal control system should effectively prevent individuals from interpreting organisational goals in their own way or indeed from pursuing conflicting goals of their own such as theft, embezzlement, computer fraud, etc. The conditions necessary for sound internal control are discussed in Chapter 2: the essentials are:
   (a) Sound organisational structure;
   (b) Management support;
   (c) Adequate staffing;
   (d) Segregation of duties; and
   (e) Internal check.
   The adequacy of the system of internal control must always be judged against these criteria. Prevention of computer related or computer assisted fraud depends upon proper control of data and data processing activities, whereas controls to prevent computer dependent fraud must focus on the activities of programmers.
3 *Internal audit*—The role of internal audit is to support and assist management in cultivating a climate of honesty and fraud prevention. In the context of preventing computer fraud, the internal audit task is to evaluate the adequacy and effectiveness of the system of internal control. There should not be a presumption of fraud but internal auditors should be alert to the possibilities for fraud to occur. They should endeavour to identify for corrective action, system weaknesses which could permit irregularities to pass undetected. System weaknesses have to be judged in terms of the criteria for internal control listed above. This evaluation requires a sound understanding of computerised data processing technology and, in certain cases, advanced technical knowledge. However,

the most critical area for consideration in the prevention of computer dependent fraud is the system by which programmers' activities are managed, including supervision, review and checking of work done.

14.0 DATA PROTECTION AND PRIVACY (DPP)

Prior to discussing this subject it is best to define the subject area:

Privacy—The individual's right to control the circulation of data relating to him or her.

Personal data—Any data which relates or can be related to an identifiable individual.

This subject area has been one of controversy. However, it is appropriate to refer first to the Lindop Report on Data Protection 1978, which made the following recommendations:

1 *Interests of individuals*—The individual should know what data is being kept about himself or herself, for what reason and use and for what timespan.

2 *Interests of users*—To handle data for stated lawful purposes without unreasonable extra cost.

3 *Interests of the community*—To enjoy the benefits that may come from the handling of personal data.

4 *Registration*—Personnel handling data for central and local government should be registered.

5 *Criminal sanctions*—The individual has redress through the criminal courts.

6 *Protective agency*—This should be self-financing from registration fees with the objective of enforcing recommendations.

14.1 Background to legislation

Other countries such as Sweden, USA and Germany now have DPP legislation. The Council of Europe has issued a Convention, to which Britain is a signatory, with the aim of protecting individuals from unscrupulous users of their personal data through the establishment of standards. The result of this Convention is that countries adopting these standards could refuse to allow information to be transferred to those that do not have such standards. Consequently, if adopted, as expected, by EC, it would inhibit Britain's commercial interests not to be able to transfer data (Sweden is thought to have already refused to allow data to be transferred.)

The 1984 Act has eight major principles regarding personal data stored by data users which are:

1 Data must be fairly and lawfully obtained, ie the user's register.
2 Data must be held for one or more specified purposes.

3 Data should not be disclosed other than for a specified purpose.
4 Data should be adequate, relevant and not excessive to its specified purpose.
5 Similarly it should be current, ie up-to-date.
6 It should not be stored for longer than needed for the specified purpose.
7 Access to such data should be made available within 40 days, when reasonable, to data subjects, who may ask for that data to be corrected or deleted.
8 It should be adequately protected against loss or disclosure.

A 'special principle' regarding bureaux and users stated that the data shuld be secure against unlawful access, alteration, disclosure, accidental loss and destruction. Internal audit is involved because where an organisation as data user unreasonably breaches the first three principles then that organisation could be criminally liable and a fine or deregristration notice could be incurred—the Act establishes a Data Protection Registrar with whom data users must be registered. Any officer of the organisation could also be liable. The following quote identifies problems that require attention:

'Internal audit should keep management informed on compliance with such legislation, eg:
1 What would constitute sufficient information for the data user to perform a search?
2 What would accurately identify the data subject?
3 What would constitute a reasonable fee?
4 What procedures could be introduced to keep within the 40-day limit?
5 How should records be edited to ensure third party anonymity?
6 How should personal data be selected from a database when the organisation has more than one register purpose?
7 How can the applicant be sure that complete erasure or change has been made? (Source based on C W Barrie *Internal Auditing*, March 1984)

14.2 Audit procedures

1 Confirm with management that the organisation is complying with the Act—Review both manual and computer phases of the system.
2 Confirm that the organisation can meet requests for information from data subjects—Undertake tests and evaluations of data held.
3 Be satisfied that the computer department is operating in accordance with the Act's principles—Review the environment that the computer system operates in, maintenance procedures (hardware and software), and systems development.
4 Determine that registration procedures have been complied with.
5 Ensure a staff member of suitable status and expertise is responsible for compliance with the Act.

Auditors must be aware of developments, both legal and technical, ensuring the organisation takes reasonable measures to protect itself against fines or other measures and it would be a wise precaution for internal auditors to consider the principles and to evaluate how the organisation might achieve a reasonable measure of compliance. Such principles would be a first stage in progressing to meet this legislation.

Some exemptions from compliance with the legislation:

1 Data held for law enforcement and Revenue purposes.
2 Data held by certain bodies for regulating those providing financial services.
3 Legally privileged data.
4 Data for 'back-up' purposes.
5 Data for statistical and research purposes.

14.3   Guideline on data privacy

Principles for the protection of the privacy of personal information in computer systems:

1   PUBLIC NOTE

All computer systems holding personal information should be publicly known and notified to the Registrar.

2   RIGHT DATA

Personal information held in computer systems should be accurate, complete, relevant and timely, ie when the specific need for retention no longer exists, it should be erased.

3   SECURITY

Personal information held in computer systems should be adequately secured against unauthorised access.

4   LEGITIMACY

Personal information in computer systems should be collected and used for legitimate purposes—As specified to the Registrar.

5   MINIMUM DATA TRAFFIC

Personal information should pass through computer systems to the minimum extent only and for the minimum time necessary for the legitimate purposes.

6   SUBJECT VERIFICATION

The data subject should be able to verify and correct all information held about him or her in any computer system and discover how it has been used.

7   INDEPENDENT SUPERVISION

Someone independent should be able to enforce these principles fairly—Data Protection Manager and the Registrar.
(Based on extracts from Paul Sieghard *Privacy and Computers* (1976).)

Further reading

Chambers, A D and Court, J M *Computer auditing* (2nd edn, 1986) (Pitman).

Computer auditing guidelines (3rd edn, 1987), CIPFA.

Data protection codes of practice (1990) (NCC Blackwell).

Disaster and contingency planning in the data processing environment (1988) (IIA-UK).

Setting up computer audit (1988) (IIA-UK).

Franks, R V in association with CIMA *Commonsense computer management* (1989) (Kogan Page).

Hearnden, K *A handbook of computer security* (1990) (Kogan Page).

Mair, C W, Wood, D R and Davies, R W *Computer control and audit* (3rd edn, 1978) (IIA Inc).

Travis, B J *Auditing the development of computing systems* (1987) (Butterworths).

CHAPTER 8   Financial security

Objectives	To describe the various methods of verifying assets and liabilities, for reviewing the audit examination and for reporting the audit findings
Contents	Vouching and verification of assets and liabilities; post audit reviews
Summary	The primary purpose of financial security auditing is to confirm that the resources of the organisation are adequately protected and controlled. The findings from recognised audit examination techniques should be carefully analysed leading to sound audit judgements. These should be presented clearly and boldly to the management concerned as the basis for positive reassurance or recommendations for action to strengthen protection or control

ASSET AND LIABILITY VERIFICATION

'Internal auditors should review the means of safeguarding assets, and, as appropriate verify the existence of such assets.' (IIA–UK)

1.0   TANGIBLE FIXED ASSETS

The purpose of asset verification is to confirm that the assets have a value to the organisation and furthermore that those assets are suitably safeguarded.

Public sector regulations

Adequate documentation should exist, appropriately authorised, to allow the purchase or disposal of an asset. All assets, their location, cost and the person responsible for them should be listed in a fixed asset register. The assets should then be classified as being either of a 'fixed' nature: land, buildings, etc which should be recorded in a legal 'terrier' and cross-referenced to legal files, or those which are financially attractive, portable and above a predetermined value which should be recorded in an inventory. The inventory should have a person nominated to be responsible for these assets, who should complete an annual check prior to forwarding the inventory to audit who may undertake a physical inspection. Where equipment is loaned to another employee, a loans record should be maintained recording the date and the name of the person 'borrowing' the item. All losses should be reported to audit, who may then notify the police and the insurance company. Where items are scrapped, audit should ensure approval is given for disposal and that any income is credited to the organisation (maybe after receiving tenders?). Pieces of equipment particularly vulnerable to disappearance include computers and photographic equipment.

Possession and ownership

Possession does not prove ownership. To verify ownership procedures include physical inspection where the inventory should be initialled and dated by the auditor. The ownership should be checked—invoice or title deeds (where the terrier should be initialled and dated). Auditors often find it difficult to identify technical equipment. It is necessry to match machine/trade number on the invoice against the inventory and the machine.

The distinction between revenue and capital expenditure is important. Generally a capital item exists for longer than a year and may be used to produce wealth. A revenue item is one that is consumed in the production of wealth, ie a trading operation. The importance in distinction is not only for budgetary control but to allow correct accounting treatment such as the method of depreciation to be considered. Similarly, the tax position should also be considered. The organisation should have a policy regarding these matters and the auditor should verify that it is being observed. It is important that assets are correctly valued, to give an appreciation of the worth to the organisation and to allow the effectiveness of the use of its assets to be evaluated and to identify those assets which are not being utilised to the full. Protection includes physical security, ie safes, locks and security patrols. Insurance should also be considered.

The following diagram illustrates the procedures used when verifying fixed assets.

ASSET VERIFICATION

Asset	In year of acquisition		Annually			
	Cost	*Authorisation*	*Valuation*	*Existence*	*Beneficial ownership*	*Disclosure report*
Property	Title deeds correspondence	Directors approval committee minute	Revaluation Depreciation	Inspection	Deeds	Correctly recorded
Plant and Machinery	Plant Register Invoices cost records Grants	Directors approval committee minute	Depreciation Obsolescence	Physical inspection of sample	Insurance Maintenance Tax records	Correctly recorded
Fittings	Invoice Inventory Correspondence	Delegated approval per above	Depreciation Obsolescence	Physical inspection of sample	Insurance Maintenance	Correctly recorded

1.1   Extent of testing

The degree of verification should have due regard to the adequacy or otherwise of the system of internal control. In addition the following general principles should be followed:

1 Larger items warrant more attention than a greater number of smaller items, as the larger items will generally have more effect on the overall picture presented in management reports and accounts.
2 If an item can be checked by an overall test, detailed checking should be kept to a minimum.
3 Excessive time must not be spent on immaterial items, except where they are of an attractive and portable nature and therefore liable to theft, eg video cassette recorders.

Before detailing some audit tests it is appropriate to define the terms 'vouching' and 'verification'.

1.2 Vouching and verification

'Vouching is an examination of documentary evidence supporting a transaction as recorded. It includes a test check of the accuracy of the recording system, the objectives being to prove the authenticity of a recorded transaction' (Pratt *Auditing*). Examples are: purchase invoices and contract documentation.

A genuine transaction is one which:

1 Actually takes place during the course of the accounting period of the audit.
2 Agrees with documentry evidence reflecting its value and nature.

It is valid when:

1 It is properly authorised.
2 It is appropriate to the organisation.
3 It is allocated to the correct account.

For the auditor to be satisfied, a check must confirm:

1 Date of transaction (within accounting period).
2 The sample test is numerically adequate.
3 The documents are addressed to the auditee.
4 The auditee normally deals with this type of transaction during the course of business (it is not *ultra vires*—outside the scope of the organisation).
5 The transaction has been properly authorised in accordance with the organisation's internal control system.
6 Quality and quantity are acceptable.
7 Conditional terms are reasonable.
8 Correct code is allocated.

Verification is defined as follows:

'Substantiate that an item is accurate and properly stated or within reasonable, permissible limits. The substantiation is through the appropriate audit procedure for that item. Verification does not imply certainty' (Thornton Baker *Audit Manual*).

1.3   Substantive tests: fixed assets and capital commitments

The amount at which fixed assets are stated in the financial statements represents all fixed assets owned by the organisation. They should be properly described and valued on a basis consistent with previous periods.

1.3.1   *Some substantive tests*

1 *Obtain or compile a schedule of fixed assets* at the date of the audit showing the cost or valuation of each type of asset and the related depreciation:
   (a) at the end of the previous audit;
   (b) at the end of the current audit;
   (c) in respect of additions and disposals in the period.

2 *Cast the schedule* and agree the total to the appropriate accounting record and with line management.

3 *Check the additions* during the year:
   (a) for approval by senior management;
   (b) with third party invoices or other independent evidence;
   (c) for correctness and consistency of accounting treatment particularly where assets have been constructed by the auditee, eg where a production department has built its own machinery;
   (d) with entries in the cash book and creditor ledgers.

4 *Check the disposals* during the year:
   (a) with supporting evidence (eg sales notes) and ensure that they were properly authorised and agreed by senior management (minutes);
   (b) with the cash book and debtor ledgers where appropriate;
   (c) have been correctly treated in the accounts, paying particular attention to any surplus or deficit arising and the elimination of cost and accumulated depreciation;
   (d) were sold at a reasonable price which includes costs relating to disposal—transport demolition.

5 *Confirm the existence and ownership* of fixed assets scheduled in 1 above, at the time of audit:
   (a) in respect of freehold property, with title deeds or confirmation from third party custodian;
   (b) in respect of leasehold property, with lease documents or confirmation from third party custodian;
   (c) in respect of plant, machinery, equipment etc by physical inspection;
   (d) in respect of motor vehicles, confirm existence by examining vehicle registration documents or chassis numbers where not registered.

6 *Review policy for assessing obsolescence.*

7 *Check the calculation of depreciation* charged in the year:
   (a) by reviewing the reasonableness of the basis used and checking that it is consistent with previous periods;
   (b) by testing the calculation of the depreciation charge for the period either on an individual basis or in total.

8 *Review revaluations* of any asset made during the period and check its treatment in the accounts. Determine whether the basis of this valuation is reasonable, taking into account the use and condition of the asset.

9 *Review the movements of fixed assets* in the period and consider whether they are in line with management's policy, eg capital budget.

10 *Review the repairs and maintenance* account for possible capital items.

An example of tests related to particular types of assets is shown here with examples of some of the tests undertaken:

Fixed assets	Special verification procedures	
Freehold land and buildings	(a)	Examine documents of title, or land register entry (terrier)
	(b)	Ensure buildings are being depreciated (SSAP12) where appropriate
	(c)	Consider appropriateness of valuation basis (usually existing use basis)
Leasehold land and buildings	(a)	Examine lease and ensure correctly classified as short or long, eg 25 years is long lease for tax purposes
	(b)	Ensure lease being amortised over period of lease
	(c)	Ensure buildings are being depreciated, where appropriate
	(d)	Review the appropriateness of valuation basis
Mines, quarries and wasting assets	(a)	Examine current projections of useful life in relation to depreciation provisions
Plant machinery and motor vehicles	(a)	No conclusive proof of ownership exists (though vehicle registration documents provide some evidence). Invoices should be checked and the number and supplier recorded on the register
	(b)	Assets should be physically verified against register at least once a year
	(c)	Assets should be identified as actually belonging to the organisation
Assets bought on hire purchase or leaseback	(a)	The agreements should be examined
Loose tools	(a)	The basis for valuation should be examined
	(b)	If the valuation method is used, the difference between opening value plus purchases, and closing value, should be charged as depreciation
Patents and trademarks	(a)	A register of patent and trademarks should be maintained, and renewal fees paid. Awareness of the value of this asset is currently growing
Works of art	(a)	A register should be maintained and the items of value regularly revalued by an expert

Note: This is only an example of some tests used.

Location	Fixed asset register		Page no	
Description	Rate of depreciation	% Asset no		Comment
Supplier	Method of depreciation	Serial no		
Date of acquisition	Cost (£)	Dep'n (£)	Written down value (£)	Location/ room no	Notes	Initial of checker

1.3.2   *Some common classifications of capital and revenue expenditure outside the public sector*

Capital charges	Revenue costs
(a) Cash price of goods acquired for use in the business	Cash price of goods purchased for conversion into cash in the normal course of business
(b) Legal fees used in acquisition of assets, patents, leases, copyright and formation of business	Legal fees for the renewal or protection of royalties, leases, etc
(c) Cost of repairs to fixed assets made to correct damage prior to acquisition	Cost of repairs to fixed assets made to correct damage after acquisition, including maintenance charges
(d) Cash value of goods bought by hire purchase	Interest element of price paid for assets bought by hire purchase

1.4   Verification of investments

Unless the organisation is a bank, insurance company, building society or similar financial institution, the ability to provide a sophisticated system of internal control is likely to be restricted. Consequently the auditor will have to rely on substantive testing.

1.4.1   *Substantive tests*

1 All purchases and sales should be verified to the brokers bought and sold notes (held by bank) with particular attention being paid to the letter of authorisation allowing transactions to take place.
2 Vouch all income received during the period subject to audit.
3 Vouch the receipt of all bonus issues, rights issues, capital distributions and other unusual items (eg free meals at certain hotels—given by a national hotel chain to shareholders). Confirmation should be made with Exchange Telegraph cards (or from the accounts of the companies concerned—unquoted companies) that all such items have been accounted for.
4 Examine documentation related to the investment; all documentation and related correspondence should be retained.

1.4.2 *Verification of title*

1 Request share certificates from bank and inspect.
2 Ensure the company holds signed blank transfers for any holdings registered in the name of nominees.
3 Ascertain the market value of quoted investments—*Financial Times* or *Stock Exchange Daily Listing*.
4 Examine the management valuation of unquoted shares and the accounts of such companies to confirm that the valuation provided is reasonable.

1.4.3 *Security*

1 Ensure a register of investments is maintained.
2 Ensure investment certificates are securely held in a fireproof place.
3 All instructions above an agreed figure should have more than one signature.

Audit profile triggers relevant to capital expenditure and fixed asset records are given on pp 366–368.

2.0 STOCK

2.1 Audit objectives

To ensure that:

1 All stock and work in progress belonging to the organisation and only that stock and work in progress has been brought into account and has been properly described, valued and classified in financial statements in accordance with methods previously applied.
2 Quantities correctly represent supplies in stock and goods in transit which are owned by the organisation.
3 Quantities are counted and recorded accurately.
4 Adequate stocktaking procedures exist.
5 Items are priced at the lower of cost and net realisable value. Slow moving and obsolete stock is identified and reported to management.
6 Long-term contract work in progress is valued at cost plus attributable profit after deducting any foreseeable losses.

The verification of stock involves a physical check of stock. In large organisations verification is often undertaken on a continuous basis by the storekeeper, eg every month a planned 10% of stock is checked, the records adjusted and the differences reported to management. Audit management must then decide upon the frequency of audit attendance at such checks and what involvement audit will have. Constant monitoring is essential for a secure system, and at all times adequate documentation should support the accounting records showing stock movement and value of that movement.

2.1.1 *Stock attendance: APC auditing guideline*

Although this guideline applies to the external auditor, it is also appropriate for the internal auditor.

In examining the effectiveness of internal control of stock, the auditor should personally observe how the system works and perform tests on that system. This would involve the following steps:

1 Prior to stocktaking—Examine stocktaking instructions with the purpose of identifying potential weaknesses and the adequacy of the instructions themselves.
2 During stocktaking—Request recounts in your presence, mainly selecting items representing significant value. Obsolete and slow moving stock should be inspected, to allow for an informed discussion with management as to its treatment.
3 Post stocktaking—Ensure 'cut off' procedures are correctly implemented with regard to movement in and out of stock at the agreed date.

2.1.2　*Cut-off procedures*

These are arrangements made to ensure that at a particular point in time there is agreement between physical stock, debtors and creditors. As such the following considerations must be taken into account:

1 Compare issues or sales to stock records to ensure goods issued or sold but not yet despatched are not counted in stock.
2 Compare purchases and stock records to ensure creditors and accrued invoices are represented by stock in hand or consumed.
3 Stock movements, both in and out, are arithmetically correct.
4 Stock held on behalf of others must be identified and excluded.

2.1.3　*Auditing stock*

The auditor should examine the soundness of procedures and the manner in which such procedures are complied with by employees.

In addition to attendance auditors should examine a sample of the stock records for material errors and for undue loss or wastage.

2.1.4　*Slow moving and obsolete stock*

1 An examination should be made as to the value and reason for such stock being held, management comments being noted.
2 The amount or value of such items should similarly be investigated—poor sales, cost of storage.
3 Management should be made aware of the situation and given recommendations on how to correct it—sell as scrap or write off, adjust re-order level.

2.1.5　*Other audit tests*

1 Test stock records (bin cards) to invoices (unit cost), orders (authorisation quantity, quality and description), costing records, etc.
2 With regard to work in progress, the allocation of overheads is important.
3 Arithmetical accuracy.
4 Stock sheet totals correctly carried forward (ie no missing pages).
5 Valuation and methods of stocktaking consistent with previous periods.
6 Tests of 'net realisable value' v cost (and replacement cost).

7 Nature and reliability of costing records (average cost, replacement cost and standard costing techniques).

8 Exception reporting procedures for variances.

9 Security of stock.

10 Reconciliation of stock movement to purchases, issues and production through to sales.

11 Stock turnover ratios and comparison with previous period stock level. Comparison standard cost to actual cost and how the final valuation of stock has been treated.

2.2 Work in progress

This area of stock causes auditors many problems, particularly in relation to the following:

1 Nature and reliability of stock count.
2 Internal checks reconciling input to output.
3 Quality control.
4 Method of allocation of overheads and profit element.

2.2.1 *Audit tests*

1 Reconciliation of change in stock levels between selected dates to records of purchases, production and sales.
2 Stock movement reconciled to production records.
3 Stock turnover.
4 Expected v actual expenditure.
5 Expected v actual consumption.
6 Where a standard costing system is in use, an examination of variances above an acceptable level should be made.

2.3 Stock valuation

COMMON METHODS OF COMPUTING COST

FIFO—first in first out
AVCO—Average cost
Replacement cost
'Standard' cost
Adjusted selling price

STOCK VALUATION (SSAP9)

SSAP9 requires stock to be valued at the lower of cost and net realisable value. A simple concept but difficult to apply in practice. Stock valuation is as important to the internal auditor as to the external auditor—it is directly related to the measurement of performance (gross profit).

ELEMENTS COMPRISING COST

1 Direct materials.
2 Direct labour and expenses.

3 Overhead allocation—a proportion based upon normal level of activity of overhead costs incurred in bringing the product to its present location and condition.

LOWER OF COST AND NET REALISABLE VALUE

Net realisable value (NRV). If it is known that some costs incurred on stock are irrecoverable, provision must be made for such losses based on:

1 The individual item.
2 Groups of items.
3 Aggregate value of items.

The following tabulation illustrates how this may be achieved:

Stock item	Cost £	NRV £	Lower of cost/NRV £
A	20	25	20
B	23	29	23
C	56	53	53
D	12	15	12
E	10	8	8
F	7	10	7
G	15	16	15
	143	156	138

The total value at cost of £143 is clearly below the total of net realisable value of £156, but when each item is taken separately, £138 is the total of the lower of cost and net realisable value. *Note*: Cost may be taken to mean all expenditure incurred directly in the purchase of materials or manufacture of an item. Net realisable value (NRV) may be taken to mean the amount that could be realised at the time of stock valuation from the disposal of items of stock on the open market less any costs still to be incurred.

Reduction to replacement price.   This method may be taken to mean the replacement of stock at current purchase price. It is applied in the following exceptional circumstances:

1 Uncertainty of net realisable value.
2 The selling price is based on current replacement prices.
3 Adjusting for losses sustained due to inefficient buying.

STANDARD COSTING

In standard costing systems, two different values must be identified:

1 Actual cost.
2 Standard cost.

Standard cost is a predetermined value based on technical specification which an item is expected to cost and being predetermined it is likely to differ from the actual cost. This difference is called the 'variance'.

Using a standard costing system an organisation would record all transactions of stock at their standard costs and 'variances' from the standard would be written off a 'variance' account as follows:

Journal entries	£	£
FAVOURABLE VARIANCES		
Debit stock (standard cost)	x	
Credit cash (actual cost)		x
Credit variance (difference)		x
UNFAVOURABLE VARIANCES	£	£
Debit stock (standard cost)	x	
Debit variance (difference)	x	
Credit cash (actual cost)		x

It is common practice to transfer the outstanding balance on a variance account to 'cost of sales' periodically. However, it may be appropriate to adjust the value of closing stock at the end of a period to 'actual' or 'revised standard cost'. This will apply when the standard cost does not comply with SSAP9.

When a standard costing system is in use the organisation's accounting system has to ensure that the correct costs have been matched against each sale and the correct standard cost has been computed and transferred to a 'cost of sales' account, the entries being:

	£	£
Debit cost of sales	x	
Credit stock or work in progress		x

The appropriate variances are then transferred to the variance account. Standard costing is an important technique used extensively in manufacturing industry. Those seeking more detailed knowledge of standard costing techniques should read one of the many excellent textbooks devoted to this subject.

STOCK MANAGEMENT PHILOSOPHY

The internal auditor should consider the overall objectives for stock management even though the audit brief may be concerned only with issues affecting financial security.

The principal objectives are likely to include:

1 Securing benefits from bulk procurement.
2 Achieving economic production runs.
3 Minimising production waiting time.
4 Facilitating production flexibility for changes in customer requirements.
5 Optimising customer service.

Constraints on achieving these objectives would include:

1 Cost—restricting capacity to store and manage the stock.
2 Time—set by shelf-life limitations or obsolescence risks.
3 Financial—imposed by a need to minimise working capital investment.

The adequacy and effectiveness of stock recording and control systems should be judged in the context of the overall objectives of the stock management policy as well as by criteria for financial security.

2.4   Some stocktaking systems

2.4.1   *Stock records not integrated*

With this system subsidiary records of stock quantities are usually kept and are updated from other documents such as goods received notes (GRN) and goods despatched notes (GDN) with stocktakes at periodic intervals. Consequently the following should be examined:

1 Differences between actual stocktake and 'book' stock (results of stock records).
2 Differences due to GRNs and GDNs not being recorded in stock records.
3 Differences between sales records and GDNs and between purchase records and GRNs.

Audit approach:

1 Check that physical quantities at the stocktake are correctly counted (this will include cut-off tests).
2 Verify that the quantities shown on the stock records reflect the results of the stocktake.
3 Check the correctness of quantities recorded on the stock records between the stocktake date and the cut-off date. In doing this comparison, stock levels at stocktake and cut-off date should be made and the reasons for unusual fluctuations examined. Quantities from goods received notes and goods despatched notes to the stock records and vice versa should be tested.
4 Determine that the quantities of stock as stated at the cut-off date have been correctly extracted from the stock records.
5 Agree the cut-off date.
6 Ensure that the cut-off date stock has been correctly valued in accordance with instructions and accounting conventions.

2.4.2   *Integrated stock accounting*

With this system, the nominal ledger stock accounts are debited with purchases (and the corresponding credit is raised in creditors or cash) and credited with cost of sales (and the corresponding debit is raised in cost of sales). Therefore the stock on hand should always correspond to the figure of stock shown in the nominal ledger stock accounts.

The nominal ledger stock accounts are adjusted to reflect the results of interim stock counts. (Any write-up or write-down will result in a credit or charge to the profit and loss account.)

The stock accounts will record all stock movements from the stocktaking date and the end of the period subject to audit as part of the double entry accounting system.

Controls include:

1 examination of differences between results of stocktaking and stock records;
2 examination of variances where standard costing is used; and
3 internal checks on entries in the nominal ledger stock accounts to underlying documentation.

Audit aproach:

1 To ensure physical quantities at the stocktake are correctly counted.
2 To ensure stock is priced correctly on the stocktake sheets (unit costs).
3 To compare the stock in hand at the stocktake date with the amount at which stock is stated in the nominal ledger and ensure that the correct adjustment is made to the stock account. The stock account must record all entries that relate to the stock on hand at the stocktake date. Entries can be tested by relating stock purchases both via goods received notes to the nominal ledger accounts (and vice versa) and by confirmation with trade creditors at the stocktake date. This procedure should ensure that both the correct quantity and the correct price have been used to value stock at the stocktake date. Such confirmation is a fundamental requirement.

If the stock accounts are correctly updated at the stocktake date, any errors or omissions from creditors for stock purchases in the period between that date and the date of audit will have a corresponding effect on the stock account. Any such errors or omissions would generally have no effect on the profit and loss account.

The main audit work on creditors for stock purchases should be performed at the stocktake date in order to ensure that all necessary adjustments at that date (most of which will affect the profit and loss account) are undertaken. Entries concerned with stock despatches should be tested by ensuring that goods despatched notes around the stocktaking date have resulted in the correct credit entries being made to the stock accounts.

4 To ensure that the value of stock has not been overstated, in respect of the period between the stocktake date and the audit, the auditor should:
   (a) Check debit entries in the stock account with underlying evidence (eg purchase invoices, goods received notes).
   (b) Check debit entries in the cost of sales account with supporting documentation and ensure that they have resulted in credit entries to the stock accounts.
   (c) Carry out an analytical review on the monthly sales, gross profit margins and cost of sales to be satisfied that the 'cost of sales' appears to be reasonable. The cost of sales should then be compared with the amounts credited to the stock accounts in the nominal ledger.

2.4.3 *Continuous stocktaking*

Continuous stocktaking occurs when an organisation counts selected items of stock throughout the year rather than counting all the stock at one annual stocktake, eg 10% every month. It usually operates as follows:

1 A schedule is prepared showing which stock is to be counted at each particular stocktake—the schedule should ensure that all stock is counted at least once during the course of the year.
2 After completion of each stocktake, the stock records are adjusted to reflect the results of the stocktake.

3 The adjusted stock records continue to be updated from goods inward and goods despatched notes to reflect all the stock movements to the end of the relevant period.
4 At the end of a year the quantities on the stock records are used as the basis for the valuation of the year end stock.

Continuous stocktaking depends upon sufficient effective internal controls to ensure the production of accurate stock quantities at the end of the relevant period. The controls should include:

1 Counting every item of stock at least once per annum.
2 Investigating the difference between physical and book quantities at stock count and reporting these differences to management.
3 Correction of stock records to reflect the results of the stocktake.
4 Sequence control of goods received and goods despatched notes to ensure that all receipts and the despatches are recorded in the stock records.
5 A discipline to ensure that cancelled notes are retained.

Audit approach:

The auditor should attend some continuous stocktakes to ensure quantities are correctly counted and should review the results.

Auditee: Location: Date: Manager (auditee) present:	*Auditor's initial*	*Ref*	*Comments*
1 Ensure that you are familiar with auditee's stocktaking instructions/procedures			
2 Inspect the area/location where you are responsible for identifying particularly the stock to be counted.			
3 Observe the stocktaking procedures, ensuring that the instructions are being carried out and that the count is being carried out in an orderly manner. (Ensure that the auditee is informed of any significant failure to count the stock accurately and make a note of the circumstances)			
4 Perform test counts and record details on working papers to allow subsequent checking to the stock sheets. These test counts should include: (a) items selected at the planning stage of the audit as being of material value (b) items selected from the actual physical stock (c) items selected from the stocktaking sheets			
5 Ensure that all differences disclosed by the count are resolved. If not resolved ensure that full details are recorded on the working papers			

Auditee: Location:	Auditor's initial	Ref	Comments
Date: Manager (auditee) present:			
6 Observe the controls over the movement of goods between areas while stocktaking is in progress			
7 Ensure that all obsolete, slow moving or damaged stock is clearly marked as such			
8 Check that all goods which do not belong to the auditee are properly identified and segregated and that they are not included in the count			
9 Observe the procedures for dealing with any goods which are received or despatched during the stocktaking. Record the details of such items to enable a subsequent check to be made (eg the serial numbers of the last goods despatched note and goods received note)			
10 Check the serial numbering of the count sheets and record details of the sheets used			
11 (a) Obtain copies of the stock sheets to ensure that they are not subsequently altered			
(b) Ensure all records are recorded in ink			
(c) Check that stocktakers initial their work			
12 Where stocks are stored in bulk, record and assess the methods used for inspecting and estimating such stocks			
13 Prepare a report giving your conclusions as to the adequacy and effectiveness of the stocktake—adherence to procedures, review of procedures, adequate staff etc			

Examples of audit profile triggers for stock are given on pp 344–346.

3.0 DEBTORS

Debtors are amounts owed to the organisation—audit objectives with respect to debtors are to verify:

1 That the debtors exist and that all are included and stated at their realisable value.
2 That balances have been correctly extracted from ledgers.
3 That income is correctly assigned to the correct period, using a method that is consistent with that adopted for previous periods.

4 That adequate provision is made for bad debts, discounts receivable, returns and accounts subject to dispute.
5 That prepayments are identified as benefits due in future periods and are consistent with previous periods.

Of critical importance to both internal audit and management is credit control—interest is earned on moneys received and lost on moneys not received. When allowing credit, an adequate system should exist for a check to be made on the 'credit rating' of the customer (Dun & Bradstreet/ banker's letter/financial press). Once credit is given, follow-up procedures should be efficient and subject to periodic review. In the last resort the services of a debt collection agency may be necessary. At no time should it become common knowledge that old debts are written off.

The finance department should periodically reconcile debtor accounts and issue a monthly management report disclosing debtors outstanding beyond the agreed credit period—Debtors Ageing Analysis, eg:

		DEBTORS AGEING ANALYSIS					
Account No	Name of customer	Amount	Months Outstanding 1 2 3 4 5 6 6+	Invoice No	First Letter	Second Letter	Comments

Similarly, accounts should not be 'chased' where they amount to less than it costs to collect. Adopting a minimum invoice value for credit sales may help to avoid this dilemma.

3.1   Recommended substantive tests—debtors

Some audit tests that should be considered when carrying out the substantive testing of debtors now follow (further tests should be introduced where necessary).

1 Obtain, or prepare, a schedule of debtors at the cut-off date.
2 Check the arithmetic of the schedule and agree the total to the general ledger.
3 Select a sample of debtors from the balances, including:
   (a) All material balances.
   (b) A sample of other smaller debtor balances.
   (c) Some credit and nil balances.
4 In respect of the balances selected in 3 above, undertake a debtor circularisation to confirm balances (often this test is left to the external auditor).
5 Test cut-off procedures either side of the cut-off date as follows:
   (a) Ensure that sales made either side of the cut-off date are recorded in the correct period by testing:
      (i) A sample of despatches on either side of the cut-off date to sales invoices.
      (ii) A sample of sales invoices on either side of the cut-off date to despatch records.
   (b) Verify that credit notes issued on either side of the cut-off date are recorded in the correct period by testing:

    (i) A sample of goods returned on either side of the cut-off date to credit notes.

    (ii) A sample of credit notes on either side of the cut-off date to goods returned records.

6 Review any material credit notes issued after the cut-off date with supporting evidence to ensure that they are recorded in the correct period.

7 Review the debtors schedules for:

  (a) Incorrect set-off against credit balances.

  (b) Balances with connected persons, eg employees.

8 Review policy for bad and doubtful debts:

  (a) Review the balances at the cut-off date for any bad or doubtful debts by:

    (i) Checking the auditee's list of bad and doubtful debts and considering whether the provisions made are reasonable.

    (ii) Reviewing the debtors accounts after the cut-off date for any outstanding accounts, payments on account or disputed items.

    (iii) Reviewing correspondence available relating to bad and doubtful or disputed debts.

  (b) Examine the basis of any general provision made against bad and doubtful debts as a consequence of previous experience.

  (c) Review the validity of any debts written off in the period examined.

  (d) Check debts written off are properly authorised.

9 Other debtors balances:

  (a) Prepayments: Obtain, or prepare, a list of prepayments at the cut-off date and:

    (i) Test the calculations.

    (ii) Check them against supporting documents, eg invoices, correspondence.

    (iii) Review them for reasonableness and compare them with previous periods.

  (b) Loans: Schedule all loans at the cut-off date including details of their repayment terms and interest. Attention should be paid to loans to employees and correct adherence to the terms of such loans.

Examples of audit profile triggers for debtors are given on pp 328–330.

4.0 BANK FUNDS AND CASH

4.1 Audit objectives

Bank and cash resources include all cash items held by the organisation in banks, in transit or on site at a certain date. Such balances require verification. In order to meet this objective, the audit should cover the following elements—custody, authorisation, valuation, existence, beneficial ownership and disclosure. All these elements should be audited.

    Reconciliation of bank statements with the accounting records at regular intervals is a fundamental accounting control.

    Bank and cash balances may not in themselves be material but the extent of their audit may need to be increased due to:

1 Weaknesses identified in certain of the organisation's financial control systems.
2 The opportunity for theft or fraud, which may exist, and the need to detect some of the more common types of irregular activity which, if undetected by audit, will continue to cause a loss to the organisation.

4.2   Some types of error and possible controls

Error	Possible controls
Cash stolen by employee and possibly concealed by: altering cash book; altering bank reconciliation, delaying deposit with bank but making up the loss at a later date	1 Cash book balances regularly reconciled to control account 2 Documented procedures for deputisation in absence of cashier 3 Bank reconciliations performed by a supervisor independent of the cashier 4 Test checks of bank reconciliations made during the year by internal audit 5 Bank statements and returned cheques delivered direct to supervisor 6 Supervisor to check cash book entries with returned cheques and paying-in slips 7 Cash book arithmetic checked and totals 'inked in' 8 Cash sales compared with audit till rolls 9 Sequence checks performed by internal audit on pre-numbered receipts for cash sales 10 Sundry receipts controlled 11 Petty cash balances regularly counted and reconciled by supervisor 12 Petty cash vouchers authorised 13 Petty cash vouchers cancelled after payment 14 'Imprest' system adopted
Cheques payable which are fraudulently endorsed	1 Ensure cheques are sent out immediately after signature, ie not returned to those who drafted them
Monies received are misappropriated and shortfall concealed by: applying another payee's payment against the first	1 Monies received listed immediately on receipt, mail being opened in the presence of at least two people—one of whom should be a line manager 2 Exception report of all non-cash credit entries on the sales ledger 3 All journal entries must be authorised

4.3   Prevention and detection of theft and fraud

4.3.1   *Misappropriation*

Cash and bank balances are the most easily transferable assets of the organisation and most susceptible to theft. Because so many items inter-relate with the cash book, the cash balance is always changing and this offers more opportunity for the concealment of a theft. The main defence against such theft is separation of duties which should prevent both 'one-off' and 'rolling' frauds.

'One-off' frauds may be concealed in an expense account, so reducing profits. Tests on the sales, purchases and payroll cycles should alert the auditor to these frauds.

'Rolling' frauds only reveal themselves when the bank and cash require reconciliation, ie the cash is always stated as being £x until counted.

Audit of the bank reconciliation should incorporate:

1 Verification of the cash book balance with third party evidence (bank statements and audit confirmation letters).
2 Ensuring that cash cut-off was effective.
3 Determining that effective internal control was in operation.
4 Supporting evidence that no material loss has occurred.

The audit of the reconciliation should be carried out in a methodical manner.

4.3.2 *Cash count*

Where controls over monies received (cheques or cash) are ineffective or lacking and where monies have not been banked at the cut-off date, it will be necessary to undertake a cash count. Cash counts are also relevant where there is a high volume of cash sales, when cash count information is required to verify the cut-off of cash sales, or where controls over cash receipts from all sources are absent or ineffective. Cash counts will also be necessary if division of duties is unsatisfactory (poor internal control), ie:

1 the person recording cash also disburses cash;
2 the person recording cash also reconciles bank accounts; or
3 custody of cash and marketable securities (certain bonds) is with one person.

Cash counts will assume greater significance in particular industries, eg banks and the catering trades, where it will be necessary to arrange carefully planned audit attendance at various locations and to issue specific written instructions. When we consider that a cash count is required, it is important that the procedure is properly planned and explained by the senior, having regard to cut-off procedures.

4.3.3 *Bank reconciliation—audit procedures*

Procedure	Special points	Potential fraud
1 Obtain the auditee's reconciliations and perform the following checks:		
(a) Agree the arithmetic of the reconciliation	This should be done even if a machine add-list is attached	Theft: List of outstanding cheques may be 'under-cast' to conceal a deficiency, or lodgements 'overcast' to conceal deficiency
(b) Verify 'balance per bank' on reconciliation to bank confirmation letter	—	—
(c) Verify 'balance per books' on reconciliation	—	—

Procedure	Special points	Potential fraud
2 Obtain bank statements for a period immediately following the cut-off date and scrutinise for evidence of erasures, alterations or frequent correcting entries	—	Falsification of bank reconciliation
3 Review bank debit notes to determine what they represent	Check debit notes do not represent reversal of fictitious or worthless lodgements. If debit notes represent bills discounted this may be indicative of cash shortage at the cut-off date	Fictitious lodgements made to disguise cash deficiency
Lodgements in transit:		
4 Verify outstanding lodgements per reconciliation to post cut-off date bank statements and also to bank stamped duplicate paying-in slips	Ensure that delay in banking is reasonable (cash book entry date to date banked)	Cash book held open after the cut-off date purporting a better liquidity position
5 Agree any lodgements in transit to the cash count	Check explanations of any differences	Theft: overstatement of lodgements in transit can disguise a cash shortage
6 When a cash count is performed after the cut-off date then reconcile the cash book at the date of the count	As above	—
7 Trace all outstanding lodgements to the cash book	Ensure all outstanding lodgements are entered in cash book prior to cut-off date	As above
Outstanding cheques:		
8 Vouch outstanding cheques per reconciliation to the cash book or cheque record to ensure that they relate to the period under review	—	—
9 From the last period select from the cash book or cheque record any material payment not covered above and to the bank statements	Ensure items are cleared by bank on or before audit cut-off date	Theft: cheques may be omitted from outstanding list but fraudulently marked as cleared to conceal a cash shortage
10 Vouch outstanding cheques per the reconciliation to the bank statements	Note date of clearance by the bank List all material items where cheques were not cleared until 10 working days after the audit cut-off and refer to supporting documentation	Cheques entered in the cash book are withheld or not despatched until after the cut-off date
11 Review items on the bank statements covering the first few working days after the cut-off date to ensure that items not already tested by us are entered in the cash book before the cut-off date	Check such items are listed as outstanding cheques on the bank reconciliation List items where the cash book date and bank clearance date appear unreasonable Audit 'ticks' should be clearly defined	Theft: A fraudulent cheque not entered in the cash book and which had not been cleared by the bank would evade detection by the bank reconciliation

Procedure	Special points	Potential fraud
Bank transfers: 12 Transfers between the company and its branches or affiliated companies, and between its own bankers, should be scheduled, and reconciliation items correlated	This may require close co-operation with other internal auditors	'Cross-firing' or 'Kiting': an outstanding lodgement is recorded in the received account but not in the paying account, in order to disguise a deficiency

4.3.4   Teeming and lading

A practice used to misappropriate funds by manipulation of the records. As a result of the 1957 Cheques Act separate receipts are not normally given for cheque payments making defalcation easier. The internal check to prevent teeming and lading is to identify cheques and cash received via a till at the time of receipt by a listing of the drawers and accounts. The reconciliation of the till should be completed by a separate person, with both persons agreeing the amount received and the analysis thereof.

Examples of teeming and lading

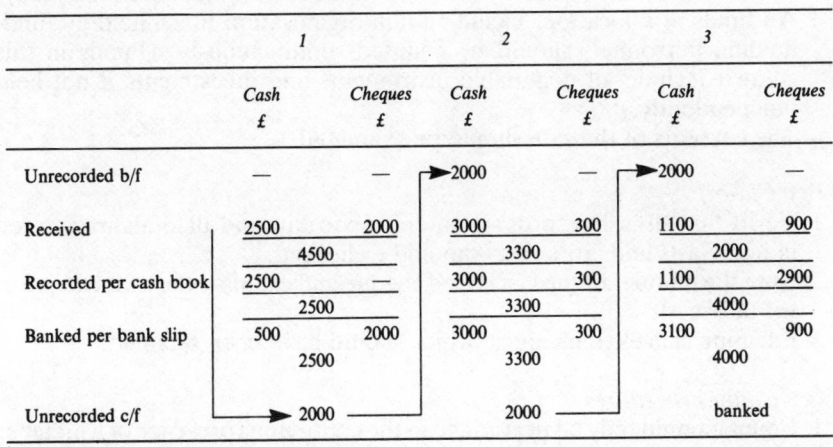

	1		2		3	
	Cash £	Cheques £	Cash £	Cheques £	Cash £	Cheques £
Unrecorded b/f	—	—	2000	—	2000	—
Received	2500	2000	3000	300	1100	900
	4500		3300		2000	
Recorded per cash book	2500	—	3000	300	1100	2900
	2500		3300		4000	
Banked per bank slip	500	2000	3000	300	3100	900
	2500		3300		4000	
Unrecorded c/f		2000		2000	banked	

ie cash has been 'borrowed', interest stolen

Teeming and lading re debtors ledgers—Receipts from debtors may be 'switched' between ledgers, ie a cheque received from Z in week 3 if for the same amount taken in cash might be used to credit that debtor who paid in cash in week 1, so restoring the balance on the ledger account. Such fraud may be minimised by:

1 Recording the amount and nature of all receipts (cash, cheques, postal orders, etc).
2 Operating a system of internal check.
3 Listing all cheques banked by date and amount.
4 Identifying the paying-in slip by day and number in the cash book.

5 Cross-referencing individual debtors ledgers to cash book.
6 Limiting cash balances held by cashiers.
7 Regular internal audit examination.

Audit checks:

1 Ensure cheque lists and paying-in book stamped by the bank and check date of stamp. Also check for cashier's initial.
2 Compare till date with date records in cash book and date banked.
3 Verify that debtors balances are reconciled to statements of account.
4 Use till which identifies cheques, cash and credit cards.
5 Examine debtors ledgers for date of entry and amount.
6 Cash count.
7 Reconcile cash received to cash banked to date of last audit.

4.3.5   *Cash count procedures*

(a) *Planning*
Planning is essential to ensure the efficient operation of cash count procedures. In particular:

1 Determine locations where cash is held and by whom.
2 For locations where a cash count is not thought necessary—because the balance and throughput are immaterial, confirmation of the balance held may be sufficient (this also occurs where audit resources are restricted).
3 All funds at a location, including non-organisation funds held by fund-holding personnel, should be counted simultaneously. (Funds in this context include all negotiable instruments and investments if not held independently.)
4 The contents of the safe should be examined.

(b) *Cut-off*
1 Verify that all cash records are entered up to date and all totals are entered in ink. Casts and cross casts should be checked.
2 Note the number of the last issued cheque and examine the next cheque as yet unissued.
3 Examine cancelled cheques, which should have been retained.

(c) *Count procedures*
1 Counts should only be performed in the continuous presence of a member of the organisation's staff who should be asked to sign that he or she is in agreement with the count performed.
2 Monies not yet lodged with the bank should be counted and checked in detail against the cash book and paying-in slips (if prepared) at the time of the count. Details should be noted on audit working papers.
3 The contents of packets of coins should not normally need counting (weighing is sufficient). In the case of packaged bank notes, each case should be considered on its own merits having regard to the type of packet and the nature and quality of the sealing.
4 Sundry items included in cash balances counted should be noted in detail on working papers—in particular: IOUs, cheques, cash for employees and cheques drawn by cash custodian. Where possible, a responsible official should sign the list to signify that these items are in accordance with acceptable practice.

5 Where discrepancies between the count and the records are revealed, a recount should be instituted. Any unexplained and material differences remaining should be reported immediately to management.

6 Full details of cash counts should be recorded on current files, ie:
   (a) Date and time of count.
   (b) Location of count.
   (c) Names of persons present at the count (including signatures).
   (d) Confirmation that records were up-to-date.
   (e) Total value of items counted.
   (f) Confirmation that all balances were counted.

FOLLOW-UP

An essential ingredient of the count is the correlation and follow-up of items noted on working papers at the time of the count. In particular:

1 Unbanked lodgements agree to bank reconciliation.
2 IOUs and cheques cashed for employees have been reimbursed.
3 Balances noted from the records have been included, unaltered, in the financial statements unless physical shortages were revealed.

It should be noted that it is considered by many to be poor practice to allow IOUs and to cash cheques for employees.

Audit profile triggers for cash and payroll audits are given on pp 273–275.

5.0 CURRENT LIABILITIES

5.1 Trade creditors

These are amounts owed for purchase of goods and services.
   Audit objectives:

1 Records relating to the purchase of both goods and services are correctly maintained in an orderly manner.
2 Payments are made only for authorised liabilities incurred for the purpose of the organisation.
3 Expenses are correctly identified to the appropriate period on a basis consistent with previous periods.

5.1.1 *Some substantive tests: creditors and contingencies*

1 Obtain or compile a schedule of creditors at the cut-off date.
2 Check additions and cross cast the schedule and agree the total to the creditors 'control' account.
3 Select a sample of creditors and reconcile them to suppliers' statements which should be retained in alphabetical order for this purpose.
4 Consider obtaining direct confirmation of the balance with the supplier.
5 Review all material discrepancies that arise from checking to the suppliers' statements and seek satisfactory evidence from the auditee as to the nature of all differences.
6 Review transactions carried forward from the previous audit for possible unrecorded liabilities by:

    (a) Examining material payments and invoices in the next period.
    (b) Examining suppliers' correspondence for disputed accounts.
    (c) Examining journal entries in the next period.
7 Ensure that proper cut-off procedures exist in respect of:
    (a) Goods received either side of the cut-off date.
    (b) Expenses incurred either side of the cut-off date.
    (c) Cash paid either side of the cut-off date.
8 Obtain or compile a schedule of accruals at the cut-off date, test the calculations and agree the total to the creditor 'control' account.
9 Compare the accrual with the last period and check the basis, accuracy and consistency of the accrual made.
10 Vouch the accruals to the supporting documentation (eg third party invoices).

5.1.2 *Analytical review*

1 Examine the level of creditors and accruals at the audit date and compare this with the level of the organisation's activity, eg stock levels or production activity and see if they are reasonable.
2 Compare expenses this period with the same period last year and explain any material fluctuation.
3 Compare the number of days purchases in creditors with previous years and explain any material variance, eg taking additional credit from suppliers, etc. (Exclude VAT to ensure comparability with prior periods in the event of rate changes.)

5.1.3 *Some errors and possible controls*

Error type	Possible controls
Materials or services received but no invoice received, and no accrual made	1 Pre-numbered goods received notes matched to suppliers' invoices and accounted for 2 Purchase orders pre-numbered and all accounted for, ie cancelled ones retained 3 Control over direct shipments from suppliers to sites or customers

Materials and invoices received but invoice not posted to ledger nor accrued	1 Suppliers' invoices controlled on receipt, and checked to ensure all posted to purchase ledger
	2 Suppliers' statements periodically agreed to individual purchase ledger accounts and that reconciliation retained
	3 Purchase ledger control account reconciled regularly
	4 Records maintained of all services received
	5 Internal debits processed matched with credit notes received from suppliers
	6 Computer controls:
	  (a) Check digits used on supplier numbers
	  (b) Supplier numbers validated against supplier file or purchaser ledger
	  (c) Posting verified by matching invoice details with outstanding purchase order file

5.1.4 *Accrued expenses*

An accrued expense may be defined as, 'expenditure relating to the period audited but for which a charge has not been made', ie when wages are paid in arrears at the cut-off date a certain sum will be owing (outstanding) and provision should be made for this in any financial management report.

5.1.5 *Examples of accruals and their verification*

Liability	Verification
Accruals:	
Rent	Reconciliation of charge to profit and loss account to the previous period's accrual and current rent agreement
Interest	Similar to above
Payroll	Check correct allocation of last period's expense by reference to the next payment and period covered
Commissions and royalties	Check total expense as a percentage of sales to that agreed
Claims under warranty	Check reasonableness by reference to statistics of past claims records, sales volumes, correspondence files, retailers' comments, etc
Liabilities:	
Pay as you earn	Normally one month's deductions. Check amount paid to Revenue by inspecting receipted annual declaration of tax paid over, or returned cheque
Value added tax	Check reasonableness to next VAT return. Verify paid cheque for last amount paid in quarter

Where difficulties arise in confirming the completeness of creditors the following relationship must be recognised:

Creditors overstated = Purchases overstated
Creditors understated = Purchases understated

5.1.6 *Particular procedures*

CIRCULARISATION OF MAJOR SUPPLIERS AND CREDITORS

Confirmation of creditor balances provides independent evidence as to the accuracy and completeness of those balances. This technique may be used whenever there are:

1 No suppliers' statements available.
2 Creditor accounts which appear to be irregularly conducted.
3 Weaknesses in internal control which could cause a material misstatement of liabilities.

Balances should always be confirmed if there are indications that the organisation may be deliberately attempting to conceal or understate liabilities. If it is considered not necessary to carry out a circularisation, other procedures should be adopted to confirm the existence, completeness, propriety and valuation of creditors.

Such procedures include:

1 Reconciliation of purchase ledger accounts with suppliers' statements, which should be retained for this purpose.
2 Scrutiny of goods received records to establish whether invoices have not been received, or have not been posted to the ledger.
3 Review of invoices posted to the purchase ledger accounts, both immediately before and immediately after the audit date, to establish the date on which the goods they refer to were received and that they have been allocated to the appropriate accounting period.
4 Review of payments after the audit date in order to ascertain whether any relate to balances which existed prior to that cut-off date and which have been omitted from the financial statements.

5.2 Provisions and accrued expenditure (accruals)

A provision is:

1 An amount written off or retained by way of providing for diminution in value of assets including depreciation of fixed assets.
2 Any amount retained by way of providing for a known liability of which the amount cannot be determined with substantial accuracy.

Unless these issues are fairly judged and taken into account on a consistent basis, the management accounts are unlikely to present a true and fair view and may mislead. Internal audit must provide assurance on these issues.

6.0 LONG-TERM AND CONTINGENT LIABILITIES

AUDIT OBJECTIVES

All long-term liabilities should be correctly described, classified and consistently reported. Interest should be charged in the appropriate period in a consistent manner. Long-term liabilities usually comprise debentures, loan stock and loans repayable at a date more than one year after the year end.

The auditor is particularly concerned that long-term liabilities are not understated in management statements. If necessary third party confirmation should be obtained.

6.1 Debenture and loan agreements

Debenture and loan agreements contain conditions with which the organisation must comply. These may include restrictions on the organisation's total borrowings and the adherence to specific borrowing ratios. The debenture and loan agreements should be read to identify any such conditions and to ensure that the organisation has complied with them.

6.2 New loans

The auditor should verify that any new loans or debentures have been properly accounted for and authorised. This may be undertaken by reviewing management minutes and the cash book for evidence of new loans taken out during the period.

6.3 Third party evidence

The best evidence that can be obtained of the outstanding balance on a long-term liability is by confirmation from the lender.

6.4 Other audit procedures

A review of changes in the amount of long-term liabilities confirming that they comply with loan agreements should be undertaken (ie that specified loan repayments have been correctly made). Failure to comply with such agreements may leave the organisation liable to legal action.

Audit procedures to confirm the correctness of the cut-off date amounts should be used, including:

1 Verify repayments of principle and payments of interest with the loan agreement and with returned cheques.
2 Verify that the correct interest charge for the year has been debited to the appropriate account.
3 Obtain or compile a schedule of long-term liabilities, cast the schedule and agree the total to the general ledger. This schedule should show:
   (a) The balance outstanding at the start and end of the period.
   (b) Other amounts advanced/repaid in the period.
   (c) Interest charged and paid in the year.
4 Agree loan details with related legal documents (eg debenture trust deed, loan agreement) and check that all terms have been complied with. Restrictions based on the accounts such as liquidity ratio requirements should be checked with the draft financial statements. (Copies should be filed on the permanent audit file, or if voluminous, a summary of the main terms.)
5 Analyse movements in the year and cash received and cash paid records and agree details to senior management instructions.

6.4.1 *Some substantive tests*

Substantive audit procedures relevant to this area are:

1 Confirm details on permanent audit file that the description, amount outstanding and dates and terms of redemption of loans and debentures are correctly recorded.
2 For loans received or debentures issued during the year, verify with minutes, debenture deed, loan agreement or other evidence. Record details on audit working papers.
3 Advise that any part of the loan repayable within the next year should be classified as a current liability if it is a material amount.

4 Obtain certificates from lenders to confirm the amount outstanding and the nature of the security they hold.
5 Check repayments during the year with paid cheques, cancelled certificates, receipts or other evidence and check premiums on redemption are properly accounted for.
6 Reconcile loans outstanding and verify from the previous period with the current period, enquiring into the reasons for repayments not made promptly.
7 Check interest charges to the terms of the loan.

6.5   Contingent liabilities

LEGAL ACTIONS

The auditor should obtain from the legal department details of all legal actions at the cut-off date and discuss their impact on the financial and management reports.

OTHER CONTINGENT LIABILITIES

The auditor should consider the nature of the organisation's business in determining whether there may be other contingent liabilities or commitments that could influence the results reported in the management accounts such as:

1 Guarantees to third parties.
2 Warranties on goods delivered or services performed.
3 Discounted or assigned debts, where the organisation is responsible for any debts that are subsequently not recovered.
4 Commitments to buy or sell assets.
5 Performance bonds in respect of long-term contracts.
6 Revenue commitments that cannot be cancelled, eg leases for plant and machinery.
7 Pension fund or superannuation fund commitments.

Examples of audit profile triggers for creditors are given on p 343 and for nominal ledger and period accounts on pp 276–280.

7.0   SURPRISE VISITS

The purpose of the surprise visit is to prevent temporary 'window dressing' by the auditee. They are still common practice in many organisations, eg public houses where a manager is employed. The purpose of the visit is to ensure cash is correct, stock is reconciled and agreed and the correct products are for sale. However, with the exception of suspected fraud, the surprise visit is often regarded as an outmoded practice due to:

1 Ill-feeling on the part of the auditee, leading to a lack of co-operation.
2 Inefficient use of audit resources, as records may not be available for inspection, auditee may be absent for various reasons.

3 Causing administrative problems for auditee who may not be able to assist the auditor.

Nevertheless the following advantages exist:

1 The auditor may witness the system in operation.
2 The auditee is prevented from 'covering his tracks' or destroying evidence where fraud is concerned.
3 The knowledge that an auditor may at some time arrive is in itself a deterrent to malpractice, fraudulent or otherwise.

8.0 INSURANCE COVERAGE

Throughout the conduct of an audit, the auditor should consider the adequacy of insurance coverage, so that the cost of a 'catastrophe' to the organisation is minimised or that management has made the decision to accommodate the risk.

Audit profile triggers for security risks and insurance are given on pp 280–282.

9.0 POST AUDIT REVIEWS

Audit management should at the end of each major audit review the manner in which it has been conducted, not only to appraise the performance of staff, but to encourage the wider adoption of new skills and to pass on information on techniques useful to other auditors.

TYPES OF REVIEW

1 Managerial review—To confirm compliance with approved audit practices and to allow for performance appraisal.
2 External audit—To satisfy the external auditor that the work undertaken by internal audit can be relied upon, so reducing duplication of audit effort.
3 Audit committee review—To apprise the audit committee of contentious issues.
4 Peer review—Where other auditors examine methods used with the idea of providing constructive criticism so maintaining an 'edge' to internal audit performance, ie upholding professional internal audit standards.

Audit profile triggers (Defined at **2.11** in Chapter 3)

CASH

CASH IN HAND
Cashiers
Petty cash
Floats

Canteen
Shops
Vending machines
Protective clothing
Club funds
Bar funds
Cash sales
Receipt procedures
Imprest systems
Domestic checking arrangements
IA checks

EMPLOYEE PAYMENTS
Expenses
Advances
Loans
Payroll

RECEIPTS
Cheques
Credit transfer/Giro
Bills of exchange
Letters of credit
Lines of credit
Direct debit
Postal/cash orders
Bank transfers
Registration
Reporting/reconciliation
Paying in procedure
Cash book entry and controls
Sales ledger aspects
Treatment of discounts
Purchase ledger refunds
Sundry income

PAYMENTS
Payment control:
  Sundry payments, cheque requisitions
  Purchase ledger payments
  Expense payments

Cheque controls
Credit transfers/Giro
Direct debits
Treatment of discounts
Sales ledger refunds

BANK STATEMENTS
Reconciliation
Routine checks
Spot checks

SECURITY
Office arrangements
Sales
Strong boxes
Insurance cover

Special arrangements:
  Bank Holidays
  Holidays
  Peak times

Access

CASHFLOW
Monitoring
Returns

PAYROLL

AUTHORISATION AND CHECKING OF MASTER FILE CHANGES

VALIDATING OF HEADCOUNT
Physical
Payroll records
Personnel records

CHECKING OF VARIABLE DATA
Hours
Overtime
Bonus
Deductions
Temporary arrangements
Extra payments

CALCULATION ROUTINES AND PAYROLL PREPARATION

RECONCILIATIONS OF CONTROLS TO PAYROLL
Gross pay
Deductions
Net pay
Other payments
Starters, leavers and transfers

PAYMENT ARRANGEMENTS
To employees
To statutory bodies
To deduction bodies

UNCLAIMED PAYMENTS AND CASH FLOATS

PENSION CALCULATIONS

ACCRUALS FOR WAGES, HOLIDAY PAY, ETC
Period
Year-end

COMPARISONS
Year on year
Average earnings
Actual to budget
Actual to forecast

RETURNS
Company:
  Personnel
  Pensions
  Other

External:
  Income tax—P9/P11, P35, P60
  DSS
  Employers' liability insurance
  Other

NOMINAL LEDGER

Timetable
Method
Integration/relationship with other ledgers

SOURCES OF DATA
Sales:
  Ledger
  Analysis
  Invoices
  Credit notes

Purchases:
  Ledger
  Analysis
  Invoices
  Credit notes

Cash book

Journal entries:
  Standing
  Special

Transfer vouchers
Payrolls
Capital expenditure records
Cost of sales
New accounts
Balancing

Controls:
  Operation
  Reconciliation

Reports:
  Interim
  Period-end
  Quarterly
  Annual

CODE OF ACCOUNTS
Structure
Objective/subjective
Department/expense
Up-dating arrangements
Integration aspects

ACCRUALS AND PREPAYMENTS
Collection of data
Period
Year-end
Valuation
Period
Year end
How processed
Part of ledger double entry
Memorandum

UNUSUAL BALANCES
Examination of unusual transactions
Sundry sales
Disposals
Sundry purchases
Staff sales
Social club/sports club funds
Advances/loans to employees
Sundry income
Rentals of company property
Interest from investments
Special staff payments
PAYE
VAT
Non-operational items
Non-trading items

PERIOD ACCOUNTS

ORDER BOOK STATEMENT
Opening orders
Order intake
Sales input

Closing orders:
  Product
  Quantity
  Value
  Price level
  Cost

Order book analysis
Forward load
Arrears, by cause

SALES AND PROFIT
Activity
Trading
Operating

COST OF GOODS SOLD
Labour
Material
Overheads
Other costs
Overhead under/over recovery

INDIRECT EXPENSES
Manufacturing
Marketing
Selling
Engineering
Administration
Research and development
Other by department type

LABOUR COST ANALYSIS
Hours, direct and indirect
Cost
Efficiency—operative and factory

PERSONNEL STRENGTH
Direct
Indirect factory
Marketing
Selling
Engineering
Research and development
Other by department and category

OUTSTANDING VACANCIES
Authorised
Unauthorised

FIXED ASSETS
Opening
Capital expenditure
Disposals
Depreciation
Revaluation
Closing

CAPITAL EXPENDITURE
Sought
Approved
Committed
Spent
Outstanding

INVENTORIES
Raw materials
Work in progress
Finished stocks—opening, intake, output, closing
Movement analysis
Adjustments
   (stated in quantity as well as value, where applicable)

CREDITORS
Trade third party
Other third party
Intra group
Inter group

WORKING CAPITAL, EG CASH

TRADING CAPITAL

CASHFLOW STATEMENT

VARIANCE ANALYSIS

RATIOS

NARRATIVE REPORT

PREPARATION
'Cut-off' arrangements
Sources of data
Integrity of data
Preparation method
Presentation
Timeliness
Distribution
Cost effectiveness/usefulness

ANALYSIS OF CONTENT
It is necessary to examine all presented data, with particular emphasis on unusual items. Useful checks can be made by examination of trends, calculation of additonal ratios, sensitivity analysis, comparisons with trade indices and other units' data. Items requiring specific examination include:
Accruals
Prepayments
Provisions
Reserves
Non-operational items
Non-trading items
Suspense accounts
Unallocated items
Excluded items
Unconventional treatment
Significant variances
Major deviation from plan
Major deviation from forecast
Major changes through external influences
CCA calculations
Effects of organisational changes
Changes in product mix
Pricing policy
Manufacturing methods

PRESENTATION OF DATA
Layout
Distribution
Frequency
How used
Degree of integration with other procedures
Extent of duplication with other data

SECURITY

SITE FEATURES
Enclosed or open premises
Freedom of access and exit
Constraints

AREAS OF SITE
Factory
Confidential processes
Stores
Warehouse
Shop
Canteen

Offices:
   Computer
   Cashier
   Wages
   Accounts
   Personnel

General
Research and development
Petrol and diesel pumps
Fuel stores

INDUSTRIAL
Machine/equipment guards
Protective clothing/helmets/spectacles
Housekeeping
Unsafe practice

ACCIDENT ARRANGEMENTS
First aid equipment
First aid staff
Surgery
Emergency facilities
Duty executive

SECURITY ARRANGEMENTS
Security guards
Watchmen
Guard dogs
TV cameras
Reception
Passes

Locks:
  Manual
  Magnetic
  Designated key-holders

CASH AND VALUABLES
Strong rooms
Safes
Security boxes

Cash and cheques:
  Unbanked
  Overnight arrangements
    Cash receipts

Payroll:
  Wages packet making up
  Payout
  Unclaimed wages

FIRE
Charts and fire drill instructions
Exits
Drill rehearsals
Alarms
Extinguishers
Sprinklers

Inflammable materials
No smoking areas
Emergency contacts
Insurance

INSURANCE

PROPERTY
Premises
Plant and equipment
New equipment, installation cover
Cash and valuables
Stocks

TRANSPORT
Commercial vehicles
Private cars

PROCESSES
Special processes
Contractors on own sites
Employees on customer sites
Employer's liability

ACCIDENT
Employee travel:
   UK
   Overseas

COMMERCIAL
Consequential loss
Liquidated damages
Fidelity bonds
Indemnity bonds
ECGD
Goods in transit
Warranty/guarantee

NATIONAL INSURANCE

Further reading

Samuels, J M, Wilkes, F M and Brayshaw, R E *Management of company finance* (5th edn, 1990) (Chapman & Hall).

Woolf, E *Auditing today* (4th edn, 1990) (Prentice Hall).

CHAPTER 9   Contract management

Objectives	To describe the audit procedures and practices which apply to major contracts from tendering, through execution to completion, while taking due account of the need to protect the organisation from loss or damage as a result of financial failure or default by other parties to the contract
Contents	Tendering procedures Contract audit objectives; roles of auditor and engineer; types of contract; stages of contract audit; post-contract review; contract fraud Liquidations
Summary	Most major contracts will involve significant commitments for expenditure and a substantial element of risk. Consequently there is a special need for sound administration and control throughout from compiling the initial tender document to the post-contract review

1.0   INTRODUCTION

In this chapter the commonly used methods of tendering are described together with the audit of such procedures. Following on from this, audit problems associated with the control of contract expenditure are examined prior to concluding with audit controls over a contract where the contractor has defaulted. The audit of capital expenditure is particularly important due to the large sums of money involved and the time taken to make such expenditure produce a return. The organisation should have developed a co-ordinated strategy to benefit from this expenditure as quickly as possible in order to gain an early return. Consequently the auditor is concerned with ensuring not only that the best value for money is obtained, but that the scheme is commissioned within the agreed timespan, within budget and according to specification. The auditor's objective is to reassure management that these criteria have been met.

2.0   TENDERING PROCEDURES

A DEFINITION OF TENDER

An offer in writing to execute work or supply goods. *(Oxford Dictionary)*

Many organisations have regulations which stipulate that once items or services above a certain value are requested their purchase must only take place after a tendering procedure. Below that sum, quotations should be obtained to achieve best value for money.

The objective of tendering is to obtain the best quality at the best price for the organisation. Where it is public money the rationale might be rephrased 'honesty with economy'. The procedure for awarding contracts is one of the very few areas specified by law for which standing orders are mandatory in the public sector. Such standing orders often state a common practice for the award of contract, eg:

Amount	Requirement
£2,000	Three written quotations
£10,000	Five written quotations
£50,000	Local advertisement
£100,000	National advertisement
£1,000,000	International advertisement

In order to prevent future areas of misunderstanding, it is important that tender documents are in agreement with project specifications and that the nature of responsibilities is clearly defined. It is often advisable to have an agreed arbitration procedure for use in the event of disputes, rather than for both parties to suffer expensive legal action and endure the resulting delays.

2.1   Methods of tendering

2.1.1   *Open competitive*

The contract is advertised and no restriction is placed on those tendering.

2.1.2   *Selective*

The organisation compiles a list of approved contractors, which is periodically reviewed by senior management or, in a public concern, by members. Contractors are admitted onto the listing based on reputation, recommendation and the organisation's experience of their work. In order to compile such a list a public notice should be issued asking for contractors to apply for work of a certain type, size and value of contract. The contractors are then evaluated, eg their performance and financial viability, prior to being allocated a certain grade and category of work.

Once the list is completed those 'approved' contractors are circulated with work to be tendered for in their category only. Such a method of tendering has the advantage of cost effectiveness, tender evaluation being costly for an organisation and unsuccessful tenders being an expensive overhead to contractors. The disadvantage is that, if not on the approved list, some potential contractors will not have knowledge of work open to tender and thus the organisation may not achieve best value for money.

2.1.3 *Restricted*

Particular firms are invited to tender—this does not presuppose an 'approved' list. A particular project might require specialised knowledge limiting to a handful of potential contractors, eg construction of communication satellites or Ministry of Defence equipment.

2.1.4 *Negotiated*

This form of tendering occurs where only one contractor is invited to tender for a very large project, eg Concorde, where there are very few organisations large enough to undertake such an operation. It is mainly used by government on vast national schemes, invitations to tender being based on an 'approved' list.

2.1.5 *Serial*

A form of standing offer whereby a contractor undertakes to enter into a series of 'lump sum' contracts in accordance with terms and conditions set out in the standing offer. Such a system aims to save time for the employer and contractor on a series of tasks whereby the tender is for one contract which is then used as a basis for the series. Essential factors are:

1 A programme of specified tasks which is planned to be completed with a time limit.

2 The series of tasks should be similar in nature.

3 The timespan should be related to the capacity of the contractor.

2.1.6 *Indicative design*

This occurs where tenderers are asked for an overall quotation for a scheme, the contractors being responsible for design, construction and commissioning of the project, eg the National Theatre, the Barbican.

2.2 Audit controls for tendering procedures

The auditor must ensure that regulations are enforced with regard to:

1 *Receipt and custody of tender*—The envelope containing the documents should be marked with the date and time of receipt and entered in a register. Thus the number received can be agreed to the number opened.

2 *Opening procedures*—The operational methods for this are normally stated in regulations and should specify at least two staff, preferably a director, or, in the public sector, the chairman of the committee and chief officer, ie a person who is independent of operational activities.

3 *Assessment*—Quotations and quality of likely performance should be appraised and recorded. In the event of a significant error the contractor may be contacted and asked to resubmit. Such a procedure must, however, be clearly laid down in the organisation's regulations.

4 *Acceptance and award*—Where the lowest tender is not accepted, reasons should be recorded as to why a particular decision was taken (eg for better quality work) and the chairman's decision recorded in the minutes of the meeting approving the award of tenders.

5 *Model regulations*—Within local government the chief inspector of audit reported to the Radcliffe Maud Committee on Local Government Rules and Conduct that more than half of all fraud cases were connected with contracts for work or supplies of goods and services. He further recommended that model standing orders were needed to demonstrate fairness in the allocation of contractors and the avoidance of undue delay in awarding the contract. Failure to comply with model standing orders opens the door to corrupt practices. Whatever the organisation, a recognised and agreed procedure, which must be adhered to, is of utmost importance in order to demonstrate that honesty and integrity are achieved.

3.0   CONTRACT AUDIT

A DEFINITION OF CONTRACT

'The writing containing an agreement.' (*Chambers Dictionary*)

In the context of this book, contract audit refers to the audit of work undertaken by outside contractors on behalf of the organisation of either a revenue or capital nature. The work of the auditor can be divided into three stages:

1 Pre-contract—Before the award of the contract.
2 Currency of the contract—Work in progress and related payments.
3 Final contract—Completed work and final payments.

3.1   Audit objectives

Whatever the stages of the contract, the following objectives should be borne in mind:

1 Compliance with the organisation's regulations and policies.
2 Compliance with professional standards (including surveyors).
3 Achievement of VFM and identification of waste.
4 An adequate system of financial and management information from planning the contract to its completion.
5 An adequate system for recovering rechargeable works.
6 An adequate system of internal control.
(Based on the *Audit of Capital Contracts* (CIPFA).)

However, these objectives are tempered by the ruling in *Wheater v Brighton Corpn* 1946 where it was held that, 'the Architect or Engineer is the responsible officer under the terms of the contract . . .'.

The internal auditor must be careful not to usurp the appropriate professional judgements of architect, engineer or quantity surveyor. The auditor's responsibility is to appraise financial and administrative aspects of the contract and to evaluate its operational impact.

3.2 Extent of audit involvement

The extent of audit work in this area is determined by many factors including the following:

1 Importance attached by the organisation to audit involvement.
2 The auditor's ability to examine technical data.
3 The relationship between auditor and technical expert.
4 The available audit resources and audit plan.
5 Recommendations from the external auditor.

3.3 Role of the engineer

'The engineer is named and is the representative of the employer for the purpose of the contract. The employer looks to the engineer to ensure that the works are properly constituted in accordance with terms of the contract. The contractor looks to the engineer for instruction and certification of invoices properly due to him.' (1983 Joint statement between CIPFA and the Institute of Civil Engineers)

3.4 Contract documents

The auditor should be familiar with all documentation associated with contracts. It is good practice to maintain a checklist of documentation on file, eg:

Contract conditions
Work specifications and drawings
Bills of quantities, rates and prices
Deeds
Architects' certificates and other certificates of work completed
Variation orders
Nominated sub-contractors
Bonds, insurance and liquidated damages
Retention monies and penalty charges

4.0 TYPES OF CONTRACT

Prior to discussing the audit of the three contract stages, various types of contract in common use are now described (please note some of these types may be combined).

4.1 Bills of quantity

This form of contract is based on a given quality and quantity of material being delivered for a given price at a given time. With such contracts the payment system may be vulnerable to overpayments when variation clauses are introduced to allow for increased deliveries. Similarly quality control may be difficult to assess. Both aspects require periodic audit check.

4.2   Schedules of rates for work completed or specifications met

Contracts may be based on certification of work completed, issued by architects, surveyors and engineers. It is for the auditor to monitor that the correct rate is being applied to the appropriate work, based on the contract document.

4.3   Cost plus basis

Under this system the contractor is reimbursed for the cost of labour, materials and plant, together with an agreed percentage to provide for overheads and an allowed profit. Such a contract may prove difficult to audit, the contractor claiming the work being undertaken requires expensive methods, though the appropriate professional manager should act as a control via the 'certification of work done' process.

4.4   Professional appointments

Professional organisations (eg architects, accountants) usually have a set scale of charges or fees. The auditor should monitor that such appointments are made in accordance with the organisation's policies and that any agreement complies with regulations concerning specific areas such as cost control and final payment. Indeed, close monitoring from the outset should ensure that only the correct fees are paid, eg in the case of aborted schemes the professional fees should only reflect the work executed to the stage reached.

4.5   Fixed price

This is a form of contract in which, the price for the work is fixed regardless of increases in costs. It has the advantage that the organisation's financial commitment is known—any change to that commitment requiring a variation order. It is the auditor's role to thoroughly examine such orders investigating the reason for their issue—inefficiency or poor tendering specifications? Variation orders must also be verified to day work schedules to ensure such work claimed for has been undertaken.

4.6   Variable price contracts

This is where the contractor states a basic price but is able to claim for additional costs incurred due to inflation since the contract was agreed.

5.0   STAGES OF CONTRACT

5.1   Pre-contract stage

Prior to the award of contracts to either internal (direct labour) or external organisations, a project appraisal should have taken place to determine the most efficient, economical and effective manner in which to achieve the objective for the organisation.

Secondly, a system should be in existence to control the manner in which that objective is achieved from its conception as an agreed idea or policy, through draft of plans and specifications, tendering process, contract work and final commissioning.

MONITORING MANAGEMENT INFORMATION

Initially the auditor's role is to monitor management information to ensure that policy decisions are based on adequate and reliable information and that specifications for the contract relate to the policy decisions made. Consequently the auditor should be an adviser and not be directly involved in the making of policy decisions.

SELECTION OF CONTRACTORS

Once all the tenders have been received and the associated procedures completed, the auditor's role is to appraise management procedures for the evaluation of the contractor. In undertaking this role the auditor should ensure management action is adequate.

The rate of business failures in the UK increased from approximately 15,000 per annum in 1985 to 20,000 in 1990. Building and engineering industries, which comprise the major contractors, are among the most likely to suffer failure. These are the industries at greatest risk especially in times of economic depression.

The financial viability of a potential contractor is vitally important, as it can be very expensive to have a contract completed if the primary contractor defaults. Use of the 'Extel' service and Dun & Bradstreet (eg Dunmatch service) are recommended, supported by an inspection of the contractor's records, eg an examination at Companies House. Time may be saved by requesting a copy of the accounts from the latter or the use of financial information provided by Prestel and Oracle. Though experts have developed complex formulae to detect potential business failure, the following three financial ratios have been identified as critical:

1 *Profitability*—This can be measured as a ratio of profit before taxation to total assets. This indicates the degree of efficiency with which management is utilising its resources when compared to others in the same industry or to previous periods. It may also indicate long-term viability.

2 *Gearing*—This can be measured as the ratio of average net borrowing to total net assets. It indicates the proportion of fixed interest that has to be paid no matter what the profit is. Thus when times are good, there are no problems; however, should profits be low, the payment of interest will still be necessary placing the organisation in a position of vulnerability as far as liquidity is concerned.

3 *Liquidity*—This is measured as the quickly realisable assets (cash, short-term investments which can be quickly realised and debtors) as compared to short-term creditors (bank loans and trade creditors). This indicates the ability of the contractor to meet any short-term claim.

The latter is important because it measures the ability of the organisation to function in the immediate term, ie to purchase materials, undertake work and meet immediate commitments (employee costs, etc). A sound assessment of the financial strength of every potential contractor is a crucial requirement. It is recommended that one of the many good textbooks concerning financial accounting be read in order to gain an appreciation of the technique of ratio analysis.

When dealing with small or newly-formed contractors, it is prudent to ask for a form of guarantee—there being no accounts available for inspection—and obtain a statement from the firm's bankers as to their financial status. With larger organisations a provision should exist within the contract for liquidated damages whereby monies are retained against failure by the contractor to fulfil his obligations. Such provision should cover loss of income and profit, together with loss of interest on capital invested in the project as well as the cost of making alternative arrangements.

ABILITY TO PERFORM WORK

Professional evaluation of another profession's work is beyond the scope of most auditors. However, an auditor should ensure that expert evaluation of the tenderer is made and that previous experience of the contractor's work is taken into account. When considering a firm for the first time it may be useful to approach previous customers of the company where the work to be undertaken is comparable in both size and complexity.

A major problem facing auditors is that of sub-contracting, where the main contractor sub-contracts part of the work. Lack of control by the main contractor may lead to poor performance and bad workmanship. To avoid such problems, the following matters should be provided for:

1 Penalty clauses for late completion—damages payable by the main contractor.
2 Progress payments for certified work.
3 Retention monies—monies retained (usually 5% of certified work) and held for an agreed period to ensure that the completed work is satisfactory.

It should be noted that penalty clauses are often difficult to enforce, sometimes due to vague terminology, eg 'due to weather permitting'. Retention monies are usually held over for a given period after the final completion date.

LEGAL CONSTRAINTS

In practice any illegal act will terminate the contract.

ADEQUATE INSURANCE

A copy of the tenderer's insurance cover should be requested for inspection to allow assessment of the cover provided re contractor third parties and other material matters.

BONDING

It is not uncommon for organisations to request a bond, as much as 10% of the contract value, to secure performance of the contract. Where cash is not available, guarantees should be taken.

Once the contractors have been evaluated, the appropriate directors or committee should award the contract in accordance with the organisation's regulations.

Once selected, the contract should be entered in a contracts register so that progress can be regularly monitored and reviewed.

5.2 Currency of the contract

CHIEF INSPECTOR OF AUDIT'S CRITICISM AND RECOMMENDATIONS

With regard to construction contracts the Chief Inspector of Audit (Local Government) noted that controls commonly existed at the pre-contract and final contract stages but were in many instances non-existent during the currency of the contract:

'This lack of audit cover at the interim audit payment stage would have been more acceptable if there were systems to exercise effective control over such expenditure. But often, once contracts were let, financial control was left in the hands of the authorities' technical officers or consultants. There was an absence of regular financial reporting to the financial directors or members of progress on schemes, against the original contract sums. Thus, finance departments did not become aware of any major variations on contracts until their record of contract payment alerted them to the fact that the original accounts had been or were likely to be exceeded. More often than not where contractors were paid on the basis of consultant architects' certificates, there was no system to ensure that proper valuations existed to support those certificates.' (1979 Annual Report)

In line with the CIPFA and ICE statement reliance, has been placed on the 'expert's' certificate, the general view being taken that:

1 An undue delay in payment might constitute a 'breach of contract'.
2 Refusal to pay the debt might be seen as interference with the professional and technical skill of the 'expert'.

In conclusion the Inspector of Audit recommended that:

1 The finance officer should not release monies until satisfied that:
   (a) They are supported by properly compiled valuations.
   (b) Each certificate is supported by a copy of the valuation.
   (c) No unauthorised variations have been included.
2 The progress of all major contracts be regularly reported to members.
3 Internal audit should examine all stages of the contract.

MEETING THESE RECOMMENDATIONS

Pre-audit work:

1 Analyse the valuation of work to date showing details of major works, day works and claims, etc.

2 From the legal section obtain and examine bills of quantities, specifications, agreements, forms of tender and correspondence files. Note information which may require examination at a later stage.
3 Identify 'preliminary' items.
4 Identify from the specifications and bills a sample of items for physical inspection on site, ie thickness of concrete, asphalt, number of doors, windows, quality of materials.
5 Check audit files and working papers for any further matters.

Preliminary work at site office:

1 Examine all correspondence, records of site meetings, site instructions, variation orders, day works and clerk of works reports, noting matters for further consideration.
2 Request a copy of the site plan.
3 Check the method of appointment of sub-contractors and suppliers.
4 Check the system for providing financial control and ensure compliance with the organisation's regulations.
5 The expert's certificate of work completed—valuation thereof:
   (a) Examine the latest and first valuations on a test basis with the rates shown in the bill of quantities or schedule of rates applicable to the contract. Request explanations for variations.
   (b) Test check the measurement per valuation with the site records, eg dimension books and sheets.
   (c) Check day work sheets to verify that day works have been properly authorised and agree arithmetical accuracy and rates applied. Check that the day work claims are properly documented.
   (d) Verify that variation orders have been issued in respect of all variations, certified by those authorised and the costs correctly applied. Such procedures should comply with the financial regulations of the organisation. Review all variations and their explanations.

Materials control:

The extent of the audit work will depend on the procedures being adopted on the site. Consideration should be given to coverage of the following matters:

1 Adequacy of documentation, eg copy orders, delivery notes, etc.
2 Where materials are supplied free of charge by the organisation, ensure that the issue of materials is adequately controlled.
3 Examine the arrangements for the disposal of scrap material—who receives the income?

Recommended site visit procedure:

Arrange a meeting with the 'expert' to:

1 Discuss matters raised during the pre-audit stage.
2 Examine work undertaken by the contractor referring to the site plan and by physical inspection, eg it is particularly important for the extent of excavations, site conditions, soft spots, etc. Record the type of construction involved (eg in a sewer contract whether pipe-jacking).

3 Examine the method of compiling the valuation:
Preliminaries.
Normal contract work.
Increased costs.
Where a remeasure is involved, physically inspect the method agreed between the 'expert' and the contractor. If necessary carry out sample checks on the measures taken.
4 Check whether variation orders have been issued in respect of all variations.
5 Physical checks:
   (a) Check preliminary items, ie visible temporary items (site huts etc).
   (b) Check specifications.
   (c) Determine plant usage at the time of the site visit and reconcile the accuracy of the plant register.
6 Discuss the following with the clerk of works:
   (a) The name of and time when an authorised clerk of works can be found on site.
   (b) The site records prepared.
   (c) The method of checking labour, plant and materials. Ensure compliance with regulations.
   (d) Discuss any other relevant matters.
(Based on *Financial Examination and Audit of Capital Contracts* (CIPFA).)

ADVANTAGES OF AUDIT INVOLVEMENT DURING THE CURRENCY OF A CONTRACT

1 The auditor is already familiar with the contract.
2 The auditor has established adequate control procedures.
3 Physical evidence of variation orders can be inspected.
4 Technician's responses are more accurate the more current the problem.
5 Prime documents are more readily available.
6 Fraud is easier to detect, there being less time to hide evidence.
7 The contractor may wait a considerable time before final settlement is made hence a long delay in the audit of the final account.
8 The close involvement of the auditor during the currency of the contract allows for close working with technical staff and an understanding of technical problems and their financial effect.
9 The appointment of sub-contractors can be investigated and their work viewed prior to problems arising.
10 Checking progress payments and variation orders during the contract reduces the work at the final account stage.
11 Adequate reporting of financial data can be ensured.
12 The intricacies of costing techniques can be readily appraised.

5.3 Final contract audit

Following involvement at current and pre-audit stages the auditor will have knowledge of areas of weakness requiring further examination, eg:

1 Comparison of work done to work in the tender for quality of materials and labour utilised. Cost per unit of material may be compared to that in the contract or, if a variation order, to a technical journal. Similarly labour rates can be compared to those for the trade for reasonableness. Materials used can be totalled to ensure errors have not occurred to date.

2 Prime cost (costs directly associated with the work) and provisional items should have been adjusted for the actual cost instead of the original provision. Supporting invoices should be used to justify costs. Similarly additional percentages can be applied to allow for overhead and profit recovery depending on the contract.
3 Any discounts obtained by the contractor (sub-contractor) should be passed on to the organisation depending on the terms of contract (cost plus contracts).
4 All variation orders accompanied by day work schedules should be appropriately authorised.
5 A report should be made summarising total cost to tender document detailing reasons for variations and time agreed and time taken.
6 Payment of retention monies should only occur upon satisfaction with the work at the agreed time.

6.0   PROBLEMS OF DAY WORK

1 Charges for work are the contractual responsibility of the contractor.
2 There can be duplication between day work and measured work (contract work).
3 Plant may be charged for longer hours than the operator.
4 There may be duplication of work between worksheets.
5 Labour may be charged at a higher rate than paid.
6 Fictitious workmen may be charged for.

It should be noted that many contracts allow the contracting party to inspect the contractor's records, eg as in local government.

6.1   Scope for malpractice

1 Labour rates above that agreed are paid.
2 Unrealistic material cost increase.
3 The price list used at the time of tender may be lower than the current price list which should have been applied at the time of tender, thereby increasing the rate of inflation.
4 Claims for apprentices at adult rates.
5 The price list may quote certain prices for certain quantities of goods, but the claim may be for smaller quantities of delivery, thereby over-claiming the cost of goods.

Again, an examination of contractor's records would detect most of these malpractices.

6.2   Problems relating to land

Problems relating to land are an inseparable part of any construction project. Other than the procedures for the purchase of land and entry on terrier, the following matters should be considered:

1 Any income transferred with title (fishing rights?).
2 Income from temporary use (car park).
3 Prevention of loss of land through encroachment.
4 Disposal of land surplus to requirements.

7.0 POST-CONTRACT COMPLETION REVIEW

Lessons should be learned from errors made and procedural, financial and technical controls improved. Similarly where ex gratia payments are made, the proper authorisation should be verified. Comparisons such as final cost to tender price, time taken to that forecast (slippage), etc should be made and finally reported upon.

Where equipment is concerned, its capability and reliability in practice should be compared to the original specifications and again finally reported upon. Where a failing is identified, management should be advised to undertake action to prevent a recurrence.

8.0 CONTRACT FRAUD

In general, capital transactions are more complex than revenue transactions, being particularly subject to the following problems:

1 The need for long-term planning to control and co-ordinate the many procedures and activities of large numbers of internal and external personnel with differing skills and professional expertise.
2 In the public sector compliance must be with the various central government standards.
3 Again in the public sector, the changing political environment may cause amendment to long-term contracts, eg 1984 moratorium.

Such complexity allows fraud to be the more easily concealed and fraud is further facilitated due to the enormous sums involved which are controlled by a small number of people, thereby reducing the number of internal checks, and indeed making collusion more rewarding. Secondly, while internal audit of revenue transactions is readily appreciated, the various experts involved in a capital scheme may strongly object to a 'mere auditor' examining their work, and as a result internal control may not be as well established. Thirdly, while performance indicators are available to auditors (unit costs) to alert them to problems as they occur, these cannot be so easily monitored with capital schemes because a capital project may be a one-off event.

8.1 Some examples of contract fraud

During the 1970s police carried out massive investigations into supplies of materials for a motorway construction and found that thousands of tons of rocks paid for by main contractors never reached the site. They revealed:

1 Ghost lorries—Registration numbers 'borrowed' from scrap lorries shown on delivery tickets.
2 Lorries being repeatedly driven round the same checkpoint, simulating deliveries.
3 The switching of number plates from one lorry to another in order to weigh loads twice.
4 Claiming payment with forged delivery tickets.

8.1.1   *Some other typical contract frauds*

1 Variation orders not assessed financially prior to issue.
2 Demolition work incomplete, although certified as having been done.
3 Private houses painted together with local authority houses.
4 Metal footbridge charged for, yet cheaper wooden one provided.

These are only a few examples of fraudulent activity, there are many more which could be listed if space allowed.

8.1.2   *Contractors in default*

The final settlement in a liquidation may take years to complete, involving changes of staff and disruption of work. It is essential for documentation to be complete and maintained in an orderly manner, thereby providing adequate evidence as to the stage of work completed. From the organisation's point of view it is important to complete the contract. This may be undertaken by either the receiver or through the appointment of a new contractor.

8.1.3   *Areas of concern*

1 *Part completed contract*—At the earliest opportunity the organisation's technical expert (architect or quantity surveyor) should complete an examination of the defaulting contractor's completed work in order to establish the following:
   (a) The value of the work completed until time of default.
   (b) An estimate of the cost of work required in order to complete the contract.
   (c) The cost of remedial work, eg the effect of the elements on an unprotected site.
   (d) The amount of outstanding claims payable to the liquidator.
   (e) A revised timescale within which to complete the contract.

2 *Completion of the contract.* The objective must be to complete the contract satisfactorily with the minimum of additional work, expenditure and delay.

8.2   Defaulting contractors

All equipment and assets should be secured so that the liquidator and not unsecured creditors (eg sub-contractors) can take possession. All payments due to the defaulting contractor should be made to the receiver and not to other claimants. A procedure should be established whereby either the receiver and his staff agree to complete the contract or a new contractor is found by tendering. In undertaking this work the auditor must ensure that the expert has carried out his investigations (see above) and that the following matters have been considered:

1 Any claims that can be made against the insurance company.
2 The withholding of guarantees.
3 Notifying the organisation's own insurance company.
4 Establishing separate records in order to identify expenditure that has been incurred as a result of the default.
5 Maintaining separate records for the defaulting contractor, for the receiver and for the new contractor.
6 Retention monies and certified payments should only be released to the receiver following agreement of work completed.
7 The releasing of performance bonds should only be made to the receiver (depending on terms) once the final certificate has been agreed.
8 When assessing the state of the contract a written agreement should be reached with the receiver, the new contractor and the organisation—the object being to avoid any later dispute which might further delay the contract.
9 Adequate documentation should be maintained to support all stages and agreements reached in concluding the contract.

Audit profit triggers—contract audit (Defined at **2.11** in Chapter 3)

Tendering procedures:
  Compliance with standing orders and regulations
    Invitation and selection of tenders
    Methods of tendering
    Selective lists
    Receipt & Custody of tenders
    Opening of tenders
    Open competitive
    Selective
    Restricted
    Negotiated
    Serial
    Indicative design
  Financial & administrative controls
  Reasons for not accepting lowest tender

Contractual arrangements:
  Pre-contract
    Appraisal of proposed contract
    Systems control procedures
    Management information
    Tendering procedures
    Financial & technical appraisal
    Adequacy of specification
    Form of contract
    Responsibility of contractor
    Award of the contract
    Legal constraints (incl insurance)

Currency of the contract:
  Site visits
  Materials control
  Variation orders & day work schedules
  Responsibility of professional experts
  Retention monies
  Orderly & timely progress reports
  Method of valuation of part completed work
  Part payment & valuation certificates

Final stage:
  Summary & comparison of costs & progress
  Comparison to tender with reasons for variations
  Performance bonds & retention monies
  Discounts received policy
  Penalty clause
  Actual: expected cost

Post contract review:
  Appraisal of performance—actual: expected
  Corrective action

Liquidations procedures:
  Protect assets
  Revised timescale to completion
  Insurance policy; retention monies; performance bonds
  Relationship with liquidator & receiver
  Minimise risk
  Cost of remedial action
  Estimated stage of completion

Further reading

Financial examination and audit of capital contracts (1979) (CIPFA)

CHAPTER 10   Operational management

Objectives	To explain the nature and techniques of operational audit and to give some detailed examples of practical application
Contents	The nature of operational audit Operational audit techniques Marketing applications: demand forecasting; market development; product development; distribution planning; sales pricing; sales promotion; sales administration Production control applications: sales order processing; production planning and engineering; material management; production scheduling
Summary	This chapter analyses the management objectives of some key operational functions and gives practical examples of how operational audit can be used to contribute positively to achieving them. The operational auditor must first gain a clear understanding of the objectives and of management's detailed plans for their achievement. The purpose and scope of each operational audit assignment must be clearly defined and agreed in advance

1.0   THE NATURE OF OPERATIONAL AUDIT

1.1   Management audit

Internal audit is a management service. It is established by the management of an organisation who will define the terms of reference within its own absolute discretion. It follows that the terms of reference will be primarily concerned with contributing in some way to achievement of the management objectives. These terms will vary considerably from one organisation to another depending upon the perceived need for internal audit services by the separate managements of each organisation. In some cases it may concentrate on financial security while in others it may be required to appraise all management activity and it may be described as internal audit, operational audit or management audit.

J Santocki in *Auditing* defines 'management audit' concisely:

'to assist management to better the performance of the organisation.'

In *Management Audits* A J Sayle expands on this:

> 'an independent examination of objective evidence, performed by trained personnel, to determine whether integrated management systems, which are required to fulfil contractual and legal obligations of the company to its customers and the community, are being effectively implemented, and the true and fair presentation of results of such examination'.

Management audit is:

> 'a systematic, comprehensive, critical appraisal of the organisation structure, management practices and methods conducted normally by external independent persons . . . its primary objective is to motivate management to take action which will lead to increased efficiency and profitability of the organisation.' (British Institute of Management)

There is unfortunately a degree of confusion about the terminology used to define some internal audit activity. The term 'management audit' in particular has been used to convey a number of distinctly different ideas:

1 The term 'management audit' is sometimes used to describe any audit function established by management for its own purposes so as to distinguish such a function from 'statutory audit' which is required by law for the benefit of shareholders or the public. Throughout this book these two types of audit are described as 'internal audit' and 'external' or 'statutory audit' respectively.
2 The term 'management audit' has been used to describe the audit of board level activity to distinguish this from the audit of management activity below board level which is described as 'operational audit'. Throughout this book the term 'operational audit' is adopted as applying to the audit of all management activity. Internal audit of board level activity does of course imply an independent line of reporting, perhaps to an audit committee, to ensure impartiality and objectivity.
3 The term 'management audit' has been used to describe audit appraisal of management efficiency in the formulation of policies and in policy decision making. This is distinguished from 'operational audit' which is then the appraisal of operational effectiveness and is concerned with verifying that management policies are being effectively implemented. Throughout this book the term 'operational audit' is used to describe audit activity which both appraises management policies and verifies their implementation.

1.2   Operational audit

Internal audit is a management service which can be used in various ways depending on the objectives envisaged when it was established. Managements should first evaluate the opportunities and risks in each major operational sector. The potential contribution of an internal audit service in giving assurance on the one hand and identifying opportunities for improved performance on the other can then be assessed against each major area of risk or opportunity.

If financial security is perceived as the predominant area of risk, this is likely to be the main objective of the internal audit function. The internal auditor will then be concerned primarily with the validity, authenticity and integrity of financial recording and reporting systems and procedures and the effectiveness of compliance.

A skilled internal auditor examining financial recording systems for security may find opportunities for recommending improvements in efficiency. This auditor is also in a position to make valid judgements on the decision making process which the records are intended to service. This can enhance considerably the value to management of the internal audit service.

When financial reporting is effectively used as a management tool, the internal audit service is likely to be directed to take the audit examination beyond the management accounts into the operational activity which they describe. At this stage the audit service has to become operational audit and will need to be equipped with a whole range of additional skills and experience.

DEFINITION

Operational audit is an impartial service to operational management which gives assurance when appropriate that operational objectives are valid; that operational control information is reliable; and that operational activities are effective and efficient. It is also an agent for change by identifying and analysing managerial problems and offering practical suggestions for improving operational effectiveness, efficiency or economy.

Operational audit is concerned with the pursuit of economy, efficiency and effectiveness throughout all operations:

Economy is the measure of input.
Effiency is the measure of the relationship between input and output.
Effectiveness is the measure of output.

The concept is illustrated in the chart below.

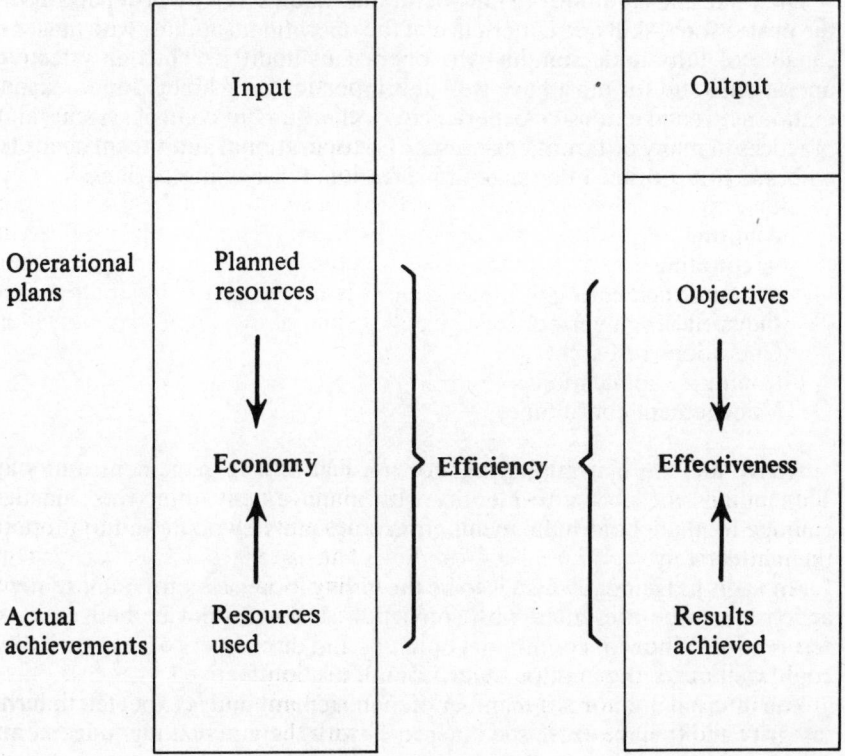

1.3   The operational auditor's role

Operational audit involves the application of all the basic audit skills of penetrating examination of relevant evidence, informed analysis of findings and making objective interpretive judgements from an impartial viewpoint.

This must be followed by effective presentation of the audit judgements to the responsible operational management and when appropriate making practical suggestions which will lead to improvements in the economy, efficiency and effectiveness of the operations.

In theory, the audit function is limited to observing and making recommendations. In operational audit terms this means identifying and analysing managerial problems. The solutions should then be clear to the responsible management who should be able to resolve the problems using its own resources.

In practice, operational managers are often acutely aware of their managerial problems. They may also have perceived valid solutions while finding other operational needs to take priority in the allocation of available resources.

In these cases an independent operational audit analysis of the problem will be reassuring. It will often bring to bear experience of similar problems which have been tackled elsewhere. It will also be beneficial in that it can enable progress to be made.

The audit recommendations can form the basis of a programme for change. The auditor can then become a valuable additional resource and is in a position to make a positive contribution by giving detailed guidance and monitoring progress. This practice also extends the auditor's experience and enhances credibility.

The value and credibility of the operational audit service will depend upon the professional skill and experience of the operational auditor who must be capable of fully understanding the operations audited. Thus an effective operational auditor must have well developed learning ability, audit examination skills and extensive experience of management control systems and practices in many different businesses. The operational audit team needs to embrace competence in a range of professional disciplines such as:

Auditing.
Accounting.
Systems engineering.
Industrial engineering.
Operations research.
Computer applications.
Management consultancy.

Above all, the operational auditor must have a management outlook. This implies the ability to identify with management objectives and the courage to make bold judgements from a unique viewpoint and to present them effectively.

An audit judgement which is to be the basis of a decision for management action has to be presented with conviction. It should not be hedged with reservations. Indeed, conditional opinions and disclaimers of responsibility could well make the auditor's view completely ineffective.

The internal auditor is a member of management and is expected to have integrity and to have exercised due professional care in making judgements on the best information available at the time. They must act like managers and be prepared to stand by the judgements they make.

For this quality, recent operational management experience is an invaluable ingredient in the operational audit team to ensure a credible and effective service to management.

All auditors must be responsible for the quality and integrity of their advice. This can be a very onerous responsibility. They will expect their advice to be taken seriously and it may well have far reaching implications which they must take into account in reaching conclusions.

1.4   Independence

The operational audit functions must be seen to be independent from the management it serves. It must protect and preserve its independence to ensure it remains capable of making impartial audit judgements which will be perceived as objective. It must never usurp the operational manager's role. The function of audit is to observe and make recommendations.

It must be clear at all times that the auditor has no authority to change operational methods, systems, procedures, practices or personnel. These are management activities and full authority for them must be seen to remain firmly with the accountable operational manager.

Operational auditors must identify totally with the objectives of the managements they serve. They must analyse the organisation and the managerial activity in the context of these objectives.

Involvement in implementing changes which the audit has shown to be necessary could jeopardise the auditor's independence and reputation for impartiality. However, operational audit work must be regarded as incomplete until the recommended changes have been either accepted and successfully implemented or positively set aside.

The auditor can often make a significant positive contribution at the implemenation stages by giving detailed guidance and monitoring progress as the work proceeds. In such circumstances auditors must take special care to ensure their independence is not compromised.

2.0   OPERATIONAL AUDIT TECHNIQUES

2.1   Service to management

Operational audit is not a universal panacea for all management problems. It is difficult, systematic and disciplined work. A first essential is a strong commitment from the management to whom the service is being provided. Effective results depend upon good collaboration between the operational auditor and the user of the service.

Ideally the user management should identify the areas needing operational audit examination and initiate the request for service. This request should always be specified as a formally agreed clearly written brief before the work starts.

The primary purpose of an operational audit brief is to ensure that both the user and the auditor have a common understanding of what has to be done. The brief will need to specify answers to such questions as:

What is the problem to be considered?
Which areas are to be examined?
When is the work to be done?
Who may be consulted?
How is progress to be monitored?
How are final conclusions to be reported?

If changes are recommended and adopted and the auditor is retained in a continuing guidance and monitoring role, it is often preferable to agree a separate brief for his work after the changes have been agreed.

2.2   Operational audit planning

Operational audit may be concerned with the full range of operational activity.

The risks and opportunities in each sector of activity should be evaluated and ranked in order of priority to determine in which areas operational audit services are likely to make the most effective contribution.

The operational audit function can then be planned and equipped with the appropriate skills and effectively directed to give maximum support to achieving corporate objectives.

By way of example, a list of the coverage areas considered most suitable for operational audit examination in the range of different businesses which comprise a major UK industrial conglomerate are listed here:

MARKETING

Price structure
Sales administration
Distribution
Debtors

MATERIAL MANAGEMENT

Purchasing
Stock control
Creditors

FIXED ASSETS

Capital expenditure
Fixed asset management

DATA PROCESSING

Operations
Security

SECURITY

Site security
Insurance
Cash
Payrolls

PRODUCTION

Production records
Planning and control

MANAGEMENT ACCOUNTING

Costing
Period accounts
Accounting records

These areas of audit coverage provide the basis for determining the annual audit plan in consultation with each chief executive responsible for the effective management of a group of operating businesses. An example of a section of an audit plan prepared in this way is given on p 306.

Having agreed the areas to be examined, detailed audit programmes and operational audit briefs can be developed for each business in collaboration with the accountable general manager of that business.

2.3 Audit profile triggers

The key to effective operational audit is in developing a programme of audit tests which will enable the auditor to make a positive contribution to management performance. Such a programme must be designed to relate specifically to the objectives of the operations to be examined and to the circumstances prevailing at the time. The auditor can be helped in forming this judgement by audit profile triggers (APTs).

Audit profile triggers represent a digest of topics to be considered under each area of coverage. Their purpose is to prompt creative thinking in the context of the operations to be appraised. They are not an alternative for a detailed programme of audit tests and checks. They are in fact the means of developing such a programme which ensures that it will be directly relevant to the objectives and circumstances of a specific business.

Examples of APT topics for particular areas of audit coverage are quoted in various parts of this book. The topics for each area should be considered within a common framework.

FRAMEWORK FOR DETERMINING AUDIT PROFILES

Organisation	How the function being examined is organised
Objectives	Objectives of this function
Authority	How authority is delegated and the limits
Accountability	Who is accountable to whom and for what
Resources	The resources provided for this function
Instructions	Procedure notes, system manuals, operating instructions
Compliance	Adherence to procedures and operating instructions
Monitoring	Systems and procedures for testing and measuring performance
Control	Action to keep to plans
Effectiveness	Achieving targets, plans and objectives
Efficiency	Optimum use of resources
Security	Protection against specific risks
Legality	Compliance with obligations imposed by law
Risks	Risks related to this function
Opportunities	Further possibilities for contributing to corporate objectives

AUDIT PLAN

Coverage

Unit	Marketing 1				Material management 2			Fixed assets 3		D P 4		Security 5				Production 6		Management accounting 7			date	days
	1.1	1.2	1.3	1.4	2.1	2.2	2.3	3.1	3.2	4.1	4.2	5.1	5.2	5.3	5.4	6.1	6.2	7.1	7.2	7.3		
3001					x			x						x						x	Jan	4
3002		x	x	x	x	x	x							x	x	x	x	x	x	x	Feb	20
3003					x	x	x			x	x	x	x	x				x	x	x	Feb	5
3004		x	x		x	x	x	x	x	x	x					x					Sep	15
3005		x	x		x	x						x	x	x	x						Jul	6
3007		x	x		x	x						x		x							Dec	6
3009		x	x		x	x						x		x							Dec	6
3010		x	x		x	x						x	x	x	x						Oct	6
3012	x	x	x	x	x			x	x	x	x					x					Sep	10
3013	x	x	x	x	x	x	x			x	x	x	x	x				x	x	x	Aug	15
3014		x			x	x	x					x		x	x			x	x			
3017	x	x	x	x	x	x	x					x	x	x	x	x	x	x	x		Oct	10
3202					x		x			x		x		x					x		Jun	15
3202	x	x	x		x													x	x		Feb	5
3203						x						x		x		x	x	x	x		Oct	10
3204	x	x	x	x								x	x	x							Oct	10
3017					x	x	x									x	x			x	Feb	10
3018					x	x	x									x	x			x	Feb	5
3501	x	x	x	x	x													x	x		Nov	4

Key to columns:

- 1.1 Price structure
- 1.2 Sales administration
- 1.3 Distribution
- 1.4 Debtors
- 2.1 Purchasing
- 2.2 Stock control
- 2.3 Creditors
- 3.1 Capital expenditure
- 3.2 Fixed asset man'gmnt
- 4.1 D P operations
- 4.2 D P security
- 5.1 Site security
- 5.2 Insurance
- 5.3 Cash
- 5.4 Payroll
- 6.1 Production recording
- 6.2 Planning and control
- 7.1 Costing
- 7.2 Period accounts
- 7.3 Accounting records

2.4 Adherence and adaptive systems

Adherence is another word for compliance: the system expects operations to conform to an original plan.

Adaptive control is a more flexible approach, operations can adapt to changes as and when they occur.

Production control is complex and tends to be subject to unexpected variations. It is usual to strike a balance between strict adherence and adaptability.

For the auditor it is important to recognise the difference between the systems and allow for it in the audit techniques adopted.

A comparison of the main features is illustrated here:

Dimension	*Adherence system*	*Adaptive system*
Information base	Historical data	Current data
Starting point	Predictable: Sales forecast and customers orders	Unpredictable: Change in any production variable
Frequency	Periodic forecasting with some updating for customer orders	Continuous monitoring of all production control variables
Lead time for decisions	Long: for reaction to forecasts Intermediate for reaction to orders	Short

Audit tests of adherence control should be based upon ensuring that an appropriate response is made to changes identified by the information system. Adaptive control testing must examine the response to environmental change which may not be recorded in the information system. Informal information is then very important.

Most management decisions involve choosing between competing demands on finite resources. The objective in allocating priorities is to achieve the optimum compromise in the interests of the undertaking as a whole. It involves management judgement. For example:

Rescheduling production to improve customer service in one area may result in pressure on warehouse capacity and stock investment in another.

Design changes to satisfy a customer request may result in obsolescent stock and redundant purchase commitments and an imbalance of production capacity.

Adaptive control action would be taken to mitigate the effect of such repercussions.

It is important in auditing adaptive control systems to obtain adequate evidence that significant changes in control variables are detected and that reasonable adjustments are made to scheduling. Particular attention should be paid to changes in:

1 Customer requirements.
2 Delivery dates.
3 Product specification.

4 Stock levels.
5 Re-order levels.
6 Purchase lead times.
7 Material availability.
8 Labour availability.
9 Plant availability.
10 Warehouse availability.
11 Transport and delivery requirements.

2.5   Cash operating cycles

An example is given here:

	Days	Days
Raw materials		
$\dfrac{\text{Value of stock}}{\text{Annual consumption}} \times 365$	= 50	
Less:		
Credit received		
$\dfrac{\text{Trade creditors}}{\text{Annual credit purchase of material}} \times 365$	= 45	5
Add:		
Production period		
$\dfrac{\text{Value of work in progress}}{\text{Annual cost of goods manufactured}} \times 365$	=	30
Finished goods		
$\dfrac{\text{Value of finished goods}}{\text{Annual cost of goods sold}} \times 365$	=	60
Credit allowed		
$\dfrac{\text{Trade debtors}}{\text{Annual credit sales}} \times 365$	=	55
Cash operating cycle		150

This is a useful guide for measuring working capital investment. It relates overall production time, stock turnover, and supplier and customer credit to give a measure of the time interval between paying out cash to suppliers and receiving payment from customers.

2.6   Example of an operational audit brief

Internal audit examination of marketing, sales order processing and finished stock

Terms of reference

Examine the marketing and selling procedures and controls, report on their adequacy and recommend potential improvements which will make them more efficient and cost effective.

MARKETING

Selling approach—how, and through what outlets.
Quotations procedures and the hit rate achieved.
Pricing structure, including the detailed treatment of pricing at the time of price changes.
Discount structure.
Sales order book controls.
Delivery times, including adherence to promised delivery dates.
Quality control procedures to ensure customer requirements are met.

SALES ORDER PROCESSING

The administration and control of sales order processing in the sales office before computer input.

DATA PROCESSING

The controls within the computerised areas of your sales order processing and stock systems to ensure completeness, accuracy, and security of data processing, and adequacy of DP service provided.

PRODUCTION PLANNING

Review briefly the relevant production planning procedures which aim at ensuring adequacy of stocks for customer service while avoiding excessive build up of surplus stocks or side runs.
Establish whether there is a need for further work in this area.

RESOURCES

Hardware and personnel resources available in the areas examined.

MANAGEMENT INFORMATION

Management information generated in all the areas covered.

SCOPE OF ASSIGNMENT

The review is to cover all products produced and will include procedures for integrating new products or fringe products into your mainstream systems.

3.0 MARKETING OPERATIONS

3.1 The nature of marketing

The pursuit of profitability by business enterprises is based upon successfully satisfying an established demand.

Marketing is the function concerned with identifying demand for the products or services the business enterprise intends to offer. It follows that the marketing function subsequently becomes involved to varying degrees in most aspects of planning the activities of the enterprise to exploit the demand it has identified. In particular the marketing function's responsibility for demand forecasting is crucial to the corporate plan and is a cornerstone of the basis of planning and performance measurement for most other functions.

For this reason the operational auditor needs to understand the role of the marketing function in every business examined. This is necessary to judge the impact of marketing forecasts on the plans developed for the other functions.

DEFINITIONS

> 'Marketing is the management process which identifies, anticipates and supplies customer requirements efficiently and profitably.' (Institute of Marketing)

> 'Marketing management is the analysis, planning, implementation and control of programmes designed to create, build and maintain mutually beneficial exchanges and relationships with target markets for the purpose of achieving organisational objectives. It relies on a disciplined analysis of the needs, wants, perceptions and preferences of target and intermediary markets as a basis for effective product design, pricing, communication and distribution.' (Koch *Marketing Management, Analysis, Planning and Control*)

The marketing function will normally include some or all of the following activities:

1 Marketing research and demand forecasting.
2 Market development.
3 Product development.
4 Distribution planning.
5 Pricing policy.
6 Promotion and sales planning.
7 Sales administration.

It is important to distinguish selling from marketing:

Marketing—To supply what the customer wants, focusing on the needs of the buyer.

Selling—To persuade the customer to buy, focusing on the needs of the seller.

Consequently marketing is a planning and co-ordinating management function to identify and maintain markets. In achieving such objectives the marketing department must identify the needs of the buyer.

Factors influencing a buying decision may be identified as either psychological or socio-economic as follows:

Psychological needs:

1 Motivation—as with Maslow's hierarchy of needs (A H Maslow *Motivation and Personality*), so customers have needs requiring satisfaction (ie to exist, security, social status, self-fulfilment).
2 Attitudes—the buyer's attitude to a product.
3 Learning—the buyer learns about a product.
4 Loyalty—an important phenomenon—buy British!
5 Personality—the buyer's behaviour is inevitably influenced by his personality.

Socio-economic needs:

6 Group influence—others may influence the buyer.
7 Size of the population—total demand will be restricted by size, per capita income, etc.
8 Demography—the numbers in the various age groups will determine a market size.
9 Regional preferences—there are many regional variations which will affect total demand.
10 Cultural preferences—as 9.
11 Social class—occupation rather than income tends to determine buying habits.

Marketing is a crucial management function. It plays a key role in corporate planning. Its work affects every other function of the business to some degree. It can have a significant influence on performance and profitability. Consequently management will have taken considerable care to get its marketing judgements right and to ensure they are properly understood and applied.

The audit objective should be to assist in enhancing the quality of marketing judgements and the effectiveness of their application. In this case it is especially important for the auditor to have a thorough understanding of the entire business—its markets, its products, its technology, its processes, its systems and its people—to be in a position to form meaningful views. Auditing skills can then be applied to evaluate the information bases and the rationale used in forming marketing judgements but the auditor must take care to stop short of 'second guessing' the experts. In this way there can be considerable potential for audit of marketing activity to contribute positively to operational effectiveness in the pursuit of corporate objectives.

Audit programmes should be developed using the audit profile framework referred to previously. The audit tests should be designed to analyse information validity and application effectiveness for the marketing judgements made in six key areas:

1 Market research and demand forecasting.
2 Market development.
3 Product development.
4 Distribution planning.
5 Sales pricing.
6 Sales promotion.

3.2 Market research and demand forecasting

To survive in a competitive world a commercial organisation must develop its operational plans on a foundation of reliable information about the market place in which it intends to offer its products. Market information is collected in a variety of ways. Most business enterprises, including nationalsied industries, will use a range of resources in varying degrees:

1 Information collected through the organisation's own salesforce about customers' attitudes and plans and about the activity of competitors. The procedures for collecting this information should be formally structured to include:

Major customers and potential customers:
product lines;
buying policies;
financial status; other main suppliers;
growth or divestment plans:
Competitors:
growth or divestment plans;
changes in resources;
product development;
pricing policies;
service and distribution policies;
main customers;
financial status.

2 Information from consumer research. The business enterprise may conduct market surveys or more usually commission specialist market
research organisations to undertake them, or they may contribute to
similar studies commissioned by industry or trade associations.

Their purpose is to explore the needs, buying habits and preferences of
potential consumers. They will take account of the psychological and
socio-economic factors which influence buyers. Research sampling techniques may vary from direct mail shots to telephone polls and street
interviews depending on the product and the market.

Conclusions from market research reports must be interpreted in the
context of the brief given for the work to be done.

3 Information gleaned from more general sources of statistics such as:
trade associations;
government statistics;
CBI;
TUC;
business schools;
OECD;
banks;
trade press and financial press;
stockbrokers;
marketing boards;
consumer organisations;
interfirm comparisons;
and there are many others.

When using this kind of information it is important to understand the
source of collection and the purpose for which it was prepared. This is
necessary in judging whether the interpretation put on the information has
any relevance to the market we are trying to predict.

In the end, demand forecasting is a matter for expert interpretation of the
available information and sound management judgement.

An auditor who has already earned management confidence for having a
sound understanding of the business can contribute by confirming the validity of the information base and the rationale for interpreting it. The auditor
must avoid both usurping the role of marketeer in expert interpretation and
second guessing the management judgement.

DEMAND FORECASTING: AUDIT QUESTIONS

1 What market research has been done? Consider relevance, penetration and conclusions. Consider alternative sources of information. What has been used, what rejected and why? What information is lacking?
2 Is the rationale sound for the projections adopted? Consider the relevance of the statistical techniques adopted. Have they been correctly applied? Consider the basis for weighting the range of influencing factors.
3 How do the projections match with 'track record' trends? Consider track records for:
   forecasting;
   performance;
   market trends;
   product evolution;
   trade cycles, fashion trends, etc;
   competition.
4 Have all functions of the business been fully consulted? Have the forecasts been fully accepted and adopted?
5 Are the forecasts feasible in terms of the potential resources and capacity of the business?

3.3 Market development

In most businesses it is necessary to plan marketing activity with the specific objective of retaining market share and to achieve effective gains.

PLANNING MARKET SHARE GAINS

Critical market and competitor information is necessary to establish market share goals and strategies for reaching them. This includes:

Current or potential developments affecting end-users.
Key product features as perceived by the end-users.
How well products fit the product lines offered by distributors.

It is necessary to define which competitors are vulnerable, to analyse why and to predict what their likely reaction will be to attempts to gain share by different methods. This competition survey should identify those product lines where share gain is thought possible and pinpoint where and how much each competitor is vulnerable to specific share gain strategies.

For an effective marketing strategy to improve market shares, it is necessary to integrate information from all functions of the business. An integrated marketing strategy should establish criteria for choosing the market segments likely to contribute most towards achieving corporate objectives. For this it is necessary to evaluate market opportunities and constraints and then to structure product design, promotional activity, pricing policy and salesforce effort to match the requirements identified for each market segment.

A detailed segmentation analysis is necessary for planning and programming marketing activities and to identify specific requirements for penetrating each market segment. It is then necessary to identify the preferred channels of distribution for each market segment and the specific requirements for securing the active co-operation of these channels.

It should then be possible to define realistic targets for volume and market share for each of the various options and to evaluate the commitments and programmes necessary for each option.

The next stage is to identify separately those products for which to plan increases in market share and to define individual marketing and sales strategies for each product line. It is necessary to distinguish the gains attributable to product innovation from those to be achieved from promotion, price or service.

Procedure for planning market share gains

1 *Information collection* Market research Competition review Salesforce information		
2 *Competition analysis* Analyse competiton profile for each product: price; service; selling effort; promotion Identify competition weaknesses Determine best share gain strategy against each competitor		

3 *Product segmentation*
(a) Dominant products
   or no gain
	(b) Low share products
	   or growing
		(c) Potential innova-
		   tion products

4 *Define objectives*
—Competitive price
 	
—Maintain good
   customer service
—product innovation
	—Define market share
	   objective
	
	—Set objectives for:
	   pricing;
	   distribution;
	   promotion.
	—Identify key accounts
		—specify
		   development
		   needed

5 *Set targets*
—Sales budgeting
	—Territory targets
	
	—Individual account
	   targets
	—Promotion targets
		—Define new
		   product
		launch programme

6 *Evaluate*	—Establish costs and
	   benefits against 'do
	   nothing' strategy
		—Prepare cost/
		   benefit
		analysis for each
		development

7 *Implement*
—Normal business
   activity
	—When benefits exceed
	   costs execute
	   programme
		—Execute
		programme where
		justified

MARKET DEVELOPMENT: AUDIT QUESTIONS

1 Consider the strategy for market share projection. Is the information base reliable and comprehensive? Is the rationale sound?
Consider action proposed to achieve changes in market share:
pricing;
promotion;
service;
product changes;
selling effort.
Consider feasibility and evaluation. Test cost/benefit calculations.
2 Consider the constraints of the sales plan.
Which elements are devised from top down analyses?
Is the information reliable and comprehensive?
Is the basis of analysis valid?
Which elements are devised from bottom up synthesis?
Is the information reliable and complete?
Is the synthesis sound?
3 Consider market segmentation analysis.
Are the bases of analyses sound?
Test the evaluation and profitability estimates for:
market area profile;
product profile;
main customer profile;
distribution profile.

Audit profile triggers (Defined at **2.11** in Chapter 3)

MARKETING FUNCTION

ORGANISATION
Marketing role in relation to:
  Market penetration
  Product development
  Selling
  Advertising
  Distribution
  Merchandising
  Industrial marketing
  Export marketing

MARKET RESEARCH
Relevance of findings to:
  Capacity planning
  Product mix
  Customer satisfaction
  Product development
  Product launches
  Selling policy
  Pricing policy

DISTRIBUTION PATTERN
Direct to customer
Direct to wholesaler
Direct to retailer
Direct to agent
Transfer to own branch/depot

Transport arrangements:
  Cost
  Efficiency

PRODUCT DEVELOPMENT
Specification
Market volumes
Stocking policy
Prototype arrangements
Production plan/capacity
Estimated costs
Price structure
Launching programme

3.4   Product development

DEFINITION

[Research and development] 'includes basic and applied research in the sciences and in engineering, and design and development of prototypes and processes. It does not include quality control, routine product testing, market research, sales promotion, sales service, research in the social sciences or psychology, or other non technical activities or technical services.' (US National Science Foundation)

From this general definition Chambers, Selim and Vinten in *Internal Auditing* (2nd edn) (1987) further identify the following three areas:

'1 Basic research—representing original work for the advancement of scientific knowledge and which has a commercial spin-off.
2 Applied research—representing work on unknown scientific problems which have a commercial spin-off.
3 Development—this involves the conversion of research findings into commercial operations.'

Lindberg and Cohn in *Operations Auditing* (1972) have stated the following guidelines for determining whether research will allow an organisation to be innovative:

'(a) A developed sense of how much innovation is needed to remain competitive.
(b) A proportion of resources should be allocated to new activities.
(c) Innovation should be directed to future needs, not mere face-lifting.

(d) New ideas resulting from research should be recognised not stifled.

(e) Decisions on innovations should be based on 'team analysis' to reduce risk.

(f) Renewal needs and resources required should be matched.

(g) Identification of needs met by others should be made to prevent wasteful duplication.

(h) A plan should exist to give researchers a purpose towards which to work.

(i) Tests of results should be performed to reduce costs, introducing new activity and reducing risk of failure in this area.

(j) Budgetary control and investment appraisal (cost benefit analysis) should not stifle occasional cross-fertilisation of new ideas.'

Product development is crucial to the continuing success of every business. Consequently it needs top level management involvement to ensure that this activity is both efficient and effective in meeting the needs of the business.

A clear policy needs to be established.

The product development function must be totally integrated into the business organisation with strong cross-functional relationships with the marketing, production and finance departments. This is necessary to ensure that it responds intelligently to the needs of the business.

Product objectives have to interpret corporate and marketing objectives and strategies in terms of detailed product development programmes. These programmes should then make the appropriate contribution to the achievement of the corporate and marketing objectives in ways which capitalise the strengths and market advantages attributable to the business.

DEFINING OBJECTIVES

First, it is necessary to determine the life cycle position of all major products and construct a life cycle profile. This profile specifies the percentage of sales and profits that fall within each stage of that life cycle.

Next, a target product life cycle profile specifies the percentage of sales that should fall in each stage of the life cycle. Several factors should be considered in designing a target profile such as:

1 Average length of product life cycles; including the rate of new product introductions and the rate of obsolescence.
2 Growth objectives.
3 Cashflow.
4 Risk, the stability of the technological environment, the volatility of consumer demand, etc.

By comparing the target profile with the current life cycle profile, preliminary product objectives can be identified. These objectives indicate the amount and timing of resources that should be allocated to development programmes or elimination programmes for each product.

ESTABLISHING CRITERIA

1 The acceptable level or range of profitability is defined with the appropriate pay back period.

2 For each product, market scope and growth targets which management intends to pursue are specified.
3 The synergy expectations for new products are identified.
4 The advantage expectations for new products are scheduled.
5 Any other guidelines that are considered appropriate in channelling new product development activities are then specified.

CONTROLLING PRODUCT DEVELOPMENT ACTIVITY

Every new product idea or product improvement should be evaluated and measured against these criteria before resources are committed for its development. New product ideas or improvements which match the policy criteria provide the foundation on which effective product development activity can be built and controlled. It will ensure that appropriate resources are planned to be available for investment when needed in the development of those products judged to have the greatest potential for contributing to corporate objectives.

Product development activity may include:

New business projects:

New products.
New markets.

Existing business:

Product modifications to extend life cycle by improving or expanding the product line.
Market extension projects aimed at opening additonal market segments to existing and modified products.
Cost engineering projects designed to improve manufacturing efficiency, processes, etc.

PRODUCTION ELIMINATION

Weak products tend to consume a disproportionate amount of management time. They require advertising and salesforce attention which might be better applied making strong products more profitable.

Unsuccessful products can cast a shadow on the company's image by causing customer misgivings.

Stage I: Identifying candidates for elimination:

1 Is the sales volume of the product line rising or falling?
2 Is the product line making an adequate contribution?
3 Is the product line generating an adequate return on investment?
4 How does the gross margin compare with other product lines?
5 Is there justification (other than 'full product line' philosophy) for retaining the product?
6 Are substitution products available in the market?
7 Are low volume sales due to 'growing pains' of a new product or ageing of a mature product?

Stage II: Profitability analysis:

For evaluating the contribution and costs attributable to retaining each suspect product, it is important to identify specific costs which could be readily eliminated separately from apportionments of the cost of general resources.

The effect on the profitability of each of the remaining products in the product line must also be evaluated.

The potential reduction of investment in inventory and receivables must also be evaluated.

There is a primary case for eliminating products which consistently fail to achieve what has been established as a minimum acceptable rate of return on investment.

When marketing considerations require retention of a product which fails to meet profitability requirements, the case for retaining it should be carefully quantified. The product may be perceived either as necessary to fill out the product line for the benefit of customers or as making an important contribution to the company's leadership image. In either case retention is then a promotional activity for which the full cost should be identified and closely monitored.

Stage III: Phasing out:

Products failing to satisfy the profitability and marketing criteria should be phased out.

There are three categories:

1 Expired products—immediate deletion from the product offer and inventory and disposal of residual stocks.
2 Expiring products—cease current production but leave on offer while stocks last.
3 Limited life expectancy—retain on offer with minimum support to optimise profitability for remainder of limited life—monitor closely.

AUDIT OF PRODUCT DEVELOPMENT ACTIVITY

The auditor should expect to see an organised and well documented system working to a plan. The skill and flair of researchers must not be stifled by excessive bureaucracy and so balance must be reached between adequate documentation and planning and scope for the researcher's own initiative.

It should be possible to quantify the possibility of success and the likely return. In so doing projects can be ranked so that the best options are chosen. Budgetary control is vitally important, as are reports on scientific progress giving expected and actual performance measured in terms of resources consumed and a revised 'expected outcome and return'. These procedures must be soundly based. This is the area upon which the internal auditor can concentrate, as all decisions will stem from this control. Knowledge needs to be freely available between employees; but obviously access to information requires restrictions. However, such controls must not discourage innovation—again a delicate balance needs to be found.

PRODUCT DEVELOPMENT: AUDIT QUESTIONS

1 Consider objectives for product development activity.
2 Is the allocation of resources clearly identified and controlled in line with these objectives?

3 Test cost/benefit calculations for new products.
4 Appraise launch plans for new products:
   technical tests;
   market tests;
   stock building and distribution;
   promotion;
   monitoring.
5 Appraise system for product elimination.
6 Verify that effective budgetary control is exercised over development costs and that project costs are properly analysed, monitored and reported.
7 Verify the arrangements for protection of industrial property.

3.5   Distribution planning

1 First it is necessary to set objectives for each distribution channel in terms of market share and profitability goals for each market segment.
2 Then the course must be chosen to achieve these objectives:
   whether to distribute direct or indirect;
   whether to use existing outlets or establish new networks;
   whether or not to use resale support programmes.
3 Then the distribution channel options can be evaluated in terms of profitability taking account of alternative product mixes.

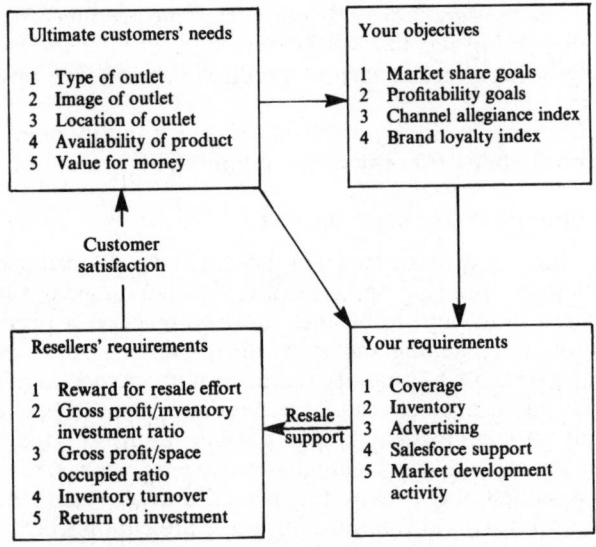

DISTRIBUTION PLANNING: AUDIT QUESTIONS

1 Consider objectives for distribution management:
   market share;
   customer service;
   cost efficiency.
2 Test profitability assessments of options.
3 Is the rationale sound for the distribution strategy adopted?

4 How is performance monitored?
  Is the information reliable and comprehensive?
5 Are changes planned? If so consider the feasibility and cost/benefit
  assessment.

3.6 Sales pricing

In any commercial undertaking sales pricing is a key management judgement area. It has a direct impact on profitability.

Offering goods at selling prices which are too low depresses profitability
but if they are too high sales will be lost.

Because of the critical nature of pricing decisions it is especially important
to ensure the information used is adequate and reliable. This will be
information about competition, about costs and about the product being
offered in terms of quality and service.

Selling price decisions also need to take account of judgements about the
needs and attitudes of buyers. Profits are earned by selling products for more
than they cost to produce. This means that you have to convince a buyer that
your product is worth more to him than it cost you.

Buyers have pressures on them too. They may be wanting to use your
product in their own manufacture or to sell it on to their own customers. In
such cases they have their own customer pressures to overcome. In other
cases the buyer may be the ultimate consumer, seeking value for money. In
almost every case there will be competitive products on offer.

It is the market which determines selling price but the seller must have the
ability to judge whether or not it will be profitable before making a commitment to sell. To do so it is necessary to have some knowledge both of the
price the market will pay and your own costs to supply.

Both factors are always indefinite. Costs will depend on future buying
terms for resources including materials and labour. They will also depend on
how efficiently these resources are used which in turn depends upon how
much business can be attracted.

It is a marketing judgement to estimate the price you can get.
It is a financial judgement to estimate what it will cost to produce.
It is a management judgement to decide whether or not to make a
  commitment to sell.

Making such a commitment involves an irreversible step which will
determine future profitability. This commitment normally occurs when a
priced offer is made. In some cases a specific price is quoted for each
customer enquiry. In others a price list is published for a standard product
range and this may be subject to negotiated discounts. In yet others discrete
contract terms are negotiated with each buyer for bulk orders and so on.

These are all critical pricing decisions; making them without adequate
information puts profitability at risk.

Risk of loss of profit through under pricing.
Risk of loss of business through over pricing.
Risk of inefficient production through inability to monitor
  meaningfully.

In this area internal audit assurance can make a positive contribution to
profitability by validating the information and systems used in the process of
making pricing decisions.

SALES PRICING: AUDIT QUESTIONS

1 *Where in the organisation are pricing decisions made?*

   Authority?
   Is there effective control?
   How are pricing decisions monitored?

2 *How are pricing decisions made?*

What consideration is given to:
   customer pressure;
   competitors;
   costings;
   marketing policy?

Consider the validity of the information used.

3 *Consider all elements of the price structure*

   Published list prices:
   discrete specifications and quotes;
   customer classification discounts;
   negotiated discounts;
   rebates;
   allowances;
   credit terms;
   supplementary services, samples, etc;
   promotional support.

4 *Appraise the validity of the cost information*

   (a) Are standard costs used to provide a common basis for measuring market prices and production efficiency?
   (b) What is the basis for ongoing verification of the validity of cost elements used in pricing decisions? Are amendments made when appropriate?
   (c) What is the basis for identifying fixed and variable elements of the cost structure? Are marginal costing and contribution accounting techniques used to assist selected pricing decisions?
   (d) Are differences between historical costs, current costs and replacement costs acknowledged when appropriate?

(5) *Assess the effectiveness of sales pricing decisions*

   Trends in conversion rate for quotations.
   Trends in sales performance:
   by product;
   by market segment;
   by distribution channel.

Consider other factors influencing sales performance.

Audit profile triggers (Defined at **2.11** in Chapter 3)

SALES PRICING

PRICING POLICIES
Market penetration
Profitability
On sales
Return on capital employed

Capacity/volume:
    Cost per unit
    Contribution
    Market conditions
    Strategy changes—consumer type, product mix, standardisation, home and export

PRICING–METHODS
Cost plus:
    Factory cost for given volume plus gross margin

Variable costs and fixed costs:
    Factory variable costs for given volume plus share of fixed costs plus gross margin

Marginal costing:
    Variable costs plus mark up to achieve contribution:
    (a) to fixed expenses
    (b) to profit
    Necessary to have details of fixed expense relating to factory, marketing/sales and administration

Cost estimating tables:
    Prices based on standard cost in estimating tables plus gross profit
    Knowledge of market (competitive-based pricing)
    Price is set against 'what the market will stand'

Value added:
    Cost of material plus value added through production, administration, selling and distribution plus net margin

Product analysis pricing:
    Attempts to equate market value with main properties from technical description

Bid/tender pricing:
    Adopts any of the above with intention to achieve most viable sealed bid to secure a contract against competitors' bids

DISCOUNTS
Revealed, standard:
    Based on order volume
    Based on customer's volume

Revealed, special:
   To secure order/capacity
   To contractor, or middleman
   Through associations

Concealed:
   For commercial reasons
   By giving services, such as transport free
   By keeping no standard price list
   By unauthorised manipulation

QUOTATIONS

TYPE
Ex price list
Standard per estimating tables
Special:
   size
   price
   discounts
   product or contract conditions
   source of estimating data

CUSTOMER DATA
Name, address, industry
Credit status
previous similar contract
Previous annual business (turnover)
Ultimate customer
Analysis codes

MARKET DATA
New/existing customer
Competition
Criteria for securing order:
   Price
   Delivery
   Reputation
   Capability
   Continuity
   Development/market penetration
   Volume/capacity

PRODUCT DATA
Description, quantity and size
Inspection requirements
Packaging
Delivery arrangements and dates
Capacity check
Design check

TIMELINESS OF QUOTATIONS
Acceptable response time
Targeted time
Actual time taken
Cause of delays and what can be done to resolve the problems

QUOTATION 'HIT RATE'
Standards and Specials

3.7 Sales promotion

Sales promotion is primarily about communication. It is not sufficient simply to identify market demand intelligently, develop a suitable product and offer it at an appropriate price. It is also necessary to make potential buyers aware of this and to persuade them to buy.

This may be done by advertising which will often include brand promotion and merchandising supported by various forms of price concessions to facilitate distribution and stock availability.

Advertising is the means of conveying messages to groups of potential buyers. The audience can be general (eg television, national press, posters), captive (eg in store advertising), selected (eg direct mail) specialist (eg special interest magazines).

Brand image is important for most consumer goods. The brand carries a promise of an established reputation for a particular quality standard which the buyer can take on trust.

Merchandising is also important for consumer goods distributed through retail stores. It is the exploitation of point of sales appeal. It involves packaging and presentation of the product and in-store presentation, availability and promotional support.

Price concessions to facilitate distribution may include promotional discounts, quotas of free product, special credit terms and there are many other forms of inducement to buy including gift schemes, competitions and lotteries. Other forms of sales promotion include exhibitions, trade fairs, and trade showings.

Criteria for promotional activities tend to be subjective and difficult to measure. Consequently, it is very important that specific marketing objectives are clearly established and rational plans made to achieve them.

The objectives may be related to market share gains, new products or new markets all evaluated in terms of profitability. The plans to achieve them may involve, in addition to promotional plans, elements of strategy for:

1 Product profile.
2 Sales pricing.
3 Distribution planning.
4 Sales service.

Next, it is necessary to plan and budget the promotional expenditure to be incurred in considerable detail, clearly identifying each separate campaign. This is important to enable effective budgetary control to be exercised.

Monitoring must include a rational assessment of the results achieved to be measured against the objectives set. This gives a measure of effectiveness.

Internal audit can make a positive contribution in this area in validating promotional plans to confirm that the rationale adopted is soundly based and that there is proper application of effective control disciplines.

SALES PROMOTION: AUDIT QUESTIONS

1 Consider objectives of sales promotion projects;
  brand image;
  market share development;
  new product launch.
2 Consider all forms of sales promotion:
  advertising;
  free product;
  launch discounts;
  free samples;
  customer support.
3 Consider how sales promotion budget is determined:
  authorisation of projects;
  how is cost controlled?;
  collection of data, analysis and reporting;
  cost/benefit analysis.

3.8   Sales administration

The major objective for the sales department should be to satisfy customers needs, achieving the best standard of service attainable within defined constraints such as cost and available resources.

Sales management involves responsibility for developing a sales plan and directing the salesforce to achieve the plan as a fully co-ordinated team effort. It is necessary to monitor the performance of the salesforce against agreed targets and against the plan continuously.

The sales manager has to analyse the expected sales over distribution channels and over key accounts. In each case he has to identify the strengths and weaknesses of competition. He has to establish goals for each major account and define the selling strategy to be adopted. He has to evaluate the plan by calculating the costs of achieving the objectives set compared with the profit to be generated for each element of the plan.

Developing the sales plan involves:

1 Research and collection of relevant information on the market demand and competitive resources, strengths and weaknesses.
2 Exercising judgement about future trends in demand and competitors' likely strategies.
3 Defining market share objectives for the product range to be offered.

DIRECTING THE SALESFORCE

Directing the salesforce involves training and motivating the team of salesmen and the supporting service staff and then planning, directing and controlling their work.

It involves educating departmental staff to ensure everyone has a clear understanding of the objectives and identifies with them.

It is then necessary to define the sales task and responsibilities.

DEFINING THE SALES TASK

Define and articulate the activities necessary to do a successful selling job. This includes using knowledge of the market to determine a selling strategy for each distribution channel, each customer and each product. These strategies have to take account of product performance and the feasibility of each available course of action.

Evaluate the effort needed for new product introduction and decide the degree of emphasis to be placed on it.

Define the basis on which salesmen should divide their time between servicing existing accounts and prospecting for new ones.

DEFINING RESPONSIBILITIES

Responsibilities for planning, directing and monitoring selling activities:

1 Commercial guidance for salesmen.
2 Review of performance by salesmen against the sales plan.
3 Analysing opportunities for market share gains.
4 Specifying duties and responsibilities of the salesforce in the field for day-to-day operations.
5 Control of paperwork to ensure it captures all essential information which is then readily retrievable.

MONITORING PERFORMANCE

Establish procedures for generating reliable and effective information which is timely and accurate to enable progress in fulfilling each element of the plan to be monitored.

This information must be analysed and acted upon to correct any unacceptable deviations from the plan or to take full advantage of any favourable changes in the environment or circumstances assumed in the plan.

SALES ADMINISTRATION: AUDIT QUESTIONS

1 Sales management—consider the effectiveness of sales management:
   management structure;
   delegation of authority;
   monitoring salesforce performance;
   salesforce training;
   motivation, targets, incentives.
2 Information systems—consider the effectiveness and efficiency of information systems:
   Salesforce support information on customers, product availability and competition;
   Collection and acceptance of orders and progress;
   Collection and recording of market intelligence on customers and competitors.
3 Salesforce performance—consider the efficiency and effectiveness of selling operations;
   selling methods;
   sales area coverage;
   costs and profitability.

Audit profile triggers (Defined at **2.11** in Chapter 3)

SALES ADMINISTRATION

ORDER INTAKE
Type of order:
  Ex quotations
  Specials
  Standards
  By hand
  By telephone
  By post

Checking processes:
  Customer data—name, address, industry, credit status, contract terms and conditions, previous business, ultimate customer, analysis codes

  Product data—description, quantity, size, inspection requirements and packaging, delivery dates and delivery arrangements, capacity check, design check

  Price data—unit price, item value, total value, discounts, where applicable, VAT rating, extra charges eg carriage, FOB, packing, delivery

  Order generation—method, circulation, internal, customer order acknowledgement, entry into order book, order intake analysis.

CUSTOMER SERVICES
Interface between customers, salesforce and production:
  Maintains or has access to progress records
  Deals with customer complaints
  Initiates action to clear bottlenecks in meeting orders
  Informs customers of potential delays
  Ensures all orders are satisfactorily completed

CREDIT NOTES
Generation and authorisation of credit notes applicable to salesforce
Analysis of causes to facilitate remedial action

DEBTORS

INVOICES
Despatch note generation

Preparation of invoices:
  Accuracy
  Timeliness
  Postal arrangements
  Discount arrangements
  Sales ledger posting

CREDIT NOTES
Sources of generation and authorities

Preparation of credit notes:
  Accuracy
  Timeliness
  Postal arrangements
  Sales ledger posting

CASH RECEIPTS
Cash
Postal order
Cheque
Credit transfer
Direct debit
Bill of exchange
Letter of credit

Reconciliation of accounts:
  Customer's remittance advice
  Ledger card
  Invoice copies
  Credit notes
  Discounts allowed
  Allocation against items
  Posting to sales ledger

OTHER SALES LEDGER ENTRIES
Origin and authority

LEDGER CONTROL ROUTINES
Posting batches/runs
Control account entries
Ledger balancing routines
Reconciliation of control accounts

CREDIT CONTROL PROCEDURES
Credit limits:
  Credit checks
  Limit authorisations
  Review arrangements
  Communication methods—customers, salesmen, accounts staff

Debt collection arrangements:
  Routine receipts
  Salesmen calls
  Credit control calls—telephone, postal, visits
  Chasing letters
  Doubtful debts
  Legal proceedings
  Bad debts

AGE ANALYSIS OF DEBTS
Procedure
Timing

Distribution and use:
  Credit control
  Sales
  Accounting

NON-TRADE DEBTORS
Examination needs to be as thorough as for trade debtors

Areas where these may occur:
  Sale of capital equipment
  Sale of scrap
  Staff sales
  Loans to employees
  Canteen
  Sports/social clubs
  Bars
  Staff advances
  Nominal ledger items
  Purchase ledger items

4.0   PRODUCTION OPERATIONS

4.1   Production control objectives

Every management activity must have disciplines to achieve its objectives and maintain effective control. When the operations concern the production of goods and services, a systematic approach to production control is necessary to ensure the production activity meets the objectives of the business. These objectives will usually be conditioned by market forces in general and customer requirements in particular.

The production resources available have to be capable of meeting current market demand economically, efficiently and effectively. Only when this condition is satisfied can customers be expected to entrust to the business their requirements for the goods and services offered. Securing contracts to satisfy these requirements is then a commercial matter influenced by price, quality, service and mutual trust.

Production control is the function by which the right resources are planned, directed and monitored to ensure they are available in the right quantities, at the right time and in the right place for producing the goods and services needed to satisfy customer needs with optimum efficiency. The resources to be so marshalled include materials, equipment, manpower and services.

Effective production control is essential to achieve efficient use of the production resources in fulfilling the commitments made to customers in terms of service and quality and so to maintain the basis for mutual trust.

It is equally important to ensure economic use of the resources in order to remain competitive and cost effective: in business terms this means remaining profitable and ultimately solvent.

Production control can be exercised informally in relatively simple businesses where very few individuals are involved in critical management decisions. The requirements rapidly become more complex with every additional area of activity to be co-ordinated when a formal system becomes essential.

KEY PRODUCTION FUNCTIONS

The chart and tables given on pp 331–333 illustrate the complex web of relation-ships between the production support functions in a manufacturing business. It demonstrates that it is imperative to ensure that the separate activities of all these functions are subject to fully integrated planning and control procedures.

Production control: key functions

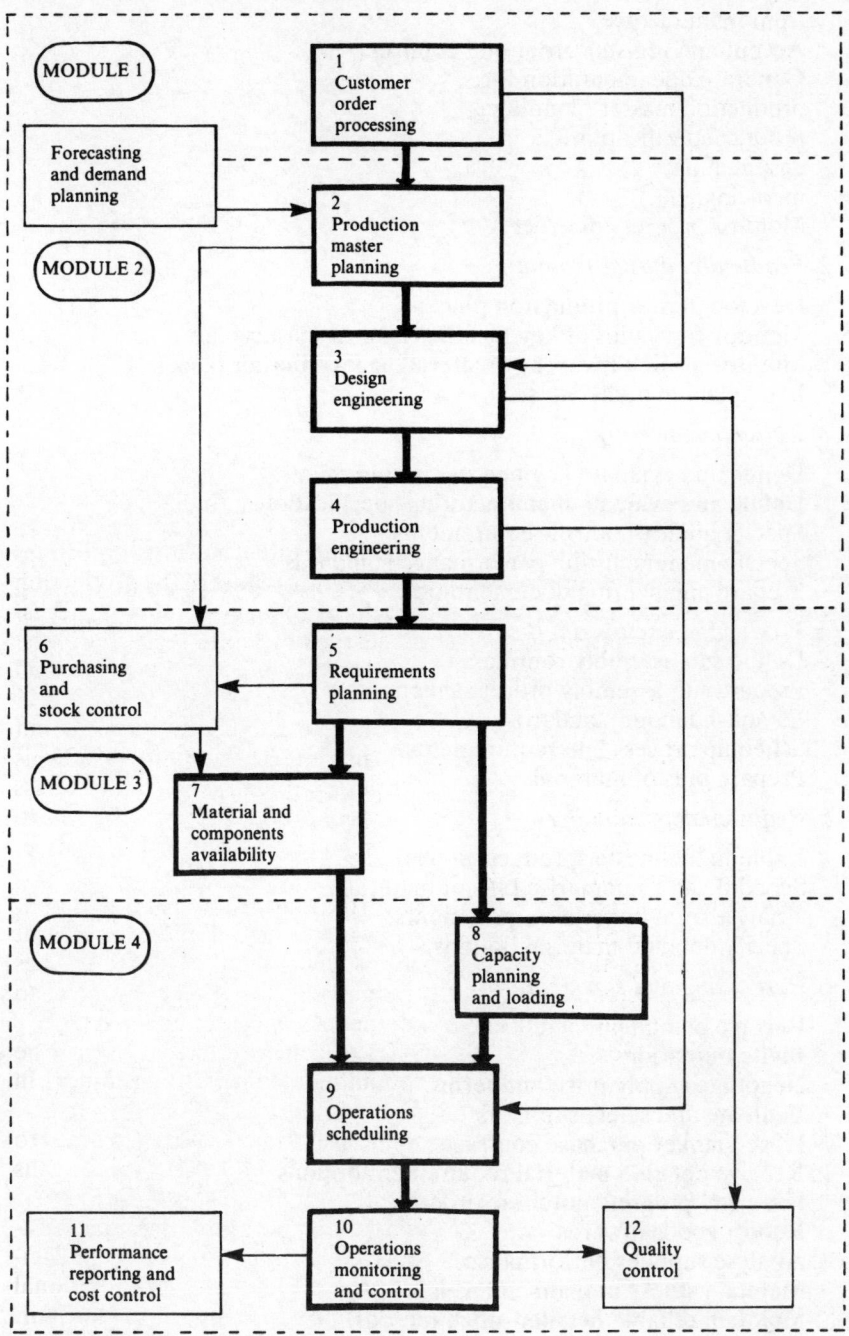

PRODUCTION CONTROL—KEY FUNCTIONS

1 *Customer order processing*

Receive customer orders.
Verify price and terms.
Check availability:
from stock;
from purchase;
from manufacture.
Accept and register order and confirm.
Generate documentation for:
production master planning;
product specification;
despatching;
invoicing.
Monitor progress of order.

2 *Production master planning*

Develop master production plan.
Monitor capacities of key facilities against master plan.
Monitor availability of key material against master plan.
Issue planning schedules.

3 *Design engineering*

Define and evaluate engineering requirements.
Define and evaluate manufacturing specifications.
Specify quality control requirements.
Specify manufacturing performance standards.
Prepare engineering documentation.

4 *Production engineering*
Define sub-assembly routings.
Prepare sub-assembly process sheets.
Establish labour standards.
Schedule process line requirements.
Prepare bills of materials.

5 *Requirements planning*

Explode the master production plan.
Schedule and summarise bills of materials.
Analyse total material requirements.
Specify detailed material options.

6 *Purchasing and stock control*

Receive planning schedules.
Invite quotations.
Negotiate supply price and terms.
Evaluate and select suppliers.
Place blanket purchase contracts.
Receive detailed material requirement options.
Issue and progress purchase orders.
Report goods inwards.
Analyse supplier performance.
Maintain stocks at planned levels.
Maintain reliable detailed stock records.

7 *Materials and components availability*

Analyse detailed materials and components requirements.
Check availability, reserve and allocate material stocks.
Monitor continuously.
Receive information on purchase orders and goods inwards.
Generate documentation for material issues.

8 *Capacity planning and loading*

Prepare shop load analysed by work centre.
Match work load to capacity.
Report adjustments:
Plant and equipment;
Labour requirements.

9 *Operations scheduling*

Prepare detailed manufacturing instructions.
Schedule operations.
Issue production start instructions.
Monitor progress, chase and control.

10 *Operations monitoring and control*

Receive detailed manufacturing instructions.
Authorise production starts.
Monitor and report continuously on progress of orders.
Investigate deviations from schedule and prompt corrective action.
Monitor and report continuously on:
lead times and priorities;
excess material, scrap and waste;
underutilised plant;
idle manpower resources and overtime;
completion time slippage.

11 *Performance reporting and cost control*

Develop operations budget.
Evaluate performance standards.
Collect and validate actual performance data.
Report actual performance against standards.
Analyse and evaluate variances.
Identify trends and interpret in terms of corrective action.

12 *Quality control*

Identify technical standards and tolerances.
Sample test or inspect:
goods in;
product in process at prescribed stages;
manufactured parts;
sub assemblies;
final production.
Monitor and report on supplier quality performance.
Monitor and report on production quality performance.
Monitor and report on waste and scrap.
Analyse customer complaints.

The foregoing refers only briefly to the key functions and activities which may be involved in production control. It is a very complex area of operational management.

A detailed example is provided on how to determine a purchasing strategy on pp 338–341.

4.2 Audit of production control

Before an audit of these operations can make any significant contribution the auditor must have a thorough understanding of the business, its markets, its products and its production processes. Only then can judgements be made about the effectiveness or the efficiency of the production control methods.

It is then necessary to study each sector of the production control system in considerable depth. The auditor must be able to judge the effectiveness of each separate function and of the whole system against alternative methods from a sound knowledge of recently developed concepts in this field preferably supported by experience gained from similar audits elsewhere.

In making these judgements the auditor must consider the impact of production control activities on closely related functions such as purchasing and quality control and also on the more remote functions like marketing or capital development.

INTERNAL AUDIT PROGRAMME FOR PRODUCTION CONTROL

Preliminary review—Before the detailed audit programmes can be prepared the auditor will need to spend time becoming totally familiar with the entire production operation in order to get the significance of each control function into perspective. For this a general audit review should be undertaken covering the following:

1 The management organisation:
   job descriptions;
   responsibilities;
   reporting relationships.
2 The production process:
   plant layout;
   operating performances;
   plant capacities;
   manning requirements.
3 Material management:
   procurement policy;
   stock turnover;
   working capital constraints;
   evidence of control.
4 Employment policies:
   industrial relations;
   skills availability;
   training and recruitment policies.
5 Information system:
   data collection;
   processing;
   reporting;
   system objectives.
6 Management accounting:
   costing relationships;
   variance analysis;
   material yields;
   complaints analysis.

Each of these aspects should be closely studied and the observations recorded.

On the completion of this stage judgements can be made and recorded about the importance of each aspect to the task of maintaining efficient production control. The audit profile framework referred to earlier in this chapter can be applied to this review.

Module basis—Production control is often a vast area to cover and the audit programme should be constructed on a modular basis so that an effective audit impact can be achieved over a period by tackling the functions separately or in groups at appropriate intervals. Separate modular audit programmes should be prepared for:

Module 1
Customer order processing.

Module 2
Production master planning.
Design engineering.
Production engineering.

Module 3
Requirements planning.
Purchasing and stock control.
Material and components availability.

Module 4
Capacity planning and loading.
Operations scheduling.
Quality control.
Performance and cost reporting.

4.3   Module 1: Customer order processing

Consideration must first be given to the sales forecast. Sales forecasting is a marketing function and probably one of the most critical elements of corporate planning. Its influence on production planning is manifest in capacity plans, employment policies, material management, budgetary control and cost allocation. For this reason it is important to measure sales performance against the forecast very carefully in order to judge the effect of variations from the sales forecast on subsequent operations.

The audit of this first stage dealing with sales orders should examine the basis of sales forecasting and how performance compares with the forecast. From this, judgements can be made about the validity of other criteria used in operating the production control system.

Audit tests on the order processing procedures should be designed to establish that:

1 The time taken to process a sample of individual orders is reasonable.
2 Delivery date promises are reasonably valid.
3 There is an effective system for despatching orders promptly on completion.
4 There is an effective procedure for dealing with customer changes requested after acceptance of order.
5 There is an effective procedure for dealing with returned goods.
6 The security of the despatching and invoicing system is sound and effective.

Audit profile triggers (Defined at **2.11** in Chapter 3)

SALES ORDER PROCESSING

The types of sales orders will have a close correlation to the types of quotations. With use of computers there is a possibility of integrating quotations records with ultimate order processing.

METHOD OF PREPARATION
Manual/mechanical
Computerised
Number of parts and their uses

INTEGRATION WITH OTHER PROCESSES
Quotations
Design/engineering
Material requirements planning
Production
Despatch
Invoicing
Marketing/sales statistics
Costing/accounting

TIMELINESS
Acceptable issue time
Targeted time
Actual time taken
Cause of delays

SALES ANALYSIS
Gross sales
Discounts
Commission
Carriage and packing charges
VAT
Product
Outlet—country, industry, wholesaler, contractor, end-user
Volume turnover

COST AND PROFIT ANALYSIS
Receipts—gross sales, less discounts and commission, plus carriage and packing charges

Factory cost—materials, labour, overheads, carriage and packing cost

Other costs—selling overhead, administration overhead, other expenses

CASHFLOW, PROFITABILITY AND YIELD DATA
Gross margin
Variable cost
Contribution

Net margin
Return on capital employed
Gross cashflow

PAYMENT
Terms:
  Standard
  Special
  Stage payments
  Security
  Guarantee/warranty
  Retention
  Bankers guarantee

Method:
  Cash/cheque
  Letter of credit
  Line of credit
  Sight draft

TERMS AND CONDITIONS
Standard
Major variations
Liquidated damages
Other penalties
Cancellation
Validity period of quotation
Nature of quotation—normal, sealed, budget, provisional

CONTROLS
Sequential numbering checks
Reconciliation of orders to order book total
Part completed orders
Completed orders
Cancelled orders
Cancellation charges
Reconciliation with depatches and invoicing
Retention of records

4.4 Module 2: Production planning and engineering

This is the function which reserves production capacity on the basis of the sales forecast to be allocated as sales orders are accepted.

The auditor should examine carefully the basis on which capacity budgets have been balanced against the sales forecast in the master production plan. This examination should be developed to establish how the master production plan is updated to reflect current order intake and changes in plant capacity.

Audit tests of the design engineering function should aim to establish that:

1 Bills of materials are maintained up-to-date by efficient methods and that they are available when required.

2 Scrap or waste allowances are properly controlled.
3 Engineering modifications are effectively controlled.

Audit tests on the production engineering function should be designed to establish that:

1 Up-to-date industrial engineering methods and performance standards are in use.
2 Performance standards are matched by current experience.

4.5   Module 3: Material management

Audit tests of the requirements planning function should seek to establish that:

1 The bases of calculation of requirements are valid for sub-assemblies and for final assemblies.
2 The system for establishing priorities is viable and effective.
3 The system is flexible in responding to design changes.

Audit tests of the purchasing function should be designed to establish that:

1 Lead time information is reliable.
2 The criteria used for supplier selection are valid.
3 The monitoring system for delivery times is effective.
4 The expediting system is effective.
5 There is an effective emergency ordering system and it is controlled.
6 Information on delivery delays is distributed to those who need to know.
7 Purchase prices are agreed and confirmed before commitment.
8 Purchasing commitments made obsolete by design changes are evaluated and reported.
9 Provision is made for alternative sources of supply for critical materials.
10 There are proper acceptance disciplines for goods inwards and satisfactory arrangements for returning faulty materials.
11 The purchasing procedures provide effective internal checks on the exercise of purchasing authority.

PURCHASING STRATEGY

Purchasing is a function which may be crucial to the overall performance of the business.

Effective systems support is essential to free buyers from pre-occupation with day-to-day problems to enable them to focus more effectively on the long-term analysis and planning.

The purchasing function also needs to be totally integrated into the business organisation with strong cross-functional relationships with other departments to ensure that it responds intelligently to the needs of the business.

The first requirement is to determine purchasing strategy by analysing the market to assess the supply risks and to identify areas of opportunity and vulnerability.

The approach should be in four stages:

1 Classify all purchased materials in terms of:
  (a) profit impact
  (b) supply risk.

2 Analyse the supply market for these materials.
3 Determine the overall strategic supply position.
4 Develop a materials strategy and action plan.

4.5.1 *Stage 1: classification of materials*

The profit impact of each supply item may be defined in terms of the volume purchased, the proportion of total purchase cost, or the impact on product quality.

Supply risk is assessed in terms of availability, storage risks and substitution possibilities.

Using these criteria, all items purchased can be classified into the following four categories:

Procurement focus	Main tasks	Required information
1 Strategic items	—Accurate demand forecasting. —Market research. —Development of long-term supply relations. —Make or buy decisions. —Risk analysis. —Contract staggering. —Inventory control. —Vendor control.	—Detailed market data. —Long-term supply and demand trends. —Competitive intelligence. —Industry cost trends.
2 Bottleneck items	—Volume insurance. —Control of vendors. —Security of inventories. —Back-up plans.	—Medium-term supply and demand forecasts. —Good market data. —Inventory costs.
3 Leverage items	—Exploitation of full purchasing power. —Vendor selection. —Product substitution. —Targeted pricing strategies. —Negotiations. —Contract/spot purchasing. —Mix. —Order volume optimisation.	—Good market data. —Short- to medium-term demand planning. —Price forecasts.
4 Non-critical items	—Product standardisation. —Order volume monitoring. —Efficient processing.	—Good market overview. —Short-term demand forecast. —Economic order quantity.

4.5.2   *Stage 2: supply analysis*

Weigh the bargaining power of your suppliers against your own strength as a customer.

Review the supply market, assessing the availability of strategic materials in terms of both quality and quantity.

Then analyse your own needs and supply lines to gauge your ability to get the kind of supply terms you want.

Supplier strength	Buyer strength
1 Market v supplier capacity.	Purchasing volume v capacity of main units.
2 Market growth v capacity growth.	Demand growth v capacity growth.
3 Capacity utilisation or bottleneck risk.	Capacity utilisation of main units.
4 Competitive structure.	Market share 'vis-à-vis' main competition.
5 Cost and price structure.	Cost and price structure.
6 Break even stability.	Cost of non-delivery.
7 Uniqueness of product and technological stability.	Own production capability or depth of integration.
8 Entry barriers, eg capital or know-how.	Entry cost for new sources v cost of own production.

4.5.3   *Stage 3: strategic thrusts*

Position the strategic materials identified in Stage 1 in a purchasing portfolio matrix.

Identify areas of opportunity or vulnerability and assess the supply risks. Then drive your basic strategic thrusts for these materials.

This purchasing portfolio matrix plots buying strength against the strength of the supply market and can be used to develop counter strategy 'vis-à-vis' key suppliers.

The cells in the purchasing portfolio matrix correspond to three basic risk categories, each associated with a different strategic thrust.

4.5.4   *Stage 4: supply scenarios*

Each of the three strategic thrusts has distinctive implications for the individual elements of purchasing strategy, such as volume, price, material substitution, etc.

In this stage you explore a range of supply scenarios in which you lay out your options for securing long-term supply and for exploiting short-term opportunities. You should clearly define the respective risks, costs, returns and strategic implications. You can then develop a preferred option with objectives, action required and contingency measures. These should be laid out in detail for general management approval and implementation.

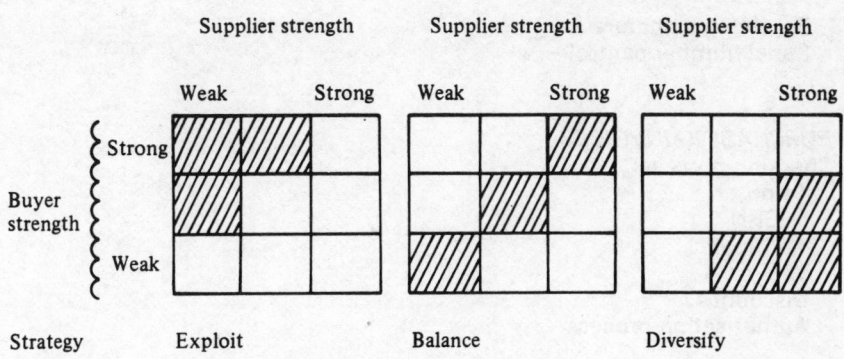

	Supplier strength			Supplier strength			Supplier strength	
	Weak	Strong		Weak	Strong		Weak	Strong

Buyer strength — Strong / Weak

| Strategy | Exploit | Balance | Diversify |

System documentation should be focused on the strategy chosen. This will include control of prices, deliveries, documentation, etc.

Policy issue	Strategic thrusts		
	Exploit	*Balance*	*Diversify*
1 Volume	Spread	Keep or shift carefully	Centralise
2 Price	Press for reductions	Opportunist negotiation	Keep low profile
3 Contractual coverage	Buy spot	Balance contracts and spot	Ensure supply through contracts
4 New suppliers	Stay in touch	Choose vendors selectively	Search vigorously
5 Inventories	Keep low	Use stocks as 'Buffer'	Bolster stocks
6 Own production	Reduce or stay out	Decide selectively	Build up or enter
7 Value engineering	Enforce supplier	Perform selectively	Start own programme
8 Logistic	Minimise cost	Optimise selectively	Secure adequate stocks

Audit profile triggers (Defined at **2.11** in Chapter 3)

PURCHASING PROCEDURES

PURCHASE ORDERS
Authorisation
Quotations obtained
Pricing
Specifications
Discounts arranged
Quantity control (economic ordering)

GOODS INWARDS
Checking process:
    Quantity
    Quality
    Condition

Preparation of goods inwards note:
    Agreed with advice note, specification, order

Receiving signature
Serial number control

PURCHASING INVOICES
Checking process:
  To order
  to GRN
  Arithmetic
  VAT
  Discounts
  Authorisation process

GOODS RETURNED
Checking process:

Preparation of return note:
  Follow up on receipt of supplier's credit note or raising of company debit
  note
  Authorisation process

SUB-CONTRACTED WORK
Despatching

Checking process:
  Quantity
  Quality
  Condition

Preparation of despatch notes:
  Sub-contract order details
  Items despatched
  Despatching signature

Receiving procedures:
  Progressing and control procedures

PURCHASE [PAYABLES] LEDGER
Control of all documents to ledger
Posting controls
Reconciliation and agreement of the ledger control accounts
Accrual procedures
Treatment of outstanding debit balances
Payment controls
Cheque controls
Discounting policies
Timeliness of settlement

SPENDING CONTROL
Budget limits
Monitoring arrangements
Authorisation of exceptions
Negotiating stance

CREDITORS

GOODS AND SERVICES RECEIVED
Invoices—registration, checking, authorisation, posting to purchase ledger

Credit notes—registration, checking, authorisation, posting to purchase ledger

Goods received not yet invoiced—accrual routines

PAYMENTS
Methods:
  Cash
  Postal order
  Cheque
  Credit transfer
  Direct debit
  Bill of exchange
  Letter of credit
Reconciliation of accounts
Customers' statements
Invoices
Other documents
Timeliness of payment
Authorisation
Preparation of cheques, etc
Security
Posting to purchase ledger

DISCOUNTS
Policy
Negotiations procedure
Practice
Posting to purchase ledger

PURCHASE LEDGER OPERATION
Timetable
Journal transactions
Method
Debit balance procedures
Integration/relationship with other ledgers/activities
New accounts
Balancing

Controls:
  Operation
  Reconciliation
  Reports

OTHER CREDITORS
Nominal/general ledger
Club accounts
Cash and petty cash systems
Credit cards

STOCK CONTROL

Audit tests in the stock control function should be designed to establish that:

1 The recording and stock management system are suitable for servicing committed and anticipated demand.
2 The system takes due account of procurement criteria such as economic order quantities and supplier lead times.
3 The stock level criteria take due account of working capital constraints.
4 The stock holding criteria take due account of obsolescence and deterioration risks.
5 The system is being operated as intended.
6 The stock records are maintained up-to-date.
7 Stock checking is adequate and properly controlled.
8 Stock discrepancies are reasonable and properly investigated.
9 The incidence of stock-outs is closely monitored.
10 Stock made obsolete by design changes is evaluated and reported.
11 There are adequate arrangements for monitoring and ageing work in process.
12 The physical layout of the stores is conducive to efficient management.

Audit profile triggers (Defined at **2.11** in Chapter 3)

STOCK CONTROL

RECORDING ARRANGEMENTS
Physical
Accounts
Computer or other mechanisation
Quantity, item and balance
Value, item and balance
Recording:
  Receipts
  Issues
  Returns to suppliers
  Returns from production
  Transfers
  Free issues
  Validation and reconciliation of balances
  Timeliness of recording

PHYSICAL PROCEDURES
Goods inwards
Stores
Handling
Measurement
A & B stocks
2 bin stocks
Picking arrangements

COVERAGE OF INVENTORIES
Raw material
Work in progress
Finished parts
Finished goods
Sub-contracted items
Customers' materials
Stock at customers' premises
Stock at suppliers' premises
Maintenance
Packaging
Canteen
Shops, sports club/bars
Stationery
Sundry

REPORTING AND CONTROL ARRANGEMENTS
Usage
Stocks in hand
Value of investment
Spending control
Stock turnover

VALUATION METHODS
Standard
FIFO
Average
Realisable or cost

OBSOLESCENCE/SLOW MOVING
Natural shrinkage
Deterioration
Obsolescence
Damaged items—scrapped/recovered
Slow moving
Accounting treatment

HOUSEKEEPING
Security
Tidiness/hazards
Colour coding
Adequacy of classification

ORDERING PROCEDURES
Minimum
Maximum
Danger level
Re-order level
Economic ordering quantities
Review arrangements

USE OF DATA
Costing
Management accounting
Purchasing
Production planning
Selling

PHYSICAL CHECKS
Cyclical checking
Perpetual inventory
Spot checks
Sample checks
Stock-takes
Treatment of discrepancies
Valuation

4.6   Module 4: Production scheduling

These functions establish the timing for all production operations by integrating the workload and work schedules of all production centres with the material resource management functions.

The audit programme for capacity planning and loading should be designed to establish that:

1 The production standards adopted for loading are sufficiently accurate for efficient utilisation.
2 Suitable control records are maintained of plant availability as affected by maintenance, breakdown, etc.
3 Plant and labour capacities are kept in economic balance.
4 Make/buy decisions are made on valid criteria.

The audit programme for operation scheduling should aim to establish that:

1 Operation scheduling is compatible with the master production plan.
2 Appropriate discipline is exercised in the preparation, authorisation and distribution of the production schedules.
3 Revisions are properly effected for priority changes or to accommodate changed resources.
4 Production releases are controlled effectively.
5 Over runs and short runs are controlled effectively.
6 The information provided to shop floor management is adequate for efficient control of operations.
7 The system for machine loading is efficient and effective, in particular, the extent to which it involves shop floor discretion.
8 The system for progress monitoring is adequate and generates appropriate action.
9 Appropriate times are allowed for set up.

It may be appropriate to include within this module some examination of the procedures and results of other closely related functions which are not strictly part of production control, such as quality control and cost control.

Examples of audit profile triggers (APTs) covering production control activities are given here.

Audit profile triggers (Defined at **2.11** in Chapter 3)

PRODUCTION CONTROL

WORKS ORDER BOOK
Total load
Under/over load
Arrears

Invoice levels:
  Weekly/monthly forecasts
  Gross sales, discounts, sales revenue cash flow

Costs:
  Weekly/monthly forecasts
  Cost of goods sold
  Gross profitability

Order book variances:
  Order intake—product and price
  Order book level—product and price

PRODUCTION PLANNING
Load:
  Total load
  Under/over load by work centre
  Remedial action
  Rephasing
  Re-routing
  Overtime
  Sub-contract
  Cost effects

Load variances:
  Capacity variance
  Volume variance
  Method variance

Performance:
  Factory—total, employee, work centre
  Output—customers, finished inventories

Performance variances:
  Efficiency—factory, employee, work centre

Output:
  Overdues
  Finished inventory levels

HEADCOUNT UTILISATION
Actual headcount against budget/forecast:
  Direct
  Indirect

Hours purchased—actual against budget/forecast:
  Saleable hours

Direct hours variance:
  Re-routing
  Method
  Planning
  Re-work
  Scrap

Indirect hours by cause:
  Maintenance
  Awaiting materials
  Awaiting work
  Tool changes

Labour variances:
  Labour rate
  Labour batch
  Labour method
  Labour efficiency
  Sub-contract capacity

MATERIALS
Usage
Yield
Production losses
Scrap

Material variances:
  Price
  Usage
  Mix
  Scrap

DELIVERY PERFORMANCE
Deliveries on schedule
Deliveries in arrears
Production delays
Transport delays
Incorrect/wrong instructions
Acts of God, eg floods, fog, ice
Cost of alternative transportation
Cost of expediting arrears

PRODUCTION RECORDING

WORKS ORDER BOOK
Product breakdown:
  Ex stock

Standard manufacture
Special manufacture
Order number
Customer name
Delivery name
Delivery date(s)
Product description
Quantity

Start date:
  Completion date
  Arrears—reasons and remedial action
  Production load each week
  Total load
  Under/over load and remedial action

ORDER DOCUMENTATION
Adequacy of details
Method of preparation
Method of amendment
Suitability of distribution
Timeliness
Use by recipients

PRODUCTION PLANNING
Machine/work centre loading charts:
  Capacity plan
  Actual plan
  Correlation to works order book
  Under/over load signals and remedial action

Routings:
  Nature of documents
  Derivation of times, set, run and batch/run length
  Authenticity of data

Issue of documents:
  Control
  Accuracy
  Completeness

Progress:
  Lead on each work centre
  Production position of each order or job
  Feedback
  Adequacy
  True times
  Problem resolution
  Customer services

ENGINEERING SUPPORT
Design
Drawings
Bills of materials
Tooling
Machine programmes

WORKS DOCUMENTATION
Work flow:
  Routing
  Order copy
  Specifications
  Instructions
  Material requisitions
  Job cards/clock cards

Work stations:
  Log sheets
  Data capturing devices—recorder charts, ticket recording, electronic
  Travelling work sheets

Adequacy of recording:
  Good work, quantity true
  Lost time and reasons
  Spoilt work and reasons
  Rectification
  Scrappage

Checking of data:
  Quantities—input, processed and output
  Links between reporting on each process

Inspection:
  Reports
  Effects on quantities, times and despatches/invoicing

DESPATCH
Despatch loading charts:
  Capacity plan
  Actual plan
  Correlation to works order book and work centre loading charts

INTREGRATION OF RECORDING
Unnecessary duplication
Missing elements
Essential data
Unnecessary data

Use of data:
  Accuracy—adequate, too precise or inadequate

Clarity and completeness of recording for:
  Customers
  Production decisions
  Inventories
  Cost effectiveness
  Accounting
  Profitability

COSTING

METHOD
Standard: process
Batch
Piece part
Unit
Operating
Job/actual
Marginal
Blanket

RELATIONSHIP TO OTHER FUNCTIONS
Cost estimating and quotations
Price setting
Production efficiency
Material management
Wage payment
Management accounts
Statutory accounts

MATERIALS
Raw materials
Components
Sub-contracted processes
Direct (special contract purchases)
Services
Work in progress
Finished products

Valuation:
   Actual
   Average actual
   FIFO
   Replacement
   Standard

Wastage—standard scrap, exceptional scrap, rework

Stocks—value and quantity

Purchases:
   Already contracted
   Forecast of vendors price movements
   Predicted usage
   Ordering pattern

LABOUR
Wage rates:
   By skills
   By operations
   Direct workers
   Indirect workers
   Basic rate
   Premiums
   Bonus/productivity payments

Hours booked:
  Direct
  Indirect
  Sub-contracted hours

Inter-departmental transfers:
  Reciprocal work
  Temporary/casual
  Extended periods

OVERHEAD
Expense classifications
Self-generated
Formula-based allocation
Objective/subjective
Arbitrary allocation
Fixed
Variable
Recovery basis
Block entry
Blanket percentage on labour
Man hour
Machine/work centre hour
Materials
Specialists
Other

CAPACITY CALCULATIONS
Sales—by product:

  Budgeted—value and units

  Forecast—value and units

Finished inventory levels:
  Budgeted—value and units

  Forecast—value and units

  Stocking policy

Conversion to production required:
  Machine hours
  People

Resource available:
  Machines
  Equipment
  People

Management decisions:
  Working hours
  Shifts
  Overtime
  Sub-contracted hours
  Policy capacity variance

External influences:
  Statutory requirements
  Union agreements

OPERATION TIMES
Process layouts/routings
Machine/work centre set time, run tune, tear down time
Batch quantities

CALCULATION OF STANDARDS OR RATES
Method
Frequency of revision

COLLECTION OF DATA
Production
Invoices
Transfers to stock

METHOD OF CALCULATING COSTS
Techniques (inc computer or manual)
Timeliness
Accuracy

VARIANCE ANALYSIS
Manufacturing expense:
  Fixed expense volume/capacity
  Fixed expense recovery
  Fixed expense spending
  Variable expense recovery
  Variable expense spending
  Variable expense, sub-contracted hours
Labour
Rate
Efficiency—batch, method, operator
Sub-contracted hours

Materials:
  Price—stock items and direct purchases
  Mix
  Usage
  Scrap
  Sub-contracted processes

PRESENTATION OF DATA
Layout
Distribution
Frequency
How used
Degree of integration with other procedures
Extent of duplication with other data

Further reading

Hostrum, G and Collins, W A *Operational audits of production control* Report No 20 (1978) (IIA Inc).

Kerin, R A and Peterson, R A *Strategic marketing problems: cases and comments* (1990) (Allyn and Bacon).

CHAPTER 11   Corporate management

Objectives	To examine the scope for internal audit to contribute to efficiency and effectiveness in the corporate management of an organisation
Contents	Corporate plans Capital development Acquisition and divestment Treasury management Human resources management Health and safety Environmental issues
Summary	Internal audit techniques can be applied to support every management activity. The potential benefits will be proportionate to the scale of risk and opportunity each activity involves and the audit skill and experience required are similarly commensurate

1.0   CORPORATE PLANS

1.1   Corporate plans and audit

A fundamental function of internal audit is to validate monitoring systems:

1 Adequacy—is the breadth and depth of the control sufficient?
2 Efficiency—is it cost effective?
3 Effectiveness—is it used properly?

The ultimate measures of corporate performance are financial:

1 Return of capital.
2 Maintaining capital intact.
3 Cashflow.
4 Relating revenue and expenditure.

Consequently internal audit is concerned first with the financial monitoring systems. However, many important activities are often better monitored initially in non-financial terms. For instance:

1 *Sales volumes and product mix*—When changes occur action has to be judged in terms of physical resource reallocation.

2 *Stock control*—The primary objective is to ensure that the right goods are available and can be found to be released promptly when required.
3 *Rates of output*—The quantitative measure is immediate and readily understood by those who can influence it.
4 *Material yields*—Subtle but important signals often get lost in translation into cost terms.

Consideration of non-financial monitoring systems leads towards operational auditing. This is the systematic appraisal of the effectiveness of major functional areas of the business against corporate and industry standards with the objective of assuring management that its aims are being carried out and identifying conditions capable of improvement.

'Internal auditors should appraise the economy and efficiency with which resources are employed.' (IIA Standard 340)

'Internal auditors should review operations or programmes to ascertain whether results are consistent with established objectives and goals and whether the operations or programmes are being carried out as planned.' (IIA Standard 350)

Management action based upon monitoring performance presumes a base against which the measured performance can be judged. This may be:

1 Management hunch (accumulated from long experience).
2 Recorded previous performance (aiming to do as well or better).
3 Corporate plan (a carefully compiled projection of the operational programmes necessary to achieve a clearly defined objective in the environment expected).

Corporate planning is essential in every large complex organisation. Effective direction of a substantial management team and workforce is only feasible with common understanding of and commitment to broadly defined pre-planned courses of action which are compatible for the whole undertaking.

Long-term commitments are a necessary feature of every management activity. For example:

1 Marketing strategy.
2 Capital development.
3 Employment policies (recruitment, training and development).
4 Procurement contracts (materials).
5 Financial resources.

The effectiveness of operational control by monitoring against a corporate plan depends upon the reliability of both the plan and the reported performance. Operational audit involves the validation of both.

Validation of corporate plans is less precise than for reported performance. There is an additional dimension. The expected environment is an area of uncertainty and management judgements have to be made by predicting critical factors such as:

1 Economic climate	Inflation
	GNP
	Cost of money
	Government policies
2 The market	Consumer purchasing power
	Customer demand
	Competition
3 Available resources	Materials
	Equipment
	Skilled personnel
	Money

It must not be part of the auditor's task to second guess these management judgements but the auditor's views can contribute to the management thinking leading up to these judgements. The auditor should apply his skills of critical analysis to the interpretation adopted of the projected environmental criteria. He should examine how these are applied to the established facts about the business. This examination will enable the auditor to reach conclusions about the validity of detailed projections in each component part of the corporate plan. He should do this in the same way as he makes judgements about reported performance. When the audit results in effective validation of variances rather than reported history it is considerably more constructive and useful to the accountable management.

1.2   Audit questions on corporate plans

Audit test should be designed to establish that the following essentials have been met:

1 Corporate policy in terms of planning criteria and parameters must be well defined and clearly communicated to the management of every function.
2 Functional heads should have delegated authority so as to accept full commitment to their own budgets and to be held fully accountable for achieving them.
3 A detailed programme with time schedules for completion of each component of the planning round should be agreed by all functions and issued with reasonable notice before the work starts.
4 Market forecasts should be properly compiled and endorsed with senior management authority. This may be the subject of a separate audit.
5 The management of every key function should be familiar with the market forecasts and the basis on which they have been prepared.
6 Each functional budget should be subject to critical examination and approval by senior management.
7 Each budget should identify benchmarks as the key operational and financial monitoring points to test if the performance is on course at predetermined review dates throughout the budget period.
8 Historical information bases from which budgets are compiled should be valid and the rationale for the projections made sound. Calculations should be tested for reliability.

9 Monitoring systems should have:
Reliable and effective data collection, processing and reporting;
Regular management review of variances;
Effective action to correct adverse trends or take advantage of new opportunities.

2.0 CAPITAL DEVELOPMENT

2.1 Introduction

Effective management of capital investment is a fundamental requirement of every enterprise.

The managements of commercial and industrial organisations are accountable for earning an adequate return on the capital funds entrusted to them and for maintaining the capital intact.

Public authorities are obliged to maximise the use of resources entrusted to them in providing adequate public services at minimum cost.

Capital investment is one of the areas of greater risk in corporate management. It usually involves decisions which will influence corporate performance quite significantly for many years into the future. The effectiveness of the capital investment will be influenced not only by market forces but also by a number of economic variables which are notoriously difficult to predict. These include interest rates, inflation, foreign exchange rates, fiscal policies, taxation and investment incentives. There is a range of potential change in all these variables which can compound over several years to project a margin of error in forecast performance so broad as to make it meaningless. Consequently it is necessary to take some care in refining the forecast variables so as to be able to make a rational investment decision.

Various techniques have been developed for projecting these influencing factors and also for evaluating capital projects to take proper account of them. Stephen Lumby's book *Investment Appraisal and Related Decision* is a good example of many books which deal with these techniques in depth. Here we shall refer only briefly to those most commonly used.

In the end capital investment decisions are a matter for management judgement and it is an onerous responsibility.

2.2 Capital project stages

PLANNING

1 Define the objective.
2 Identify the specific requirements.
3 Prepare feasibility studies.
4 Evaluate the options.
5 Appraise and select the most suitable project.
6 Secure quotations for procurement and finance.
7 Prepare implementation plan and network analysis.
8 Sanction the project.

IMPLEMENTATION

1 Release the implementation plan and network analysis.
2 Allocate responsibilities, consult and secure commitment.
3 Establish budgets and project control procedures.
4 Establish procedures for monitoring project progress.
5 Establish procedures for monitoring achievement on completion.
6 Proceed with the project according to plan.
7 Monitor and report progress.
8 Establish basis for monitoring and control of commissioning costs.
9 Commission the project.

POST IMPLEMENTATION

1 Collect performance data and analyse in a form comparable with estimates used in the project proposal.
2 Compare actual performance achieved with project proposal and analyse differences.
3 Interpret the results of this comparison as a basis for:
action to correct adverse trends;
action to take advantage of unforeseen opportunities;
lessons to be learned for future projects.

2.3   Types of capital investment

ACQUISITIONS

When acquiring the equity of another business the objective may be to hold it as an investment or to integrate it with an existing business to realise some synergy: in either case the management task will be different from that of purchasing new equipment for the existing business. The principles of evaluation and control are nevertheless the same.

ASSET ADDITIONS

This is the purchase of additional tangible fixed assets (land, buildings, plant and equipment) to provide increased capacity for a growing market or to exploit an additional market. It is also most likely to involve further investment in additional working capital.

ASSET RENEWAL

This is the purchase of tangible fixed assets to replace assets which have reached the end of their useful lives. This may be due to fair wear and tear, depletion or obsolescence. The renewal becomes necessary to continue to service an established market demand. These cases would not normally involve further investment in working capital.

SYSTEM DEVELOPMENTS

These are system developments necessary to improve operational performance by providing more effective control and better management information and probably using computers. The investment represents the cost of designing, implementing and retraining. It is often substantial but for sound accounting reasons it may be written off as it is incurred.

Such developments are likely to influence long-term future performance and should be considered with the same care as an investment in tangible assets.

Internal audit is often involved in the development of new control systems to give assurance on the security and control aspects as they are designed.

KEY PERSONNEL

A further important area of investment is the recruitment and training of key staff. Again it is not normal accounting practice to account for this as capital expenditure. Nevertheless undertakings which provide professional services have to recognise the importance of this investment.

2.4   Capital investment appraisal methods

PAYBACK PERIOD

This is a simple method for evaluating projects expected to yield immediate and substantial benefits.

Net cashflow expected from the excess of cash receipts over payments from start up is accumulated to the point where it matches the full cost of capital investment in the project. Due account is taken of taxation as a payment.

No account is taken of inflation or interest. Clearly these are material omissions especially if the payback period is several years.

This method has the advantage of simplicity and so long as its limitations are realised it is a useful device for ranking projects where a short payback is essential, eg expenditure to upgrade the performance of process plant which will become obsolete within a few years.

ACCOUNTANTS' RATE OF RETURN

This is a simple method of calculating a rate of return on investment by relating the average annual net earnings after tax, expected over the life of the investment, to the average capital to be invested. This is normally working capital plus half the fixed asset value.

This return is compared against a weighted average cost of capital (WACC). This is the rate of return for the business calculated as a weighted average for dividends paid on equity and interest paid on loan capital less tax relief. This method can sometimes provide a simple guide for priority ranking of competing claims on limited resources but it is not a satisfactory criteria for investment decisions which must take account of risk. The greater the risk the higher the return required.

DISCOUNTED CASHFLOW (DCF)

By this method the present value is calculated for every item of forecast cashflow in and out throughout the life of the proposed investment.

Present value is that sum which with compound interest at a defined rate will accumulate to the actual amount receivable or payable by its due date. It is thus calculated by the process of discounting the actual amounts back to the present.

A series of discounting calculations is made for the life of the proposed investment for a range of discount rates.

The DCF rate of return is that rate at which the aggregate of discounted flows for the project is zero. It may be necessary to find this by interpolation.

NET PRESENT VALUE (NPV)

This technique adopts a minimum rate of DCF return and projects are evaluated using the DCF basis at this rate. Projects must then produce a positive NPV for further consideration. Projects with negative NPVs are rejected.

DISCOUNTED PROFITABILITY INDEX (PI)

This is the ratio of total discounted cashflow in, to total discounted cashflow out, for a whole project using a predetermined discount rate. Projects with zero NPV will have a PI equal to one. Projects with a positive NPV will have a PI exceeding one. Projects with a negative NPV will have a PI less than one.

DISCOUNTED PAYBACK

This technique is similar to the payback method except that the cashflow elements are discounted to present values at a predetermined rate of interest. The result is more meaningful by taking account of the timing of receipts and payments.

3.0 CAPITAL EXPENDITURE CONTROL

Since investment in fixed assets is such an important factor in strategic development and also because it is likely to have a significant impact on cashflow it must be firmly controlled.

The policy on capital expenditure should aim to ensure that all proposals are carefully evaluated, formally approved at an appropriate level of management and implemented strictly in accordance with clearly defined control procedures.

The capital expenditure control system should deal with:

Planning.
Authorisation.
Control.
Post-completion review.

Here are some guidelines on what the control system should cover.

3.1 Planning

Capital development needs should become apparent as a result of regular strategy reviews of the enterprise. At this stage judgements have to be made about the scale and timing of the projects. All major projects should then be evaluated for inclusion in the annual budget or business plan as an integral part of implementing the overall strategy.

The annual budget should be a key stage in the planning process for capital expenditure. Approval of the budget will effectively give approval in principle to the capital projects in it.

3.2   Authorisation

Formal authorisation of all capital expenditure projects is a necessary discipline before any commitment is made. There should be clearly defined levels for delegated authority to be related to the total cost of each project, and rules for submission of proposals. In some organisations capital expenditure proposals may be examined by a committee for clearance and priority ranking before authorisation.

A standard format for the detailed documentation supporting all capital expenditure proposals helps to ensure consistency in the application of delegated authority.

A capital expenditure proposal should include the following essential information for consideration when taking the decision to proceed or not to proceed:

1 Detailed description of the project.
2 Strategic reasons as identified in the strategy review and the annual budget.
3 Key factors, eg technologies, market shares, competition, etc.
4 Total cost, to include gross capital expenditure, incremental working capital and exceptional revenue costs.
5 Time schedule for spending.
6 Phased financial returns expected.
7 The risks involved in both proceeding and not proceeding.

Capital expenditure proposals should be considered in the light of expert evaluation by those marketing, technical and financial executives in the management team who will have the responsibility for implementing each respective project and achieving the projected results. With this objective in mind it makes sense for the formal proposal document to be accompanied by signed supporting statements from each respective executive.

Here are some suggestions for the content of these supporting statements.

3.3   Marketing statement

This should concentrate on key marketing issues relevant to the project and should identify the marketing opportunities and risks involved.

It should refer to any market research studies undertaken for the project and also quote the source of any other statistics adopted for making the market projections.

It should analyse changes in sales volume, selling prices and profit margins for the products concerned over the last five years and explain the changes projected in the proposal.

The impact on production resources and costs, on industry capacity, on market shares, and on competitor reaction should be assessed. The competition expected should be evaluated and an explanation given of how market shares have been arrived at.

The probable impact on other products should be assessed.

The plan for marketing the output from the project should be described in some detail covering branding, price structure, promotion, selling and distribution.

3.4 Technical statement

This should give a technical description of the production processes of the project with technical specifications for the equipment, processes and products.

It should schedule the detailed cost specification for the project with a timetable for issuing contracts or placing orders, delivery and cash outlay.

It should state the rationale for the capacity chosen, and for the choice of equipment and suppliers.

It should briefly describe the alternative technical solutions considered and the reasons for rejecting each of them. If new or unproven technology is involved, an opinion should be expressed on the degree of confidence to be placed in it.

Details should be scheduled of the impact on production services and utilities and on material and manpower resources.

The project management plan and proposed control system should be described.

Details should be provided of any relevant environmental considerations.

A history of capacity utilisation with a projection after the new capacity comes on stream may be required.

3.5 Financial statement

This statement should contain key financial information to augment that given in the formal proposal document. It should provide schedules evaluating the commercial implications of the marketing and technical assumptions and showing the computation of incremental profit or cost savings.

Detailed schedules should be provided supporting the total project cost and its phasing, including capital expenditure, incremental working capital and exceptional revenue expenditure.

Detailed information should be given on the available capital grants, subsidised financing or tax concessions.

Details should be given of financing arrangements proposed for the project and also of the alternative facilities considered and the reasons for the choice made.

The financial statement has to contain a detailed evaluation of the project profitability and cashflow. This can be presented in several different ways to enable the viability of the project to be judged from different viewpoints. It should include discounted cashflow (DCF), payback period and return on investment calculations.

It is also useful to have a sensitivity analysis when considering capital development proposals. It should be expressed in terms of DCF yield and return on investment. The evaluation of the project will have been based on the most likely outcome taking account of a number of key assumptions. The crucial assumptions would normally include, start up date, volumes, selling prices and profit margins, overhead costs, capital costs and working capital levels. These key factors should be listed with the range of variation believed feasible for each. Calculations can then be made of the effect on project profitability for a given change in each factor in either direction. If practical, a bandwidth of possible outcomes should be identified, with 'worst' and 'best' assessments quoted.

The recommended approach to sensitivity analysis is to measure the effect of change in each crucial factor separately with all other assumptions remaining unchanged. If this approach produces an inconclusive result, another approach would be to test the sensitivity of the DCF yield, assuming as great a variation in each key assumption as is considered a real possibility, and to express an opinion on the likelihood of such variations occurring.

3.6 Control

After authorisation it is necessary to stabilise the cost exposure as early as possible by entering fixed price contracts where possible and arranging forward cover for foreign currency transactions.

Once authorised the detailed project proposal becomes the authentic working plan and the basis for controlling implementation. A capital project control system is essential to identify for prompt action all significant differences from the approved project plan. This system should monitor changes in expenditure on fixed assets, the amount employed in working capital, sales volume, expected profit or cost savings and the consequential impact on profits and cashflow. It is important that the system should record purchase commitments as well as actual liabilities and payments to enable capital spending and cashflow to be projected.

It is important to have a discipline which requires every significant deviation in capital spending, design of the project, cashflow or expected profitability to be reported to the approving authority as soon as it is foreseen. This requirement should apply equally to timing deviations such as delivery slippage or commissioning delays. The report should explain the measures being taken to correct such deviations and to maintain or restore the commercial viability of the project.

3.7 Post-completion review

The appropriate timing for a performance review is normally after a full financial year of operation. The main purpose of reviews is to learn from past experience so as to improve the quality of future decisions. Analysing the reasons for success can be as helpful as identifying why a project has fallen short of expectations.

Post-completion reviews should cover:

1 The original justification and key assumptions.
2 What actually happened, identifying the differences from the original proposal. Controllable differences should be distinguished from those attributable to outside influences.
3 Comparison of financial returns now foreseen with those forecast in the proposal.
4 Any significant changes in the project.
5 A summary of the benefits the project has contributed to the organisation.

3.8   Audit and capital investment

Capital investment management can be considered in three stages:

> Planning.
> Implementation.
> Post implementation.

Internal audit can make a positive contribution to the effective management of capital investment at all three stages.

At the planning stage capital investment proposals will normally be prepared by operational managers for consideration and sanction by senior management. Internal audit validation of the information used and its application may strengthen the case and give a measure of comfort for making the decision to proceed. For the implementation stage the internal audit contribution is concerned with the adequacy of the project control systems and procedures and how effectively they are applied.

Post-implementation review and evaluation is an important management function. Internal audit can contribute here by validating the information collected on performance and interpreting the comparison made with the original projections in the project plan in the light of all the changes which have occurred in the interval between.

An important objective of these studies will be to assist management to improve the quality of investment decision making.

Most of this work requires the application of well developed audit skills by an experienced operational auditor. It involves audit judgements at all stages which can only be made from the basis of a sound and thorough knowledge of the business, its markets, products, processes and technology.

In the post-implementation review stage the auditor's impartial view will be particularly valuable in making an objective assessment of the effect of various elements of the changes which will have occurred over a period of several years. Not all of them will have been anticipated.

3.9   Capital development—audit questions

CAPITAL INVESTMENT PROPOSALS

1 Consider how authority is delegated and how it is exercised.
2 Consider the relationship of capital authority to corporate planning procedures and practice.
3 Have criteria been established for approval of capital projects?
4 Consider the project evaluation:
   capital costs;
   commissioning costs;
   working capital;
   revenue projections.

IMPLEMENTATION

1 Confirm the control system is adequate and properly applied.

POST IMPLEMENTATION

1 Consider all relevant changes in the business, the environment and the economy since the project plan was prepared and endeavour to evaluate how these have influenced performance.

Audit profile triggers (Defined at **2.11** in Chapter 3)

CAPITAL EXPENDITURE

APPLICATIONS
Justification:
    Cost reduction
    Maintaining the business
    Capacity expansion
    Statutory requirement
    Product development
    Technological development
    Market penetration

Description:
    Technical specification
    Anticipated life
    Capacity
    Equipment category

Cost:
    Main asset
    Ancillary equipment
    Delivery cost and insurance
    Installation cost
    Investment grant
    Capital allowances

Method of payment:
    Phasing
    Currency risk and cover
    Retention money—guarantee and warranty

Working capital:

Return on investment:
    Method of evaluation
    Cashflow

Authorisation:
    Technical
    Fiscal
    Management

POST-IMPLEMENTATION REVIEW
Assessment of actuals against application data:
    Costs
    Working capital

Return on investment
Cashflow
Market penetration
Capacity utilisation
Capital allowances
Investment grants

PROJECT RECORDS

Capital application—preparation, submission, authorisation

Expenditure—purchase contract, committed, spent, outstanding

Monitoring/control procedures—cashflow, underspend, overspend

Passing of title
Collection of data against justification criteria
Recording in fixed assets records

OPERATION OF PROCEDURES
Method:
  Manual
  Mechanical
  Computerised
  Integration
  Capital expenditure records
  Costing rates
  Nominal ledger
  Period accounts
  Calculations
  Depreciation
  Revaluation
  Completeness
  Inclusions
  Exclusions—reasons and authority
  Additions
  Disposals
  Physical validation
  Frequency—total, rotational, date of last check
  Persons responsible
  Adjustment routine

FIXED ASSET REGISTER
All or part of this information should be recorded in the fixed asset register or in other records which individual units may consider appropriate:

Asset reference number
Capital authority reference
Asset classification
Index for revaluations
Description and location of asset
Supplier
Invoice reference
Date of purchase
Date of use
Cost: (a) to the company, (b) to the group (if transferred)
Grants received
Net cost after grant
Additional costs and dates of additions

Acquisition costs
Revaluations and dates
Market valuations and names of valuers
Depreciation rate and expected life
Anticipated residual value
Accumulated depreciation
Net book amount
Disposal value and date of disposal
Transfers: (a) Transferor or transferee, (b) Date, (c) Value
Profit/loss on disposal
Insurance value

4.0   ACQUISITIONS

4.1   Rationale for acquisitions

To survive in today's world of increasingly rapid and fundamental change all major corporations must strive to achieve growth and advantage in a climate of intense global competition. This will often involve a need to change shape through acquisitions or divestments.

Acquisition is a transaction by which one corporation acquires an ownership interest in another as a going concern. It may involve acquiring either shares or assets and the result may be either a wholly-owned or a controlling interest.

Divestment is any transaction by which a corporation relinquishes the whole or part of its ownership interest in a business or other corporate activity as a going concern.

Acquisitions or divestments may be very substantial transactions which could have far reaching effects on the performance of a corporation. This is a factor recognised by capital markets throughout the world. The London Stock Exchange, for instance, imposes extensive reporting and control requirements on listed companies contemplating a major acquisition in order to ensure that the long-term interests of shareholders are protected.

Similarly the directors of a corporation pursuing an acquisition need to consider the opportunities and the risks very carefully indeed. For this they need the highest standards of independent professional advice and also strong internal support for pre-acquisition technical and financial evaluation and post-acquisition control.

The rationale attributed to acquisitions may include any of the following reasons:

Concentrating the industry base of the group.
Broadening the industry base of the group.
Acquiring management strength.
Extending market presence.
Extending the product range.
Synergy in production, distribution or administration.
Acquiring technology or specialist skills.
Acquiring intellectual property or commercial reputation.
Securing a source of supply of strategic materials or services.
Acquiring production facilities.
Acquiring distribution facilities.

Securing a captive outlet.

Filling a gap in an investment portfolio.

The organistions of the acquirer and the acquired company may be distinctly different for reasons of history, culture and the personalities of the people involved in them. Considerable adjustment of attitudes and practices will then be necessary to achieve the advantages expected.

Because of the many areas of differences between corporations, growth by acquisition could very rapidly result in an unwieldly conglomerate with so many problems of adjustment that it fails to achieve any of the advantages envisaged when the acquisitions were made. For this reason it is wise to develop a bold strategy for changing shape as the basis for a clear policy which can be firmly applied.

4.2 Acquisitions strategy

Growth by acquisition is often a key strategic objective of major corporations. Reshaping to fulfil this objective may also involve divestment. These transactions need to be totally integrated with the corporation's plans for growth of its established activities by developing markets and products and by capital renewal.

Strategic planning involves forecasting trends in markets, in technological developments and in the economic environment and making medium- and long-term projections into the future. This provides a scenario within which to evaluate all options for the development of the corporation's business, and to rank the alternative courses available in order of priority. The result will be a schedule of preferred development options and among them there may well be a strategic objective to change shape by way of acquisitions and possibly divestment also.

The next stage is to develop a feasible acquisitions strategy. Having identified the general direction in which growth by acquisition has to go, it is necessary to set the criteria against which to measure potential acquisitions: they could be expressed in terms of market strengths, technical strengths, people strengths and financial strengths. A research programme can then be launched to identify target companies which measure up to these criteria. This research should result in an acquisition 'shopping list'.

Once the strategic objectives have been established there needs to be a clear policy for achieving them. There must also be a set of procedures for ensuring the policy is adhered to with such controls and safeguards as are appropriate to this critical activity.

4.3 Acquisitions policy and procedures

This is an area of business activity where the stakes are high. The transactions are usually very substantial with correspondingly attractive opportunities and serious risks. Successful acquisition may lead to substantial improvement in performance but getting it wrong can be disastrous or at least very costly and mistakes can cause irreparable damage. For these reasons it is most important to have a clearly defined policy with explicit essential procedures which should be strictly observed. It has to be recognised that time pressure is often used to reinforce bargaining power in negotiations. To accommodate this situation, shortcuts would need to be made in some detailed procedures. It is important then to identify clearly those specific procedures which must never be omitted. They would clearly have to include such formal steps as securing any necessary Stock Exchange approval or board confirmation or the sanction of shareholders at an extra-ordinary general meeting when this was necessary. There would also be other essential steps in the procedure which ensure that control is firmly maintained from board level; these should be clearly identified as steps which may not be shortcut under any circumstances.

The procedures should provide guidelines for:

Initial contacts.
Preliminary studies.
Authorisation.
Post-authorisation procedures.
Post-acquisition procedures.
Post-acquisition reviews.

Here are some suggested guidelines for a policy on acquisitions.

4.4   Initial contacts

For security, a code name should be allocated to every proposed acquisition from the start and it should only be referred to by its code name from then on.

For each proposed acquisition an individual should be nominated to be the co-ordinating executive through whom all contact and communication is made.

Until an acquisition proposal has been formally authorised all options must be kept open on price and the form of consideration and no written or verbal commitment may be made.

All necessary professional advisers should be selected and instructed by the head of the appropriate corporate function. For example:

Legal advisers	—Company Secretary
Merchant bankers	—Finance Director
Reporting accountants	—Finance Director
Stockbrokers	—Finance Director

All written communication with the other party must be agreed first with the legal advisers instructed for the transaction.

4.5   Preliminary studies

These should include:

A preliminary estimate of financial viability.
Major shareholdings.
A search of published financial information.
Significant market and technical factors.
Potential synergy.

Monopolies or anti-trust considerations.
Any special studies which may be required.

4.6 Authorisation

It is most important to ensure that all critical factors about the undertaking to be acquired have been collected and analysed to be considered at the time the decision to proceed or not is taken.

Delegated authority levels and rules for submission of proposals should be determined and made known to all who are likely to be involved in acquisition activity.

For each case a detailed formal acquisition proposal should be prepared in a prescribed format for authorisation at the appropriate level: this will often be at board level.

The team to prepare the acquisition proposal and conduct the negotiations should be specifically nominated to represent all the appropriate disciplines.

The value of the acquisition to be authorised should include:

Purchase consideration, whether in cash, shares or otherwise.
Borrowings to be assumed.
Additional capital to be injected (if any).
Pension fund deficiency (if any).
Rationalisation costs (if any).
Legal and other acquisition costs.

The acquisition proposal should be supported by detailed documentation covering:

Detailed description of the undertaking to be acquired.
Market and technical profiles and prospects.
Financial record.
Detailed financial statements and projections.
Information on the present ownership.
Rationale for the acquisition.
How the acquisition will satisfy strategic objectives.
Impact of take over on the corporation's current operations.
Proposed future management.
Rationalisation plan.
Other issues such as contingencies, litigation, environmental problems, industrial problems, constraints, etc.

4.7 Post-authorisation procedures

The acquisition team has to work closely with the professional advisers to negotiate acceptable terms and complete a formal agreement. It has to be recognised that the process of negotiating major transactions of a non-routine nature may present opportunities for irregular inducements to be offered. Disciplines must be established which will protect both the company's interests and its executives involved against the risks of such possibilities. All negotiating should be conducted by a small negotiating team, of which only one member is empowered to offer or accept bargains within terms agreed in advance as acceptable. All members of this negotiating team should attend all meetings and be present for all discussions.

It is important to ensure the authorising body is made aware immediately of any material correction or other change uncovered in the course of negotiations, to the details which formed the basis of authorisation. Formal arrangements should be established for reporting the progress of the negotiations regularly to the authorising body.

No commitments should be made which are not strictly in accordance with the acquisition proposal as authorised.

For major acquisitions it is usual to commission an independent accountants' report on the undertaking to be acquired. This work is often assigned to the acquiring company's auditors. The report should be received and considered before terms are finally agreed and negotiations closed.

4.8   Post-acquisition procedures

Before completing the acquisition, it is most important to determine where in the parent company organisation, responsibility is to rest for the newly acquired subsidiary: accountability will start immediately from acquisition.

It will be necessary to visit the new subsidiary to establish personal links and to inform employees in both organisations how they are affected by the takeover.

It will be necessary to inspect assets and examine the accounting records. The post-acquisition balance sheet should be compared with the acquisition proposal and the acquisition agreement with particular reference to the warranty clauses.

It will be necessary to establish as early as possible, group reporting procedures which will enable the performance of the new subsidiary to be monitored from acquisition.

Special care may be necessary to ensure continuity of services which may have been provided by a previous parent company such as computer and insurance services.

4.9   Post-acquisition reviews

It is important to monitor how effective the acquisition policy is in satisfying strategic objectives. This needs to be demonstrated not only in physical and practical achievements but also in terms of financial performance.

In general, a meaningful assessment of the performance of a newly acquired subsidiary cannot be made until it has completed at least one full financial year under its new ownership.

Frequently the principal reason for an acquisition is the pursuit of synergy. This usually means that completion of the acquisition is rapidly followed by a programme of rationalisation and integration. It then becomes difficult to identify the contribution attributable to the newly acquired business. Where this is the case and it was planned to be so in the acquisition proposal, forecasts should have been made of expected results with and without the proposed acquisition. It will then be feasible to measure the performance actually achieved against those forecasts.

One of the benefits of preparing a post-aquisition reivew is that it may reveal some unexpected successes and some disappointments. In both cases lessons can be learned for future projects.

The preparation of the post-acquisition review should be the responsibility of the executive in charge of the acquisition project. It should be submitted for consideration by the authorising body and there should be a group consolidation procedure to enable the effectiveness of the overall strategy to be monitored.

4.10 Divestments

Divestment proposals should be subject to authorisation on a similar basis to acquisitions.

For a major divestment the proposal submitted for authorisation would need to be supported by detailed information similar to that needed for a major acquisition. This would apply to the sale of a substantial business unit as a going concern in the process of changing shape. It could also apply to the sale of part of a recent acquisition because it did not fit the strategic plan being pursued; unless it was fully dealt with in the acquisition proposal.

When the transaction is to be treated as a major divestment similar post-authorisation procedures to those for acquisitions should also apply.

A post-divestment review is helpful to confirm that the transaction was completed as authorised. This should follow as soon as possible after completion.

The following minimum information would normally be required in support of a proposed disposal or closure:

> Reason for the divestment.
> Trading record.
> Financial statements.
> Forecast for the business if retained.
> Asset book values for disposal and expected realisation.
> Number of employees to be transferred or declared redundant.
> Termination costs.
> Prospective buyers.
> Contingent liabilities and warranties to be given.
> Impact on continuing operations.
> Any constraints or external approvals required.

There are particular risks to be alert to in a closure situation. Established security procedures may have lapsed when operations ceased. There may be unrecorded assets of considerable value represented by consumable stores or equipment which for accounting convenience has been written off on purchase. The loyalty of employees serving out redundancy notices will have been put under considerable strain. Whenever possible all responsibility for custody of assets and their disposal for value should be placed with employees with a sound basis for a continuing loyalty to the corporation. Special care must be taken to identify and protect all assets of value which are the corporation's property, especially those which may not be recorded.

4.11 Audit of acquisition and divestment activity

Corporate reshaping is an area where internal audit techniques can be developed to provide valuable protection against the significant risks involved. The sequence of steps from developing a strategy for acquisitions through to successful achievement of the objectives is important. It is not always clearly specified or documented because acquisitions are not a routine activity, there is a need for secrecy, and only a very few, very senior, executives are involved. An experienced operational auditor can give reassurance in this important area using the 'gap analysis' technique.

Internal audit techniques should also be applied to verify that the control procedures are soundly based and adequate for the purpose, and that they are being strictly observed. In the case of pre-acquisition activity the time scale may not always allow for concurrent audit review and in these circumstances the lessons learned through the audit have to be taken particularly into account for subsequent projects.

Internal audit techniques are particularly appropriate in establishing effective post-acquisition control. An early internal audit evaluation of all financial control systems should be standard practice for all newly acquired businesses. This will provide an authentic basis from which the necessary changes can be introduced to bring reporting, monitoring and control into line with group standards.

All post-acquisition reviews should be subject to internal audit examination to ensure consistency in preparation.

Internal audit should provide a special service for projects to close down operating units. This would involve a pre-closure review to take account of the closure proposal: it would identify the risks and recommend protective measures. There would then be a follow-up audit to confirm whether or not adequate control was being maintained.

5.0 TREASURY MANAGEMENT

5.1 Planned funding

Cash resources are an essential requirement for all business activity and conversely, all transactions of a business result in cashflow. For a corporation to be adequately equipped for survival and to have growth potential, control of funds is crucial. This is the role of the corporate treasurer: it involves raising funds, safeguarding money and regulating its use.

The principal objective of corporate treasury management is to ensure the fight funds are available for the needs of the corporation whenever they are required. The source and application of funds statement in the annual report will show how effectively this objective is being achieved. It is also an important indicator of the financial health of the corporation.

The task involves balancing the inflow and outflow of funds. Funds are normally generated continuously by trading operations and there will usually be a steady outflow requirement for servicing existing borrowings, taxation and profit distribution. Requirements for capital development and retirement of borrowings may be less regular and any acquisitions or divestments will add an additional dimension. To balance supply and demand it will sometimes be necessary to invest a temporary surplus and at other times to raise additional money on a short-term basis or on a long-term basis depending on the projected needs.

Funding for major capital developments or long-term debt maturity can be planned in detail well in advance. Every option may be fully explored and evaluated and advantage can be taken of the most favourable market conditions. A corporation pursuing growth by acquisition should have a contingency plan for arranging the necessary funding when a suitable acquisition opportunity arises.

Effective treasury management depends upon full consideration being given to the funding needs at every stage of corporate planning activity. Budgeting parameters will be set to achieve strategic objectives including a prospective financing profile. Cashflow projections are an essential element of budgeting. These projections have to take account of dividend policy, tax planning, all capital developments and extraordinary trading activities such as the launch of new products as well as the cashflow expected from normal trading operations. All detailed planning must include the funding needs and the consolidated result will then include an integrated corporate financing plan.

5.2 Capital markets

A public corporation can raise funds in many different ways and the range of choice continues to expand in response to competition in the capital markets. There are, however, a number of fundamental principles which a corporation must recognise to earn credibility in the marketplace. A good profit record is the first requirement for attracting investors. A healthy return on capital with evidence of steady growth is a favourable omen both for equity capital and loan capital. It holds the promise of dividends and capital growth for shareholders and of security for interest and capital for lenders. Maintaining a reasonable balance between borrowings and share capital, the debt/equity ratio, is an important criterion for a well managed corporation.

Interest rates may vary significantly between world markets. However, the advantages of cheap money in a foreign currency may be outweighed by exchange risks.

Available funding methods include:

Equity capital (ordinary shares).
Preference shares.
Secured loan stock (mortgage debentures).
Unsecured loan stock.
Bank overdraft.
Finance leasing.
Hire purchase.

There are many variations designed to meet particular needs: they include deferred ordinary shares, participating preference shares, redeemable mortgage debentures, convertible loan stock, convertable notes, bearer bonds, revolving financing facilities, etc.

Specialist advice and guidance from merchant bankers and stockbrokers is essential when participating in capital markets. They are highly specialised markets and an inept approach could be disastrous. In addition to the need for sound financial logic in defining the requirements, there are statutory obligations and constraints as well as the rules and conditions of the market to be strictly adhered to.

Raising funds by public subscription requires a prospectus to be published inviting subscription and the shares or loan stock issued then become marketable investments. In the case of a public issue of loan stock, a trustee is appointed as guardian of the interests of the loan stock holders. The trustee contracts with the corporation as borrower on behalf of the loan stock holders as lenders and takes on responsibility for monitoring performance of the terms agreed for the loan stock. These terms are embodied in the formal deed of agreement or borrowing instrument which is known as the trust deed.

5.3   Control of borrowing

The articles of association of most public corporations confer borrowing powers up to a specified limit. It is usual for the limit to be defined by reference to the aggregate of paid up share capital of the corporation and the consolidated reserves of the corporation and its subsidiaries. It may for instance, be expressed as equal to, or perhaps, one and a half times that amount.

In the process of negotiating a loan, the lender will seek to protect security of capital by imposing conditions which restrict the borrower's right to contract further borrowings. Consequently most borrowing instruments will contain conditions which set a limit on total borrowings, sometimes with an inner limit on secured borrowings. For instance, it is a normal condition of an unsecured loan that secured borrowings must not exceed the amount outstanding when the loan was made: this is because secured creditors would stand in front of unsecured creditors in the event of a liquidation. Similarly, a limit on total borrowings will restrict the total of unsecured claims ranking *pari passu* against the residual fund of assets available in the event of liquidation.

Borrowing limits usually apply to the total of borrowings by the corporation and by its subsidiaries. The interests of a lender to the parent company would rank behind those of lenders to the subsidiary in a liquidation of the subsidiary.

Major corporations will normally endeavour to arrange their borrowings in various categories to allow maximum flexibility in meeting funding needs as they arise. Due consideration has to be given to the terms and other conditions attached to different classes of borrowing including the interest rate or 'coupon' and the repayment terms.

Each borrowing instrument will set borrowing limits and its is unlikely they will be identical in all cases. Much more usual is a complex pattern of restrictions on borrowing in various forms. There is normally provision in each instrument or deed for regular annual certification by the auditors of the corporation that the prescribed borrowing limits have not been exceeded.

There will often be a condition that the loan becomes immediately repayable in the event of breach of certain key terms, one of which would certainly be the borrowing limitation requirement. Serious default in one borrowing instrument is also generally a reason for requiring immediate repayment of all others so there is a 'domino' effect.

Effective control of all borrowings is thus a key treasury function. It is clearly of the utmost importance to apply strict disciplines throughout the corporation and its subsidiaries for dealing with mortgages, loans, bank overdrafts, acceptance credits and financial guarantees to ensure limits are not exceeded. In some cases leasing commitments and long-term credit may also be classified as borrowings.

The control system for borrowings should be based upon a clear statement of policy promulgated from the corporate centre and acknowledged by every management centre: it would need to be supported by guidelines and mandatory rules. The rules would probably include a requirement to obtain approval from the corporate centre for any proposed change in borrowing exposure, such as an increase in overdraft facility or arranging a new loan or mortgage. The system should incorporate a routine reporting procedure to enable borrowing exposure to be continuously monitored at unit level and at the centre as appropriate.

Guarantees represent an area of particular vulnerability. A financial guarantee is a significant risk. It must be treated as a borrowing for the purposes of borrowing limits. However, accounting convention recognises an important distinction between the two: the liability under a guarantee will not materialise unless some other event occurs and it is only then that it will be recorded in the balance sheet. The threat posed by an undeclared open ended guarantee given by a subsidiary for a liability of some other party is obviously unacceptable. The secure way to avoid this kind of risk is by making it absolutely clear throughout the organisation including all subsidiaries that guarantees must not be given or offered except by specific and explicit authority of the parent company board. The most usual form of guarantee is that required by a bank or financial institution from the parent company for a local currency loan to an overseas subsidiary.

Another area of financial vulnerability is in the relationship with associated companies. Major corporations sometimes take a minority interest in an otherwise independent specialist company as a basis of partnership pursuing a mutual interest in the marketplace or to share technology or some similar practical objective. If this associate then took advantage of its relationship with a major corporation in obtaining substantial credit and possibly overtrading, the corporation might be at risk through its minority shareholding. The risk could materialise in a need to inject substantial financial resources to protect the corporation's own interests in the joint development. With hindsight it will then be obvious that the corporation should have secured and exercised a right of involvement in the management of the associate from the start of the joint venture. Firm treasury management would ensure such risks were foreseen and acted upon.

5.4 Cashflow management

Cash is an extremely volatile resource: it generally weaves a cyclical pattern with peaks and troughs occurring at monthly intervals reflecting trading custom. Cashflow planning, monitoring and control are critical features of budgetary control. It is necessary to ensure cashflow is properly controlled to serve the best interests of the business. Ensuring funds are available when required is a key treasury function. It is essential to monitor cashflow very closely in order to manage it efficiently and avoid liquidity problems. This will entail weekly and, for some aspects, daily reporting and analysis of trends measured against budget.

Major corporations usually comprise many separate management units in which the day-to-day business activity occurs. There is then a need for corporate treasury influence to be exercised in each separate unit. This will be achieved by effectively pooling all cash resources in a central bank account and setting rules for administering it. The rules have to be defined in the context of local management accountability for return on capital, cashflow and maintenance of the asset base.

Pooling cash resources is probably simplest to achieve by using the Memorandum Account Statement System (MASS) service offered by bankers. This requires a single central bank account with multiple local operating facilities. The bank provides separate memorandum statements of all transactions originated by each unit to support single monthly entries on the central account statement. Each unit uses its respective memorandum statement in the same way as it would its own bank statement. It is, in effect, banking with the corporate centre.

The arrangements may include setting up a separate regional pooled banking facility for each local currency. However, it may not be feasible to include every unit in these arrangements. Isolated foreign units and partly-owned subsidiaries, for example, may have to maintain individual banking arrangements. It is important that the corporate treasury gives specific approval for all local banking arrangements made. Due regard has to be paid to the corporation's exposure to risks in its total involvement with each major international banking group. Terms for every local facility must stand comparison with those secured by the corporation for banking services elsewhere. Borrowings must be strictly controlled

5.5   Currency management

This is a complex treasury management task which has assumed significant importance as currency movements have become volatile and major corporations have extended their businesses far beyond their home country.

Changes in the rates of exchange between the currencies in which an international corporation does business will affect its financial performance in various ways. The commercial incentive in international trading transactions, profit contributions and dividends from overseas operations and interest on currency borrowings can all be significantly influenced by movement in the exchange rates.

Similarly, the carrying value in consolidated financial statements for assets and liabilities denoted in foreign currency will need to be revalued to reflect movement in the exchange values of those currencies.

The objective of currency management should be to match opposing currency risks wherever it is feasible; for example, by matching currency borrowings against investment in assets in the same currency, exchange losses in the one will be offset by gains in the other and vice versa.

There are some well developed and reliable techniques for hedging exposure to changes in the world economic environment. Such techniques can be applied to commercial and financial risks in import and export transactions and also to matching investment and funding for foreign subsidiaries and overseas operations generally.

It is sound practice to adopt a rule for all significant commercial transactions involving more than one currency, that concurrent arrangements must be made for the exchange risk to be underwritten, unless the legitimate business is currency dealing. For example, a contract for importing goods into the UK to be paid for in US dollars should be covered by a forward contract to purchase the necessary currency on the day payment for the goods falls due. Similarly, when goods are exported and priced in the local currency for payment at some future date, a forward sale contract should be made for the currency receipts expected. Clearly it helps if firm settlement dates can be agreed for all international transactions.

Some major international corporations will have many different commercial and financial transactions involving more than one currency. It may then be possible to match currency risks by selecting from a range of opposing obligations in each currency. In such circumstances skilled management of the settlement arrangements can reduce the amount of forward cover needed with consequent savings in premium.

5.6 Security

Treasury management involves specific risks. The transactions are substantial and cash is by far the most attractive reward for the thief: it is immediately usable and very difficult for the rightful owner to trace. The corporation must take particular care to protect itself against the risk of loss through theft, misappropriation, embezzlement and fraud or just plain carelessness on the part of its staff entrusted with handling cash. Equally it must ensure that those staff are adequately protected against any possibility of being wrongly accused if cash is missing.

The essence of good protection against the risks associated with handling cash is in rigorous internal control procedures. Whenever conducting negotiations in the money market, there should be at least two representatives of the corporation present throughout. Every decision taken should be recorded and endorsed by two authorised signatories. Responsibility for separate critical elements of every type of transaction to be undertaken should be assigned to different individuals as far as this is feasible. For instance the person giving telephoned instructions to the bank to transfer funds on short-term deposit should not be involved in maintaining the cash book or in preparing the bank reconciliation. All routine work should be checked by a second person: this work may be computer aided, when the program could be so designed to accept only identical data received from two different input sources. There should be a procedure for monitoring closely that all internal control procedures are being strictly observed.

Pratten in Company Failure (1991) ICAEW examines the circumstances of ten major private sector corporation failures in 1990. A feature common to all these cases was exceptionally high rates of growth before the collapse. In some cases the organisation's resources were committed by a sole executive exercising ostensible authority in major deals or in money market transactions; these involved risk exposure which materialised as significant losses. In the public sector substantial losses have been incurred by local authorities in money market transactions which have been the subject of litigation to establish whether these transactions were ultra vires. All these cases serve to emphasise the scale or risk associated with the management of financial resources.

Bonding may be considered for key treasury executives handling large amounts of cash. This is an insurance contract by which the corporation's risk of loss is covered by an insurance underwriter. One of the principal benefits may be in the disciplines imposed by the underwriter as a condition of cover. These disciplines will apply to the selection, vetting and appointment of treasury staff, to the adequacy of the internal control procedures and the arrangements for ensuring they are being strictly adhered to.

5.7   Audit of the treasury function

Internal auditing has a key role in giving positive support and assurance in this high risk area. Validating the corporate financing plan is a support role which should be extremely useful to treasury management. The financing plan is a crucial element of corporate management: getting it wrong could lead to disaster. Its credibility depends upon sound perception of the financing requirements of each of the separate activities which contribute to the corporation's performance. Internal audit should be examining the forecasts and procedures adopted in the preparation of business plans and budgets including cashflow projections as a service to local management. This work provides a sound basis from which to judge the validity of the foundation on which the corporate financing plan has to be constructed.

Challenging the effectiveness of internal control and frequent regular review and evaluation of the systems of control are important aspects of treasury audit. Changes occur in staffing, the funding needs of the corporation are continuously changing and the financial marketplace changes rapidly all the time. To handle these changes, it may be necessary to amend control systems or to introduce new ones or drift may occur in the application of the existing systems. A minor weakness in a treasury control system could just be all that was needed for a major leakage of funds to occur. This is a risk which has to be guarded against and no system weakness should be tolerated in this area. The objective of the audit in reviewing treasury control systems must be to give assurance that the systems remain adequate as a basis for effective control in the prevailing environment. There must also be an element of flexibility to accommodate environmental change.

Compliance testing is also important in treasury audit. However, the emphasis here needs to be on the effectiveness of the treasury's own internal monitoring system. Strict observance of the established control procedures is critically important in this area. Treasury management should not be depending upon internal audit to ensure compliance.

Compliance auditing of treasury operations takes place at two levels: at the corporate centre where the consolidated resources and borrowings are managed and at operating units where trading cashflow is generated and where major capital spending occurs. Strict adherence to defined procedures and sound control systems is a fundamental requirement in the management of cash resources at both levels. Routine compliance audit coverage at operating units should include tests to verify that corporate treasury rules for operating bank accounts, for transactions in foreign currency and for controlling borrowings and guarantees are being followed.

Internal audit can give considerable support in dealing with borrowings. Compliance with the onerous conditions imposed by borrowings trust deeds is a critical requirement for the entire organisation. Internal audit can help to ensure that there is universal understanding of the conditions and the rules for ensuring they are met. It is also an area where there is scope for useful liaison with the statutory auditors for the annual certification of borrowings.

6.0 HUMAN RESOURCES MANAGEMENT

6.1 People count

Probably the most important asset of most business undertakings is its people. The employees of each major corporation collectively represent a formidable resource.

Accounting convention stops short of attributing an asset value to this resource. Indeed, employing people involves responsibility and cost so the workforce could be considered a liability. The expense of training them could be perceived as spending money on a potentially fugitive asset, in which case the prudent accounting treatment should be to write it off as incurred.

There is, of course, a fundamental difference between employees and inanimate assets: employees have wills of their own. In fact, the employee's ability to think and exercise judgement is one important quality which makes the workforce a particularly valuable resource. It is important to acknowledge the worth to an enterprise of a committed team of individuals with an appropriate range of aptitudes and skills and an identity of interest in the continued progress of their employer.

The accountant's reluctance to record this worth does not inhibit a full recognition in most successful corporations that people count and that the performance of the corporation can only be as good as the quality of its people allows. This recognition will be manifest in an employment policy designed to attract the most suitable people and to encourage their development in the mutual interests of the corporation and of each individual employee.

Human resources management is about developing such a policy and implementing it. Maintaining an effective workforce is a fundamental responsibility of general management for which specialist professional guidance is usually wise and sometimes indispensable. This is the role of the personnel manager.

6.2 Investment in people

Recruitment is critical; so much will depend on recruiting the right people; getting it wrong can be costly. Starting with unsuitable material makes the task of matching it to the needs of the business difficult or even impossible. This is wasteful and may be unnecessarily traumatic for the individual. Good recruitment requires disciplines and skills which have to be learned. It is necessary to identify the needs accurately, to seek suitable candidates in the right marketplace while promoting the corporation's reputation as a good employer. Selection involves matching the need and the talent offered. It requires a particular skill to extract the relevant information from applicants and to judge their potential objectively. Even so, it is possible to misjudge individuals and seeking references should be routine practice. Particular attention should be paid to references when recruiting for positions of considerable trust or responsibility.

For a major corporation to build a resourceful workforce with potential to match all projected needs for people, there has to be a consistent policy on recruitment which is applied throughout the organisation. This objective is normally achieved by communication, through functional guidance of personnel management in each operating unit from the corporate centre.

Training is an important management responsibility and a necessary investment for the long-term interests of the business. It requires special skills not just to perform the task but also to comprehend the methods and principles involved and to communicate them to others. All tasks for which people are employed require particular skills which may be general or unique. In every case it is important to analyse the requirement and make due provision for it. This usually means establishing a training programme.

Training is a continuous process. In addition to the recruitment of new unskilled employees, the requirements of most jobs are subject to change to keep pace with changes in product design or in the environment. Individuals progress in their ability and their expectations. Every operating unit which employs people needs to maintain suitable training facilities. Major corporations often maintain formalised training schemes into which they recruit individuals judged to have particular potential to be trained for various key responsibilities, generally in management or specialist functions.

Development of employees as individuals is probably one of the most challenging of management responsibilities. The objective must be to develop resources to match the projected needs of the business and also to encourage each employee to strive to achieve his or her full potential. All line managers have a primary responsibility to pursue these objectives for every member of their staff.

Annual appraisal interviews provide the appropriate opportunity for identifying the training and development needs of each employee, planning the action necessary to satisfy them and monitoring progress. Training and development programmes should be devised to focus on the needs of the business and the potential of the individual in both medium- and long-term perspectives.

Management development is best achieved working under a successful manager who is dedicated to developing staff. This needs to be supported by participating in formal courses of training from time to time. It is sometimes appropriate to establish specific jobs as training appointments to provide exposure to specific areas of experience and responsibility.

6.3   Managing human resources

A contract of employment is the formal arrangement between employee and employer by which the employee undertakes to work for a reward. The nature of the work and of the reward are normally explicit with conditions including those relating to working times, holidays, sickness absence, how the reward is to be paid and how the employment may be ended. In the UK contracts of employment are required by law to be in writing with certain minimum conditions specified. There is also a substantial body of employment legislation designed for the protection of both employees and employers. There are also statutory requirements to be met for paying remuneration and for accounting for income tax and national insurance. This is the legal framework and management will usually need specialist guidance to ensure it is properly observed.

Remuneration is a key element in motivation: it covers pay and all other benefits included in the remuneration package to place varying emphasis on incentive values. It must be perceived as adequate and fair by employee and employer alike, but their different viewpoints can result in distinctly different judgements about what is adequate or fair. It is a crucial personnel management task to achieve a resolution of these two perspectives. A competitive market rate must be offered to attract new recruits and fairness demands that all remuneration scales must be kept competitive and loyalty must not be abused. To achieve these objectives requires a well developed system of job analysis and evaluation.

Job analysis is a key element for effective management since it provides the basis of a clear understanding between manager and operative about the nature of the work and the detailed tasks involved. Job analysis for many jobs is a field requiring the specialist skill of the industrial engineer; it must also take account of the conception of the job held by both employer and employee.

Job evaluation is the management task of assessing the contribution made by each element of the job specification towards fulfilling the objectives of the business. It represents an endeavour to rank elements of the job content such as problem solving and accountability and to define the degree of skill and experience needed and the scale of influence of the job. This inevitably involves subjective judgement but a carefully designed job evaluation scheme helps this judgement to be exercised intelligently and with consistency. Having rated all jobs it is then necessary to attribute a competitive monetary value to them. It is a fundamental requirement of good personnel management to have an up-to-date and comprehensive grasp of employment market rates. Sound job evaluation provides an essential foundation from which to negotiate rates of pay and other aspects of remuneration.

The management task is to motivate and effective team management is dependent upon good personnel administration. This means efficient pay administration, good working conditions and facilities, a positive approach to training, development and promotion prospects and effective communication systems and employee involvement programmes. For the purposes of personnel administration, the employer needs to have access to a significant amount of personal information about each employee. The employer has a clear duty to respect the confidentiality of personal data and when it is on a computer file it may have to be registered under the Data Protection Act.

All businesses have to address continuous change in the environment, in their markets, in their methods and their technology. The necessary response to such changes will not occur just by introducing a new organisation or structure. It needs to be supported by a change in employee attitudes and behaviour. This is crucial because success or failure of the new arrangements will depend upon keeping employees motivated while their work environment is being transformed. The trauma caused to employees in the process of adapting to change must not be overlooked. Re-orientation of attitudes is notoriously one of the most difficult of management tasks to achieve.

Good communication with employees is essential. The success of any project may well depend upon the initiator's effectiveness in communicating the needs and the desired outcome. People will only be motivated if they are encouraged to feel involved in the successful working out of a sound strategy. When it comes to working together to achieve corporate objectives, relationships which are based upon mutual trust will usually provide a more powerful incentive than those defined by contract or by law.

6.4   Audit of human resources management

Internal audit can contribute to the achievement of personnel management objectives in a number of ways. One risk area is recruitment. A sound personnel policy should have proper safeguards against the risk of appointing a person with a criminal record of fraud or theft to a position of trust, for example. However, if the procedures for applying the policy have been allowed to lapse so that references were not taken up or were ignored, it could happen.

For recruitment, training and management development activities, audit work should be in three phases. First, appraisal of the policies: this should highlight any gaps in meeting the corporation's strategic objectives for manpower planning.

Second, evaluation of the systems for implementing the policies: when policies are determined at the corporate centre for implementation at operating unit, procedures for communication and monitoring call for particular attention.

Third, compliance testing to give positive assurance that the policies are being properly applied. Compliance testing would thus be applied to the disciplines adopted in recruitment for adequate job specification, for using adequate interviewing skills, for taking up references, etc. In training and development the tests would focus on practices for anticipating training needs and preparing for them, the procedures for regular employee performance appraisals and how they are followed up.

Operational audit work in other functions of the business can sometimes bring to light issues of importance in personnel management. For instance, where employees may be at risk because of the nature of their work or responsibilities or the environment they have to work in. In other cases the motivation of one group of employees may be in jeopardy due to frustration caused by failures in the system or poor performance elsewhere.

Finally, all personnel administration procedures can benefit from regular internal audit examination. The objective of this examination would be to give assurance that the procedures were adequate to satisfy the purposes they had been set up for and that they were being properly applied. This examination would need to establish that adequate arrangements had been made to ensure compliance with all legal requirements. The audit examination of the employee records system could well be undertaken as an integral part of the payroll audit.

7.0   HEALTH AND SAFETY

7.1   Health and safety risks and the law

Social history, particularly since the industrial revolution, provides numerous examples of debilitating injury, impaired health and loss of life from industrial diseases and accidents at work. Those directly involved in producing goods or services, those using them and the general public sharing the same environment, may all be at risk.

Health and safety legislation has been progressively enacted and a regulatory structure developed for the protection of those at risk.

7.1.1 *Legislation*

The principal UK legislation is the Health and Safety at Work Act 1974. The Factories Act 1961, and the Offices, Shops and Railway Premises Act 1964 also have health and safety provisions which currently supplement those of the 1974 Act. These will ultimately be replaced by regulations and codes of practice under the 1974 Act.

The general principle behind this legislation is that industry should be self-monitoring.

The primary purpose is to promote safety awareness on the basis that safety at work can only be achieved when all involved have clear understanding of the hazards and how they can be avoided, and a personal commitment to prevent accidents.

The legislation identifies areas of responsibility for employers, employees and others involved with the working environment. A range of duties is imposed on employers which are subject to enforcement by the inspectorate. Breach of these duties gives rise to criminal liability.

7.1.2 *The regulatory framework*

The 1974 Act provides the basis for the regulatory framework by establishing the Health and Safety Commission and the Health and Safety Executive.

The role of the Health and Safety Commission is:

1 To develop policy.
2 To propose health and safety regulations.
3 To draft codes of practice.
4 To disseminate information.
5 To promote the concept of safety committees having both management and operative representation.

The Health and Safety Executive is responsible for enforcement of the legislation. This is achieved in conjunction with local authorities through health and safety inspectors. The Executive also provides an advisory service for employers and employees.

Health and safety inspectors have wide powers. They may:

1 enter premises, examine, sample, test, dismantle and ask questions; and
2 when they judge there has been a breach of health and safety regulations, they may issue notices of prohibition or improvement, with or without prosecution; and
3 they may seize or destroy dangerous substances.

7.1.3 *Employers' duties*

The 1974 Act prescribes duties for employers:

1 To prepare, keep up-to-date and promulgate a written statement of safety policy which also specifies the organisational arrangements for implementing the policy.

2 To keep the workplace safe and provide adequate access and egress.
3 To provide machinery and equipment which is safe to use and to maintain it in safe working order.
4 To provide safe working methods.
5 To provide proper training and supervision.
6 To maintain a safe working environment and adequate welfare arrangements.
7 To conduct operations in a way which avoids undue risk to the safety or health of others who may be affected by the organisation's activities.

7.2   Management policy

Health and safety at work is a crucial issue to be addressed by all organisations and a carefully considered management policy is essential. Failing to provide adequate protection for all exposed to injury resulting from the organisation's activities would be socially unacceptable, criminally unlawful and ruinous.

The management policy should:

1 Confirm acknowledgement of the principle of accident prevention based upon safety awareness by all.
2 Define management responsibilities and accountability for making the policy work.
3 Define the role and duties of safety officers.
4 Define arrangements for safety committees including role, membership and methods of working.
5 Identify health and safety hazards which are critical in relation to the organisation.
6 State the principles to be applied in the adoption of safety standards.
7 Define the basis for developing safe working practices.
8 Define the arrangements for training in safe working practices.
9 Specify critical monitoring requirements.
10 Confirm the philosophy adopted for provision of medical services, health care and health and fitness amenities for employees.

7.2.1   *Responsibilities*

Safety should be perceived as an essential element of the function of every line manager and indeed of every employee.

Every line manager has to be accountable for applying corporate safety policy throughout his or her area of responsibility and each must be aware of the obligations imposed upon them by law. It is an integral part of the management role and cannot be directed effectively as a separately managed function of the organisation. However, specialist advice may be appropriate in the design and use of protective devices, in the development of safe working methods and in safety training for employees.

Every individual employee has the potential ability, both to cause and to prevent accidents. Consequently, an attitude of accident prevention has to be cultivated in each. Each must be made fully aware of the hazards and of the preventive measures available for their protection and each must be trained and kept up-to-date in safe working practices. Each must acknowledge responsibility for his or her own safety and also for that of those working with them.

7.2.2 *Safety standards*

Safety standards constitute a crucial element of the corporate safety policy to ensure consistency and compliance with the law throughout the organisation. They should be set to take account of the requirements of the law and the accumulated experience of the insurance industry and factories inspectorate as well as the circumstances particular to each organisation.

Many processes are inherently dangerous and it is not possible to eliminate the risk of accident completely. Safety measures must provide adequate safeguards, firstly to reduce the likelihood of an accident and secondly to contain the damage, if one occurs. Deciding what is adequate is a matter of judgement against prescribed criteria for safe working conditions and practices and for the protection of those involved.

Operations will usually have been analysed by an industrial engineer and a method or procedure prescribed for doing the job with due regard to safety. It is then necessary to train operatives in these procedures. It is an important part of the training process to ensure they understand what the hazards are and the critical elements of safe practice built into the method.

7.2.3 *Monitoring*

The establishment of safety committees as recommended by the Health and Safety Commission provides a forum for promoting safety awareness throughout the organisation. It thus assists implementation and development of the corporate health and safety policy and facilitates continuous review of how effectively the policy is being applied.

Many organisations adopt the practice of establishing a functional structure of safety officers covering every management centre. They should have specialist training which enables them to act in an advisory capacity and a key objective of the role is to monitor safety compliance in the workplace. Corrective management action can then be taken promptly whenever an unsafe practice, a lack of proper protection or a breach of safety regulations is observed.

The law requires all accidents at work to be recorded in the accident book and every employer must maintain a policy of insurance for employer's liability to cover valid claims for compensation to employees injured at work.

7.3 Health and safety risks

Those at risk may include employees, sub-contractors' employees, suppliers, customers and other visitors to the premises, ultimate users and consumers of the organisation's products and services and members of the general public affected in any way by the organisation's activities.

The risks to be addressed by the organisation may include injury from:

1 Unguarded machinery, machinery or equipment out of control due to breakdown or overloading, falling objects.
2 Unsafe buildings or other structures, explosion, fire or flood hazards, restricted or obstructed exits, slippery or uneven floors, obstructed thoroughfares, insecure stairs or walkways, low headroom, poor lighting, inadequate ventilation.

3 Health or injury hazards from materials or processes, noxious effluents or emissions, radiation, electrocution, burns.
4 Health hazards from infectious or contagious diseases when the work involves contact with people who may be unwell, disease carriers, sick animals or organic products.
5 Failure to use appropriate protective clothing or equipment such as goggles, ear muffs, helmets, safety boots, protective aprons or overalls, masks and gloves.
6 Failure to follow prescribed procedures for using potentially dangerous substances or equipment such as guillotines, power presses, lifting tackle, grinding tools, furnaces, processing tanks and vats, some agricultural machinery, some mining and quarrying plant, etc.
7 Failure to observe 'no go' area restrictions or smoking restrictions, etc.
8 Failure or neglect of warning systems and protective devices (eg fire alarms, sprinklers, fire fighting equipment, safety doors, audible or flashing warnings, warning notices for hazardous areas).
9 Failure of the organisation's products or services in use (eg transport services), undesirable side effects (eg pharmaceutical drugs) or contamination (eg food products).

7.4   Health and safety audit

We have seen that health and safety at work is an issue of critical concern to management at all levels which requires a carefully thought out corporate policy. Management has also to be satisfied that the policy continues to serve the needs of the organisation adequately within the requirements of the law and that working practices continue to fulfil the intentions of the policy. Providing assurance of this is within the scope of the internal audit role, and to be effective, the internal auditor must have a full understanding of the requirements of the law and considerable knowledge of the activities of the organisation.

All employers are required by law to maintain an up-to-date policy and to promulgate among employees a written statement of the health and safety policy of the organisation and the arrangements for carrying it out. It is not part of the internal auditor's role to second guess those responsible for formulating the policy. However, changes may have occurred in the law, in the organisation's circumstances or in public attitudes to particular health and safety risks. It is thus necessary for the internal auditor to consider the impact of change since the current policy was adopted or last updated. The internal audit assignment should then be concerned with evaluating both the policy directives and the monitoring procedures in terms of continuing adequacy, effectiveness and compliance. Routine monitoring of activities for the purpose of achieving compliance with a defined policy is not audit but a management control function.

The internal audit programme should be based upon questions designed to address the specific health and safety risks to which each organisation is exposed. Here are some examples:

1 Has a statement of policy on health and safety been prepared for the organisation?
   Is it comprehensive?

Is it up-to-date?
Is it readily available to all employees?
2 Have safety standards been adopted for the organisation?
Are they soundly based?
Do they incorporate the appropriate principles established by the Royal Society for the Prevention of Accidents (RoSPA)?
Do they match the legal regulations for the Control of Substances Hazardous to Health (COSHH)?
Do they cover all necessary activities?
Are they being effectively applied in working practices, methods, job instructions amd training procedures?
3 Have hazards been researched, identified and ranked as the basis for providing appropriate protective measures?
4 Are safety committees established?
Do they have appropriate representative membership?
Are they properly directed in terms of contributing to making management policy effective?
Is the purpose clear to all involved?
Do they meet regularly?
Are the meetings well run including appropriate agenda, informed reporting, making collective judgments in pursuit of defined objectives and issuing meaningful minutes?
5 Have safety officers been appointed?
Is their role clearly defined?
Are they adequately trained for the role?
Is the role properly understood, particularly as to authority and responsibility?
Are they effective in fulfilling the role?
6 Is appropriate attention given to health and safety and safe working practices in operator training programmes?
7 Have any parts of the organisation been the subject of adverse reports from the safety inspector?
Have all safety inspectors' recommendations been implemented?
8 Are there adequate arrangements for regular testing of potentially hazardous equipment such as lifts, cranes, vehicles, pressure vessels, etc?
Are these arrangements being strictly observed?
9 Are fire regulations being strictly observed?
Is the fire alarm and fire fighting equipment appropriate and adequate?
Is it regularly tested?
Are there sufficient staff who are adequately trained to use it?
Are fire drills held regularly for all employees?
10 Are all those employer's duties prescribed by the Health and Safety Act 1974 being properly observed?
11 Is protective clothing provided for employees and others working where conditions may be hazardous?
Is it adequate?
Is it being properly used?
12 Is a complete record of all accidents at work maintained as required by law?
Is the information obtained analysed to identify trends as a basis for modifying working practices or protective devices?
13 Does the health and safety policy include providing facilities for health care or for actively promoting health and fitness among employees?

Are such facilities effectively controlled?
Are they fully used by employees?

7.4.1 *Reporting*

In most cases, internal audit involvement with health and safety matters arises in the course of local internal audit assignments as a service to local management. Then it is likely to be one of a number of areas of management activity included by rotation in the coverage planned for examination at the periodic internal audit visit. The internal auditor is then concerned with the adequacy of arrangements in force for implementing corporate policy and statutory obligations and how well those arrangements are being adhered to. The report is addressed to the accountable local manager who is in a position to act on the internal audit recommendations.

In some cases, a corporate health and safety officer may have been appointed with special responsibility for development policy and overseeing compliance throughout the organisation. In these cases it would be appropriate to establish an arrangement which ensured that this officer received a copy of all internal audit reports dealing with health and safety procedures and compliance.

Corporate management may specifically commission a comprehensive internal audit examination of corporate health and safety policy and compliance. The objective for such an examination could be to assess the scope of the policy and its feasibility in terms of current conditions and to report on compliance throughout the organisation. Much of the examination work already done on local health and safety procedures would be relevant, subject to updating, summarising and interpreting from a corporate viewpoint. In all such cases, the report must be addressed to the chief executive or other officer or members of the management board, who with due authority, commissioned the assignment. It is then a matter for the addressees to decide what further distribution may be required.

8.0 ENVIRONMENTAL ISSUES

8.1 Environmental concern

An important trend in the second half of the twentieth century has been the growing awareness throughout the world of the escalating environmental damage to the planet being caused in pursuit of economic aims. There is concern on two counts: the damage is seen to be impairing the environment for subsequent generations and it involves threats to human health or life.
Damage is occurring through:

1 Depletion of scarce or finite resources, particularly fossil fuels.
2 Pollution of land, rivers, lakes, ground water, the atmosphere and the oceans.
3 Destruction of elements of the natural environment which have ecological significance including species, habitats, rain forests, soil fertility, the ozone layer.

These issues are being progressively researched and considered internationally and nationally by many organisations established for the purpose by the United Nations, or by national governments.

8.2 Corporate response

Concern for the environment is adding a new dimension to the way in which corporate policies are developed. Industry now faces the challenge of reconciling profitability with consumer and shareholder demands for responsible environmental behaviour. This necessitates taking a longer term view than is normally associated with a market philosophy.

The response to environmental issues has to be qualified in terms of competitive costs. In isolated cases, 'the polluter pays' principle can be directly applied; the *Exxon Valdez* oil spillage in Alaska was one such example. Otherwise, generally accepted conventions for measuring economic performance fall short of attributing a value to the environmental resources consumed or destroyed along the way.

Attitudes to economic measurement are likely to change progressively, if slowly, as more and more cost attributable to past neglect falls as a burden on the present and future. This process may be reinforced by taxation policies such as taxing undesirable products and accounting practices such as attributing a cost value to depletion of critical resources. 'The Greening of Accountancy' project of the Chartered Institute of Certified Accountants is an example of pioneering work in this field.

A 'green image' of environmental friendliness is becoming recognised as having a commercial value; it is also likely to influence the calibre of recruits attracted to an organisation. Many organisations, and responsible multinational corporations in particular, perceive considerable economic value in having a clean environmental record; this is important since they are often in a position to influence international response to environmental issues.

The International Chamber of Commerce in supporting the UN Environment Programme has developed a 'Business Charter for Sustainable Development' which has been signed by some 200 international corporations. It commits participants to making environmental management a corporate priority and to developing the concept of environmental auditing.

Another important initiative is the 'Prince of Wales Business Leaders Forum' which has been established by Business in the Community International. The philosophy is that international business is a powerful agent of change in the modern world and should assume its responsibilities. Top executives of the world's major international corporations participate in sessions of the Forum held throughout the world. The purpose is to promote better corporate citizenship.

The environmental agenda is vast and affords much scope for divergent views on the many issues which threaten achievement of environmentally secure economic development. These issues include:

Energy conservation:

Depletion of non-renewable resources
Atmospheric pollution, health hazards, acid rain, and global warming
Wasteful use of energy

Nuclear radiation:

Health hazards
Risk of disaster
Disposal of nuclear waste

Depletion of the ozone layer:

Health hazards
Global warming

Water management:

Health hazards
Irreversible damage to finite resources

Waste management

Health hazards
Pollution of land, water, atmosphere and oceans
Hazards from past indiscriminate dumping
Potential for recovery and conservation

Intensive farming

Pollution of soil and water
Food contamination
Health hazards
Destruction of soil fertility
Ecological damage
Depletion of fish stocks
Threats to endangered species
Cruely to animals

Depletion of rainforests:

Ecological damage to habitats and species
Damage to soil structures and fertility
Global warming
Climatic changes

Third World deprivation:

Human suffering
Population explosion
Health threats
Famine threats
Potential for escalation of environmental damage
Pressing need for aid for development

Health:

Third World health hazards and needs
Affluence diseases
Medical research hazards

A clear corporate policy is essential for any organisation to be effective in addressing these issues. Without policy direction, every executive of the organisation acts on the basis of individual priority judgements. The corporate response will not then be consistent or effective.

A corporate environmental policy has to be focused on the organisation's interests in order to secure commitment throughout the management structure. There must then be procedures for applying the policy and for monitoring compliance. Internal audit has an important role here in appraising the continuing effectiveness of these procedures.

8.3 Corporate policy

The purpose of a corporate environmental policy is to define the attitudes to be adopted towards such issues throughout the organisation. It is first necessary to consider all the major issues and judge the potential impact of each on the organisation. It is then equally important to judge what scope there may be for the organisation to influence solutions. A code of behaviour can then be developed for these criteria.

A corporate environmental policy needs to be developed for serious consideration by the most senior level of management of the organisation. The policy, when agreed, would then be formally confirmed by board minute or similar authentic record. It might be expected to cover:

Objectives and attitudes:

Specification of the organisation's environmental objectives and a definition of the attitudes to be adopted to achieve them.

A code of practice as the basis for setting standards of environmental behaviour and performance.

Scope:

Guidelines for the application of the environmental policy to the following areas:

1 Routine operations within the organisation, particular concern for energy efficiency and waste management.
2 Development of new products with emphasis on conservation, avoiding pollution and avoiding ecological damage.
3 Development projects; particular concern for sources of energy, avoiding pollution, sound management of waste and safety.
4 Marketing attitudes including demonstration of environmental concern in; choice of markets and sectors, distribution options, advertising and sales promotion.
5 Personnel management attitudes to recruitment, training, development, welfare, remuneration and incentives, responsibilities, retirement.
6 Procurement of products and services, including choice of suppliers and sources in promoting environmental concern.
7 Support for community projects such as health care, education, recreation and cultural activities.
8 Support for international environmental causes such as Third World development projects.
9 Compliance with the law.

Responsibilities:

Definition of how authority for decisions on environmental issues is to be delegated with prescribed limits where appropriate.

The basis on which departmental goals are to be set within the policy framework and the establishment of accountability for achieving the goals.

Communication:

A declaration that the corporate environmental policy and code of practice with the rationale (or a synopsis or selected extracts) is to be made known to all managers, employees, customers and potential customers, shareholders, suppliers and others as appropriate.

Confirmation that the environmental policy is to be incorporated in training programmes wherever appropriate including induction courses for new employees.

Confirmation that there will be internal audit examination to verify adherence to the corporate environmental policy.

Implementation:

It is not essential to incorporate the implementation plan in the policy statement but it is necessary to develop a programme of action to make the policy work. This is likely to cover:

1 An analysis of the operational activitities to which the environmental policy is likely to apply.
2 Outlines of the programmes which need to be established for achieving the long-term objectives of the environmental policy.
3 Arrangements for designing procedures for implementation of the policy in specific areas.
4 Definition of the responsibility framework and training requirements for making the procedures work.
5 Arrangements for setting budgets and establishing monitoring and reporting procedures.
6 Specification of a structure for regular review of the environmental policy.

8.4   Environmental audit

There can be no environmental audit until the parameters of environmental policy have been established. It is then important that the statement of corporate environmental policy should contain an express requirement for internal audit examination of procedures and compliance.

Environmental audit can be conducted using the normal internal audit practice of regular review of local arrangements for reporting to accountable managers. It would be one of the items of audit scope for cyclical inclusion in the assignment plans for regular audit visits. An annual report on environmental performance would then review the local assignment work from a corporate viewpoint for reporting to the board.

As with all operational auditing, it is necessary for the internal auditor to have an extensive understanding of the organisation, its culture, markets, operations, products and people. There is also a need to comprehend the environmental policy fully and especially its rationale. The internal auditor must be able to identify with the objectives of the corporate policy even though he or she may take a different stance personally on some of the issues.

The plan for environmental audit should cover regular review of policy to verify that appropriate revisions are being made for changes in environmental threats, public attitudes, legislation or circumstances of the organisation.

The audit work should include:

1 Testing observance of the code of practice.
2 Reviewing arrangements for communication of the policy internally including training and testing their effectiveness in application.
3 Reviewing arrangements for communication of the policy externally.
4 Evaluating the procedures designed to meet the objectives of the policy and of the organisation and testing compliance.
5 Reviewing budgets and verifying the reliability of monitoring information and how effectively it is used.
6 Reviewing progress on programmes with long-term objectives.
7 Reviewing product development activity to verify compliance with policy objectives.
8 Examining major development projects to confirm that policy objectives and criteria are being adhered to.

8.5 Major environmental issues

Environmental issues tend to be inter-related so that it is often difficult to recognise cause and effect in the process of determining appropriate action to correct damage already done. Here by way of example are synopses of some major environmental issues. The list is not claimed to be comprehensive.

8.5.1 *Energy consumption*

The most significant feature of industrialisation has been the progressively increasing demands for energy. World energy consumption increased by 64% over 20 years up to 1988 and the industrialised nations account for 76% of the total. The main sources of energy have been fossil fuels. These are finite resources and current rates of consumption will exhaust them within a few generations.

Oil spillages are among the most serious causes of oceanic pollution and all fossil fuels are environmentally damaging in use as atmospheric pollutants.

1 Soot is a health hazard causing respiratory diseases.
2 Oxides of sulphur and nitrogen cause acid rain which impairs soil fertility whole forests have died.
3 Carbon dioxide (CO_2) in the atmosphere before the industrial revolution, as measured from glacial samples, was 75% of today's concentration. This trend is contributing to global warming to cause climatic changes with serious implications for world food production and a rising sea level to submerge some land areas which are currently inhabited.

Advanced living standards are dependent on high energy consumption and the world is committed to fossil fuels as the principal source for several decades into the future. Alternative energy sources have been developed including nuclear and hydroelectric power generation. Further possibilities include solar energy and wind and tidal power systems.

However, there is evidence that much energy is consumed wastefully especially in transport and space heating. Meanwhile, the potential for energy demands to escalate with the development of Third World countries is enormous.

International co-operation is essential to curtail further environmental damage throughout the world. Development of alternative energy sources is a long-term option. The immediate practical options are energy conservation and pollution control. Improving efficiency in the use of energy will curb growth in demand. Technologies are available for improved control of pollutants from power generation and to achieve cleaner vehicle exhausts. The process of cleaning up will inevitably add significant cost.

8.5.2   *Nuclear radiation*

The sun is a source of radioactivity which occurs naturally in the environment. Man has also developed technology for generating radiation associated with both creative and destructive aims.

Uses of radioactivity include:

1 Radiography in health care, research, industry and security.
2 Radiotherapy in medicine especially the treatment of cancer.
3 Irradiation as a preservative treatment for foodstuffs.
4 Thermonuclear power generation.
5 Thermonuclear weapons for mass destruction.

From Hiroshima and Nagasaki in 1945 to the Partial Test Ban Treaty of 1963 nuclear testing had added 7% to natural levels of radiation in the atmosphere: since then it has fallen to 1%.

Exposure to raised concentrations or for long periods is hazardous for all living organisms. It may be fatal, or may result in genetic mutation or various forms of cancer; often the illness takes years to develop. Contamination may also be passed on through the food chain. Consequently, special care is necessary to prevent radioactive leakage, to deal safely with contaminated waste and to shield all those in close proximity to any radioactive source.

Thermonuclear power generation is a particularly controversial issue. The advantages against coal or oil fired power stations are freedom from dependence upon a fast depleting non-renewable resource and the avoidance of atmospheric pollutants. However, the potential for accidental damage is catastrophic and there are unresolved problems of disposal of nuclear waste.

Chernobyl has demonstrated the scale of radiation contamination, loss of control of a nuclear power generator can cause. This disaster and the earlier accidents at Windscale (1957) and Three Mile Island (1979) tend to inhibit public confidence in the safety of this form of power generation, particularly for Third World countries in the process of development.

Uranium-238, the radioactive element used in nuclear power generation has a half-life measured in billions of years, which for practical purposes means for ever. Disposal of high level waste is therefore a matter of enormous responsibility. None has been disposed of so far and the International Atomic Energy Agency, which represents 24 nations, is developing strategies. The US Department of Energy is conducting extensive studies in the development of plans for creating a high level waste burial site at Yucca Mountain on the Nevada Test Site.

Low and intermediate level wastes had been dumped in selected oceanic sites up to 1983 since when there has been a moratorium on sea dumping by international consensus.

8.5.3 *Depletion of the ozone layer*

The ozone layer is a natural feature of the stratosphere. It prevent's the sun's ultraviolet radiation from reaching the earth where it would otherwise be harmful to human beings, causing sunburn and skin cancer. Since 1975, when a hole in the ozone layer over Antarctica first appeared, progressive depletion has been recorded.

Ozone gas occurs in the stratosphere from ionisation of oxygen. It reverts to oxygen by catalytic action attributable to traces of certain gases notably chloroflourocarbons (CFCs). The catalytic action is most effective at the low temperatures of the polar regions.

CFCs are inert gases used for refrigerators, aerosol propellants, air conditioning and foaming agents. The relatively small quantities released into the atmosphere reach the stratosphere unchanged as traces sufficient for the catalytic breaking down of ozone.

International agreement to reduce the production and use of CFCs in stages to 50% of 1986 levels by 1998 was reached in 1987 by signing the Montreal Protocol to the Vienna Convention on the Protection of the Ozone Layer 1985. The United States, Canada, Norway and Sweden had banned the use of CFCs for aerosols and refrigerators from 1978. In the UK the Department of the Environment has assigned to industry responsibility for monitoring the UK obligations under the Montreal Protocol.

8.5.4 *Water management*

Toxic and pathogenic contamination of drinking water are health hazards. The contamination may be caused by agricultural leaching, industrial effluents or domestic sewage. Domestic consumption accounts for no more than 6% of the world's water usage; crop irrigation takes 72% and industrial uses 22%.

Ground water is the earth's main store of fresh water which is normally replenished from surface water. Excessive extraction has depleted some of these reservoirs beyond restoration. Others have been contaminated by toxic chemicals and purification is virtually impossible.

A number of rivers and lakes throughout the world are now virtually dead water as a result of agricultural and industrial pollution: examples include Lake Erie in North America and the River Elbe in Europe. River water often has to be cleansed and recycled many times over as it flows to the sea.

Much industrial pollution may be preventable by the use of closed systems for recycling on the principle that any effluent returned must be as clean as the water withdrawn. Eutrophic polluted water is nitrogen enriched from agricultural leaching; it encourages excessive algae growth which depletes the water of oxygen. This destroys aquatic life and inhibits the natural microbial breakdown of organic pollutants which requires oxygen. Pathogenic contamination is controlled by chlorination.

The United States, Canada and EC countries have introduced legislation to protect ground water against pollution and there are OECD water recommendations and EC water directives relating to water management and pollution control.

8.5.5 *Waste management*

Waste is a feature of the life-style of developed nations. It reflects extravagant consumption of resources which are often non-renewable and disposing of the waste often causes damage to the environment through pollution.

In addition to solid waste which requires sound management for safe disposal, industrial waste occurs as emissions which can pollute the atmosphere and effluents which can pollute the land or water courses. While domestic waste also occurs as sewage requiring hygienic treatment to avoid epidemic disease.

Most solid waste is currently disposed of in landfill tips. There is a legacy from the past of unsafe disposal sites in Europe and North America where hazardous waste has been dumped without adequate environmental protection. Contamination of the soil or ground water is already occurring or is expected to occur. Biodegradation of organic waste in landfill tips also releases methane gas with a consequent risk of explosion and as an atmospheric pollutant, methane contributes to global warming.

Substances which can be recycled or recovered for reuse from domestic or industiral waste include paper, plastics, glass, metals, chemicals, oily products and construction materials. Extracting these substances is costly but it considerably reduces the quantity of residual waste to be disposed of. This may then be incinerated, buried with due protection or treated for controlled biodegradation: all three processes are costly.

Incineration adds to atmospheric pollution but generates usable heat energy. Biodegradation releases methane which can be collected as a usable fuel and the residual product is a stable organic compost, useful for aiding soil fertility.

Conservation and prevention of pollution have been addressed by the OECD Recommendations of 1987 and Basel Convention of 1989 and the 1989 EC Framework Directive. These measures establish a framework for control based upon responsible voluntary constraint by member nations. They require national controls to be established to ensure waste is disposed of without harming the environment by encouraging recycling, controlling the movement of hazardous waste and applying the 'the polluter pays' principle.

Managing waste disposal in ways which are both environmentally sound and economically viable is a developing industry based on advanced technologies in the USA and in EC countries. The factors influencing this trend include: concern to observe the principles of OECD and EC waste disposal measures; the need to deal safely with increasing quantities of hazardous waste; and increasing difficulty in finding suitable safe disposal sites.

The United States and most EC countries including the UK have introduced legislation which aims to tackle pollution at source. Responsibility for treatment, storage and disposal of hazardous wastes rests with the producer. Strict conditions are imposed for waste disposal in landfill sites. An International Maritime Organisation agreement effectively prohibits incineration at sea after 1992. These developments make it necessary for manufacturers to take account of waste disposal as an integral part of product life cycles in planning operations.

8.5.6   *Intensive farming*

The potential agricultural capability of the world is adequate for feeding its entire population for the foreseeable future. In the developed countries there is over-production of food and ecological damage is being caused by intensive farming. The Third World has sufficient suitable land but for various reasons cannot use it effectively for feeding the impoverished inhabitants of these regions. The result is that two-thirds of the world's population are undernourished and many die from starvation. The weakness is thus in communication and distribution rather than in technology.

Throughout the developed world there has been considerable develop-ment in agricultural productivity, particularly in Europe, during the second half of this century. Crop yields and meat and dairy productivity have all been greatly increased through the application of new technologies, mech-anisation and intensive methods of husbandry. Modern farming is supported throughout the developed world by a multi-national agrochemical industry.

Chemical fertilisers are used for concentrated plant nutrition, part leaches out to pollute rivers, lakes and ground water. Over reliance on chemicals depletes the soil of humus leaving it vulnerable to erosion by wind and rain. These practices have already caused ecological damage both to the soil and to water resources needing urgent correction. The need is particularly acute in Europe where nitrogenous fertilisers are applied to the soil at a rate four times that of the USA. The practice of recycling crop residues to maintain soil fertility is common in the USA but not in Europe.

Some selective herbicides and pesticides used have been toxic to wild life and human beings and some are persistent in the soil. Some residues may remain in the crop to contaminate the food chain. Use of organochlorine compounds which include DDT and dieldrin have been banned in the USA and Europe since 1972 but they continue to be used in the Third World.

An International Code of Conduct on the Distribution and Use of Pes-ticides has been published by the UN Food and Agricultural Organisation and the World Health Organisation. The aim is that manufacturers and users should agree voluntary standards. In the USA the American Society for the Testing of Materials and the American Petroleum Institute establish standards and codes of practice which are adopted by the multi-national chemical corporations as applying throughout the USA and the EC.

Animal husbandry involving intensive management of livestock includes: selective breeding; hormone treatment to promote productivity; concen-trated nutrition and in some cases forced feeding; and confining animals in enclosures which severely restrict movement. These practices prompt con-cern about contamination of the food chain and cruelty to animals.

These developments have been largely led by domestic market demand but influenced in some cases by government intervention. In particular the Common Agricultural Policy of the European Community in aiming for abundant and cheap food for the community has also created 'mountains' of surplus produce.

Fishing is closely related to agriculture, and should be considered here along with other forms of hunting wild life. Food is the principal objective of these activities. Other aims may include hunting for sport or for animal products such as pelts and tusks or culling for the protection of other species or to protect crops and livestock. These activities raise specific environ-mental issues which include: conservation of fish stocks; protection of endangered species; and cruelty to animals.

8.5.7 *Destruction of rainforests*

The tropical rainforests of the world provide habitat for nearly half the world's species of plants and animals. They also have a high capacity for absorbing atmospheric CO_2. They often thrive on soils too fragile for other vegetation and they provide protection against soil erosion.

Large scale forest clearance is likely to disturb the ecological balance and could result in elimination of species or changes in climate with significant effects on agriculture.

Between 1980 and 1989 the world's total area of tropical forests had been reduced from 14 million to 8 million square kilometres. Latterly however, the rate of depletion has slowed down significantly. South America has more than half the world's total area of tropical forest: some 37% occurs in the Amazon basin. Other significant areas are in Zaire (12%) and Indonesia (10%).

The driving force behind tropical rainforest clearance is population pressure to make the land available for agriculture and industrial development. Exports account for about a quarter of the timber, most of the rest is burned on site adding to atmospheric CO_2.

Areas where tropical rainforests have flourished tend to have fragile soil so that agricultural productivity is likely to be poor with high incidence of crop failure. Forest clearance then becomes progressive with the adoption of a practice of shifting agriculture, whereas the natural vegetation is often capable of yielding economically valuable products such as rubber, aromatic oils, medicinal extracts, edible fruits and nuts as well as timber. Realising the economic potential of the forests depends upon sound management of these resources. This lends important economic support to the ecological argument for ending deforestation.

There are no international constraints upon any country wishing to destroy its forests. However, UNESCO's Biosphere Programme provides a limited measure of protection in some areas and there are also a number of national programmes for preservation of specific ecological systems.

8.5.8   *Third World deprivation*

United Nations and World Bank sources estimate that five billion people currently inhabit the earth: three-quarters of them in the undeveloped countries of the Third World. World population is increasing with an estimated growth rate of 1.74% per annum. The demographic prediction is that population growth will slow down during the next century to stabilise at a world population of between 8 and 12 billions before the end of the twenty-first century.

Over the last half century the population of the Third World has been expanding rapidly with no economic progress. Whereas over the same period in the developed countries there has been substantial economic progress and an almost stable population.

The economic progress achieved by developed countries has led to progressive improvements in living standards represented by advances in nutrition, comfort, health care, education, and recreation. By contrast, most of the inhabitants of the Third World exist on the threshold of starvation and lack most amenities of life. This contrast brings a crucial perspective to all the major environmental threats.

The issues raised by this division of the world were analysed in both socio-economic and environmental terms in the Brandt Report of 1980 and Brundtland Report of 1987. These studies identified wealthy nations broadly as those inhabiting the north of the globe and impoverished nations the south. Both reports urge greater economic co-operation between the two.

The objectives for addressing Third World deprivation have to be:

1 Improvement in living standards in the Third World based upon substantial economic development.
2 Stabilisation of population growth in the Third World.
3 Effective control to minimise environmental damage throughout the world.

There is unlikely to be any significant economic development in the Third World without substantial aid from the developed nations. However, aid has to be carefully targeted to promote sustainable economic development. There have been successes and failures among past aid programmes. They include groundnut cultivation, forestry, land reclamation and civil engineering projects. Small scale projects, developed in collaboration with local communities have achieved a good success record by consolidating local traditional skills. Some major projects have foundered through fundamental weakness such as inadequate research, inappropriate technology, insensitive direction or unnecessary intervention.

Major capital intensive aid projects usually involve transferring advanced technology to be applied in a Third World country where culture, educational standards, and experience will all be different. The risk of damage from industrial accidents is then likely to be greatly increased calling for special attention. At Bhopal in India in 1984, toxic gas escaping from a chemical plant caused 3,323 deaths, 26,000 chronically ill and over 300,000 other cases of lung damage. Industry in the developed world may be no less accident prone but is usually better able to contain potential damage through experienced management, contingency planning and technology.

High birth rates, high infantile mortality, shortlife expectancy and progressive population increase are characteristics common to all impoverished communities. This places severe constraints on potential economic growth. The experience of the developed countries demonstrates that improvements in education, hygiene, health care and nutrition, bring not only reduced infantile mortality and extended life expectancy, but also a fall in the birth rate to a level which maintains a stable population. Meanwhile family planning programmes have been adopted with marked success in some countries.

Severe famine frequently occurs in some regions of the Third World, particularly in Africa, inflicting a heavy death toll. Recurrent drought is the principal cause but crop failure may also be due to flooding or pest damage and in some cases starvation results from growing cash crops for export instead of food for the native population. Recurrent flooding in Bangladesh is related to forest clearance in the Ganges basin.

A critical feature which inhibits economic development in the Third World is the urban concentration of population distribution. There is a common pattern of persistent migration from rural to urban areas in hopeful search for employment. These aspirations are rarely fulfilled and invariably, the urban structures are hopelessly inadequate to cope with the influx. It results in conditions of extreme degradation and epidemic disease for very large numbers of the inhabitants of most Third World cities.

8.5.9 *Health*

Medical research has contributed much to the increased expectancy of life in developed countries. Many human diseases, which were previously fatal, have been controlled or eliminated by immunisation, preventive therapy or treatment with drugs such as antibiotics. Most of the benefits have yet to penetrate Third World populations where progress will depend upon the development of education and more robust structures for health care.

Some drugs developed for chemotherapy have had undesirable side effects, which were not always known at the time of treatment. Thalidomide was one such example. Public concern has led to legislation in European and North American prescribing standards, requiring extensive testing, and controlling production and use of new medicinal drugs.

A major cause of epidemic disease and high morbidity rates in the Third World is contamination of natural water supplies by sewage particularly in the squalor of over-populated cities.

Infectious diseases do not now cause a significant number of deaths in developed countries; heart disease and cancer are more common terminal illnesses. Diet, smoking, lack of exercise and stress are believed to be contributory causes of heart disease. Smoking is a significant cause of death from lung cancer.

Narcotic addiction threatens social structures; drug traffic is illegal virtually worldwide with severe penalties; this serves to raise the price demanded from addicts.

As a threat to human health, AIDS also gives cause for concern because it is a transmittable terminal disease for which no cure is known.

Another area of health concern has been the development of additives in food products as preservatives or to add colour or flavour. Some additives cause undesirable reactions in some individuals. Disclosure of additives is now required by law.

Chemotherapy in health care and chemical additives in food are controversial issues. The alternative view claims that equivalent research effort focused on the world's estimated 17,000 plant species not used for food could well yield more effective and less harmful natural remedies.

The environmental health challenge is to improve water management and health care in the Third World and to curb the health threatening dietary and other habits of affluent peoples.

Further reading

Cairncross, F *Costing the earth* (1991) (Economist Books).

Cuming, M W *The theory and practice of personnel management* (6th edn, 1989) (Heinemann).

Lumby, S *Investment appraisal and related decisions* (1988) (Van Nostrand Reinhold).

Samuels, J M, Wilkes, F M and Brayshaw, R E *Management of company finance* (5th edn, 1990) (Chapman & Hall).

Simpson, S *The Times guide to the environment* (1990) (Times Books).

CHAPTER 12   External audit and corporate governance

Objectives	To describe the duties and responsibilities of external auditors and audit committees and their relationship with internal audit
Contents	The role and purpose of external audit, public accountability and types of audit. Auditing standards and guidelines. Co-operation between external and internal auditors. The role and purpose of audit committees. Corporate governance and the regulation of investment, reporting and audit
Summary	External auditors and audit committees perform critical roles in ensuring proper corporate governance. An effective internal audit function will give constructive support to both. Legislation provides for a self regulatory framework with legally sanctioned parameters

1.0   THE ROLE OF EXTERNAL AUDIT

The explanatory foreword to 'Auditing Standards and Guidelines' developed by the Auditing Practices Committee and approved by CCAB governing bodies gives the following definition:

'An audit is the independent examination of, and expression of opinion on the financial statements of an enterprise. (When reading Auditing Standards and Guidelines, the term "enterprise" should be read as embracing any form of entity, whether profit oriented or not.)

Unless the relevant Auditing Standard or Auditing Guideline indicates to the contrary, the term "audit" applies:

(a) where there is a statutory requirement for the auditor to express an opinion in terms of whether the financial statements give a true and fair view (for example under the Companies Acts or the Industrial and Provident Societies Acts);

(b) where there is a statutory requirement for the auditor to express an opinion in terms other than whether the financial statements give a true and fair view (for example audits of government departments or local authorities); and

(c) where the terms and scope of the engagement are agreed between the auditor and his client (for example the audit of a sole trader or partnership) or where they are specified in a legal document (for example a trust deed).'

1.1 Public accountability

Commercial corporations are accountable to those who provide the capital, such as shareholders and lenders. Public service organisations are accountable to the public as taxpayers. Accountability implies a requirement for those charged with responsibility for managing such organisations to report on their performance. Moreover, for the reporting to be credible there is a need for independent confirmation that it is correct, or indeed both true and fair. This is the role of external audit.

The relationships between shareholders, management and auditors in a public company are illustrated in Figure 1 below.

Figure 1

Shareholders, management and auditors—Relationships

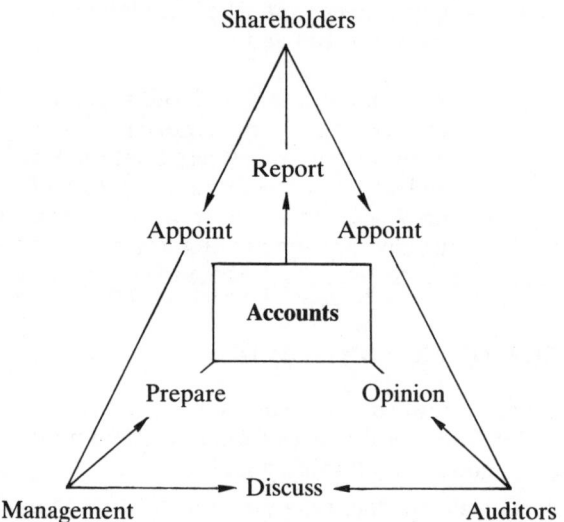

1.2 Types of external audit

External audit in the public sector often carries duties and responsibilities additional to expressing an opinion on financial statements. These may include:

1 Reporting on and contributing to the achievement of value for money.
2 Reporting in the public interest where appropriate, for example, where there has been a failure to comply with legislation, policies or directives.

The authority and purpose of the external audit role in a number of different organisations are summarised in Figure 2 on pp 405–406.

Figure 2

Types of external audit

Organisation	Legislation	Auditor	Additional duties
Public companies	Companies Acts 1985 and 1989	Private accountants appointed by members	Proper accounting records; Adequate returns from branches; Financial statements agree with records.
Central government	National Audit Act 1983	National Audit Office	Achievement of value for money; Report in the public interest.
Local government	Local Government Finance Act 1982	Audit Commission	As for central government; Use of government grants.
National Health	Health Circular 85/3	DSS Approved	As for central government; Use of monies granted.
Nationalised industries	Appropriate Industry Act	Approved by Secretary of State	As for public companies; Compliance with Ministerial Directives.
Housing Associations	Housing Act 1974 Industrial & Provident Societies Act 1968	Private accountants	As for public companies; Compliance with trust deeds and Agreements.
Charities	Charities Act 1960	Private accountants	Agree donations and fund raising, grants and loans, special fund and legacies.
Building Societies	Building Societies Act 1986	Private accountants	Right to pass information to Building Society Commission where investors need protection.
Friendly Societies	Friendly Societies Act 1974	Private accountants	Submission of annual return to Registrar of Friendly Societies

Organisation	Legislation	Auditor	Additional duties
Insurance funds	Insurance Companies Act 1974	Private accountants	Compliance with margin of safety; Security of capital; Adequate procedures for reinsurance; Adequate asset cover; Relevant actuarial valuation; Suitable management.
Investment companies	Companies Acts 1985 and 1989	Private accountants	Gain approved status; Portfolio valuation.
Pension funds	Independent audit required to satisfy the Inland Revenue		Solvency of fund; Valuation of assets.

2.0   AUDITING STANDARDS AND GUIDELINES

The purpose of auditing standards and guidelines is to prescribe the basic principles auditors are expected to follow in the conduct of an audit. Members of CCAB accounting bodies are expected to abide by the auditing standards; failure to do so may lead to disciplinary action; Audit guidelines are indications of best practice.

2.1   The auditor's operational standard

This auditing standard is effective for the audit of financial statements relating to accounting periods starting on or after 1 April 1980 and it applies whenever an audit is carried out.

1 The auditor should adequately plan, control and record his work.
2 The auditor should ascertain the enterprise's system of recording and processing transactions and assess its adequacy as a basis for the preparation of financial statements.
3 The auditor should obtain relevant and reliable audit evidence sufficient for him to draw reasonable conclusions therefrom.
4 If the auditor wishes to place reliance on any internal controls, he should ascertain and evaluate those controls and perform compliance tests on their operation.
5 The auditor should carry out such a review of the financial statements as is sufficient in conjunction with the conclusions drawn from the other audit evidence obtained, to give him a reasonable basis for his opinion on the financial statements.
6 General guidance on procedures by which this standard may be compiled with are given in auditing guidelines:

Planning, controlling and recording
Accounting systems

Audit evidence
Internal controls
Review of financial statements

2.2 The audit report

This auditing standard applies to all audit reports issued as a result of audits as defined in the Explanatory Foreword and issued on or after 1 September 1989. Although it is not primarily intended to apply to other forms of report provided by auditors many of the principles will normally be applicable to them.

The audit report should state clearly:

1 The addressee.
2 The financial statements audited.
3 The auditing standards followed.
4 The audit opinion.
5 Any other information or opinions prescribed by statutory or other requirements.
6 The identity of the auditor.
7 The date of the report.

If the auditor is unable to express an audit opinion without reservation, he should qualify his report by referring to all those matters which he considers to be material and about which he has reservations.

This standard is supported by explanatory notes covering:

1 Standards followed.
2 The audit opinion.
3 Qualified audit reports.
4 Circumstances giving rise to qualification.
5 Forms of qualification.
6 Disclosure of reasons for qualification.
7 Uncertainty and management representations.
8 Emphasis of matter.
9 Other information or opinions prescribed by statutory or other requirements.
10 Dating of the audit report.

2.3 Qualified audit reports

Much of the guidance relates to qualifications in audit reports. There are two important reasons for this:

1 In many cases the audit report provides reliable assurance that the subject matter examined is as it should be. But, when this is not so, the audit report must communicate, with precision and clarity, that such assurance cannot be given, by stating why and to what extent.
2 Most external audit reports have to be addressed to a body of people such as the members of a company. There is a need to ensure consistent interpretation.

Reasons for such concern may be:

(a) uncertainty which prevents the auditor from forming an opinion on a matter; or
(b) disagreement where the auditor is able to form an opinion but it conflicts with the view given by the financial statements.

The impact of the uncertainty or disagreement on the financial statements then has to be judged as immaterial, material or fundamental and an opinion expressed accordingly (see Figure 3 below).

Figure 3

Qualifications in audit reports

Reason for concern	Impact on financial statements		
	Immaterial	*Material*	*Fundamental*
Uncertainty	Unqualified opinion	'subject to' opinion	Disclaimer of opinion
Disagreement	Unqualified opinion	'except for' opinion	Adverse opinion

2.4   Errors and irregularities

The primary responsibility for prevention and detection of errors and irregularities rests with management.

Management establishes systems and procedures for internal control purposes. Errors and irregularities may be caused by (a) unintentional mistakes or (b) intentional distortions. These are manifestations of weakness in control and therefore a cause of concern to the accountable management.

Management control systems frequently contribute to the process of compiling the financial statements on which the external auditor is required to express an opinion. He must then ascertain and record these systems and carry out compliance tests. If errors are uncovered in the course of this work the auditor is concerned primarily with the impact they have on the view presented by the financial statements.

However, it is in the interests of both auditor and management that when such weakness is uncovered it should be brought to the attention of the management so that it can be remedied. The auditor should explain that the errors came to light in the course of audit examination for the purpose of establishing the reliability of information used in compiling the financial statements. It is important that he makes clear the limitations of the findings for other purposes.

The auditor is not required to report irregularities he may uncover to the shareholders. Indeed his duty of confidentiality debars him from doing so unless he is instructed to the contrary by the court in any case where a criminal offence has been committed. Auditors do however have a public duty to disclose information coming to their knowledge of any serious criminal offence if it is likely to affect a large number of people or to cause serious harm to any individual.

3.0 CO-OPERATION BETWEEN AUDITORS

There are two CCAB guidelines of particular significance to internal auditors because they establish the basis on which internal audit is able to contribute to the quality of corporate governance in both the private and public sectors. The two guidelines are:

1 *Guidance for internal auditors*—This guideline relates to internal audit as a control tool for management. This aspect is fully discussed in Chapter 2 and the full text of the guideline is quoted in Appendix 1.

2 *Reliance on internal audit*—This guideline addresses internal audit from the external auditor's viewpoint and is considered below.

Internal and external auditors pursue different objectives. While the external auditing perspective is focused on the truth and fairness of financial reporting, internal auditing is totally concerned with the quality of the result to be reported. There is often, however, an element of common ground both in the audit evidence collected and the techniques used for collecting it. The significant difference is in the viewpoint from which the relevance of the evidence is judged.

Thus there are benefits to be secured from co-operation in the course of their separate pursuits. The conditions necessary for successful co-operation are, mutual trust and each understanding the role of the other and respecting the other's competence.

Co-operation should include consultation in planning audit work, and each making available to the other working papers, audit reports and management letters.

The benefits include:

1 Each auditor is able to take account of the other's audit plans in formulating their own; this is particularly helpful where audit coverage is arranged on a rotational basis.
2 Unnecessary duplication of work in collecting audit evidence and clashing schedules for local audit visits can be avoided.
3 Detailed audit programmes can sometimes be modified to meet the needs of both without compromising the objectives of either.
4 Each auditor is able to take account of evidence uncovered by the other which may have relevance to audit judgements other than those for which it was collected.

Arrangements for co-operation between auditors need the full support of management: they involve sharing information received in confidence and the benefits of an effective combined audit service accrue to the organisation.

3.1 Reliance on internal audit

Internal audit is a key element of the management's system of internal control. It is a control which functions by evaluating the adequacy and effectiveness of other controls. Internal audit work is therefore of interest to the external auditor.

The auditing guideline on reliance on internal audit developed by the Auditing Practices Committee issued by the governing bodies of CCAB recognises that the scope and objectives of internal audit may vary widely depending on the responsibilities assigned to it by management. It lists the areas where internal audit may operate as follows:

1 Review of accounting systems and related internal controls.
2 Examination of financial and operating information for management, including detailed testing of transactions and balances.
3 Review of the economy, efficiency and effectiveness of operations and of the functioning of non-financial controls.
4 Review of the implementation of corporate policies, plans and procedures.
5 Special investigations.

The guideline recognises that the external auditor may wish to place reliance on internal audit as a means of reducing work in the following areas:

1 Documentation and evaluation of accounting systems and internal controls.
2 Compliance and substantive testing.

Before determining the level of reliance the external auditor should make an assessment of the effectiveness and relevance of the internal audit function. In doing so the following areas need to be appraised:

1 *Degree of independence*—Although an employee of the organisation, reporting to senior management, the internal auditor should be able to carry out audits without the burden of conflicting obligations and have access to the highest level of management and be free to communicate with the external auditor.

2 *Scope and objectives*—The external auditor should examine the formal terms of reference (charter) for the internal audit function and judge the relevance of the work to external audit purposes.

3 *Due professional care*—Internal audit work should be properly planned, controlled, recorded and reviewed to ensure that audits are undertaken in a professional manner.

4 *Technical competence*—Internal audit staff should be adequately trained and experienced for the work involved.

5 *Reporting*—Internal audit reports should be of adequate quality and taken seriously by management.

6 *Resources*—The external auditor should consider the adequacy of the internal audit resources.

Although the extent of the external auditor's work may be reduced by placing reliance on work done by internal audit, the responsibility to report is that of the external auditor alone, and therefore is indivisible and is not reduced by this reliance. As a result, all final judgements relating to matters which are material to the financial statements or other aspects on which he is reporting, must be made by the external auditor.

The main differences between internal and external auditing are summarised in Figure 4 below.

Figure 4

Comparison of internal and external audit

Area of difference	Internal audit	External audit
Legislation	Only in the public sector	Companies Acts 1985 and 1989 and Appropriate Acts for public sector
Appointment	By management	By the owners or the Secretary of State
Independence	Non-operational role as determined by top management and confirmed by internal audit charter	Independence prescribed by statute and monitored by regulatory bodies
Accountability	To management	To the owners or the Secretary of State
Status	Employee of the organisation	External to the organisation
Remuneration	Salaried employee	Paid by fee
Timespan of work	Continuous review	Annual appointment
Scope of work	Determined by management	Determined by statutory requirement
Standards of practice	Best practice as defined by professional bodies	Standards and guidance defined by professional bodies and endorsed by regulatory bodies
Techniques	Standard audit techniques focused on management objectives	Standard audit techniques focused on financial statements
Concern with internal control	All management control systems of the organisation	Financial controls and directly related systems

Area of difference	Internal audit	External audit
Concern with information	Sufficient to support sound management decision	All information needed to support financial statements
Concern with organisational performance	Principal objective	A key objective of most public sector audits
Concern with corporate governance	Freedom to examine corporate activity to ensure probity and compliance with the law for the management and audit committee	Duty to confirm if accounts considered true and fair and if not to report why not to members

4.0   AUDIT COMMITTEES

4.1   Precedents

Audit committees have been developed in USA and Canada which include the following objectives:

1 To increase public confidence in the credibility and objectivity of published financial information.
2 To assist directors to meet responsibilities concerning financial reporting.
3 To strengthen the independence of external auditors by providing a channel of communication through directors who are free of operational accountability.

A DEFINITION

'A committee of directors of a corporation whose specific responsibility is to review the annual financial statements before submission to the Board of Directors. The committee generally acts as liaison between the auditor and the Board of Directors and its activities may include the review of the nomination of the auditor, overall scope of the audit, results of the audit, internal financial controls and financial information for publication.' (Canadian Institute of Chartered Accountants 1976)

4.1.1   *Canada*

In Canada as a consequence of several spectacular business failures in the 1970s attention was drawn to:

1 Boards of directors failing to control dominant executives.
2 Directors failing to take their responsibilities seriously.
3 Directors being unaware of important transactions taking place.
4 External auditors failing to alert management where problems exist.

The establishment of audit committees was seen as a means of addressing these problems. The Canadian Business Corporations Act now requires every Canadian corporation which accepts deposits from the public to set up an audit committee.

4.1.2 *USA*

In the USA the Equity Funding fraud prompted concern about corporate governance while the Foreign Corrupt Practices Act 1977 imposed on directors of public corporations a statutory responsibility to maintain adequate systems of internal control. A need for audit committees was acknowledged, particularly by the Securities and Exchange Commission (SEC) and the New York Stock Exchange (NYSE). In 1978 they introduced a condition of listing requiring every US-listed company to have an audit committee which must have a majority of non-executive directors in its membership.

In 1987 the National Commission on Fraudulent Financial Reporting (Treadway) made a number of recommendations for strengthening the effectiveness of audit committees. It has been followed by changes to strengthen the regulatory framework for US corporations covering auditing standards and communication with audit committees.

4.1.3 *Europe*

In Europe a draft EC directive proposes a requirement for public corporations to have a two tier structure of directors. The board of management is to submit an annual report and accounts with the auditor's report annexed to it, to a supervisory board, to be considered at a joint meeting. Similar requirements have applied for many years in a number of European countries, notably Germany and Holland.

4.2 Audit committees in the UK

Interest in the audit committee concept has been developing in the UK for a number of reasons:

1 Concern by the directorate to ensure that their corporate policies are being implemented by management with effective control.
2 An increasing burden of personal responsibility imposed upon directors by legislation; eg successive Companies Acts, Financial Services Act 1986, Banking Act 1987, Building Societies Act 1986.
3 Pressures on the board from increasingly competitive capital markets.
4 Growing public concern about the credibility of financial reporting prompted by a crop of corporate failures. In some cases ineptitude or malpractice have come to light.

Consultative papers from various bodies including CBI (1977) and the Bank of England (1987) have recommended that major public corporations should have audit committees which should be comprised mainly of non-executive directors.

PRO NED, a body set up by the Stock Exchange in 1982, issued a code of practice for non-executive directors in 1987. It recommended that:

1 Roughly one-third of the board of larger quoted companies should be independent non-executive directors with a minimum of three.
2 There should be an audit committee comprised wholly or mainly of non-executive directors.
3 Non-executive directors should have a right of access to the auditors.

A private member's Bill requiring every large public company to consider the appointment of an audit committee at its AGM was passed by the House of Commons in 1988 but foundered in the House of Lords.

The Institutional Shareholders Committee (ISC) published a code of practice for directors in 1991 which recommends the appointment of more non-executive directors.

4.3   Terms of reference

It is clear that there is a substantial body of opinion in favour of the establishment of audit committees in large UK public corporations and that they should be board committees of predominantly non-executive directors. Indeed a large number of these organisations have already established an audit committee. Some others have appointed non-executive directors who are in a position to bring an independent and objective viewpoint to the board's deliberations.

In the absence of prescription by statute or other sanction, the terms of reference for the audit committee is a matter for the board's discretion at the time it sets it up. In this, it is usual to take into account the recommendations and codes of practice published by the various interested bodies.

The function of the audit committee is to be the focus of control for the corporation.

1 It is the custodian of the board's collective conscience for fulfilling all its obligations and acting with propriety.
2 It serves as the focal point for verifying that the board's policies and directives are being effectively implemented throughout the organisation.
3 It provides a forum for discussion between the board and the auditors permitting more detailed consideration of audit issues than would be feasible at a meeting of the full board. Auditors may discuss issues with individual directors but in the absence of an audit committee, their access to the board as the governing body is restricted.

Some, if not all, of the following duties will normally be specified in the audit committee's terms of reference:

1 Reviewing the appointment and remuneration of the external auditors.
2 Reviewing with the external auditors:
   (a) audit plans;
   (b) accounting policies; and
   (c) financial statements

   including:

   (d) interim statements before publication;
   (e) annual report and accounts before adoption by the board;

   (f) material issues on which the auditors seek confirmation of expert judgement from the board;

   (g) any statements to be issued by the board with audit involvement before adoption by the board.

3 Considering the external auditor's report.

4 Seeking the external auditors' views on:

   (a) the quality of internal control;

   (b) compliance with the law; and

   (c) corporate conduct.

5 Concurring in the appointment or removal of the chief internal auditor.

6 Reviewing the quality of internal control with the chief internal auditor. This involves consideration of:

   (a) the terms of reference for internal audit;

   (b) the adequacy of internal audit resources;

   (c) any limitations on internal audit rights of access;

   (d) the internal audit plan of work;

   (e) the standards adopted for internal audit practice;

   (f) the extent of planned internal audit work completed;

   (g) the extent of co-operation with external auditors; and

   (h) internal audit conclusions.

The terms of reference determined by the board need to be fully specified and recorded in a board minute. This is necessary to ensure that all members of the board and the auditors have a clear understanding of the committee's purpose, its powers and any limitations. The deliberations of the audit committee also need to be formally recorded and reported to the full board for directing management action when necessary.

4.4 Methods of working

Non-executive directors of public corporations usually have other demands on their time. Consequently arrangements for audit committee meetings must be formally programmed well in advance. The frequency and duration of meetings will depend upon the range of duties specified in the terms of reference. The committee may meet monthly to match meetings of the full board; or it may need only one or two meetings for specific tasks.

An outline plan for a typical programme of audit committee meetings is shown in Figure 5 on p 416.

4.5 Relationship with internal audit

The internal audit function has an identity of purpose with the audit committee in the pursuit of high standards of internal control. There has to be a close working relationship. Internal audit is primarily a management tool for ensuring systems of internal control continue to be adequate and effective. The audit committee performs a similar role on behalf of the board. The only way this role can be fulfilled is by having the full support of the internal audit resources. The independence of the internal audit function is reinforced by having direct access to the audit committee.

Figure 5

Plan for audit committee meetings

Purpose of meeting	Invited to attend	Timing
1 Review of audit plans *	External audit partner Chief internal auditor	Start of financial year
2 Review of internal control *	Chief internal auditor External audit partner	End of financial year
3 Review of interim statement	External audit partner	Specific date (mid-financial year)
4 Review of annual report and accounts **	External audit partner Chief executive Financial executive	Specific date (after year end)
5 Consider auditors' report **	External audit partner Chief executive Financial executive	Specific date (after year end)
6 Review of other statements issued by the board	Chief executive Financial executive External audit partner	When necessary

Notes:

* These purposes may be combined in a single meeting.

** These purposes may be combined in a single meeting.

The Institute of Internal Auditors Inc. has issued a statement on the relationship between internal auditors and audit committees. This statement makes the following recommendations concerning audit committees:

1 *Need*:
   (a) every public company should have one as a board committee; and
   (b) other organisations should be encouraged to have one.

2 *Membership*:
   (a) all should be board members; and
   (b) all should be independent of management.

3 *Role*:
   (a) to assist the board to fulfil its statutory and accounting obligations;
   (b) to maintain liaison between the board, auditors, internal auditors and financial management; and
   (c) to review regularly the authority, scope and quality of performance of internal audit.

4 *Rights*:
  (a) to concur in appointment or removal of the chief internal auditor;
  (b) to expect internal audit to assess the quality of internal control; and
  (c) to use internal audit as a source of information on irregularities.

5 *Liaison with internal audit*:
  The chief internal auditor should:
  (a) have direct access to audit committee members;
  (b) meet with the audit committee at least annually; and
  (c) report significant findings to the audit committee.

5.0 CORPORATE GOVERNANCE

Corporate organisations are governed by boards of directors who have a duty prescribed by law to account for their stewardship to shareholders who have invested in the organisation. The directors are thus in a position of trust and investors are entitled to expect the affairs of the corporation to be directed in pursuit of their best interests with competence and honesty. The performance of a board of directors is judged by how well the corporation services its investment and this is measured in terms of earning a competitive return on the capital and maintaining its value.

This measure of performance requires revenue and expenditure to be allocated to accounting periods. There are many cases where this involves a considerable element of judgement; for example: expenditure on intangible assets such as goodwill; and dubious items such as unrealised gains or losses caused by foreign currency exchange fluctuations.

Various influences may encourage boards of directors to favour short-term options in exercising judgement on these issues. They include competitive pressure in the capital market and operational priorities overtaking shareholders' interests.

The quality of corporate governance depends upon establishing a structure capable of resisting these pressures. Elements which give strength to the structure include:

1 *Accounting standards*—Which are definitive and comprehensive and endorsed by legal sanction.

2 *Statutory audit*—To give an independent and competent opinion on whether the directors' stewardship accounts give a true and fair view.

3 *Non-executive directors*—As board members to add independent viewpoint in corporate policy and decision making.

4 *Audit committee*—Of the board comprised essentially of non-executive directors to provide a forum between the board and the auditors and to act as the focus of control for the corporation.

5 *Internal audit*—Reporting to top management, with access to the audit committee and an unrestricted brief to examine all corporate activity.

6 *Orderly capital markets*—Which are well regulated to curb excesses of competitive pressure for short-term benefits.

In the UK, investment and the raising and servicing of capital are driven by free market forces within a regulatory framework. The regulation is intended to protect investors against abuse of trust. The framework primarily consists of self regulating bodies with responsibilities conferred upon them with the authority of the law. The Companies Acts and the Financial Services Act 1986 are the principal enabling statutes for these self regulatory arrangements.

The Companies Acts prescribe conditions to be satisfied when raising capital by public subscription and also define the responsibilities and duties of directors and auditors. The Financial Services Act 1986 prescribed conditions for regulating investment business.

The Companies Act 1989 strengthened:

1 Accounting requirements for directors' financial reporting.
2 Requirements for appointment, qualification and practices of auditors.
3 The regulatory framework covering capital markets.
4 The investigative powers of DTI inspectors.

5.1   Accounting

Investment and shareholding are spreading and there is a need for reliable bases for comparison. Variations in accounting practice make comparison difficult and possibly misleading.

In accordance with the 1989 Act the DTI has established the Financial Reporting Council and its supporting Accounting Standards Board (ASB) whose role is to set accounting standards, to oversee application, and to investigate departures from statutory accounting requirements. The Act requires companies to state in their accounts that they have been prepared in accordance with the applicable accounting standards.

The declared aim of ASB is to devise a framework which ensures that accounts are more consistent and easier to read. It acknowledges a need for radical change in the structures of both the profit statement and the balance sheet. It has also indicated support for the view that the earnings per share calculation needs to be standardised by gradually restricting the ability to write off heavy costs as extraordinary items below the line.

5.2   Regulation of auditors

Since the Companies Act 1989 CCAB has replaced APC by a more independent Auditing Practices Board (APB) whose role is to supervise the setting of auditing standards and the monitoring of compliance. Its membership includes representatives of government, the legal profession, industrialists and academics.

The 1989 Act permits auditors to be incorporated as limited companies provided certain conditions are satisfied. It also requires auditors to be subject to regulation by supervisory bodies whose duties include ensuring that audits are carried out with integrity and independence by persons with appropriate qualifications. It prescribes conditions to be satisfied by way of professional qualification to hold office as auditor: these relate not only to individuals seeking to qualify but also to the bodies offering an appropriate qualification. Conditions of entry, content and standard of examinations and the extent of practical training must satisfy specified criteria. The bodies must apply rules which ensure the critria are met and they must monitor continued compliance effectively.

A succession of corporate failures followed by revelations of various forms of inadequacy or malpractice has put at risk public confidence in the worth of audit certificates. The Polly Peck case emphasised this point because the collapse of the company followed shortly after the publication of audited accounts which gave no warning of impending disaster. The Caparo case has also contributed a degree of public anxiety. In this case the House of Lords held that the auditor's duty of due professional care was to the general body of shareholders for the time being and not to individual members.

The auditor's independence and competence are crucial to the basis for confidence. It is thus most important that the recognised supervisory bodies for auditors have adequate rules for securing these qualities and they must also be seen to be enforcing these rules effectively.

5.3 Regulation of capital markets

The Securities and Investment Board (SIB) was established under the provisions of the Financial Services Act 1986. This Board has issued ten 'Statements of Principle' which define the framework for 'Core Rules' to be established by self regulating organisations (SRO): SIB is to exercise its disciplinary powers to enforce them. The 'Core Rules' have to provide adequate protection for investors while ensuring the cost to them of compliance is reasonable. The right of investors to sue for loss caused by breach of Core Rules is restricted to private individuals. Core Rules are supported by 'Third Tier Rules' over which SROs have complete discretion.

Two regulatory bodies have been set up under SIB for investment advisers. Those advisers who are tied agents having contracted to offer the products of one financial institution exclusively, have to be registered as members of the Life Assurance and Unit Trust Regulatory Organisation (LAUTRO). Independent advisers must be members of the Financial Intermediaries, Managers and Brokers Regulatory Association (FIMBRA). A feature of these regulatory bodies is that they impose a levy on members to provide a fund from which to compensate investors for losses resulting from malpractice or default by members.

The EC Second Directive on Banking which is to apply from 1993 will free banks from obligation to join a regulatory organisation. Regulation of investment business carried on by banks may then have to be exercised by the Bank of England as a condition of banking licences.

Since the 1986 Act, public concern has been aroused by two cases involving alleged attempts to rig the market for companies' shares in support of take over bids. In the Guinness case the High Court found the defendants guilty. The other case was sub judice at the time of going to press.

The Institutional Shareholders Committee has published a 'Code of Practice for Directors'. It distinguishes the respective roles in corporate governance of owners and managers and urges the appointment of more non-executive directors to ensure the company's interests take priority over those of the executives.

Amendment of the 1986 Act by the Companies Act 1989 allows judgement to be exercised in compliance with the spirit of the code of practice by moving away from strict interpretation of a legalistic rule book. Thus responsibility for protecting the investor lies firmly with SIB and the SROs to establish sound rules and to be seen to be enforcing them.

Further reading

Auditing and reporting, UK auditing standards, guidelines and exposure drafts (1990) (ICAEW).

Buckley, F *Audit committees, their role in UK companies* (1979) (ICAEW).

Financial Services Act 1986: a guide to the amended legislation (1990) (Butterworths).

Jennings, M *The guide to good corporate citizenship* (1990) (Director Books).

Walmsley, K *Butterworths company law handbook* (8th edn, 1991) (Butterworths).

CHAPTER 13   The public sector

Objectives	To examine the arrangements for both external and internal audit in major public sector organisations with emphasis on features which distinguish the requirements from those which apply in the private sector
Contents	External and internal audit in central government, local authorities, the National Health Service; non-departmental public bodies and shared systems. The concept of value for money auditing in the public sector. Competitive tendering for internal audit services
Summary	All public administration is under increasing pressure from the public to demonstrate effective control and accountability and to achieve value for money. The most recent changes in the laws governing all the major public sector organisations concentrate on these two requirements in both the management and the audit requirements. This is a trend which extends the responsibilities of the internal audit function and increases the opportunities for it to contribute to the achievement of management objectives

1.0   AUDIT IN CENTRAL GOVERNMENT

1.1   The need for audit

'The output from public administration is seldom sold on the open market and its value is difficult to measure. In most cases the administration has a monopoly of its activities: this accentuates the problem of assessing the administration's effectiveness.'

This statement from the Controller of Audit at the Swedish National Audit Bureau identifies the essential feature which differentiates public sector activities from a commercially motivated private sector.

In recent years political pressure has focused on the need for more effective accountability in the use of public funds. In the absence of readily quantifiable performance indicators, the trend has been for increasing emphasis on achieving value for money. This trend is reflected in the developments of both external and internal auditing in the public sector.

Indeed the legal framework now imposes external audit requirements on most public sector organisations by which their performance in terms of achieving value for money is to be independently appraised and publicly reported upon. The role of internal audit in this process is to examine operations on behalf of the accountable managers and to recommend management action for achieving better value for money. In this way internal audit contributes to improved management performance.

Internal auditors are not expected to comment on policy or indeed to challenge it. Their role is to examine the effects of the policy in a changing environment as compared with declared intentions.

'It is the function of testing the data or the situation which exists with that which might be expected to exist.' (Chief Inspector of Audit, Local Government 1981)

1.2   National Audit Act 1983

The National Audit Office (NAO) and the Public Accounts Commission were established by the National Audit Act 1983. The NAO is independent from the government. The Comptroller and Auditor General (C&AG) is head of NAO although this office existed long before NAO. The 1983 Act authorises access by NAO for value for money examinations to over 5,000 bodies in receipt of public funds.

The independence of the C&AG is assured in his appointment by Letters Patent from the Crown on recommendation from the Prime Minister and the Chairman of the Public Accounts Committee with House of Commons support: only the Sovereign can remove him from office on the recommendation of both the Commons and the Lords. He has complete freedom in determining the selection, scope and reporting of audit examinations, and in the appointment, remuneration and employment conditions for staff. His salary is not subject to annual approval by parliament.

The role of C&AG includes:

1 Authorising the issue of public funds to government departments.
2 Certifying the accounts of all government departments.
3 Examining and reporting to parliament on the economy, efficiency and effectiveness in the use of resources by government departments and other public organisations.

An important feature of the current philosophy of NAO is to encourage the development of effective internal auditing in government departments. The objective is to promote an efficient comprehensive service from the combined audit resources. That is to say, a service which:

1 contributes to, and
2 publicly reports on:
   the quality of control, and the achievement of value for money in the application of public funds.

1.3   Internal audit in central government

Central government is accountable to parliament for substantial spending on the provision of services such as further education, and on the management of major programmes such as motorway construction. There is thus a need to consider the results of government expenditure in terms of value for money.

In 1979 the Exchequer and Audit Department (whose functions are now undertaken by the National Audit Office) had reported serious inadequacies of internal audit in central government. This gave rise to the Wass/Bancroft initiative and in 1981, the 9th Report of the Committee for Public Accounts urged the development of a more effective internal audit function in central government. The Government Internal Audit Manual (GIAM) was prepared by HM Treasury and first published by HMSO in 1983. In its introduction, it states that it consolidates and brings up-to-date existing guidance and supports the development of internal audit in government. Its purpose is to provide direction, advice and information on internal audit to government departments and non-departmental public bodies.

The section of GIAM which deals with objectives contains the following statements:

'In his memorandum of responsibilities an Accounting Officer is charged with paying particular attention to the adequacy and effectiveness of his arrangements for internal audit.'

'The Accounting Officer should specify terms of reference which will enable the Head of Internal Audit to give him the quality of assurance he requires.'

'An internal audit should be established with responsibility for giving assurance to the Accounting Officer on the department's internal control system. It also assists managers by measuring, evaluating and reporting on the elements of the internal control for which they are responsible.'

'Internal audit is not an extension of or a substitute for line management. Responsibility for internal control rests fully with line managers who ensure that appropriate and adequate arrangements exist without regard to audit activity. It is for management to decide whether or not to implement audit findings and recommendations.'

An example of the role of internal audit within a major department is provided by the Ministry of Defence, where the principal duties are to provide assurances to management that:

1 The policies, procedures and systems of internal control established by management ensure the efficient, economic and effective use of resources.
2 Those policies and procedures are being complied with and are effective in meeting the objectives of the Department.
3 The assets and interests of the Department are properly controlled and safeguarded against losses of all kinds.
4 The accounting and other records form a reliable basis for the preparation of appropriation and other accounts (including management and trading accounts).
5 The financial and other data furnished to management in connection with decision-making processes is reliable.
6 The business systems established are sufficient to ensure the accomplishment of established objectives and goals.

1.4   Review of performance

In 1987 NAO conducted a review of internal audit performance within central government against standards established by HM Treasury. The review covered:

1 Scope of work.
2 Independence.
3 Staffing and training.
4 Due professional care.
5 Planning, controlling and recording of work.
6 Audit conduct.
7 Reporting.
8 Fraud and irregularity.
9 Relationships.
10 Computer audit ability.

NAO reported as a result of this review that while progress was being made towards achieving the standards the rate of progress was disappointing.

2.0   OTHER PUBLIC SECTOR AUDITS

2.1   Local authorities

The Audit Commission was established under the Local Government Finance Act 1982 with responsibility for the local government audit service. It is headed by the Controller of Audit and it is independent of both central government and local government. Its members are appointed, from a range of professions and interests, jointly by the Secretaries of State for the Environment and for Wales.

The objectives of the Audit Commission include promoting efficiency and integrity in the management of local government affairs. It performs its role mainly by:

1 Appointing external auditors to examine and report on the accounts of all local authorities in England and Wales.
2 Undertaking value for money audit examinations of local authority operations for the purpose of recommending improvements.

Local authority audits are concerned with:

1 The auditor's opinion as to the truth and fairness of the local authority's financial statements.
2 The adequacy of the local authority's arrangements for achieving economy, efficiency and effectiveness in its use of resources.
3 Whether any items dealt with in the accounts are contrary to the law or losses or damage have been caused by wilful misconduct.

Local authority auditors are required to report by certifying the authority's financial statements. If, however, they consider there is a case for reporting in the public interest this will be addressed to the local authority who must then inform the public through the press that the report is available for inspection.

Reports on special studies by the Commission are published by Her Majesty's Stationery Office.

The Audit Commission superseded the District Audit Service which had been established for many years under central government authority. The title 'district auditor' has continued in use for the Commission's own auditors appointed to audit the accounts of local authorities as distinct from private sector firms appointed by the Commission.

Local government audit in Scotland is provided for by the Local Government (Scotland) Act 1973. This legislation established the Commission for Local Authority Accounts in Scotland. The Commission assumed responsibility for external audit of local authority accounts in Scotland in 1975. Value for money studies became a statutory requirement in local authority auditing in 1988.

In Northern Ireland the Local Government Act (Northern Ireland) applies as amended by a Local Government Order of 1985. This legislation empowers the Department of the Environment (NI) to appoint local government auditors. Their role is primarily to certify local authority accounts but since the 1985 amendment order it also includes undertaking comparative and other studies of economy, efficiency and effectiveness.

2.2 National Health Service

The National Health and Community Care Act 1990 introduced changes in the management philosophy for the National Health Service aimed at achieving more effective accountability. Significant among these changes were new arrangements for independent audit. Responsibility for provision of audit services is now vested in the Audit Commission. The Local Government Finance Act of 1982 by which the Audit Commission was established has been amended to incorporate the audit requirements for the National Health Service. The established twofold role of the Commission to appoint auditors to certify accounts and to undertake value for money studies is now extended to the Health Service.

A key element in the changed management philosophy is a need for major changes in management information and appropriate financial reporting systems. In this context an important development has been initiated by the Chartered Institute of Management Accountants (CIMA) in developing a series of guides on financial management in the National Health Service. These are:

1 Financial Management and the Family Health Services;
2 The Application of Strategic Management Accounting to NHS Business Plans;
3 The Financial Management of GP Practices;
4 Return on Capital Employed Techniques in Hospitals; and
5 Activity Based Costing Applied to the NHS.

There is also to be a research report:

Costing Methods and Techniques for an NHS Internal Market.

These developments will provide bases for measurement and control and can be expected to contribute to the establishment of more effective accountability and help in the pursuit of value for money.

There has been a developing internal audit function in the National Health Service for some years. The Health Service internal audit manual has been developed since 1983 and is very comprehensive. It provides an operational audit service with emphasis on achieving value for money. There is already a significant element of co-operation between internal and external audit functions. The involvement of the Audit Commission, concentration on achieving value for money and emphasis on accountability must create challenging opportunities for the internal audit function.

2.3　Non-departmental public bodies

Major financial support is provided to certain non-departmental public bodies (NDPBs) from central government funds. There is then a need for accountability within a framework of operational autonomy. A sponsoring department's internal audit unit has a key role in assessing the quality of control exercised in providing such financial support and appraising the achievements in terms of value for money.

The Government Internal Audit Manual provides detailed guidance for internal auditors of sponsoring departments concerning funds advanced to NDPBs. The accountability issues involved in funding NDPBs are described in GIAM as follows:

> 'The public sector contains a great variety of bodies apart from government departments and local authorities. In every case a minister looks to the bodies he sponsors to be effective, efficient and economical in the conduct of their affairs. His department needs appropriate arrangements to follow through his interests which will depend on, for example, the function of the NDPB, why it was set up and the scale of its activities. Departments' aims and objectives in this area, and therefore their arrangements and procedures, are developing. The internal auditor needs to understand these aims and objectives in order to appraise current developments.'

> 'The main task of the internal audit unit is to appraise the adequacy and effectiveness of the department's systems for its dealings with its NDPBs. This may involve some work within NDBPs. The unit's terms of reference may also provide that it should examine specific activities within NDPBs and/or participate in, or undertake, periodic reviews or other examinations.'

2.4　Shared systems

Throughout the public sector common data sources have to be referred to by more than one department. This is particularly true within the civil service where there is considerable centralisation of records. For example: individual departments prepare input information for pension awards, whereas subsequent recording, payment and accounting are the responsibility of the Paymaster General's Office. Similarly, the administration for recruitment by many departments is the responsibility of one central office. In these circumstances it is important that there is a sound basis for confidence in the reliability of shared records and information. The internal audit service has a key role in maintaining this confidence and this is recognised in the Government Internal Audit Manual (GIAM) which states:

'Some systems are used by more than one department and a department may be responsible for identifiable components of a system, use data produced by another's system, or carry out functions on behalf of others. The Head of internal audit should satisfy himself that the responsibilities for such systems have been identified and agreed, and that the internal controls and internal audit arrangements adequately protect his Accounting Officer.'

Clear identification of responsibilities for system maintenance, communication of information and data integrity are critical factors which the internal auditor must consider and it will often be necessary to place some reliance on work done by internal auditors in other departments.

The Government Internal Audit Manual provides detailed guidance for internal auditors about the audit of shared services based upon the principle that all such arrangements are in effect supplier/user relationships and this provides the basis for identifying responsibilities.

3.0 VALUE FOR MONEY (VFM)

In commercial undertakings profitability is the recognised measure of management performance. Internal audit scrutiny of the application of scarce resources aims to enhance the achievement of greater profitability.

Without profitability, public organisations lack an easily understood measure of performance, though the public will readily understand what an improved or declining level of service is. To manage scarce resources, management must guard against inefficiency and needless bureaucracy.

The National Audit Act 1983 and Local Government Finance Act 1982 require the external auditors to consider the provision of value for money when conducting public authority audits. It is interesting to note that the Post Office Users Council stated:

'Government sets financial targets for nationalised industries but customers have difficulty knowing whether they are getting value for money. It is necessary to relate financial requirements, operational performance and quality of service.'

Value for money auditing is a form of operational audit and is concerned with the pursuit of economy, efficiency and effectiveness throughout all operations. In understanding VFM it is important to define the terminology in use:

Economy is the measure of input.
Efficiency is the measure of the relationship between input and output.
Effectiveness is the measure of output.

The inter-relationship between these measures is illustrated on p 428.

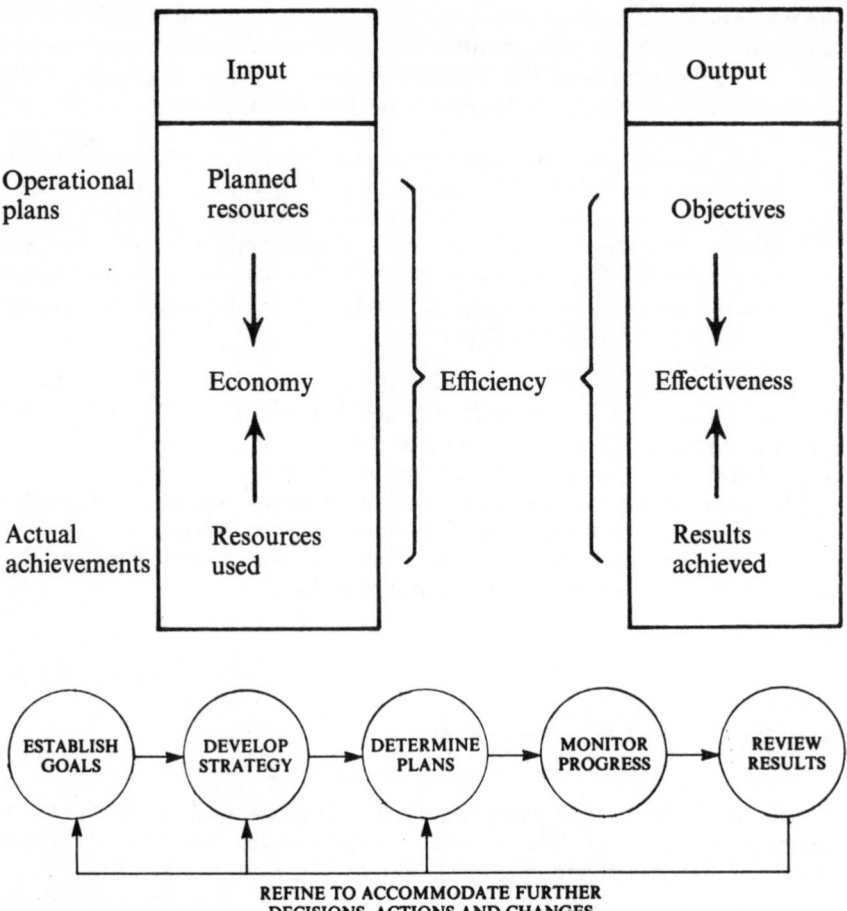

The Audit Commission's Code of Local Government Audit Practice, 1983, states:

> 'the achievement of economy, efficiency and effectiveness depends upon the existence of sound arrangements for planning, appraisal, authorisation and control of the use of resources. It is management's responsibility to establish these arrangements and to ensure that they are working properly.'

Needless to say, it is for internal audit acting on behalf of management to review the adequacy and effectiveness of these arrangements. In order to undertake this task internal audit needs to consider the following elements of organisational activity:

3.1   Elements of organisational activity

Vision—What the organisation is seeking to achieve. Vision is the guiding concept or statement concerning future areas of organisational activity. It may take the form of a corporate statement of policy objectives. From such ideas goals and individual objectives can be determined and clarified.

Strategy—The translation of vision into reality. With a large organisation rapid change is often difficult to achieve; nevertheless, it is important for organisations to have a plan as to how targets are to be met and against which performance can be monitored. Such a plan must itself be subject to periodic review to reflect the changing environment within which the organisation operates, thereby allowing for objectives to be restated to meet current need.

Style—'The way we do things.' It is appropriate to quote from the Audit Commission manual:

> 'Perhaps the single greatest handicap to securing improved value for money with many local authorities is what might be termed management style or the prevailing culture of the organisation. Time and again possibilities are blocked—or slowed down—by cultural constraints . . . the power of style can be managed—by the way members and chief officers reinforce things that are important.'

Although this quotation refers to local government, it is nonetheless relevant to many bureaucracies.

Structure—The manner in which the organisation is organised to implement the strategy. Structure is the framework which enables objectives to be analysed into separate functions. The Audit Commission identified some common characteristics which have proved conducive to achieving effective value for money:

1 Simplicity—Fewer committees may lead to quicker decisions.
2 The management structure should support the Committee structure.
3 Clear identification of tasks.
4 Individual accountability.

Systems—The manner in which people plan, organise, direct and control day-to-day operations that support the agreed strategy.

Management systems are the procedures that make the organisation work. The elements comprising an effective system include:

1 Procedures for reviewing objectives and evaluating performance in the light of changing circumstances.
2 Planning procedures for allocating resources and assigning individual performance objectives.
3 Monitoring procedures to show whether progress is being made in the direction required.

Supervision—Co-ordinating and controlling systems. Systems require continuous supervision and review in order to reflect the changing needs placed upon them. Management looks to internal audit for advice on the effectiveness of control systems in maintaining an efficient organisation.

Staffing—The manner in which those operating the systems work. Changes in strategy, structure or system require people to make the organisation function, ie having the right person in the right job at the right time.

Skills—Utilising the human resource more effectively. Those operating the systems need to have the appropriate skills and be updated in their work techniques to meet future needs of the organisation and to achieve their potential level of ability.

3.2   Structure for value for money audits

Auditors should not be involved in or comment on policy making and this will include setting objectives. Depending upon the organisation and the nature of the audit, examination should embrace the following areas of activity:

1 Identifying policy objectives.
2 Establishing that the organisational structure is appropriate to the activity involved—Codification of responsibilities, authority and accountability.
3 Establishing that line managers fully understand and implement policy as defined and intended by senior management. Plan, budget and control income and expenditure.
4 Reviewing the effectiveness of performance indicators (eg cost per patient bed per week).
5 Examining the performance of each section of the organisation against the organisational objectives. Achieving economies of scale, manpower management.
6 Ensuring that the information reaching decision makers is reliable and adequate for all options to be reasonably appraised. Monitoring results against pre-determined performance objectives and standards, to ensure that outstanding performance is encouraged and unacceptable performance corrected.

It is interesting to note that the Audit Commission published the diagram reproduced on p 431 showing the inter-relationship between regularity (compliance) audit and value for money audit, revealing how the regularity audit comprises part of the VFM audit.

Although identified with an external audit viewpoint, such a framework is nevertheless applicable to internal audit. Similarly the techniques described below are identified with VFM auditing.

3.3   The scope of internal audit work

The terms of reference for the Department identify the nature of work to be undertaken by internal audit in order to fulfil its responsibilities. Such work may be provided by three forms of audit:

1 FINANCIAL AND REGULARITY (COMPLIANCE) AUDIT

Such an audit is used to verify that the financial statements and reports presented to management fairly present the financial position of the organisation or subsection of the organisation, and that line managers have understood and complied with the instructions and directives of senior management. This requires application of the auditing techniques described in Chapters 5 and 8.

2 ECONOMY AND EFFICIENCY

The examination of economy and efficiency is now fundamental to auditing in the public sector. Expenditure is substantial and so too are the needs that have to be met. In order to maintain standards of service, management need to be vigilant in the use to which resources are put. Internal audit is needed

Framework for VFM audit of a public authority

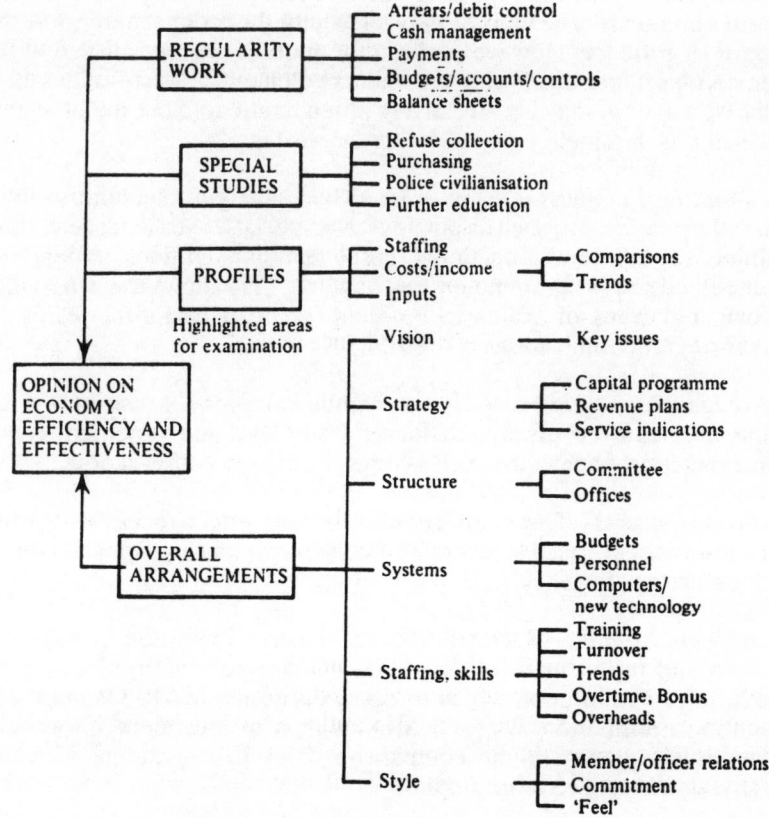

(*Source*: Audit Commission Report—Basildon District Council 1984.)

to make management aware of the adequacy of its monitoring systems and to provide advice where improvements are needed.

3 EFFECTIVENESS (PROGRAMME AUDITING)

Internal audit has had included in its remit the effectiveness with which both line and senior management achieve agreed goals and policies, so that 'value for money' can be appraised. Such audits are used to evaluate whether or not the goals of the organisation or programme of work have been achieved or are being met. Increasingly, internal audit is now being asked to review how management manages.

3.4   Audit methodology

It is now appropriate to examine some of the more specialised auditing techniques used within the government sector in order to monitor the effectiveness of the organisation or programme of work.

3.5   Some audit techniques

Value analysis—This technique represents 'an organised procedure for the efficient identification of unnecessary cost' (*The Waste Watcher's Guide*

(CIPFA)). By way of illustration a car-seat covering could be made of leather, cloth or a synthetic product, each requiring differing manufacturing processes and costs. The market associated with the product determines the standard of product. However, where the market can be satisfied with a lower standard, and this is not met, then an element of waste is identified. Similarly, a system may be excessively bureaucratic to meet the objectives for which it is designed, again allowing for wastage.

Functional cost analysis—Many organisations analyse expenditure by its nature of commitment, such as employees, materials, overheads, etc: this is a subjective analysis. Functional cost analysis identifies expenditure objectively, eg by programme or area of work. This allows the programme of work, eg award of grants to be identified with performance, eg the number of grant applications processed.

Cost reduction programme—This technique involves the use of a multi-disciplinary team of experts to identify and evaluate potential savings against the cost of achieving such savings, eg energy conservation.

Input-based studies—These studies examine the effectiveness with which scarce resources are used to achieve objectives, comparing input and output as a measure of efficiency.

Systems-based studies—Such studies are concerned with the management structure and procedures for providing management with adequate and reliable information upon which to make decisions: MAIS (Management accounting information system). MINIM is a management information system which allows for the comparison of each programme of work's objectives and resource consumption.

INFORMATION SYSTEM

Output-based studies—Operational achievements may be difficult to quantify. These studies are concerned with determining effective performance measures by which to evaluate the achievement of policy.

Inter-organisation comparison—This technique involves the use of accepted statistics for organisational comparison, eg Centre for Inter-Firm Comparisons (CIFC) and CIPFA Statistics. Within central government it is difficult to identify such acceptable measures.

Goal analysis—This technique is used to examine an organisation's ability to translate policy into operational goals for line management. It should be possible at any point in the organisation's operations to compare actual results with those planned for in the corporate plan. Where a change occurs, a gap is identified. Such gap may be identified with current plans and various methods used to extrapolate to the future, and to reconsider with future plans.

Systems review—This includes the process of verifying the continuing relevance and suitability of operational procedures to the organisational objectives. Divergence from such objectives will lead to inefficiency and waste.

4.0 COMPETITIVE TENDERING FOR INTERNAL AUDIT SERVICES

Continuous pursuit of value for money in the provision of public sector services leads to consideration of the competitive value of all internally established activities including internal audit. It may be feasible to consider an external agency as suitable for providing internal audit services in some public sector organisations. This is because there is often an element of common ground in the control systems, procedures, codes of practice and statutory obligations. It is thus a feature of internal auditing in the public sector that tenders to undertake the work may be invited from external agencies and some will be accepted.

The specification for bought out internal auditing services is of course crucial to the quality and effectiveness of the service to be provided. This specification needs to be prepared with considerable care taking into account the needs and circumstances of all operations expected to benefit from it. In particular, it should define clearly:

1 *Objectives:*

These should be determined by the chief executive with due emphasis on those fields in which internal audit is perceived as offering the greatest contribution to the achievement of management goals. Specified objectives might include:
(a) accuracy and reliability of records;
(b) security of assets;
(c) evaluation of the system of internal control;
(d) assessment of value for money in specific areas;
(e) adherence to policy:
(f) compliance with statutory obligations.

2 *Standards:*

It is necessary to identify the standards of internal audit practice to be applied, including the discipline for ensuring they are adhered to. Standards can be identified as those prescribed in the Government Internal Audit Manual or those published by CIPFA, or by IIA–UK.

3 *Scope:*

It is important to define the scope of internal audit examination required and to confirm the rights of access to premises, activities, records, staff, management and executives with specified limits if any.

4 *Reporting:*

The channels for reporting internal audit findings, conclusions and recommendations need to be clearly identified.

5 *Staffing:*

Minimum qualifications need to be defined for the various grades of internal auditing staff including specialists and management; the specification should be stated in terms of educational standards, professional qualifications and experience.

6 *Availability:*

Minimum requirements need to be stated for the availability of internal audit staff and the arrangements for training and for continuity of the internal audit service.

Further reading

Buttery, R and Simpson, R K in association with CIPFA *Auditing in the public sector* (2nd edn, 1989) (Woodhead-Faulkner).

Computer auditing guidelines (3rd edn, 1987) (CIPFA).

Glynn, J J *Public sector financial control and accounting* (1987) (Basil Blackwell).

Henley, Likierman, Holtham, and Perrin *Public sector accounting and financial controls* (3rd revised edition, 1990) (Chapman & Hall).

Government internal audit manual (1983) (HMSO).

Price Waterhouse *Value for money auditing* (1990) Gee & Co.

CHAPTER 14   Fraud and other irregularities

Objectives	To examine: Civil and criminal law of fraud Admissible evidence and its presentation in court Alarm signals for the auditor Preventative measures
Contents	Fraud defined; audit role; alarm signals; detection; action after discovery; relationships with police and senior management; preparation of evidence for court use; psychology of interrogation; Police and Criminal Evidence Act 1984; civil law and fraud
Summary	Fraud may result in loss or damage to the organisation; it is also a criminal offence. For both of these reasons the auditor must be constantly alert to the possibility of fraudulent practice and the scope for prevention. This involves vigilantly pursuing weaknesses in system or organisation which could allow malpractice to go undetected and boldly urging the accountable management to apply suitable safeguards. Auditors need to be familiar with the techniques for apprehending anyone suspected of fraud and the procedures for bringing them to justice

1.0   INTRODUCTION

Due to the sensitivity of this area of audit activity, both the definition of what constitutes fraud and audit objectives must be well understood. Prior to considering these matters, references should be made to the 'terms of reference' (charter):

'Internal audit promotes, in common with general management, an environment of fraud prevention. There is a specific requirement throughout the group for managers to notify every known or suspected fraud to the audit manager who will then ensure there is a prompt and thorough investigation of every incident.' (Reed International plc)

Similarly professional statements clearly establish the role of the internal auditor:

'The Internal Auditor shall endeavour to reveal any serious defect in systems of internal control which might lead to the perpetration of fraud and must have regard to the possibility of malpractice in areas under examination. He shall be alert to the possibility of corruption and be prepared to inform the appropriate level of management of any justifiable suspicions.' (CIPFA Statements 1979)

'Internal auditors should review the measures used to safeguard assets from various types of losses such as those resulting from theft, fire, improper or illegal activities, and exposure to the elements.' (IIA Guideline 330.01)

1.1   Definitions of fraud

When investigating areas which are subject to the suspicion of fraudulent activity, it is essential that the investigating auditor is aware of what constitutes fraud, irregularity and error. Advice on this subject is provided by the IIA:

'1 Fraud encompasses an array of irregularities and illegal acts characterised by intentional deception. It can be perpetrated for the benefit or to the detriment of the organisation and by persons outside as well as inside the organisation.
2 Fraud designed to benefit the organisation generally produces such benefit by exploiting an unfair or dishonest advantage that also may deceive an outside party. Perpetrators of such frauds usually benefit indirectly, since personal benefit usually accrues when the organisation is aided by that act.
    Fraud perpetrated to the detriment of the organisation generally is for the direct or indirect benefit of an employee, outside individual or another firm.' (IIA Guieline 280.01)

Meanwhile, 'irregularity' refers to financial statements: 'Any intentional financial misrepresentation of financial information' (Audit Commission).
'Errors' are not intentional and may be of commission or omission. Omission means that something is missing thereby causing information to be incorrect. Commission is an error of principle, such as the treatment of revenue expenditure as capital expenditure. Where an error is intentional it will be fraudulent if intended to deceive.

1.2   Criminal conduct

Before a person can be convicted of a crime it is necessary for the prosecution to prove beyond reasonable doubt that:

1 A certain event or state of affairs that is forbidden by criminal law has been due to his or her action: *actus reus*.
2 Actions are accomplished by a prescribed state of mind: *Mens rea* (of guilty mind).

It is to be noted that a guilty act may consist of a failure to take action where action is required.

1.3 Management fraud

Such frauds may be to the advantage or disadvantage of the company. The operation usually is by falsification of the state of affairs of the company. This may be represented as follows:

Action	*Benefactor*
Financial statements are used to commit an act of fraud	Company/perpetrator
Financial statements are used to disguise an act of fraud	Company/perpetrator

1.4 Contract fraud

A contract needs to consist of three basic elements:

1 *Offer*—An expression of willingness by one party to enter into an agreement with another on particular terms.

2 *Acceptance*—An agreement to abide by the terms of the offer by the party or person to whom the offer was made.

3 *Consideration*—'Some right, interest, profit or benefit accruing to one party or some forebearance, detriment, loss or responsibility given, suffered or undertaken by the other' (*Currie v Missa* (1875)).

Lord Hirshall defined when a contract may be fraudulent as follows: 'A misrepresentation made knowingly or without belief in its truth or recklessly not knowing whether it is true or false' (*Derry v Peek* (1889)).

A contract that is fraudulent may be both void and subject to legal action under the tort of deceit, while a contract the subject of misrepresentation may be void or actionable under the tort of deceit, but not both. As a consequence of action subject to the tort of deceit, damages may be awarded.

1.5 Criminal fraud

Criminal fraud may be one of the following four main activities:

Fraudulent trading	Objective: to obtain funds in order to continue trading	'If a company continues to carry on business and to incur debts at a time when there is, to the knowledge of the directors, no reasonable prospects to the creditors of ever receiving payment of those debts, it is in general a proper inference that the company is carrying on business with intent to defraud' (*Re: William C Leith Bros Ltd* (1932))

Long-term fraud	Objective: to obtain assets without payment	This may take the form of the acquisition of property by various forms of deception. Ownership is transferred without the knowledge of the owner
Investment fraud	Objective: the acquisition of money	This activity takes the form of deceiving investors to part with their monies on an investment from which only the perpetrator gains
Insider dealing	Objective: to take advantage of personal knowledge of price sensitive information for personal gain	The employee having possession of confidential information purchases and sells company shares for short-term personal gain

Note: It is worthy of note, that with regard to 'insider dealing', employees should be requested to sign a 'Code of conduct' acknowledging that they are aware of these particular provisions of the Companies Act 1985.

2.0   CRIMINAL STATUTE LAW: A SUMMARY

2.1   Theft

DEFINITION

'A person is guilty of theft if he dishonestly appropriates property belonging to another with the intention of permanently depriving the other of it'. (Theft Act 1968 s 1)

2.2   Deception

1 A person who by a deception dishonestly obtains property belonging to another with the intention of permanently depriving that other of it commits an offence. (Theft Act 1968 s 15)
2 By inducing or attempting to induce another person to recklessly invest by making any statement he knows to be false or misleading. (Prevention of Fraud (Investments) Act 1958 s 13)

2.3   Manipulation of accounting entries

Destroying, defacing, concealing or falsifying accounting records or knowingly furnishing false information. (Theft Act 1968 s 17)

2.4   Conspiracy

The Criminal Law Act 1977 s 1 defines statutory conspiracy as conspiracy to defraud and it remains a common law offence. Previously the Criminal Law

Act 1967 s 5 described conspiracy as an unlawful agreement between two or more persons to carry out an unlawful act by unlawful means.

2.5 Forgery and counterfeiting

This is described as the making of a false document in order that it may be used as genuine with intent to deceive or defraud. The mere act of forgery as defined in the Criminal Law Act 1977 s 1 is of course a crime. The more common methods in such frauds are the use of an eraser, chemical bleaching, washing and overwriting. More recently, under the Forgery and Counterfeiting Act 1971, in *R v Donnelly* a false valuation has been held to be a forgery, the certificate issued not being supported by jewellery.

2.6 Other terms defined

1 Falsify—A document is false if it is not what it purports to be or if it has been materially altered without authorisation since it was made.
2 Making of a false document—Deceitfully altering or attaching a seal or stamp to the document. It includes the addition or deletion of material words, letters or figures.
3 Intent—A deliberate purpose, eg to defraud or deceive.
4 Uttering—Putting into circulation, eg a fraudulent offer.
5 It should be noted that the use of a photocopy of a forgery is an offence (*R v Harris* (1965)).

3.0 CONCEALING OFFENCES

Where an indictable offence has been committed, if someone else knowing of that offence and having information which might be of material assistance in securing the conviction of the offender, accepts or agrees to accept consideration, an offence is committed (Criminal Law Act 1967 s 5). Exceptions to this law are:

1 Where consideration is to make good of loss or injury caused by the offence.
2 Compensation for loss or injury due to that offence.

4.0 BRIBERY AND CORRUPTION

4.1 Bribery: a definition

'Any circumstances where an inducement or reward is offered or given . . . which may influence the actions of others.' (Audit Commission)

LEGISLATION

Prevention of Corrupt Practices Acts 1896–1916. Generally these Acts apply to those who contract with public organisations. However, the 1916 Act increased penalties against contractors convicted of corrupt practices and further stated that any money, gift or consideration paid or received shall be deemed to have been paid or received corruptly as an inducement or reward unless the contrary is proved.

4.2   Corruption: a definition

> 'The offering, giving, soliciting or acceptance of an inducement or reward which may influence the actions taken by the authority, its members or officers.' (Prevention of Corrupt Practices Act 1896–1916)

It is important to mention the Code of Practice for External Auditors of Local Authorities (Audit Commission) which states that, 'It is the duty of the authority to take reasonable steps to limit the possibility of corrupt practices.' In connection with corruption it should be noted that where a bribe has been received, the recipient cannot use as a defence the fact that he did not provide what the bribe was designed to procure (*R v Carr* (1957)). This decision was reinforced in *R v Graham* (1983) where the judge directed that admission of receipt of a bribe was consideration, ie corruption had taken place. And in the case of *Reading v A-G* (1951) it was held that an officer who receives secret profits shall be accountable for such sums to his employing organisation.

More recently, the Local Government Act 1972 expanded on this area of legislation:

s 94 Members must disclose a pecuniary interest.
s 117 Officers must disclose a pecuniary interest. Also an officer shall not accept any fee whatsoever other than his appropriate remuneration.

With regard to promotional offers, CIPFA in conjunction with the Institute of Purchasing and Supply have issued a statement concerning sales promotional offers. The statement refers to a regularly updated list of promotional offers available to buyers. The list gives details of:

1 Name of organisation making sales promotion offer.
2 Nature of goods and services promoted.
3 Nature of offer.
4 Duration of offer.
5 Source of information.

It is intended that such a list will be renewed on a monthly basis and can be used as guidance of auditors on offers currently available. It is appropriate at this stage to mention the comment made in the Final Report to the Secretary of State for the Environment by the Wardale Touche Rosse Enquiry (following dismissal of 61 employees from the Property Services Agency for irregularities 1977–82):

> 'management reluctance to acknowledge that problems exist . . . this indicates a degree of complacency towards dishonesty and fraud.'

Some of the matters the Enquiry highlighted were:

Collusion with long-term contractors.
Collussion over stores misappropriation.
Excessive expense claims.

It can only be said that internal audit must make management aware of the potential for fraud.

5.0 THE AUDIT ROLE WITH REGARD TO FRAUD

It is an important function of internal audit to detect fraud, thereby safeguarding the organisation's assets. Using techniques involving the identification of weakness in control procedures and continuous monitoring of systems, internal audit aims to prevent and detect fraud. Prior to discussing the prevention and detection of fraud, it is useful to examine some of the basic circumstances which can foster fraud.

These circumstances can be analysed by primary and secondary causes of fraud and irregularity.

5.1 Primary causes

Concealment—The chance of remaining undetected. The perpetrator needs to assess the likelihood of detection and consequent punishment.

Opportunity—The perpetrator needs to be in the right place at the right time in order to take advantage of particular weaknesses within the system and also to avoid detection.

Motivation—The perpetrator requires motivation to undertake such activity, a personal need such as greed or financial pressure, and there are many other motivators.

Attraction—The target of the envisaged fraud needs to be attractive to the perpetrator.

Success—The perpetrator needs to assess the chance of success, which can be measured by either avoiding prosecution or detection.

5.2 Secondary causes

A perk—Where controls are lacking, the taking advantage of the organisation's assets may be considered as a fringe benefit by employees.

Poor employee/employer relationship—Where mutual trust and respect has failed the perpetrator may reason that the fraud is only what is due to him or her.

Revenge—Intense dislike for the organisation may lead the perpetrator to attempt to harm that organisation.

Challenge—Employees who become bored with their work environment may seek stimulation by attempting to 'beat the system', thereby gaining a sense of achievement, or relief of frustration.

Indeed, R K Elliot and John Willingham in *Management Fraud, Detection and Deterrence* (PBI Books) identify the cause of fraud by the following three stages:

1 The feeling that a personal financial problem is unshareable.
2 The knowledge of how to solve the problem in secret, but thereby violating a personal trust.
3 The ability to find a formula which describes the act in terms which do not conflict with the image of oneself as a trusted person.

6.0 PREVENTION OF FRAUD

The following matters can assist the auditor in the prevention of fraud.

6.1 Internal control

The provision of an adequate system of internal checks supported by sound reporting procedures is the foundation to an environment which discourages fraudulent activity. This is essential in order to ensure that the potential fraudster realises that the opportunity for fraud is considerably reduced and that concealment is unlikely.

6.2 Review of systems

Continuous review and appraisal of information, eg the monitoring of actual against expected results, together with the identification of responsibility for functions is a disincentive: the potential fraudster is aware that systems are monitored. This is one justification for maintaining an internal audit function.

6.3 Personnel policies

Adequate personnel procedures regarding the recruitment of staff are essential to reduce the chance of employing not only those who already have experience of fraudulent activity but also those who are subject to pressures that may make them succumb to fraud. Similarly, adequate staff training is necessary to ensure that the employee is both familiar with the working environment and of the importance of controls. As such the following pitfalls should be avoided:

1 POOR PAY

The employment of staff at too low a rate of pay both in relation to type of work and compared to pay offered by other employers in the locality. This situation can lead to discontent which may foster fraud. It is particularly dangerous to pay those in fiduciary (money handling) positions poorly, and of course fiduciary insurance cover may be provided to alleviate loss should it occur.

2 POOR RECRUITMENT

Careful selection of staff, including the taking up of references and the identifying of reasons for gaps in a person's employment record are essential in order to reduce the chance of the recruitment of a fraudster.

3 POOR SUPERVISION

All employees should be made to take their annual holiday allowance. Many employers have learned to their cost that a loyal, hardworking and trusted employee is only able to commit a fraud because he is always there, with no-one checking or supervising his work or deputising for him. Similarly unsupervised overtime should not be allowed.

4 AWARENESS OF THE CAUSE OF CHANGED CIRCUMSTANCES

Dramatic improvement in living style may have a straightforward explanation, eg an inheritance, but may also indicate a fraud occurring. The auditor must be aware of the legislation concerning slander and libel.

5 AWARENESS OF EMPLOYEE'S PERSONAL PROBLEMS

These can also be the cause of change in an employee's circumstances, or may cause the employee to behave in an abnormal manner. Again, the auditor must be sure of the evidence.

6.4 Climate of honesty

A climate of honesty is a fundamental requirement for fraud prevention. Crime will be perceived as repugnant where honesty and probity are actively promoted as essential features of the pursuit of efficiency. This is a management responsibility which involves setting the tone and encouraging exemplary standards of probity throughout the organisation.

> 'Crime is contagious . . . The company that creates the right climate of honesty can reduce crime. It can ensure that the factors unfavourable to crime exceed those favourable to it.' (Comer, M J *Corporate Fraud*, 2nd edn 1987)

6.5 Organisational policy re fraud

Policy on fraud should be clearly stated and be seen to be enforced, eg 'All perpetrators will be dismissed and prosecuted'. Often such policy is seen as harsh and controversial, eg many take the view that the fraudster suffers enough by losing his job, or 'he's been a fool not a knave', is often said by those with sympathy.

For situations where regulations are deliberately flouted a disciplinary procedure should be laid down beforehand so that corrective action can be seen to be just, following predetermined lines.

7.0　DETECTION OF FRAUD

A first step in the detection of fraud is the compilation of a risk analysis identifying the areas most vulnerable/open to exploitation. Having undertaken this task, the auditor should be on the alert for symptoms (alarm signals) that might indicate the existence of a fraud, for example:

7.1　Failure to correct serious weaknesses in internal control

1 The existence of unauthorised transactions.
2 Unusual recording of transactions.
3 Transactions with inadequate supporting documentation.
4 Failure to take holidays or doing unsupervised overtime.
5 Records non-existent—no audit trail.

7.2　Problems of an accounting nature

1 The existence of discrepancies between related accounts.
2 Loosely controlled suspense and expense accounts.
3 High volume of corrections.
4 Records rewritten.

7.3　Problems regarding information

1 Difficulty in obtaining information.
2 Lack of co-operation accompanied by 'guarded' comments to auditor.
3 One employee being regularly given the problems to resolve.

7.4　Other risk areas

1 Diverse and poorly controlled operations at remote sites.
2 Weaknesses in internal control.
3 Lack of internal audit function.
4 High turnover of senior financial staff.
5 Insufficient financial staff.
6 Growth of organisation outstripping controls.
7 An unsupervised change of systems.

8.0　SOME FRAUDULENT TECHNIQUES

This list could be endless. However, the auditor should be aware of the more common methods:

1 Teeming and lading—See cash audit.
2 Creditors overpaid—Refund requested and pocketed.
3 Customers undercharged or not charged.

4 Perfect goods marked 'reject' or 'seconds'.
5 Cheques altered after signature.
6 Doctored expense claims.
7 Pocketed unclaimed wages.
8 Using employer's equipment for personal gain.
9 Bribery.
10 Fictitious employees on payroll—'ghosts'!
11 Sales of confidential information to a competitor.
12 False documentation.
13 Short deliveries, the difference removed in transit.
14 Sales invoices inflated and the commission shared between invoice clerk and sales person.
15 Fully depreciated assets removed.
16 Profit overstated (eg via stock valuation) allowing larger bonuses.
17 Overcharged expense accounts.

9.0 PROCEDURES TO BE ADOPTED WHERE FRAUD IS SUSPECTED

Where an auditor is 'placed on guard', he should probe the matter to the bottom. Once the auditor considers that the grounds for suspicion of fraud are reasonable, the following procedures should be adopted:

1 Carefully recheck facts (preferably done by another auditor).
2 Restrict questioning to establishing that the suspicion appears to be well founded.
3 Retain all records that may be involved—Remember that such documentation should be handled as little as possible—it may be subject to scientific examination by the police.
4 Establish all the areas of activity of the suspect in order to attempt to establish the potential size of the fraud.
5 Communicate with the chief internal auditor by confidential means.
6 Where cash is involved, 'cash up' in the presence of suspect and a witness—see cash count procedures.

10.0 ADMISSIBLE EVIDENCE: POLICE AND CRIMINAL EVIDENCE ACT 1984

Under the Police and Criminal Evidence Act (PACE) 1984, any statement made by an accused person should be voluntary, any suspicion that a statement has been obtained by coercion or inducement from a person in authority (auditor or management) renders that statement inadmissible in a court of law, ie it is not allowed for consideration.

Prior to January 1986, 'Judges' Rules', a body of rules formulated by a committee of judges of the Queen's Bench Division, were required to be applied. These rules have now been superseded by the Code of Practice for the detention, treatment and questioning of persons by police officers and under the Police and Criminal Evidence Act 1984 s 67(9), it applies to persons other than police officers under authority to investigate offences, eg internal auditors. Management should be advised to report any suspicion of fraud to the police, who are experienced in conducting investigations and obtaining evidence for prosecution. However, it is recognised that there are many occasions where this is not possible, eg an unexpected confession of fraud by a frightened clerk. The auditor needs to know when the various cautions are required so that evidence gained is admissible in a court of law. The main requirements of the Code of Practice prescribed by the 1984 Act are given on pp 447–448.

10.1   The Code of Practice

The Code expressly warns against the use of duress or the offering of inducement to obtain admissions from interviewees. Auditors might well think that this provision could not apply to them since the popular concept of duress involves physical threat or force, but the courts recognise that more subtle forms of duress exist and can be equally effective. It is important that auditors are aware of the possibility of an allegation of duress, etc being made by the defence in the course of a trial, and to ensure that an innocent remark or action cannot later be misconstrued as improper by the court.

Finally, auditors should be aware that the Code, unlike the Judges' Rules, has the force of law. Although breach of the Code is not a crime or tort *per se*, failure to comply with it will normally lead to any admission or statement thereby obtained being held inadmissible in evidence.

Although an auditor is not concerned with 'oppression' when conducting an investigation, he should scrupulously observe the provisions of the Code relating to the comfort of the interviewee, eg standard of the interview room, provision of a chair, meals and rest breaks, etc since any breach might result in a submission that a confession was 'unreliable'. Breach of the Act or Code will not necessarily be a ground for excluding evidence unless it renders the admission or confession unreliable or is so severe that it amounts to oppression.

10.2   Taking the statement

Although it is quite rare for a suspect to write his own statement, it is still necessary to invite him to do so. If the suspect does, in fact, elect to write his own statement he should not be prompted in any way other than where necessary to clarify ambiguities and to ensure relevance. The Code does not require the suspect to read through his statement to check for errors, etc before signing it when he has written it himself, but it is good practice to suggest it and to record the fact.

If, as usual, the statement is recorded by the investigator at the suspect's dictation, no attempt should be made to 'tidy up' his wording or to prompt what he should say beyond what is necessary to clarify any ambiguities, etc. Use the suspect's own words: it will sound more natural in court.

When taking the statement make sure to use the correct caution, endorsements and certificates as set out in the Code and get the suspect to write them out before signing them. No gaps should be left by indenting for paragraphs, etc so that there can be no suggestion of later additions, and errors should be deleted by drawing a single line through the words before being initialled by the suspect.

Do not become impatient or officious with the suspect: much better results are obtained by establishing a rapport with the person so that he relates and, perhaps, 'opens up'.

10.3 The court room

It is sound practice to read through one's notes before a court appearance; try to anticipate which questions might be put by the defence. Never memorise evidence parrot fashion: it sounds wrong in court. Witnesses may refresh their memory by consulting notes made at the time, but the defence may well object to a witness reading the notes in evidence.

Finally, answer defence questions as briefly as possible, if possible with a simple yes or no. The more one says the more ammunition one provides for counsel to ask additional questions, sometimes to one's embarrassment: the witness box can be a very lonely and exposed place!

10.4 Police and Criminal Evidence Act 1984. Some provisions of the Code regulating the interviewing and obtaining of statements from persons suspected of fraud, etc

Circumstances	Action
As soon as an investigation officer has grounds to believe that a person has committed an offence, he must caution him. The caution must in any event be given before any questions, or further questions, relating to that offence are put	Caution: 'You do not have to say anything unless you wish to do so, but what you say may be given in evidence.'
Suspect has already been cautioned and is about to be interviewed	Cautioned again at the beginning of the interview. All persons identified by name and rank
Short break in interview, eg to visit the toilet	Reminder that he is still under caution when interview resumed
Break in interview lasting more than one hour	Caution again administered in full
Lengthy interview	Breaks from interviewing to be made at recognised meal times. Short breaks for refreshments to be provided at intervals of approximately two hours—but may be delayed on specified grounds

Circumstances	Action
Person elects to make a statement. Writes it himself	Person writes himself at head of form: 'I make this statement of my own free will. I understand that I need not say anything unless I wish to do so and that what I say may be given in evidence.' Person signs directly under above caution. At close of statement should be invited to read through the statement and make any alterations, etc before signing
Person elects to make a statement. Recorded by another at his dictation in his own words and without prompting	Person writes himself at head of form: 'I (name) wish to make a statement. I want someone to write down what I say. I understand that I need not say anything unless I wish to do so and that what I say may be given in evidence.' Person signs directly under above caution.
At the close of a statement recorded at the person's dictation	Person directed to read through statement to make any corrections, alterations or additions before signing the following endorsement: 'I have read the above statement and I have been able to correct, alter or add anything I wish. This statement is true, I have made it of my own free will'.
Person asked to sign an interview record and refuses to sign	Appropriate record made

10.5   Notes on Code and procedure

10.5.1   *Cautioning*

Whereas the Judges' Rules required a caution to be administered as soon as an investigator had 'evidence to afford reasonable ground for suspecting that a person had committed an offence', the Code requires the caution to be given when the investigator has 'grounds to believe that a person has comitted an offence.'

With the Code of Practice much depends on how the courts interpret the term 'grounds', but clearly the caution must now be given earlier than under the former Judges' Rules: there is a radical difference between 'grounds to believe' and 'evidence affording reasonable suspicion'. When is the right time to caution? This is a matter of judgement which develops with experience. On the one hand, it is bad practice to caution prematurely since it might well inhibit a hitherto talkative suspect, and it could cause resentment if administered without good cause to an innocent person; on the other hand, delay in cautioning could mean that evidence is held inadmissible. Care should be taken to use the official caution, although minor deviations might be overlooked by the court if satisfied that the essential sense of the caution is preserved. But it should be remembered that it is common for defence counsel to question prosecution witnesses on the caution administered, and to make capital out of minor deviations from the official version. The only safe course is to keep a copy of the caution, endorsements, etc on a pocket-sized card for reference purposes.

10.5.2 *Records*

The Code requires that an accurate and full record be kept of all interviews, questions, cautions, refreshments breaks, etc. It is vital that any such record be precise and accurate since the defence will pounce on any discrepancy. Where two or more investigators are involved in an interview, great care should be taken to avoid discrepancies in their individual records. The court will not object to investigators consulting together when preparing records, provided a note is made to that effect.

10.5.3 *Duress*

The common law test of voluntariness was abolished by the 1984 Act which introduced a dual test of admissibility: oppression and/or unreliability.

The Act provides that where the prosecution seeks to submit a confession in evidence, the defence may plead that it was, or may have been, obtained by oppression, or in consequence of anything said or done which was likely in the circumstances existing at the time to render the confession unreliable.

In such circumstances the onus is on the prosecution to satisfy the court beyond reasonable doubt that the confession was not so obtained. Unless the court is so satisfied, it must not allow the confession to be admitted in evidence, notwithstanding that its contents may be true.

Moreover, the court has power in its discretion to require the prosecution to satisfy it on these matters with representations first having been made.

What conduct will amount to 'oppression' is not clear despite the definition of the term: 'Torture, inhuman or degrading treatment and the use of threat of violence, whether or not amounting to torture', but it is likely to be restricted to the more serious type of conduct postulated in the definition, and, consequently, of acadamic interest only to the auditor.

11.0 AFTER THE FRAUD

Action to be taken once fraud is suspected. Depending on where it has occurred, the following checklist is an example of recommended action. Investigations to estimate the loss should cover an area wider than that to which the suspect employee had access—he may well have been operating in more than one area! For instance, where cash is missing, the following actions should occur:

1 Determine the degree of authority and nature of duties of the suspect
  employee.

2 Reconcile the cash book to bank statement.
3 Vouch cash book against bank statements, paying particular attention to dates of lodgements to ascertain whether receipts were promptly banked and examine original paying-in slips at the bank and compare them with the counterfoils, as this may reveal the practice known as teeming and lading.
4 Circularise debtors.
5 Record any apparently irregular cash payments.
6 Scrutinise cancelled cheques and compare names of payees with details in cash book and invoices.
7 Vouch all amounts shown as directors' drawings or loans.
8 Obtain duplicates of any missing expenditure vouchers.
9 Reconcile petty cash book.
10 Check names of all employees shown on wages lists with senior officials, and amounts payable to them.
11 If fraudster had access to all records, all postings should be checked and a trial balance produced.
12 Agree bad debts written off, discount allowances and returns.
13 Verify order book with sales day book or copy sales invoices to detect any sales which have not been recorded.
14 Cash sales should be checked against any available evidence.
15 Check purchase invoices against the purchases record to ensure that an invoice has not been entered twice.
16 Obtain copies of all missing and cancelled purchase vouchers.
17 Reconcile creditors' statements to purchaser ledger balances.
18 Agree goods inwards book or order book to invoices to ensure that the latter relate to recognised purchases.
19 Advise management to notify the police of suspected fraud.

11.1 Preparation of the fraud case for court

It is unlikely that judges, juries and legal counsel will have a detailed understanding of financial systems, consequently admissible evidence must be presented to both police and counsel in a well ordered manner. Matters requiring consideration are:

1 Presentation of admissible evidence.
2 Statements of persons able to throw light on any aspect of the enquiry.
3 A résumé from the investigating auditor.

To consider these three operations the following actions should prove useful:

1 File statements in order of reference.
2 Sort documentary evidence into order which closely follows that of the statements.
3 Reference each piece of documentation.

11.1.1 *Audit report*

It is to be noted that the auditor's report should be concise and relevant, though the length can only be defined as being reasonable given the circumstances.

11.1.2 *Audit opinion*

Apart from the suspect the auditor may be the only other person who totally understands the issue. It is therefore important that the auditor gives his opinion as he is able to make a complete picture from individual witnesses' statements.

11.1.3 *Witnesses*

When investigating a fraud the auditor must assess the integrity of the persons acting as witnesses. The following matters could cause problems:

1 The motive of the witness in agreeing to give evidence.
2 Reluctance to disclose information because either this shows witnesses to have been incompetent in his duties or may incriminate him.

In conclusion a witness is generally 'at his prime' when the statement is made, and from that moment on deteriorates as a witness due to lapse of memory etc, and secondly 'it has been said that only the defence gains anything from confusion' (D Campbell *The Investigation of Fraud*) eg this may occur where the auditor has failed to extract all relevant information and the witness unexpectedly reveals new information in court. With these two points in mind it is worthwhile to remember that charges may be added but not deleted. Thus it is expedient to prefer a well defined charge which may later be amended upon receipt of further evidence.

11.1.4 *The auditor in the witness box*

This section deals with the 'memory refreshing rule', which was clarified in *R v Richardson* (1971): 'A witness may refresh his memory by reference to any writing made or verified by himself concerning and contemporaneous with the facts to which he testified.'

The term 'contemporaneous' merely means writing made at the first practicable opportunity. The old rule is that only the original document can be referred to, however, recently a copy derived from the original has been accepted (*R v Cheng* (1976)).

11.1.5 *Other forms of admissible evidence*

1 Tape-recorded evidence—to be admissible, procedures must have been in operation to secure the integrity of the tapes. The case law on this matter is *R v Robson and Harris* (1972): 'In considering the question of admissibility, the court is required to do no more than satisfy itself that what the prosecution alleges to be original tapes are shown, prima facie, to be original, by evidence which defines the source and history of the recordings up to the moment of production in Court.'
2 Microfilm—Under the Police and Criminal Evidence Act 1984 s 64, enlargements of authenticated microfilm are to be admissible.
3 Hearsay evidence—This is not usually admissible.
4 Documentary evidence (best evidence)—Many frauds involve documentary evidence to some extent and on occasions such evidence requires expert examination other than by an auditor or accountant. Examples of this are:
   (a) Where the authenticity of a signature needs to be determined.
   (b) Where a genuine document may have been altered.

(c) Where a document can be proved false by scientific means.
(d) Where the authorship of anonymous letters or instructions requires investigation.
(e) Where sealed envelopes may have been opened.
(f) Where two pieces of paper were originally one, eg torn into pieces.
(g) Where partially damaged or burnt documents need deciphering.
(h) Where fingerprints need to be taken from a document.

It should be noted that normally only the original copy of the document is admissible, though subject to professional advice, a duplicate may be admissible, eg where the original has been destroyed. Furthermore under the proposed Police and Criminal Evidence Act 1984 s 61 a document will be admissible where it is compiled by another, acting under a duty, from information supplied by another who could reasonably be considered to have the relevant expertise.

12.0   AUDIT RELATIONSHIP WITH THE POLICE AND SENIOR MANAGEMENT

CIPFA is categorical as to when the police should be notified of the detection of fraud—immediately. Needless to say, this may not hold in practice, being dependent on the organisation's policy, if any, towards such matters. However, the following basic rules apply:

1 Discuss with senior management the matter of notifying the police.
2 Urge management to notify police.
3 Advise management to notify insurance company.
4 Persuade senior management to suspend employee pending investigations. Ideally, that person should be sent directly home—the representative taking care of personal possessions.
5 The employee should not be allowed access to evidence.
6 Implement disciplinary procedures.

It must be remembered that in many instances for there to be a successful claim on an insurance policy, the police must be informed.

Finally the police may well have an advantage in being able to gain certain evidence (as under the Banker's Books Evidence Act 1879 they are able to gain access to a suspect's bank acount (subject to certain conditions)), that is not available to the auditor.

13.0   THE PSYCHOLOGY AND USE OF INTERROGATION

13.1   A definition of interrogation

'To question; to examine by asking questions.' (*Chambers Dictionary*)

OBJECTIVES OF INTERROGATION

1 To complete gaps in evidence.

2 To obtain a statement of denial, excuse or self-justification.
3 To obtain a balanced picture.
4 To place the suspect 'beyond suspicion'.

13.2   Qualities required of the auditor when interrogating a suspect or witness

Prior to examining the specific qualities the following quote is of use:

> 'No lawyer can be successful in the highest sense of the term unless he is master of the difficult art of examining witnesses. It requires a greater combination of qualities than almost any other breach of advocacy, the most important of which are patience, coolness, courage and tact.' (Wrottesley *Examination of Witnesses in Court*)

Such qualities are appropriate to the auditor.

DETERMINATION TO OBTAIN THE TRUTH

The auditor must be articulate and able to use language that the interviewee can understand without 'leading' him. Where an element of confusion exists in the response elicited, the auditor should ask for further clarification.

ABILITY TO ADAPT QUESTIONS ACCORDING TO THE NATURE OF THE INTERVIEWEE

People react differently to questioning, particularly concerning their work, and consequently a well balanced interrogation of direct and indirect questions is advisable. The interrogator must be on guard against verbose responses leading away from the objective of the interrogation.

SILENCE ON THE PART OF THE AUDITOR

It must be remembered that the interviewee should provide information and not the auditor.

13.3   Attitude of interviewee

This will largely depend on the interrogator and the subject under discussion. In deciding the format of the interrogation the auditor should take account of the following factors concerning the interviewee:

1 Age.
2 Apparent intelligence.
3 Evidence of capacity of memory.
4 Attitude to audit, ie co-operative or not.
5 General demeanour, ie nervous or confident.
6 Whether evidence is hearsay or not.

13.4   Some pitfalls the auditor should avoid

1 Creation of the impression on the interviewee that the interrogation is an inquisition because this may cause the interviewee to 'freeze', ie not release information.

2 The pretence by the auditor of knowing more than he does. When examining technical areas, involving interviewing experts, the exercise of tact on the part of the auditor is necessary to avoid stupid questions—a courteous and respectful approach should be adopted.
3 The auditor should not prejudge the issues being investigated.
4 The presence of a witness at the interrogation is essential.
5 The auditor should not confuse an articulate response with honesty, nor nervousness with guilt. It has been said that, 'innocence has a serenity which the most agitated cannot conceal and the whole manner of the interviewee should be considered. Physical mannerisms may disclose what the face and speech have repressed.'

13.5   Concluding the interrogation

A summary of relevant issues discussed, points made and conclusions reached should be made, both the auditor and witness signing the summary as being a true reflection of the discussion that took place. This is not intended to be used as 'admissible evidence', as the Code has not been complied with—where the Code of Practice can be complied with and admissible evidence gained, this is preferable.

14.0   CONCLUSION

Statistics on fraud are few and far between, though many think it is rapidly increasing—or are methods of detection improving? However, without doubt it is proving to be costly: in 1977 it was stated that fraud accounted for 5% of gross national product, ie £7 billion in 1977: A Robart *Accountancy* December 1978, 'What the Auditor needs to know about Fraud'.

Indeed in 1984 Alex Fletcher, Minister for Corporate and Consumer Affairs, said 'that accountants should develop a tough new standard on fraud in the "the public interest".' This view was further supported by Ray Whittaker (Deardon Farrow) in a paper presented to the Chartered Insurance Institute:

'Too frequently a fraud is politely covered up, somebody is removed from his job, life goes on as before. The real fault often lay with "soggy" management which was afraid to prosecute because its own mistake in hiring the person would be shown up.'

Nevertheless, it must be stressed that in providing 'positive reassurance' the internal auditor's overall objective is to enhance organisational performance, the detection of fraud being merely one aspect of audit work.

The Auditing Guideline on fraud and other irregularities advises:

'It is not the main purpose of audit to discover defalcations and irregularities, and an audit should therefore not be relied on for that purpose'.

Though applying to external audit this statement is also relevant to internal audit where prevention and detection of fraud must be considered in the context of the ultimate objective, to enhance organisational performance. Where fraud is suspected, adherence to a strict set of procedures, many of which have been described, must be adhered to.

It is important to emphasise that management is responsible for the deterrence of fraud. Internal auditors are responsible for examining and evaluating the adequacy and effectiveness of actions taken by management to fulfil this obligation.

Furthermore, internal auditors need to be able to assess all facts so that weaknesses revealed can be strengthed and that appropriate controls can be introduced to detect or preferably deter future fraudulent activity.

> 'They [Internal Auditors] should also be alert to those conditions and activities where irregularities are most likely to occur. In addition, they should identify inadequate controls and recommend improvements to promote compliance with acceptable procedures and practices.' (IIA Guideline 280.01)

Audit profile triggers: (Defined at **2.11** in Chapter 3)

THE PREVENTION AND DETECTION OF FRAUD

FRAUD & ERROR
Criminal conduct
Bribery & corruption
Lack of 'intent to defraud'
Actus & mens rea

PREVENTION OF OPPORTUNITIES FOR FRAUD
Internal control
Poor pay: responsibilities
Poor supervision
Changed organisational structure, without a review of systems to take account of changed personnel
Insurance cover
Systems review
Poor recruitment procedures
New machinery, computer systems and operational procedures without a review of systems to take account of change

ACTION TO BE TAKEN ONCE FRAUD IS SUSPECTED
Determine scope of perpetrator(s) actions
Assess extent of damage or loss
Notify police
Close 'loopholes': review systems
Reconcile all work undertaken

Further reading

Bologna, J *Corporate fraud, basics of prevention and detection* (1985) (Butterworths).

Investigation of fraud in the public sector (1989) (CIPFA).

Comer, M J *Corporate fraud* (2nd edn 1987) (McGraw Hill).

Elliot, R K and Willingham, J J *Management fraud, detection and deterrence* (PBI Books).

Appendix 1 Auditing Guideline 308—Guidance for internal auditors

(Issued by the Auditing Practices Committee of CCAB and reproduced with permission of the Chartered Accountants of Scotland June 1990)

PREFACE

This guideline provides advice to internal auditors about the main issues and procedures which they need to consider as part of their work. It should also be of benefit to organisations considering establishing an internal audit function.

The guideline is written in the context of internal audit work in both the commercial and public sectors. It should be read in conjunction with the Explanatory Foreword to Auditing Standards and Guidelines and the Auditing Guidelines 'Reliance on internal audit' and 'The auditor's responsibility in relation to fraud, other irregularities and errors'. Internal auditors may also find it helpful to refer to the Audit Brief 'Value for money audit' issued by the Auditing Practices Committee of CCAB Limited (June 1990).

Internal auditors should also have regard to the ethical statements issued by the accountancy bodies and also to any requirements regarding internal audit set out in relevant statutes or regulations.

A glossary of terms used in the guideline is given in the appendix.

OBJECTIVES AND SCOPE OF INTERNAL AUDIT

1 Internal audit is an independent appraisal function established by the management of an organisation for the review of the internal control system as a service to the organisation. It objectively examines, evaluates and reports on the adequacy of internal control as a contribution to the proper, economic, efficient and effective use of resources.

2 The essentials for effective internal auditing are:

(a) *Independence*
The internal auditor should have the independence in terms of organisational status and personal objectivity which permits the proper performance of his duties (paragraphs 11 to 14).

(b) *Staffing and Training*
The internal audit unit should be appropriately staffed in terms of numbers, grades, qualifications and experience, having regard to its responsibilities and objectives. The internal auditor should be properly trained to fulfil all his responsibilities (paragraph 15 to 26).

(c) *Relationships*
The internal auditor should seek to foster constructive working relationships and mutual understanding with management, with

external auditors, with any other review agencies and, where one
exists, with the audit committee (paragraphs 27 to 37).

(d) *Due Care*
The internal auditor should exercise due care in fulfilling his
responsibilities (paragraphs 38 to 44).

(e) *Planning, Controlling and Recording*
The internal auditor should adequately plan, control and record his
work (paragraphs 45 to 58).

(f) *Evaluation of the Internal Control System*
The internal auditor should identify and evaluate the organisation's
internal control system as a basis for reporting upon its adequacy and
effectiveness (paragraphs 59 to 62).

(g) *Evidence*
The internal auditor should obtain sufficient, relevant and reliable
evidence on which to base reasonable conclusions and recommendations (paragraphs 63 to 69).

(h) *Reporting and Follow-up*
The internal auditor should ensure that findings, conclusions and
recommendations arising from each internal audit assignment are
communicated promptly to the appropriate level of management
and he should actively seek a response. He should ensure that
arrangements are made to follow up audit recommendations to
monitor what action has been taken on them (paragraphs 70 to 78).

3 The terms of reference for the internal audit function should be formally
confirmed by the organisation and should have proper regard to the
contents of this guideline; demonstrable independence of the function is
crucial to its effectiveness.

4 For certain public sector organisations the need for an internal auditing
function is prescribed by statute and this provides a basis for defining
specific standards and guidance for the practice of internal auditing in
those organisations. The Government Internal Audit Manual and the
National Health Service Internal Audit Manual are examples of internal
auditing standards and guidance prescribed for specific organisations.

5 To achieve full effectiveness the scope of the internal audit function
should provide an unrestricted range of coverage of the organisation's
operations, and the internal auditor should have sufficient authority to
allow him access to such records, assets and personnel as are necessary
for proper fulfilment of his responsibilities.

6 It is a management responsibility to determine the extent of internal
control in the organisation's systems which should not depend on internal audit as a substitute for effective controls. Internal audit, as a service
to the organisation, contributes to internal control by examining, evaluating and reporting to management on its adequacy and effectiveness.
Internal audit activity may lead to the strengthening of internal control as
a result of management response.

7 One of the objectives of internal auditing is to assist management in the
pursuit of value for money. It is achieved through economic, efficient
and effective use of resources.

8 It is a management responsibility to maintain the internal control system
and to ensure that the organisation's resources are properly applied in

the manner and on the activities intended. This includes responsibility for the prevention and detection of fraud and other illegal acts.

9 The internal auditor should have regard to the possibility of such malpractice and should seek to identify serious defects in internal control which might permit the occurrence of such an event.

10 An internal auditor who discovers evidence of, or suspects, malpractice should report firm evidence, or reasonable suspicions, to the appropriate level of management. It is a management responsibility to determine what further action to take.

INDEPENDENCE

11 Independence is achieved through the organisational status of internal audit and the objectivity of internal auditors.

Organisational status

12 The status of internal audit should enable it to function effectively. The support of management is essential. Internal audit should be involved in the determination of its own priorities, in consultation with management. Accordingly the head of internal audit should have direct access to, and freedom to report to, all senior management including the chief executive, board of directors and, where one exists, the audit committee.

Objectivity of the internal auditor

13 Each internal auditor should have an objective attitude of mind and be in a sufficiently independent position to be able to exercise judgement, express opinions and present recommendations with impartiality.

(a) The internal auditor, notwithstanding his employment by the organisation, should be free from any conflict of interest arising either from professional or personal relationships or from pecuniary or other interests in an organisation or activity which is subject to audit.

(b) The internal auditor should be free from undue influences which either restrict or modify the scope or conduct of his work or overrule or significantly affect judgement as to the content of the internal audit report.

(c) The internal auditor should not allow his objectivity to be impaired when auditing an activity for which he has had authority or responsibility.

(d) An internal auditor should be consulted about significant proposed changes in the internal control system and the implementation of new systems and make recommendations on the standards of control to be applied. This need not prejudice that auditor's objectivity in reviewing those systems subsequently.

(e) An internal auditor should not normally undertake non-audit duties but where he does so, exceptionally, he should ensure that management understands that he is not then functioning as an internal auditor.

14 Where any of the situations referred to in paragraphs 13(a) to (c) arise, this should be clearly declared by the internal auditor so that consideration can be given to the need for alternative arrangements for the audit assignment.

STAFFING AND TRAINING

15 The effectiveness of internal audit depends substantially on the quality, training and experience of its staff. The aim should be to appoint staff with the appropriate background, personal qualities and potential. Thereafter, steps should be taken to provide the necessary experience, training and continuing professional education.

Staffing

16 The internal audit unit should be managed by a head of internal audit who should be suitably qualified and should possess wide experience of internal audit and of its management. He should plan, direct, control and motivate the resources available to ensure that the responsibilities of the internal audit unit are met.

17 The full range of duties may require internal audit staff to be drawn from a variety of disciplines. The effectiveness of internal audit may be enhanced by the use of specialist staff, particularly in the internal audit of activities of a technical nature.

18 The internal audit unit should employ staff with varying types and levels of skills, qualifications and experience in order to satisfy the requirements of each internal audit task.

19 The head of internal audit should participate in the recruitment and selection of his staff. New entrants to internal audit work should have time to familiarise themselves with the activities of the internal audit unit and the organisation, and to demonstrate their suitability for audit work.

Training

20 The organisation has a responsibility to ensure that the internal auditor receives the training necessary for the performance of the full range of duties.

21 Training should be tailored to the needs of the individual. It should include both the theoretical knowledge and its practical application under the supervision of suitably competent and experienced internal auditors. Account should be taken of:

(a) internal audit objectives and priorities;
(b) the type of internal audit work;
(c) previous training, experience and qualifications; and
(d) personal development in the light of the needs of the organisation and the internal audit unit.

22 Training should be a planned and continuing process at all levels and should cover:

(a) basic training—providing the knowledge of basic auditing principles and practices which all internal auditors should possess;
(b) development training—in general audit skills and techniques and inter-personal skills, to improve the effectiveness of those currently employed in internal audit; and
(c) specialised training—for those responsible for the internal audit of activities which require special skills or knowledge.

23 Other forms of staff development should be considered according to particular needs. These may include periods of attachment to other parts of the organisation or secondment to other organisations.

24 The internal auditor should keep abreast of current developments, improvements, new techniques and practices in auditing.

25 The internal auditor should maintain technical competence through professional development which may include:

(a) private reading and study; and
(b) participation in professional activities such as attending meetings, courses and conferences, lecturing, writing articles and papers and contributing to research groups.

26 The head of internal audit should co-ordinate, and keep under review, the training requirements of internal auditors. He should be responsible for preparing training profiles which identify the training requirements for different grades of internal auditor, and should maintain personal training records for each individual. In large organisations this may be performed by a designated training officer.

RELATIONSHIPS

27 In order that the internal auditor may properly perform all his tasks, it is necessary for all those with whom he has contact to have confidence in him. Constructive working relationships make it more likely that internal audit work will be accepted and acted upon, but the internal auditor should not allow his objectivity to be impaired.

Organisational relationships

28 The head of internal audit should prepare the internal audit plan in consultation with senior management. The internal auditor should arrange the timing of internal audit assignments in consultation with the management concerned, except on those rare occasions where an

unannounced visit is a necessary part of the audit approach. Consultation can lead to the identification of areas of concern or of other
interest to management.

29 Matters which arise in the course of the audit are confidential and
discussion should be restricted to management directly responsible for
the area being audited unless they have given express agreement to
broaden the discussion.

30 Discussions with management are necessary when preparing the audit
report. This is an essential feature of the good relationship between the
auditor and the management.

Relationships with external audit

31 The relationship between internal and external audit needs to take
account of their differing roles and responsibilities. Internal audit is an
independent appraisal function within the organisation and internal
auditors are direct employees. The external auditor usually has a
statutory responsibility to express an independent opinion on the financial statements and stewardship of the organisation.

32 The aim should be to achieve mutual recognition and respect, leading to
a joint improvement in performance and the avoidance of unnecessary
over-lapping of work. It should be possible for the external and internal
auditors to rely on each other's work, subject to limits determined by
their different responsibilities, respective strengths and special abilities.
Consultations should be held and consideration given to whether any
work of either auditor is adequate for the purpose of the other. The
internal auditor does not automatically have a right of access to the
records of the external auditor. However, the relationship between the
internal and external auditor will usually be such that the external
auditor will be able to allow access to the necessary records.

33 Since internal audit evaluates an organisation's internal control system
the external auditor may need to be satisfied that the internal audit
function is being planned and performed effectively. This review needs
to be seen by both parties as a necessary part of the working relationship
(see the Auditing Guideline 'Reliance on internal audit').

34 Regular meetings should be held between internal and external auditors
at which joint audit planning, priorities, scope and audit findings are
discussed and information exchanged. The benefits of joint training
programmes and joint audit work should also be considered.

Review agencies and specialists

35 Certain information obtained during an internal audit assignment may
assist a review agency, such as management services or consultants,
which is seeking to secure improvements in the organisation's performance. Management's formal approval should be obtained before releasing any audit report or other information to a review agency.

36 The internal auditor should establish a regular dialogue with review agencies and obtain their reports for information, for review and for comment where proposals may affect internal control arrangements.

37 Where it is necessary for the internal auditor to have contact with other specialists the same basic principles about information apply as in the case of review agencies.

DUE CARE

38 The internal auditor cannot be expected to give total assurance that control weaknesses or irregularities do not exist.

39 In order to demonstrate that due care has been exercised the internal auditor should be able to show that his work has been performed in a way which is consistent with this guideline.

40 The internal auditor should possess a thorough knowledge of the aims of the organisation and the internal control system. He should also be aware of the relevant law and the requirements of relevant professional and regulatory bodies.

Ethical standards

41 The ethical statements issued by the accountancy bodies are relevant to the work of internal auditors.

42 The internal auditor must be impartial in discharging all responsibilities; bias, prejudice or undue influence must not be allowed to limit or over-ride objectivity. At all times, the integrity and conduct of each internal auditor must be above reproach. He should not place himself in a position where responsibilities and private interests conflict and any personal interest should be declared. Gifts or other rewards should not be accepted.

43 The internal auditor should not improperly disclose any information obtained during the course of his work.

Quality of internal audit performance

44 The head of internal audit should promote and maintain adequate quality standards in the internal audit unit. He should establish methods of evaluating the work of his staff to ensure that the internal audit unit fulfils its responsibilities and has proper regard to this guideline.

PLANNING, CONTROLLING AND RECORDING

45 Internal audit work should be planned, controlled and recorded in order to determine priorities, establish and achieve objectives, and ensure the effective and efficient use of audit resources.

Planning

46 The main purposes of internal audit planning are:

(a) to determine priorities and to establish the most cost-effective means of achieving audit objectives;
(b) to assist in the direction and control of audit work;
(c) to help ensure that attention is devoted to critical aspects of audit work; and
(d) to help ensure that work is completed in accordance with pre-determined targets.

47 The stages of internal audit planning are:

(a) to identify the objectives of the organisation;
(b) to define internal audit objectives;
(c) to take account of relevant changes in legislation and other external factors;
(d) to obtain a comprehensive understanding of the organisation's systems, structure, and operations;
(e) to identify, evaluate and rank risks to which the organisation is exposed;
(f) to take account of changes in structures or major systems in the organisation;
(g) to take account of known strengths and weaknesses in the internal control system;
(h) to take account of management concerns and expectations;
(i) to identify audit areas by service, functions and major systems;
(j) to determine the type of audit: eg systems, verification or value for money;
(k) to take account of the plans of external audit and other review agencies; and
(l) to assess staff resources required, and match with resources available.

48 The internal auditor should prepare strategic, periodic and operational work plans.

49 The strategic plan should usually cover a period of between two to five years during which all major systems and areas of activity will be audited. It should set out the audit objectives, audit areas, type of activity and frequency of audit and an assessment of resources to be applied.

50 The periodic plan, typically for a financial or calendar year, translates the strategic plan into a schedule of audit assignments to be carried out in the ensuing period. It should define the purpose and duration of each audit assignment and allocate staff and other resources accordingly and should be formally approved by management.

51 Operational work plans should be prepared for each audit assignment as it is arranged covering:

(a) objectives and scope of the audit;
(b) time budget and staff allocation; and
(c) methods, procedures and reporting arrangements, including super-vision and allocation of responsibilities.

52 All internal audit plans should be sufficiently flexible to respond to changing priorities.

Controlling

53 Control of the internal audit unit and of individual assignments is needed to ensure that internal audit objectives are achieved and work is performed effectively. The most important elements of control are the direction and supervision of the internal audit staff and review of their work. This will be assisted by an established audit approach and standard documentation. The degree of control and supervision required depends on the complexity of assignments and the experience and proficiency of the internal audit staff.

54 The head of internal audit should establish arrangements:

(a) to allocate internal audit assignments according to the level of and proficiency of internal audit staff;
(b) to ensure that internal auditors clearly understand the responsibilities and internal audit objectives;
(c) to communicate the scope of work to be performed and agree the programme of work with each internal auditor;
(d) to provide and document evidence of adequate supervision, review and guidance during the internal audit assignment;
(e) to ensure that adequate working papers are being prepared to support internal audit findings and conclusions; and
(f) to ensure that internal audit's performance is in accordance with the internal audit plan or that any significant variations have been explained.

55 The head of internal audit should establish arrangements to evaluate the performance of the internal audit unit. He may also prepare an annual report to management on the activities of the internal audit unit in which he gives an assessment of how effectively the objectives of the function have been met.

Recording

56 Internal audit work should be properly recorded because:

(a) the head of internal audit needs to be able to ensure that work delegated to staff has been properly performed. He can generally do this only by reference to detailed working papers prepared by the internal audit staff who performed the work;
(b) working papers provide, for future reference, evidence of work performed, details of problems encountered and conclusions drawn; and
(c) the preparation of working papers encourages each internal auditor to adopt a methodical approach to his work.

57 The head of internal audit should specify the required standard of internal audit documentation and working papers and ensure that those standards are maintained.

58 Internal audit working papers should always be sufficiently complete and detailed to enable an experienced internal auditor with no previous connection with the internal audit assignment subsequently to ascertain from them what work was performed and to support the conclusions reached. Working papers should be prepared as the internal audit assignment proceeds so that critical details are not omitted and problems not overlooked. These should be reviewed by internal audit management.

EVALUATION OF THE INTERNAL CONTROL SYSTEM

59 Controls ensure that processes act to meet the system's objectives.

60 The main objectives of the internal control system are:

(a) to ensure adherence to management policies and directives in order to achieve the organisation's objectives;
(b) to safeguard assets;
(c) to secure the relevance, reliability and integrity of information, so ensuring as far as possible the completeness and accuracy of records; and
(d) to ensure compliance with statutory requirements.

61 When evaluating internal control systems the internal auditor should consider the effect which all the controls have on each other and on related systems.

62 As part of the planning process the internal auditor should identify the whole range of systems within the organisation. For those systems to be examined, the internal auditor should establish appropriate criteria to determine whether the controls are adequate and assist in achieving the objectives of the system. The stages of a systems audit would normally be:

(a) to identify the system parameters;
(b) to determine the control objectives;
(c) to identify expected controls to meet control objectives;
(d) to review the system against expected controls;
(e) to appraise the controls designed into the system against control objectives;
(f) to test the actual controls for effectiveness against control objectives;
(g) to test the operation of controls in practice; and
(h) to give an opinion based on audit objectives as to whether the system provides an adequate basis for effective control and whether it is properly operated in practice.

EVIDENCE

63 Internal audit evidence is information obtained by an internal auditor which enables conclusions to be formed on which recommendations can be based.

64 The internal auditor should determine what evidence will be necessary by exercising judgement in the light of the objectives of the internal audit assignment. This judgement will be influenced by the scope of the assignment, the significance of the matters under review, the relevance and the reliability of available evidence and the cost and time involved in obtaining it.

65 The collection and assessment of internal audit evidence should be recorded and reviewed to provide reasonable assurance that conclusions are soundly based and internal audit objectives achieved.

Sufficiency

66 An internal auditor should obtain the evidence considered necessary for the achievement of the internal audit assignment objectives. This is influenced by, for instance:

(a) the level of assurance required;
(b) the objectives and scope of the internal audit assignment;
(c) the scale of activity under review and the degree of risk involved;
(d) the cost and time involved in obtaining evidence; and
(e) the reliability of the evidence.

Relevance

67 The relevance of the internal audit evidence should be considered in relation to the objectives of the internal audit assignment.

Reliability

68 Reliable evidence can be achieved through the use of the appropriate internal audit techniques which should normally be selected in advance, but which may be expanded or altered as necessary during the internal audit assignment.

69 In order to place reliance on evidence an internal auditor should be satisfied with its nature, extent, adequacy, consistency and relevance to the internal audit assignment and with the methods governing its collection.

REPORTING AND FOLLOW-UP

70 The primary purposes of internal audit reports are to provide management with an opinion on the adequacy of the internal control system, and to inform management of significant audit findings, conclusions and recommendations. The aim of every internal audit report should be:

(a) to prompt management action to implement recommendations for change leading to improvement in performance and control; and

(b) to provide a formal record of points arising from the internal audit assignment and, where appropriate, of agreements reached with management.

71 Reporting arrangements, including the format and distribution of internal audit reports, should be agreed with management. The head of internal audit should ensure that reports are sent to managers who have a direct responsibility for the unit or function being audited and who have the authority to take action on the internal audit recommendations. Internal audit reports are confidential documents and their distribution should be restricted to those managers who need to know, to the audit committee and to the external auditor.

72 While the internal auditor may clear minor matters which do not indicate a consistent or systematic weakness with members of staff directly involved, matters of consequence should be reported formally in writing to managment.

73 The internal auditor should produce clear, constructive and concise written reports based on sufficient, relevant and reliable evidence, which should:

(a) state the scope, purpose, extent and conclusions of the internal audit assignment;

(b) make recommendations which are appropriate and relevant, and which flow from the conclusions; and

(c) acknowledge the action taken, or proposed, by management.

74 The internal auditor should make an interim report, orally or in writing, where it is necessary to alert management to the need to take immediate action to correct a serious weakness in performance or control, or where there are reasonable grounds for suspicion of malpractice. Consideration should also be given to interim reporting where there is a significant change in the scope of the internal audit assignment or where it is desirable to inform management of progress. Interim reporting does not diminish or eliminate the need for final reporting.

75 The internal auditor should normally meet with management to discuss the audit findings at the completion of fieldwork for each internal audit assignment and the formal written report should be presented to management as soon as possible thereafter.

76 Before issuing the final report, the internal auditor should normally discuss the contents with the appropriate levels of management, and may submit a draft report to them, for confirmation of factual accuracy.

77 If the internal auditor and management disagree about the relevance of the factual content of the draft audit report, the internal auditor should consider whether reference should be made to this in the final report.

78 It is management's responsibility to ensure that proper consideration is given to internal audit reports. The internal auditor should ensure that appropriate arrangements are made to determine whether action has been taken on internal audit recommendations or that management has understood and assumed the risk of not taking action.

APPENDIX

Glossary of terms used in the guideline

Organisation
The body for which the internal auditor is providing an internal audit service.

Audit committee
A committee of directors, usually without executive responsibility, or top-ranking managers, which considers both the external and internal audit plans and activity with a specific brief to review internal control arrangements.

Management
A comprehensive term including all persons who have responsibility at various levels for activities which may be the subject of internal audit.

Internal auditor
An individual who takes responsibility for carrying out internal audit work within an organisation whether as an employee or as an external agency.

System
A series of inter-related procedures, composed of processes and controls designed to operate together to achieve a planned objective.

Internal control
The regulation of activities in an organisation through systems designed and implemented to facilitate the achievement of management objectives.

Internal control system
The whole system of controls, financial and otherwise, established by the management in order to carry on the business of an organisation in an orderly and efficient manner, ensure adherence to management policies, safeguard assets and secure as far as possible the completeness and accuracy of records.

Controls
The individual components of an internal control system are known as 'controls' or 'internal controls'. These ensure that processes work to meet the system's objectives.

Appendix 2   Extracts from standards and guidelines for the professional practice of internal auditing

(Reproduced with permission of the Institute of Internal Auditors United Kingdom)
(Aug 1988 as amended May 1991)

STATEMENT OF RESPONSIBILITIES OF INTERNAL AUDITING

The purpose of the statement of responsibilities is to provide in summary form a general understanding of the responsibilities of internal auditing.

Objective and scope

Internal auditing is an independent appraisal function established within an organisation to examine and evaluate its activities as a service to the organisation.

The objective of internal auditing is to assist members of the organisation including those in management and on the board, in the effective discharge of their responsibilities. To this end, internal auditing furnishes them with analyses, appraisals, recommendations, counsel and information concerning the activities reviewed.

The scope of internal auditing encompasses the examination and evaluation of the adequacy and effectiveness of the organisation's system of internal control and the quality of performance in carrying out assigned responsibilities. Internal auditors should:

1 Review the reliability and integrity of financial and operating information and the means used to identify, measure, classify, and report such information.
2 Review the systems established to ensure compliance with those policies, plans, procedures, laws and regulations which could have a significant impact on operations and reports, and should determine whether the organisation is in compliance.
3 Review the means of safeguarding assets and, as appropriate, verify the existence of such assets.
4 Appraise the economy and efficiency with which resources are employed.
5 Review operations or programmes to ascertain whether results are consistent with established objectives and goals and whether the operations or programmes are being carried out as planned.

Independence

Internal auditors should be independent of the activities they audit. Internal auditors are independent when they can carry out their work freely and objectively. Independence permits internal auditors to render the impartial and unbiased judgements essential to the proper conduct of audits. It is achieved through organisational status and objectivity.

The organisational status of the internal auditing department should be sufficient to permit the accomplishment of its audit responsibilities. The chief internal auditor should be responsible to an individual in the organisation with sufficient authority to promote independence and to ensure a broad audit coverage, adequate consideration of audit reports, and appropriate action on audit recommendations.

Objectivity is an independent mental attitude, which internal auditors should maintain in performing audits. Drafting procedures for systems, and designing, installing and operating systems are not audit functions. Performing such activities is presumed to impair audit objectivity.

Responsibility and authority

The internal auditing department is an integral part of the organisation and functions under the policies established by management and the board.

The purpose, scope, authority and responsibility of the internal auditing department should be defined in a formal written document (charter). The chief internal auditor should seek approval of the charter by management as well as acceptance by the board. The charter should make clear the independence of the internal auditing department, and that it must not be restricted when carrying out its responsibilities.

Compliance with the concepts enunciated by the 'Standards for the Professional Practice of Internal Auditing' is essential before the responsibilities of internal auditing can be met.

Members of the Institute of Internal Auditors–United Kingdom accept the obligation to abide by the Institute's 'Code of Ethics' which includes the requirement that members shall adopt suitable means to comply with the 'Standards'.

Note:
The Statement was originally issued by the Institute of Internal Auditors Inc in 1947. It is a summary of the role and responsibilities of internal auditing and now derives its authority from the Standards and Guidelines and the Code of Ethics.

STANDARDS AND GUIDELINES

Note:
This extract reproduces all the Standards and the principal Guidelines published by the Institute of Internal Auditors. Some detailed interpretations are not quoted and where these occur the text is marked '**'. For the complete text, readers should refer to the Institute's booklet 'Standards and Guidelines for the Professional Practice of Internal Auditing' published by IIA–UK August 1988 and as amended May 1991.

GENERAL STANDARD 100

Independence

Internal auditors should be independent of the activities they audit.

Guidelines and interpretation

> 'Internal auditors are independent when they can carry out their work freely and objectively. Independence permits internal auditors to render the impartial and unbiased judgements essential to the proper conduct of audits. It is achieved through organisational status and objectivity.'

SPECIFIC STANDARD 110

Organisational status

The organisational status of the internal auditing department should be sufficient to permit the accomplishment of its audit responsibilities.

Guidelines and interpretation

> 'Internal auditors should have the support of management and of the board of directors so that they can gain the co-operation of auditees and perform their work free from interference.'**

SPECIFIC STANDARD 120

Objectivity

Internal auditors should be objective in performing audits.

Guidelines and interpretation

> 'Objectivity is an independent mental attitude which internal auditors should maintain in performing audits. Internal auditors are not bound to subordinate their judgement on audit matters to that of others.'

> 'Objectivity requires internal auditors to perform audits in such a manner that they can have an honest belief in their work product and that no significant quality compromises are made. Internal auditors are not to be placed in situations in which they feel unable to make objective professional judgements.'**

> 'The internal auditor's objectivity is not adversely affected when the auditor recommends standards of control for systems or reviews procedures before they are implemented. Designing, installing and operating systems are not audit functions. Also, the drafting of procedures for systems is not an audit function. Performing such activities is presumed to impair audit objectivity.'

GENERAL STANDARD 200

Professional proficiency

Internal audits should be performed with proficiency and due professional care.

Guidelines and interpretation

'Professional proficiency is the responsibility of the internal auditing department and each internal auditor. The department should assign to each audit those persons who collectively possess the necessary knowledge, skills and disciplines to conduct the audit properly.'

SPECIFIC STANDARD 210

Staffing

The internal auditing department should provide assurance that the technical proficiency and educational background of internal auditors are appropriate for the audits to be performed.

Guidelines and interpretation

'The chief internal auditor should establish suitable criteria of education and experience for filling internal auditing positions, giving due consideration to scope of work and level of responsibility.'

'Reasonable assurance should be obtained as to each prospective auditor's qualifications and proficiency.'

SPECIFIC STANDARD 220

Knowledge, skills and disciplines

The internal auditing department should possess or should obtain the knowledge, skills and disciplines needed to carry out its audit responsibilities.

Guidelines and interpretation

'The internal auditing staff should collectively possess the knowledge and skills essential to the practice of the profession within the organisation. These attributes include proficiency in applying internal auditing standards, procedures and techniques.'

'The internal auditing department should have employees or use consultants who are qualified in such disciplines as accounting, economics, finance, statistics, electronic data processing, engineering, taxation and law as needed to meet audit responsibilities. Each member of the department, however, need not be qualified in all these disciplines.'

SPECIFIC STANDARD 230

Supervision

The internal audit department should provide assurance that internal audits are properly supervised.

Guidelines and interpretation

'The chief internal auditor is responsible for providing appropriate audit supervision. Supervision is a continuing process, beginning with planning and ending with the conclusion of the audit assignment.'

'Supervision includes:

1 Providing suitable instructions to subordinates at the outset of the audit and approving the audit programme.
2 Seeing that the approved audit programme is carried out unless deviations are both justified and authorised.
3 Determining that audit working papers adequately support the audit findings, conclusions and reports.
4 Making sure that audit reports are accurate, objective, clear, concise, constructive, and timely.
5 Determining that audit objectives are met.

Appropriate evidence of supervision should be documented and retained.'

'The extent of supervision required will depend on the proficiency of the internal auditors and the difficulty of the audit assignment.'

'All internal auditing assignments, whether performed by or for the internal auditing department, remain the responsibility of the chief internal auditor.'

SPECIFIC STANDARD 240

Compliance with standards of conduct

Internal auditors should comply with professional standards of conduct.

Guidelines and interpretation

'The Code of Ethics of the Institute of Internal Auditors sets forth standards of conduct and provides a basis for enforcement among its members. The Code calls for high standards of honesty, objectivity, diligence and loyalty to which internal auditors should conform.'

SPECIFIC STANDARD 250

Knowledge, skills and discipline

Internal auditors should possess the knowledge, skills and disciplines essential to the performance of internal audits.

Guidelines and interpretation

'Each internal auditor should possess certain knowledge and skills as follows:

Proficiency in applying internal auditing standards, procedures, and techniques is required in performing internal audits.**

Proficiency in accounting principles and techniques is required of auditors who work extensively with financial records and reports.

An understanding of management principles is required to recognise and evaluate the materiality and significance of deviations from good business practice.**

An appreciation is required of the fundamentals of such subjects as accounting, economics, commercial law, taxation, finance, quantitative methods and computerised information systems.'**

SPECIFIC STANDARD 260

Human relations and communications

Internal auditors should be skilled in dealing with people and in communicating effectively.

Guidelines and interpretation

'Internal auditors should understand human relations and maintain satisfactory relationships with auditees.'

'Internal auditors should be skilled in oral and written communications so that they can clearly and effectively convey such matters as audit objectives, evaluations, conclusions and recommendations.'

SPECIFIC STANDARD 270

Continuing education

Internal auditors should maintain their technical competence through continuing education.

Guidelines and interpretation

'Internal auditors are responsible for continuing their education in order to maintain their efficiency. They should keep informed about improvements and current developments in internal auditing standards, procedures and techniques.'**

SPECIFIC STANDARD 280

Due professional care

Internal auditors should exercise due professional care in performing internal audits.

Guidelines and interpretation

'Due professional care calls for the application of the care and skill expected of a reasonably prudent and competent internal auditor in the same or similar circumstances. Professional care should therefore be appropriate to the complexities of the audit being performed. In exercising due professional care, internal auditors should be alert to the possibility of intentional wrong-doing, errors and omissions, inefficiency, waste, ineffectiveness and conflicts of interest. They should also be alert to those conditions and activities where irregularities are most likely to occur. In addition they should identify inadequate controls and recommend improvements to promote compliance with acceptable procedures and practices.'**

'Due care implies reasonable care and competence, not infallibility or extraordinary performance. Due care requires the auditor to conduct examinations and verifications to a reasonable extent but does not require detailed audits of all transactions. Accordingly, the internal auditor cannot give absolute assurance that non-compliance or irregularities do not exist. Nevertheless, the possibility of material irregularities or non-compliance should be considered whenever the internal auditor undertakes an internal auditing assignment.'**

'When an internal auditor suspects wrong-doing, the appropriate authorities within the organisation should be informed. The internal auditor may recommend whatever investigation is considered necessary in the circumstances. Thereafter, the auditor should follow up to see that the internal auditing department's responsibility has been met.'**

'Exercising due professional care means using reasonable skill and judgment in performing the audit. To this end, the internal auditor should consider:

1 The extent of audit work needed to achieve audit objectives.
2 The relative materiality or significance of matters to which the audit procedures are applied.
3 The adequacy and effectiveness of internal controls.
4 The cost of auditing in relation to potential benefits.

Due professional care includes evaluating established operating standards and determining whether those standards are acceptable and are being met.'**

GENERAL STANDARD 300

Scope of work

The scope of the internal audit should encompass the examination and evaluation of the adequacy and effectiveness of the organisation's system of internal control and the quality of performance in carrying out assigned responsibilities.

Guidelines and interpretation

'The scope of internal auditing work as specified in this standard, encompasses what audit work should be performed. It is recognised however that management and the board of directors provide general direction as to the scope of work and the activities to be audited.'

'The purpose of the review of adequacy of the system of internal control is to ascertain whether the system established provides reasonable assurance that the organisation's objectives and goals will be met efficiently and economically.'**

'The purpose of the review for effectiveness of the system of internal control is to ascertain whether the system is functioning as intended.'**

'The purpose of the review for quality of performance is to ascertain whether the organisation's goals have been achieved.'

'The primary objectives of internal control are to ensure:

1 The reliability and integrity of information.
2 Compliance with policies, plans, procedures, laws and regulations.
3 The safeguarding of assets.
4 The economical and efficient use of resources.
5 The accomplishment of established objectives and goals for operations and programmes.

A control is any action taken by management to enhance the likelihood that established objectives and goals will be achieved.'**

'Management plans, organises and directs in such a fashion as to provide reasonable assurance that objectives and goals will be achieved.'**

'Internal auditing examines and evaluates the planning, organising, and directing processes to determine whether reasonable assurance exists that objectives and goals will be achieved. Such evaluations in the aggregate, provide information to appraise the overall system of control.'**

SPECIFIC STANDARD 310

Reliability and integrity of information

Internal auditors should review the reliability and integrity of financial and operating information and the means used to measure, classify and report such information.

Guidelines and interpretation

'Information systems provide data for decision making, control and compliance with external requirements, therefore internal auditors should examine information systems and as appropriate, ascertain whether:

1 financial and operating records and reports contain accurate, reliable, timely, complete and useful information; and

2 controls over record keeping and reporting are adequate and effective.

SPECIFIC STANDARD 320

Compliance with policies, plans, procedures, laws and regulations

Internal auditors should review the systems established to ensure compliance with those policies, plans, procedures and applicable laws and regulations which could have a significant impact on operations and reports, and should determine whether the organisation is in compliance.

Guidelines and interpretation

'Management is responsible for establishing systems designed to ensure compliance with such requirements as plans, procedures and applicable laws and regulations.'

'Internal auditors are responsible for determining whether the systems are adequate and effective and whether the activities are complying with the appropriate requirements.'

SPECIFIC STANDARD 330

Safeguarding of assets

Internal auditors should review the means of safeguarding assets and, as appropriate, verify the existence of such assets.

Guidelines and interpretation

'Internal auditors should review the means of safeguarding assets from various types of losses such as those resulting from theft, fire, improper or illegal activities, and exposure to the elements.'**

'Internal auditors, when verifying the existence of assets, should use appropriate audit procedures.'**

SPECIFIC STANDARD 340

Economical and efficient use of resources

Internal auditors should appraise the economy and efficiency with which resources are employed.

Guidelines and interpretation

'Management is responsible for setting operating standards to measure an activity's economical and efficient use of resources.'

'Internal auditors are responsible for determining whether:

1 Operating standards have been established for measuring economy and efficiency.
2 Established operating standards are understood and are being met.
3 Deviations from operating standards are identified, analysed and communicated to those responsible for corrective action.
4 Corrective action has been taken.'

Audits related to the economical and efficient use of resources should identify such conditions as:

1 Under-utilised facilities.
2 Non-productive work.
3 Procedures which are not cost justified.
4 Overstaffing or understaffing.'

SPECIFIC STANDARD 350

Accomplishment of established objectives and goals for operations or programmes

Internal auditors should review operations or programmes to ascertain whether results are consistent with established objectives and goals and whether the operations or programmes are being carried out as planned.

Guidelines and interpretation

'Management is responsible for establishing operating or programme objectives and goals, developing and implementing control procedures and accomplishing desired operating or programme results.'

'Internal auditors should ascertain whether such objectives and goals conform with those of the organisation and whether they are being met.'

'Internal auditors can provide assistance to managers who are developing objectives, goals and systems by determining whether the underlying assumptions are appropriate; whether accurate, current and relevant information is being used; and whether suitable controls have been incorporated into the operations or programmes.'

GENERAL STANDARD 400

Performance of audit work

Audit work should include planning the audit, examining and evaluating information, communicating results and following up.

Guidelines and interpretation

'The internal auditor is responsible for planning and conducting the audit assignment, subject to supervisory review and approval.'

SPECIFIC STANDARD 410

Planning the audit

Internal auditors should plan each audit.

Guidelines and interpretation

'Planning should be documented and should include:

1 Establishing audit objectives and scope of the work.
2 Obtaining background information about the activities to be audited.
3 Determining the resources necessary to perform the audit.
4 Communicating with all who need to know about the audit.
5 Performing as appropriate an on-site survey to become familiar with the activities and controls to be audited, to identify areas for audit emphasis, and to invite auditee comments and suggestions.
6 Writing the audit programme.
7 Determining how, when and to whom audit results will be communicated.
8 Obtaining approval of the audit work plan.'

'When conducting fraud investigations, internal auditors should:

1 Assess the probable level and the extent of complicity in the fraud within the organisation.**
2 Determine the knowledge, skills, and disciplines needed to carry out the investigation effectively.**
3 Design procedures to follow in attempting to identify the perpetrators, extent of the fraud, techniques used, and cause of the fraud.
4 Co-ordinate procedures with management personnel, legal counsel, and other specialists as appropriate throughout the course of the investigation.
5 Be cognisant of the rights of alleged perpetrators and personnel within the scope of the investigation and the reputation of the organisation itself.'

SPECIFIC STANDARD 420

Examining and evaluating information

Internal auditors should collect, analyse, interpret and document information to support audit results.

Guidelines and interpretation

'Information should be collected on all matters related to the audit objectives and scope of the work.'

'Information should be sufficient, competent, relevant and useful to provide a sound basis for audit findings and recommendations.'**

'Audit procedures, including the testing and sampling techniques employed, should be selected in advance where practicable and expanded or altered if circumstances warrant.'

'The process of collecting, analysing, interpreting and documenting information should be supervised to provide reasonable assurance that the auditor's objectivity is maintained and that audit goals are met.'

'Working papers that document the audit should be prepared by the auditor and reviewed by the management of the internal auditing department. These papers should record the information obtained and the analyses made and should support the bases for the findings and recommendations to be reported.'**

SPECIFIC STANDARD 430

Communicating results

Internal auditors should report the results of their audit work.

Guidelines and interpretation

'A signed written report should be issued after the audit examination is completed. Interim reports may be written or oral and may be transmitted formally or informally.'**

'The internal auditor should discuss conclusions and recommendations at appropriate levels of management before issuing final written reports.'**

'Reports should be objective, clear, concise, constructive and timely.'**

'Reports should present the purpose, scope and results of the audit; and where appropriate, reports should contain an expression of the auditor's opinion.'**

'Reports may include recommendations for potential improvements and acknowledge satisfactory performance and corrective action.'**

'The auditee's views about audit conclusions or recommendations may be included in the audit report.'**

'The chief internal auditor or an audit manager designated by him should review and approve the final audit report before issuance and should decide to whom the report should be distributed.'**

SPECIFIC STANDARD 440

Following up

Internal auditors should follow up to ascertain that appropriate action is taken on reported audit findings.

Guidelines and interpretation

'Internal auditing should determine that corrective action was taken and is achieving the desired results, or that management or the board has assumed the risk of not taking corrective action on reported findings.'

GENERAL STANDARD 500

Management of the internal audit function

The chief internal auditor should properly manage the internal auditing department.

Guidelines and interpretation

'The chief internal auditor is responsible for properly managing the department so that:

1 Audit work fulfils the general purposes and responsibilities approved by management and accepted by the board.
2 Resources of the internal auditing department are efficiently and effectively employed.
3 Audit work conforms to the Standards for the Professional Practice of Internal Auditing.'

SPECIFIC STANDARD 510

Purpose, authority and responsibility

The chief internal auditor should have a statement of purpose, authority and responsibility for the internal auditing department.

Guidelines and interpretation

'The chief internal auditor is responsible for seeking the approval of management and the acceptance by the board of a formal written document (charter) for the internal auditing department.'

SPECIFIC STANDARD 520

Planning

The chief internal auditor should establish plans to carry out the responsibilities of the internal auditing department.

Guidelines and interpretation

'These plans should be consistent with the internal auditing department's charter and with the goals of the organisation.'

'The planning process involves establishing goals, audit work schedules, staffing plans and financial budgets, and activity reports.'**

SPECIFIC STANDARD 530

Policies and procedures

The chief internal auditor should provide written policies and procedures to guide the audit staff.

Guidelines and interpretation

'The form and content of written policies and procedures should be appropriate to the size and structure of the internal auditing department and the complexity of its work.'**

SPECIFIC STANDARD 540

Personal management and development

The chief internal auditor should establish a programme for selecting and developing the staff of the internal auditing department.

Guidelines and interpretation

'The programme should provide for:

1 Developing written job descriptions for each level of the audit staff.
2 Selecting qualified and competent individuals.
3 Training and providing continuing educational opportunities for each internal auditor.
4 Appraising each internal auditor's performance at least annually.
5 Providing counsel to internal auditors on their performance and professional development.'

SPECIFIC STANDARD 550

External auditors

The chief internal auditor should ensure that internal and external audit efforts are properly co-ordinated.

Guidelines and interpretation

> 'The internal and external audit work should be co-ordinated to ensure adequate audit coverage and to minimise duplicate efforts.'**

> 'Co-ordination of audit efforts involves:

> 1 Periodic meetings to discuss matters of mutual interest.**
> 2 Access to each other's audit programmes and working papers.**
> 3 Exchange of audit reports and management letters.**
> 4 Common understanding of audit techniques, methods, and terminology.'**

SPECIFIC STANDARD 560

Quality assurance

The chief internal auditor should establish and maintain a quality assurance programme to evaluate the operations of the internal auditing department.

Guidelines and interpretation

> 'The purpose of this programme is to provide reasonable assurance that audit work conforms with these Standards, the internal auditing department's charter and other applicable standards. A quality assurance programme should include supervision, internal reviews and external reviews.'**

> 'Supervision of the work of internal auditors should be carried out continually to assure conformance with internal auditing standards, departmental policies, and audit programmes.'**

> 'Internal reviews should be performed periodically by members of the internal auditing staff to appraise the quality of the audit work performed. These reviews should be performed in the same manner as any other internal audit.'**

> 'External reviews of the internal auditing department should be performed to appraise the quality of the department's operations. These reviews should be performed by qualified persons who are independent of the organisation and who do not have either a real or an apparent conflict of interest. Such reviews should be conducted at least once every three years. On completion of the review, a formal written report should be issued. The report should express an opinion as to the department's compliance with the Standards for the Professional Practice of Internal Auditing and as appropriate, should include recommendations for improvement.'**

Bibliography

Chapter 1   Introduction

Brink, V Z and Witt, H *Modern internal auditing* (1982) Wiley.

Chambers, A, Selim, G and Vinten, G *Internal auditing* (2nd edn, 1987), (Pitman).

Stearn, H J and Impey, K W in association with IIA–UK and ICSA *Manual of internal audit practice* (1990) (ICSA Publishing).

Chapter 2   The role of internal audit

Auditing and reporting 1990/91, UK auditing standards, guidelines and exposure drafts (1990) (ICAEW).

Drucker, P J *Management: tasks, responsibilities and practices* (1988) (Heinemann).

H M Treasury *Government internal audit manual* (1983) (HMSO).

Standards and guidelines for the professional practice of internal auditing (1988 as amended May 1991) (IIA–UK).

Chapter 3   Internal audit management

Patton, J M, Evans, J H and Lewis, B L *A framework for evaluating internal audit risk* Research report No 25 (1986) (IIA Inc).

Risk analysis for internal auditing (1987) (IIA–UK).

Woolf, E *Auditing today* (4th edn, 1990) (Prentice Hall).

Chapter 4   Audit skills and attitudes

Bromage, Mary C *Writing audit reports* (2nd edn, 1979) (McGraw Hill).

Gowers, Sir E, Greenbaum, S and Whitcut, J *The complete plain words* (3rd edn 1986) (HMSO).

Heeschen, P and Sawyer, L B *Internal auditor's handbook* (1984) (IIA Inc).

Matthew, H W *Fact finding interviews* Accountants digest No 90 (1980) (ICAEW).

Mints, F E *Behavioural patterns in internal audit relationships* Report No 17 (1972) (IIA Inc).

Chapter 5   Systems evaluation

Rutteman, P J *Flowcharting for auditors* Accountants digest No 32 (1976) (ICAEW).

Chapter 6   Information management

Doswell, R and Simons, G L *Fraud and abuse of IT systems* (1986) (NCC Publications).

Tricker, R I *Effective information management* (1982) (Beaumont Executive Press).

Chapter 7   Computer security

Chambers, A D and Court, J M *Computer auditing* (2nd edn, 1986) (Pitman).
Computer auditing guidelines (3rd edn, 1987) (CIPFA).
Data protection codes of practice (1990) (NCC Blackwell).
Disaster and contingency planning in the data processing environment (1988) (IIA–UK).
Franks, R V in association with CIMA *Commonsense computer management (1989) (Kogan Page).*
Hearnden, K *A handbook of computer security* (1990) (Kogan Page).
Mair, W C, Wood, D R and Davies, R W *Computer control and audit* (3rd edn, 1978) (IIA Inc).
Setting up computer audit (1988) (IIA–UK).
Travis, B J *Auditing the development of computing systems* (1987) (Butterworths).

Chapter 8   Financial security

Samuels, J M, Wilkes, F M and Brayshaw, R E *Management of company finance* (5th edn, 1990) (Chapman & Hall).
Woolf, E *Auditing today* (4th edn, 1990) (Prentice Hall).

Chapter 9   Contract management

Financial examination and audit of capital contracts (1979) (CIPFA).

Chapter 10   Operational management

Hostrum, G and Collins, W A *Operational audits of production control* Report No 20 (1978) (IAA Inc).
Kerin, R A and Peterson, R A *Strategic marketing problems: cases and comments* (1990) (Allyn and Bacon).

Chapter 11   Corporate management

Cairncross, F *Costing the earth* (1991) (Economist Books).
Cuming, M W *The theory and practice of personnel management* (6th edn, 1989) (Heinemann).
Lumby, S *Investment appraisal and related decisions* (1988) (Van Nostrand Reinhold).
Samuels, J M, Wilkes, F M and Brayshaw, R E *Management of company finance* (5th edn, 1990) (Chapman & Hall).
Simpson, S *The Times guide to the environment* (1990) (Times Books).

Chapter 12   External audit and corporate governance

Auditing and reporting, UK auditing standards, guidelines and exposure drafts (1990) (ICAEW).
Buckley, F *Audit committees, their role in UK companies* (1979) (ICAEW).
Financial Services Act 1986: a guide to the amended legislation (1990) (Butterworths).
Jennings, M *The guide to good corporate citizenship* (1990) (Director Books).
Walmsley, K *Butterworths company law handbook* (8th edn, 1991) (Butterworths).

Chapter 13   The public sector

Buttery, R and Simpson, R K in association with CIPFA *Auditing in the public sector* (2nd edn, 1989) (Woodhead–Faulkner).
Computer auditing guidelines (3rd edn, 1987) (CIPFA).
Glynn, J J *Public sector financial control and accounting* (1987) (Basil Blackwell).
Henley, Likierman, Holtham, and Perrin *Public sector accounting and financial controls* (3rd revised edition, 1990) (Chapman & Hall).
Government internal audit manual (1983) (HMSO).
Price Waterhouse *Value for money auditing* (1990) (Gee & Co.)

Chapter 14   Fraud and other irregularities

Bologna, J *Corporate fraud, basics of prevention and detection* (1985) (Butterworths).
Comer, M J *Corporate fraud* (2nd edn, 1987) (McGraw Hill).
Elliot, R K and Willingham, J J *Management fraud, detection and deterrence* (PBI Books).
Investigation of fraud in the public sector (1989) (CIPFA).

Glossary of terms

Access	A person has access to information when records which contain that information are intentionally or otherwise available and intelligible to that person to use or to change.
Account	A formal record of transactions of a defined classification maintained in monetary terms in a ledger.
Accounting records	Those records maintained to record and explain the transactions of an enterprise in monetary terms.
Accounting system	The system of records, books and documents by which an enterprise records and accounts for its transactions. The purpose of the accounting system is to record information: the internal control system should ensure that the information is correct.
Accounts	The basis for financial reports to management.
AHST	Association of Health Service Treasurers.
APC	Auditing Practices Committee.
APT	Audit profile triggers.
Audit	An examination by an authorised person.
Audit Commission	Statutory external auditors to local government and the Health Service.
Audit committee	A committee of directors of a corporation or organisation whose specific responsibility is to review the annual financial statements before consideration by the board of directors. It is common for the committee to act as liaison between the external auditors and the board. Its activities include the nomination of auditors, overall scope of both external and internal audit; consideration of the reports of both external and internal auditors; review of internal financial controls; review of financial information to be published.
Auditor	Person authorised to undertake an audit.
Audit programme	Written schedule of basic tests and examinations that the auditor should carry out in order to complete the audit.
Audit trail	A series of information links enabling a transaction to be pursued from its inception together with its supporting documentation through to its reporting in the accounts.

Audit tick	An identifing mark for an audit check.
Auditing Standards Guidance and Guidelines	Standards, guidance and guidelines for general audit practice issued by member bodies of CCAB or by IIA–UK.
CAAT	Computer assisted auditing techniques.
C&AG	Comptroller & Auditor General of the NAO.
CACA	Chartered Association of Corporate and Certified Accountants.
CAKE	Cumulative auditing knowledge and experience.
Chief internal auditor	The manager of the internal auditing function or a person fulfilling that role in an internal audit department.
CIMA	Chartered Institute of Management Accountants.
CIPFA	Chartered Institute of Public Finance and Accountancy.
CPA	See PAC.
Confidence	The assurance the auditor has, that conclusions based on audit evidence are likely to be correct.
Cut-off	The interruption of continuity in recording transactions to establish the state at a point in time and so to allow the reconciliation of separate accounting records, or to ensure that the accounting records reflect the physical situation.
DBMS	Data base management system. Programs together forming a system, designed to permit proper access to the database both for reference and for amendment and to protect the database from corruption either in its content or in its links to the user system.
Database	A single data file organised to contain all the basic data needed for a number of information processing systems which is available for access by an authorised user or program.
Due professional care	The application of that measure of skill and care which might reasonably be expected of a competent auditor relative to the specific duties undertaken.
Evidence	Information obtained by the auditor in arriving at conclusions on which the audit opinion is based.
E & AD	Exchequer & Audsit Dept: see NAO.
Financial audit	Audit examination to form an opinion about financial security and the validity of financial statements.
Flowchart	A map of inter-related operations specially arranged to indicate the sequence and type of these operations as part of a larger unit.

ICAEW	Institute of Chartered Accountants in England & Wales
ICAS	Institute of Chartered Accountants of Scotland.
IIA	Institute of Internal Auditors.
Independence	The property of a relationship between two parties in which neither party is in a position to exercise any form of control over the other so that judgements made by one party will be influenced only by the evidence discovered.
ICEQ	Internal control evaluation questionnaire.
ICQ	Internal control questionnaire.
Internal audit	An independent appraisal function established within an organisation to examine and evaluate its activities as a service to the organisation. The objective of internal auditing is to assist members of the organisation in the effective discharge of their responsibilities. To this end internal auditing furnishes them with analyses, appraisals, recommendations, counsel and information concerning the activities reviewed. (IIA)
Internal auditing department	Includes any unit or activity within an organisation performing internal audit functions.
Internal check	The checks on day-to-day transactions which operate continuously as part of information routine processing systems, whereby the work of one person is proved independently of or is complementary to the work of another, the object being the prevention or early detection of error and irregularity.
Internal control	Co-ordinated methods and measures adopted within an organisation which in conjunction with the organisational structure: (a) Safeguard its assets. (b) Secure the reliability of accounting records. (c) Promote operational efficiency. (d) Ensure adherence to prescribed managerial policies and procedures.
Judgemental	Describes a decision made on the basis of subjective criteria by a person who is familiar with the situation to which the decision relates and is capable of exercising informed and unbiased discretion in coming to that decision.
KCQ	Key control questionnaire, otherwise known as ICEQ.
Management audit	See operational audit.
Materiality	In an accounting sense a matter is material if its non-disclosure, misstatement or omission would make possible a distortion of the view given by management reports or financial statements.

MUS	Monetary unit sample.
NAO	National Audit Office, formerly Exchequer and Audit Department. The external auditors of government departments.
NDPB	Non-departmental public body.
Operational audit	Internal audit with the objective of assisting management to improve organisational performance. (Sometimes described as management audit.)
Opinion	The conclusion drawn by an auditor as the result of an audit examination.
PAC	Public Accounts Committee.
Population	The field of individual items to be tested.
Precision	A measure of accuracy applied in audit tests.
Reassure	Restore to confidence; confirm again in opinion or impression (*Oxford Dictionary*). Positive confirmation of performance as intended.
Regularity audit	An examination of internal control procedures to ensure compliance with the rules and regulations of the organisation.
Representative sample	A sample which is believed to be typical of the population from which it is drawn.
Risk	The chance of error or damage occurring.
SSAP	Statement of Standard Accounting Practice.
Sample	A selection of items from a population.
Statistical	The use of the 'laws of probability' to evaluate an audit test.
Substantive test	Those tests of transactions and balances and other procedures such as analytical review, which seek to provide audit evidence as to the completeness, accuracy and validity of the information contained in the accounting records or in the financial statements.
Standards	Defined minimum levels of internal audit proficiency.
VFM	Value for money, comprising economy efficiency and effectiveness. This term applies to operational audit . . . an examination of how the organisation is achieving its objectives.
Verification	To substantiate that an item is properly stated and accurate or within reasonable and permissable limits.
Vouch	An examination of documentary evidence supporting a transaction recorded in the organisation's records to prove its authenticity.
Walk through test	Following a transaction through the system to confirm the auditor's knowledge of the system. Such a test can be developed to test the operation of internal controls within the system to ensure compliance with the recorded system.

Index